Artificial Intelligence in Perspective

DATE DUE

Special Issues of *Artificial Intelligence: An International Journal*

The titles in this series are paperback, readily accessible editions of the Special Volumes of *Artificial Intelligence: An International Journal*, edited by Daniel G. Bobrow and produced by special agreement with Elsevier Science Publishers B.V.

Qualitative Reasoning about Physical Systems, edited by Daniel G. Bobrow, 1985.

Geometric Reasoning, edited by Deekpak Kapur and Joseph L. Mundy, 1989.

Machine Learning: Paradigms and Methods, edited by Jaime Carbonell, 1990.

Artificial Intelligence and Learning Environments, edited by William J. Clancey and Elliot Soloway, 1990.

Connectionist Symbol Processing, edited by G. E. Hinton, 1991.

Foundations of Artificial Intelligence, edited by David Kirsh, 1992.

Knowledge Representation, edited by Ronald J. Brachman, Hector J. Levesque, and Raymond Reiter, 1992.

Constraint-Based Reasoning, edited by Eugene C. Freuder and Alan K. Mackworth, 1994.

Artificial Intelligence in Perspective, edited by Daniel G. Bobrow, 1994.

Artificial Intelligence in Perspective

edited by
Daniel G. Bobrow

A Bradford Book
The MIT Press
Cambridge, Massachusetts
London, England

First MIT Press edition, 1994

Reprinted from *Artificial Intelligence: An International Journal*, Volume 59, Numbers 1–2, 1993. The MIT Press has exclusive license to sell this English-language book edition throughout the world.

Printed and bound in the United States of America. This book is printed on acid-free paper.

Library of Congress Cataloging-in-Publication Data

Artificial intelligence in perspective / edited by Daniel G. Bobrow — 1st MIT Press ed.
    p.   cm. — (Special issues of Artificial intelligence, an international journal)
  "A Bradford book."
  Reprinted from Artificial intelligence, an international journal, vol. 59, nos. 1–2, 1993.
  Includes bibliographical references and index.
  ISBN 0-262-52186-5 (alk. paper)
  1. Artificial intelligence. I. Bobrow, Daniel Gureasko. II. Series.
Q335.A7871442 1994
006.3—dc20   93-21601
                                                CIP

CONTENTS

Artificial Intelligence 59 (1993) 1–3
Elsevier

ARTINT 1021

Dedication

Daniel G. Bobrow

Xerox Corporation, Palo Alto Research Center, 3333 Coyote Hill Road, Palo Alto, CA 94304, USA

This volume of *Artificial Intelligence* is dedicated to the memory of Allen Newell who died July 19, 1992. As a retrospective on AI, it is most appropriate for Newell, who is one of the founders of the field of artificial intelligence. Allen was a scientist with grand dreams. He wanted to develop a scientific model of intelligence—one that would capture the architecture of the human mind. He worked all his life to achieve that dream.

Allen was a very special human being. He had the capacity to see through to the core of a problem and to propose interesting first steps towards a solution. And he shared his great skills. He carried on his broad shoulders a large enthusiastic group of students, collaborators, friends and organizations. He always made time for an interesting conversation, an organization that needed focusing, or a friend who needed counselling. His wisdom was admired by scientists young and old. As Marvin Minsky wrote (personal communication):

> Allen Newell was among the most profound thinkers of our century, right along with Freud, McCulloch, and Piaget (and Simon, of course). It was a privilege to know Allen—and what great times we had in those early days. Although we were roughly the same age, I sometimes imagined him as a sort of superior being dwelling out there, be it at CMU or RAND, who could always be depended on to resolve any sort of conceptual impasse that might arise. The world seems less resourceful now.

Allen was given many of the scientific communities highest honors for his contributions. These include the A.M. Turing Award of the ACM (with

Correspondence to: D.G. Bobrow, Xerox Corporation, Palo Alto Research Center, 3333 Coyote Hill Road, Palo Alto, CA 94304, USA. E-mail: bobrow.pa@xerox.com.

Simon), the Harry Goode Award of AFIPS, the Emanuel R. Piore Award
of the IEEE, the Distinguished Scientific Contribution Award of the APA,
the Career Research Excellence Award of IJCAI, the Franklin Institute's
Louis E. Levy Medal, and the National Medal of Science. He was the first
president of the AAAI, and served as Chair of the Cognitive Science Society.

Allen lived for his science. When he found out about his cancer, he thought
about what he wanted to do for what he estimated as his last five years.
His conclusion was that continuing his research was the most fun and most
important thing he could do. He was determined to make as much progress
as he could on his lifetime goal: building an understanding of the human
mind.

Allen's work on this dream is represented in this volume in several ways.
The main body of this volume is a set of retrospectives by authors of highly
cited papers that have appeared in *Artificial Intelligence*. This includes an
essay by Newell commenting on his paper "The knowledge level".

In a separate section devoted to Newell, we start with a look at how
Newell came into (and helped found) the field of artificial intelligence
though a short essay by Newell's long-time friend and collaborator, Herbert
Simon. Allen Newell's recent views on the possibilities of developing an
architecture of intelligence are summed up in his book *Unified Theories of
Cognition*. We are happy to include in this volume a set of reviews of this
book gathered and edited by the *Artificial Intelligence Journal* Book Review
Editors, Mark Stefik and Stephen Smoliar. These reviews were written before
Allen's death, with the happy expectation that Allen would respond to the
criticisms and alternative proposals of the reviewers. Although Allen knew
about this project, he did not have a chance to write his own response. Paul
Rosenbloom and John Laird, former students and current collaborators of
Newell, have provided an excellent response in his stead. But we all wish
that Newell himself were still here to continue the intellectual/scientific
discussion he so enjoyed.

Finally, we have the opportunity to hear Allen's own words as he reflects
on his book, and his approach to the grand challenge. In the summer of
1991 Phil Agre[1] held an extended interview with Allen. Phil edited the
transcript of the tape, and Allen commented on that draft of the interview.
This published version reflects Phil's understanding of the changes that Allen
requested, but Newell never saw the final form. The interview is a different

---

[1] Philip E. Agre is an Assistant Professor in the Department of Communication at the
University of California, San Diego. He received his Ph.D. in Computer Science from the
Massachusetts Institute of Technology in 1989. Along with Stanley J. Rosenschein, he is
currently editing a forthcoming special issue of *Artificial Intelligence* entitled "Computational
Theories of Interaction and Agency". His book, whose working title is *Computation and Human
Experience*, will be published by Cambridge University Press in the foreseeable future.

genre than the papers usually published in *Artificial Intelligence*, but the significant insight it provides on Newell's thinking justifies its inclusion in this journal of record. Not all members of the Soar community agree with all of Newell's comments; I think that is a reflection of the intellectual depth and diversity of that community and was a source of great pride for Allen.

Allen had a deep regard for process and history in science. He was excited by the prospect of this volume, building links between past and present in our science. His participation in this volume, as with his participation in the fields of AI and cognitive science, has enriched all of us. It is with great love and appreciation that we dedicate this volume to him.

Artificial Intelligence 59 (1993) 5–20
Elsevier

ARTINT 1022

Artificial intelligence in perspective: a retrospective on fifty volumes of the *Artificial Intelligence Journal*

Daniel G. Bobrow

Xerox Palo Alto Research Center, 3333 Coyote Hill Road, Palo Alto, CA 94304, USA

1. History of this issue

When the *Artificial Intelligence Journal* (*AIJ*) put out its fiftieth volume in 1991, it seemed an appropriate time to look at the field through the perspective of the publication of the journal. The growth from one volume of 300 pages in 1970 to six volumes of almost 2400 pages in 1991 reflects the academic growth of the field. The fifty volumes include almost six hundred published papers.

To capture the intellectual highlights of the *AIJ* publication history, we decided to look at what has happened to ideas published in some of the most influential papers from the journal. As a measure of influence, we used references from other papers as determined from SCI's databases, the Science Citation Index and the Social Science Citation Index. We obtained from each index a list of the fifty *AIJ* papers that were most cited in the five years following their publication. There was significant overlap between the two lists, and the combined bibliography of sixty-nine items is appended to this introduction. About thirty of the papers in this bibliography had twenty-five or more citations. The authors of these highly cited papers were asked to write a short essay looking at their original work from their current perspective. We suggested that they might respond to some or all of the following questions:

Correspondence to: D.G. Bobrow, Xerox Palo Alto Research Center, 3333 Coyote Hill Road, Palo Alto, CA 94304, USA. E-mail: bobrow.parc@xerox.com.

(1) How did this paper come about? What was the context (people, institutions, projects) that made this paper seem important to write?

(2) What was the key intellectual contribution of this paper? What was misunderstood or lost, if anything?

(3) What was critically left out that is still an open issue? What open issues from that paper now look central?

(4) What could people build more easily as a result of this paper? Here the emphasis is on products and the field's ability to build new kinds of programs/artifacts.

(5) What part would you have written/done differently given what is known today. This is important for the novice who might assume these papers are the gospel of AI research.

(6) What (small number of) current papers reflect the future of work that was in the paper?

This volume contains essays from those authors who responded to this request. As can be seen, these range in style from thorough overviews of current work to speculative essays about what might come next. In addition, we decided to include in this volume a set of book reviews of Allen Newell's *Unified Theories of Cognition*. Newell's book is a retrospective itself on a long line of work in artificial intelligence, and the comments from leading researchers representing many points of view provides another way of putting the field into perspective. Allen died during the process of pulling this volume together, and did not have a chance to respond personally to the reviews. Two close collaborators, John Laird and Paul Rosenbloom, wrote a response in his stead. To give Newell the last word, we conclude this volume with an interview with Allen Newell.

2. The contents of this issue

The influential papers represented in this collection span a space of methodologies, from mathematical foundations to systems architecture—and a wide variety of domains such as chemical structure analysis, diagnosis of faulty circuits, and understanding of visual scenes. This is a reflection of the spectrum of publications encompassed by *Artificial Intelligence*, and the health of both the field and the journal. But this is not necessarily a fair sampling; the newest approaches and the oldest may both be under-represented. The newest may be missing because of the cutoff date which allowed five years of records; the oldest such as robotics and natural language processing have significant overlap with other strong research communities that have their own journals of record that predate the *AI Journal*. The full bibliography, however, includes important examples of all the fields that impinge on artificial intelligence.

2.1. Foundations

At the heart of the methodology of artificial intelligence is symbolic manipulation. Newell and Simon's early program, the Logic Theorist, showed how machines could manipulate formal logic. This research foreshadowed a long line of work in which logic played an important role as a representation of knowledge. For many, logical reasoning was believed to be a useful way not only of solving problems, but of mimicking some human reasoning.

John McCarthy was an early advocate of logic and formal methods. But John felt this was taken too literally. Most people believed that logic was confined to "absolutely correct reasoning", which John thinks is not sufficient to model intelligent thought processes. In his influential paper "Circumscription—a form of non-monotonic reasoning", he took on the task of formalizing a set of mechanisms he felt crucial to common-sense inference. It is necessary to reason about minimal models that make sense of given sentences of logic and to make assumptions about where the world should be "closed". There have been many variants of nonmonotonic reasoning developed since McCarthy's initial foray. McCarthy believes that future work on making logical reasoning useful will require formalizing currently informal notions such as communication acts between reasoners, and context of use of logical sentences.

Robert Moore's "Semantical considerations of nonmonotonic logic" developed the idea of using logic and a reasoning engine for a system to reason about its own beliefs. Moore called this an "autoepistemic" logic. It provides an intuitive basis for certain kinds of default reasoning, and one sees echos in this of the recursive engine in the Soar work of Newell et al. It is strongly related to the work on nonmonotonic logics. The most significant open questions today are the completeness, complexity, and processing strategies to be used in extensions of autoepistemic logic when extended to full first-order logic.

There has been a continuing tension in the AI community between expressing knowledge in terms of *knowing what* (often identified with a logic-based representation of knowledge), and *knowing how* (often identified with a program/implementation that implicitly uses such knowledge). In "The knowledge level", Newell used the Bell/Newell concepts of systems levels in computer hardware to explicate this issue. Newell proposed an independent knowledge level for AI that would just explain the knowledge necessary to achieve rational behaviors. The mapping to the next lower level, called the symbol level by Newell, introduces resource bounds, brings in architectural considerations, and supports alternative implementations. Newell's principal surprise (and regret) was that this way of looking at systems had never been worked out in any technical detail—a step he thought necessary to clarify the power of this distinction. He thought that use of logic in AI was most appropriate at the knowledge level.

Although logic is often thought to be a "universal representation" by the so-called "logicists" in the AI community, an obvious infelicity in modeling human reasoning processes is the binary nature of truth values for sentences. Adding probabilities to the logic increases the expressiveness of the resulting language. Nilsson's "Probabilistic logic" was an early step in formalizing a method for dealing with uncertain information. Nilsson developed a formal procedure for computing bounds on the probability of a sentence given probabilities of other sentences.

Diagnosing and suggesting treatments for medical patients was an important early use of uncertainty in reasoning. Medical diagnosis is characterized by a hierarchical space of possibilities, where evidence may tend to support or exonerate a set of diseases without providing information about the distribution of the weight of the evidence among these candidates. Describing this problem and providing a tractable approximation to the Dempster–Shafer method is the principal contribution of Gordon and Shortliffe's "A method for managing evidential reasoning in a hierarchical hypothesis space". This paper spawned renewed interest in capturing subjective probabilities, and building models and systems to use them.

Judea Pearl's influential paper "Fusion, propagation, and structuring in belief networks" brought together many of these strands of probabilistic reasoning. Pearl's development of belief networks, a graphical representation, has proved very useful in representing the structure of probability relations. Belief networks support a variety of reasoning methods such as those described by Nilsson and by Gordon and Shortliffe. Pearl's belief networks have found significant application in such diverse tasks as interpreting pictures, diagnosis of medical conditions, and story understanding. Updating belief networks incrementally and extracting potential "causal" links from such networks are the focus of recent exciting research stemming from this work.

Another basic AI description technique is to represent systems through a set of constraints among variables characterizing the system. One of the earliest applications was in understanding line drawings. David Waltz introduced an algorithm to identify mutually constrained vertices in a diagram of a three-dimensional figure. This algorithm had surprisingly good performance properties; this led to much work in the development of other specialized constraint algorithms. Mackworth and Freuder's "The complexity of some polynomial consistency algorithms for constraint satisfaction problems" moved the field from heuristic explanations of the success of these algorithms to formal analytic methods for determining worst-case behavior as a function of the size of the problem.

One of the most useful tools to assist in solving specialized constraint problems is the ATMS, written up in Johan de Kleer's influential "An assumption-based TMS". In some tasks, the problem solver has to keep track of multiple problem solving contexts—for example if it needs to compare several possible problem solutions. The ATMS minimizes computational costs by using a mechanism that supports maximally sharing computations across contexts. The ATMS was initially used for qualitative reasoning, providing explanations of how circuits worked. It was adapted for the task of diagnosing circuits. Later, de Kleer made the ATMS a generally useful tool by defining a standard interface between the inference engine supported by the ATMS and the problem solver. The ATMS has now been used for a wide range of tasks from qualitative reasoning, to vision and natural language processing. The basic ATMS idea has been generalized to support full clausal reasoning, circumscriptive minimization, and abductive reasoning.

2.2. Vision

Since its beginning, an important driving force in *Artificial Intelligence* has been connecting reasoning to real-world problems. Understanding visual scenes was one such forcing function. As with a number of subfields of AI, it was an area of interest for researchers in many disparate fields, such as psychophysics, neurophysiology, signal and optical processing, and photogrammetry. In 1981, to bring current research in vision to the AI casual reader, and to enable vision researchers from fields outside of AI to see how an AI approach might help, Michael Brady edited a special volume on Computer Vision. Four of the papers in that special issue are represented in this retrospective. All take the approach that multiple sources of information are required in the interpretation of visual scenes and that proposed modules should not be unreasonable with respect to data about the human visual system.

Barrow and Tenenbaum's "Interpreting line drawings as three-dimensional surfaces" used information about boundaries in an image in deconvolving the intrinsic scene characteristics from the externals of illumination and the reflectance of surfaces. They classified the varieties of 3-D curves that might appear in a scene and developed plausible constraints on the curve shape and surface that could contain those shapes. Although continued work has been done on algorithms to recover shapes before going on to do tasks that require the knowledge of such shapes, the principal open question is whether this is needed. Barrow and Tenenbaum suggest that perhaps task-specific algorithms would be more useful and provide a better integration of goal-oriented and scene-oriented analysis.

"Determining Optical Flow" by Horn and Schunck presents another approach to integrating multiple sources of information in scene analysis. Optical flow is the distribution of apparent velocities of brightness patterns between two sequential images of a scene. This flow can arise from the motion of the objects, change of illumination, or the relative motion of objects and viewer due to viewer motion. Optical flow can be used for segmentation of the frame into objects, and recovery of the relative motion of those objects. The most important result of this work was to encourage a variational approach to machine vision. In this approach, scene interpretation depends on optimizing an error function over the whole scene, thus supporting incorporation of information from many parts of the scene into the interpretation of a single point or boundary.

Ikeuchi and Horn in "Numerical shape from shading and occluding boundaries" formalized this variational approach. To solve problems of noise influences, they introduced a smoothness constraint (which required neighboring points to have similar surface orientations). To solve the problem of singularities at points of maximum brightness, they used points on occluding boundaries as the starting point for their computation. Each of these ideas has led to its own line of work. For example, the smoothness constraint has been justified by looking at properties of the human visual system. Analyses are now augmented with information from binocular stereo and approximate reflectance maps.

Kanade's "Recovery of the three-dimensional shape of an object from a single view" developed more world-specific constraints on the image to use for analysis. He used the Origami world as a metaphor for understanding line drawings in terms of the images that produce them, converting non-accidental properties in the world to constraints on plausible shapes. Qualitative shape recovery algorithms are inherently very ambiguous; by combining them with quantitative domain regularity constraints, one can obtain a "best" natural interpretation of a real scene. Follow-up work has formalized many of the geometric contraints used, and has started to incorporate constraints based on the physical nature of the image data and the human system that is processing the images.

2.3. Qualitative reasoning

Understanding how designed objects work (and how they sometimes don't work) has been a major research thrust in artificial intelligence. Sometimes this research has been couched in terms of building an "artificial engineer" (AE). From engineering knowledge and an explicit description of an artifact, an AE should be able to do such tasks as explaining how an artifact works, suggesting tests to validate its behavior, and generating hypotheses about faulty components to explain misbehaviors. Engineers and technicians rely on their common-sense intuitions to perform day-to-day tasks using models not couched in the conventional scientific language of differential equations. How this reasoning could be captured was the subject of a number of the most highly cited papers. A 1984 special volume of the *AI Journal* on Qualitative Reasoning about Physical Systems, edited by D. Bobrow, focused on these issues.

In de Kleer and Brown's "A qualitative physics based on confluences", lumped parameter devices were modeled using a simple qualitative calculus, where quantities and their derivatives were mapped into just three values [+], [0], and [-]. Device models were composed to build composite models for the circuits. De Kleer and Brown used their technique to envision all possible behaviors of devices with this topology (and arbitrary real values for circuit parameters), and compared expected and observed behavior to support failure diagnosis. This paper laid out many of the principles that have dominated the research programme in qualitative physics. De Kleer followed with other important work on the theory and implementation of diagnostic systems. De Kleer's retrospective decries a tendency in current QP research to examine mathematical issues for their own sake; he suggests that it rather should be driven by the very interesting and hard problems that come from the world of real problems.

Contrasting with the component-centered approach of de Kleer, Ken Forbus in "Qualitative process theory" (QPC) uses models of physical processes to organize reasoning about physical systems. This was driven in part by his group's development of a tutoring system to explain a steam propulsion system for a boat. Heat transfer and fluid flow are more naturally modeled with process models. Forbus' group, among others, is now exploring how to combine qualitative and numeric simulations to produce *self-explanatory simulators* and *action-augmented envisionments* which can integrate action with analysis.

A third approach to qualitative modeling from the special issue was Kuipers' "Common-sense reasoning about causality: deriving behavior from structure". Kuipers QSIM methodology abstracts from the ordinary differential equations that characterize a physical system to build what he terms qualitative differential equations (QDEs). Reasoning with these QDEs leads to qualitative descriptions of the systems behavior. Comparison of expected and observed behavior is used for diagnosis and model refinement. Kuipers further extended the QSIM modeling paradigm in "Qualitative simulation" where he proved that QDEs were abstractions of ODEs. Because QDEs are an abstraction with fewer constraints, simulation using them produces a large class of qualitative behaviors. Some of these are unrealizable by any ODE, and Kuipers' group has developed global filters that eliminate many such spurious solutions. There have been interesting recent attempts to align Kuipers' QSIM and Forbus' QPC and to develop a common language for sharing models.

Although models in classical physics eschew the notion of causality in favor of expressing constraints among variables defining a system, humans (even physicists) seem to use causality ubiquitously in their qualitative reasoning.

Each of the qualitative reasoning systems described above includes some notion of causality. De Kleer and Brown identify causality with the flow of information in their reasoning engine. Forbus builds causality explicitly into the models of a process. If there are two different ways a process can be driven (voltage driving the current in a resistor, or vice versa) two different QPC models would be used. Kuipers relates causality to the sequence of transitions in the state of a system. Iwasaki and Simon's influential paper "Causality in device behavior" gave rise to an interesting debate in the AI community about where the locus of causality should reside, in the modeler or in the world. Iwasaki and Simon placed it in the dependency structure of variables in equations used to define models, as Simon had in his earlier work in economics. In the debate, it became apparent that causality was primarily influenced by the modeling process; this shifted the focus of the discussion to the more fruitful one of how to construct models designed for particular tasks.

2.4. Diagnosis

Qualitative reasoning and solving constraint systems both play a prominent part in AI work on diagnosis. In "Diagnostic reasoning based on structure and behavior", Davis uses two different models of composite artifacts to diagnose different classes of faults. Using a composed device model like de Kleer's, he can identify faulty components. Using a model of the physical structure of a printed circuit board supports postulating a bridge fault, a connection of two supposedly independent wires. This would be "unthinkable" if the topology of the circuit is assumed fixed. Davis' paper deals with management of multiple models in the diagnostic process and use of constraint suspension as a mechanism for managing the complexity of the troubleshooting process.

Genesereth's "The use of design descriptions in automated diagnosis" examined the tradeoffs between modeling a diagnostic process using rules, and a general diagnostic engine (Dart) that uses a declarative device model. Dart supported diagnosis at multiple levels of abstraction, doing diagnosis in a hierarchical fashion. In recent work, Genesereth's group has extended the use of hierarchical models to other engineering tasks. Within his group's Helios system the same set of models is being used for such tasks as semi-automated design debugging, automated test pattern generation, and testability analysis.

Medical diagnosis has many difficulties not usually faced in the diagnosis of designed systems. Szolovits and Pauker emphasize these differences in their comments in their influential review article, "Categorial and probabilistic reasoning in medicine". In designed systems, it is plausible to assume that only one component has failed. However, ill people often have multiple interacting disorders. Symptoms are not definitively associated with a particular disorder, and there is often significant uncertainty about whether a symptom is present or not. Reasoning in simple cases can be done at a different level of detail—and perhaps with different models—than is necessary for more complex cases. Because of the real-time nature of human illness, it may be necessary to reason about therapy without having a clear diagnosis. Finally, as with many AI systems designed for real problems, there is an increasing need to integrate reasoning into systems designed for monitoring, storing, and displaying large amounts of data.

Probably the most famous AI medical diagnostic system was Mycin, one of the first rule-based expert systems. In their "Production rules as a representation for a knowledge-based consultation program", Davis, Buchanan, and Shortliffe demonstrated that a few hundred rules with weighted (uncertain) associations could be used to perform a nontrivial consulting task. Task knowledge substituted for search, allowing reasonably rapid response. Mycin demonstrated the possibility of using the same knowledge to do both reasoning and explanation. Explanation in Mycin was limited to a trace of rules involved in coming to a conclusion. Crucially though, Mycin acted as model for the development of many other "expert" systems, and the authors trace the family history of the subsequent research systems.

Clancey's "Heuristic classification" is an early example of the power of careful formulation of an AI method. Arising out of the Mycin experience, Clancey carefully distinguishes the problem domain (medical diagnosis), implementation (rules), and the method, which for Mycin he characterizes as heuristic classification. In this general method, a set of inputs is abstracted and classified, and this classification is used to select one of a known set of diagnoses. Heuristic classification is most appropriate for analytic systems where solutions are selected from a pre-enumerated set. It is less so for synthesis problems where solutions to a problem are composed from more primitive elements. Clancey has continued his work of analyzing modeling methods and representations as coupled in task-specific reasoners.

Problems with explanation in the Mycin system were one of the driving forces for the work reported by Clancey in "Epistemology of a rule-based system". His paper characterizes the inference structures used by Mycin to elucidate for students the dual role of knowledge about diseases and reasoning processes, and the "compiled" nature of the rules used in reasoning. The philosophy taken in building Mycin was that it was a medium to transfer knowledge from the head of the expert into the rules making up the system. Then from this medium, a transfer could take place to students who would use the system, understand the rules and learn from them and the system behavior. Clancey's retrospective suggests that we must move from this view of knowledge transfer as the primary driving force for building and using expert systems. In his opinion, it is more important to seek to understand the role a system like Mycin can play in helping students learn about the practices of the community engaged in medical diagnosis and therapy, and hence become a part of that community.

2.5. Architectures

Some papers have been influential because they illuminated a new system architecture. Aikins' architecture in "Prototypical knowledge for expert systems" showed the power of using a hybrid representation system. In contrast to Mycin, where control and domain knowledge are all embedded in the same set of rules, Aikins used frames to represent prototypical consultations. Slots are used to represent steps in the process. This model is used to guide the interaction with the user and the reasoning process. Knowledge acquisition and reasoning were captured by rules. This paper led the way towards "hybrid" architectures combining frames and rules; this architecture underlies many current commercial expert system shells.

Hayes-Roth's "A blackboard architecture for control" contains a number of specialized mechanisms to support intelligent control. The blackboard is a central global memory system that drives the activity in the system. Actions whose condition part matches the global memory are put on an agenda to be considered. A scheduler rates the actions and chooses one, and when fired this action makes changes to the blackboard. This opportunistic planning model works well, both to build expert systems of certain classes and to model certain aspects of human cognition. The blackboard model has been extended recently to incorporate perception machinery and a model of a dynamically changing environment, allowing it to support the reasoning of adaptive, active, intelligent systems that can interact with a changing world.

Many techniques and architectures for expert systems design appeared in the literature in the late seventies and early eighties. It was difficult for a novice to understand what choices to make in building a new expert system. As the result of a small workshop on expert systems, Stefik, Aikins, Balzer, Benoit, Birnbaum, Hayes-Roth, and Sacerdoti wrote "The organization of expert systems, a tutorial". This tutorial characterized tradeoffs in expert system design using, as dimensions to guide the choice of methods, the size of the search space, reliability and stability of the data being process, and the reliability of knowledge available to guide search. There is a continued and increasing trend to more careful descriptions of AI methods, with analyses of costs and tradeoffs. This supports use by domain specialists who want to incorporate into a larger system methods from artificial intelligence. Tutorials such as this one (and textbooks in the same vein) are important contributions to our understanding our field.

2.6. Systems

Some of the most influential papers in the *AI Journal* were those that described systems embedded in real-world problem solvers. One of the earliest was the STRIPS system that was part of the control system for Shakey, the Robot. Fikes and Nilsson, in "STRIPS: a new approach to the application of theorem proving to problem solving", introduced a simple logic-based representation for states of the world with operators that expressed all and only those changes that affected a state. A planner for Shakey's actions tried to find a sequence of operators that would move from an initial state to a specified desired state. This basic model was generalized in a later paper by the authors, and has since been used in many systems.

Dendral was the mother of all expert systems. Work started on the Dendral system in 1965, leading to a system that had profound effects both on how chemistry was done, and how AI systems were built. In their article "Dendral and Meta-Dendral: their applications dimension", published thirteen years after the start of the project, Buchanan and Feigenbaum reported on the AI import of work that had already been reported to chemists. What was most obvious from this work was the importance of domain knowledge in the task competence of the system. This contrasted strongly with the early hope of many people in AI that the discovery of general principles would obviate the need for much knowledge beyond first principles. Rules (condition–action pairs) were used in Dendral to capture some of the knowledge; this inspired the architecture of the Mycin system. Meta-Dendral was a return to an original interest of the authors in theory formation, and led to significant generalization in the field of machine learning. However, learning itself has yet to be important in a significant AI application.

McDermott, in "R1, a rule-based configurer of computer systems", also stressed the importance of the use of a great deal of domain knowledge. R1, and its industrial spinoff, XCON, used this knowledge to configure computer systems without engaging in time-consuming search. Using the Match method of Newell, R1 decides both what is appropriate to do next, and how to do it. A later reimplementation of R1, using the RIME methodology, decomposed this task more explicitly into problem spaces; some problem spaces determined interesting facets of the problem at hand, and others knew how to use the facets in focus. In addition to the technical contribution of this work, R1/XCON demonstrated the importance of a fit between the system and the work practice of the company to achieve significant benefit.

3. Conclusion

This retrospective has provided us a chance to take a long view of the field of artificial intelligence through the eyes of many authors. From these essays, and current research reported in the journal, we can see the emergence of two important themes, specialization and integration.

The early hopes for artificial intelligence (and indeed much of the early hype) centered around the discovery of general techniques that would "solve" the intelligence problem. We understand the problem with this now. Knowledge of specialized domains is a necessary part of any system that is to perform. The other cross-cutting specialization is based on the structure of the problem; methods such as heuristic classification work over a broad spectrum of domains—it only requires that the form of the evidence, and the form of the solutions meet specified criteria.

Integration begins with combining multiple representations and processing techniques. We are seeing hybrid systems that combine neural network front ends with rule-based reasoners. Reasoning engines are integrated with communication modules and database systems. Specialized problem solvers are combined in a system that can call on the right one for a specific task. Symbolic methods combined with numeric methods provide a more understandable simulation of a designed artifact. But perhaps the most important integration we must seek for our AI systems is with the work practice of human communities in which they are embedded. The R1 experience exemplified how only after mutual adjustment of systems and work practice could the system maintain the quality of its output, and contribute to the quality of life of those who interact with it.

4. Bibliography of highly cited papers

This bibliography contains citations of all the papers found in our two requests for fifty most cited papers published in the *Artificial Intelligence Journal*. Citations were gathered from the Science Citation Index and the Social Science Citation Index.

Aikins, J.S.
  Prototypical knowledge for expert systems   **20** (1983) 163–210
Allen, J.F.
  Towards a general theory of action and time   **23** (1984) 123–154
Ballard, B.W.
  The *-minimax search procedure for trees containing chance nodes   **21** (1983) 327–350
Ballard, D.H.
  Parameter nets   **22** (1984) 235–267
Barrow, H.G. and J.M. Tenenbaum
  Interpreting line drawings as three-dimensional surfaces   **17** (1981) 75–116

Foundations

Artificial Intelligence 59 (1993) 23–26
Elsevier

ARTINT 1020

History of circumscription

John McCarthy

Computer Science Department, Stanford University, Stanford, CA 94305, USA

Introduction

My 1980 circumscription paper should be considered as part of a sequence of three papers [7–9] which introduced successively more expressive forms of circumscription. Circumscription is one way of making nonmonotonic reasoning formal in the sense of mathematical logic.

My 1959 paper [6] contains some hints about the need for nonmonotonic reasoning, but it seems to me that I thought about it in terms of what facts the theorem proving and problem solving mechanism took into account rather than in terms of putting the nonmonotonic reasoning in the logic itself. Others, especially Marvin Minsky [10] thought about the need for nonmonotonic reasoning as an objection to the use of mathematical logic.

Here I will assume that formalized nonmonotonic reasoning in general and circumscription in particular are good ideas. Arguments for the proposition are given in the papers. That being the case, we need to ask why it wasn't invented much earlier, any time after the work of Frege [2] and Pierce.

It seems to me that the basic reason is that everyone thought about logic as being confined to absolutely correct reasoning. The fact that nonmonotonic reasoning, which generates conjectures, requires formal tools of the same character as deductive reasoning was not obvious. In fact, I and the others who started formal nonmonotonic reasoning sort of backed into the idea that the very same tools were appropriate.

My opinion is that formalizing nonmonotonic reasoning won't be the final step in applying logic to understanding thought and making computers think well. Formalizing contexts, so far just begun, is another step.

Correspondence to: J. McCarthy, Computer Science Department, Stanford University, Stanford, CA 94305, USA. E-mail: jmc@cs.stanford.edu.

1. What else are we all missing?

The ideas of nonmonotonic reasoning in general have had a mixed reception.

(1) The most vigorous uses of circumscription and other nonmonotonic formalisms have been in expressing common-sense facts and reasoning. The frame, qualification, and ramification problems all involve nonmonotonic reasoning in their general forms. Circumscription and default logic have been applied to them, but unfortunately the most obvious and apparently natural axiomatizations tend to have unintended models, and this has been observed in several examples, especially the Yale Shooting Problem (Hanks and McDermott [3]). This has led to revised formalizations which work but don't seem so natural. It isn't clear whether there is a problem with the systems of nonmonotonic reasoning or whether we simply don't yet have the right axiom sets. Anyway the existing formalizations don't have enough of what I call *elaboration tolerance*. The idea is that formalizations should follow human fact representation in being modifiable primarily by extension rather than by replacement of axioms.

Thus the axioms that allow a program to plan an airplane trip don't take into account either the possibility of losing a ticket or the necessity of wearing clothes. However, a human can modify a plan to take into account either of these requirements should they become relevant but would not revise its general ideas about planning airplane trips to take them into account explicitly. I have an axiomatization of airplane travel that handles losing the ticket nicely, i.e. no axioms about the consequences of losing a ticket or buying a replacement are used in the planning, but if a sentence asserting the loss of a ticket is added, then the original plan can no longer be shown to work and a revised plan involving buying a replacement ticket can be shown to work. The ideas will need to be extended to handle the need to wear clothes.

Etherington, Kraus and Perlis [1] have discussed another problem—the fact that asserting the existence of nonflying birds spoils using the usual axiomatization to show that Tweety flies. Their solution, introducing the notion of *scope* is obviously in the right direction, but multiple scopes will be required. We hope to handle this using formalized contexts.

(2) Mathematical logicians have mainly seen circumscription and the other forms of nonmonotonic reasoning as a worthwhile addition to their subject matter. For example, Kolaitis and Papadimitriou [4] discuss the collapsibility of circumscription and its computability, and Lehmann and Magidor [5] discuss general axioms for nonmonotonic logics.

(3) Researchers interested in applications of logic to AI have also worked on the mathematical logical foundations of nonmonotonic reasoning and its relation to other fields of computer science, e.g. logic programming.

Others have applied nonmonotonic logical formalisms to axiomatization and reasoning in common-sense domains—mainly to formalization of the results of action. Today the main treatments of the frame, qualification, and ramification problems use nonmonotonic reasoning formalisms.

(4) People taking a probabilistic, i.e. Bayesian, approach to AI have mostly misunderstood nonmonotonic logic. Probabilities and nonmonotonic logic are complementary rather than rival formalisms. Nonmonotonic methods, e.g. circumscription, are necessary to form the propositions to which probabilities are to be assigned.

For example, suppose a person knows of some things wrong with his car and intends to get them fixed. The proposition that there is nothing else wrong with his car is most conveniently formed by circumscribing the predicate "is wrong with the car". After forming it, he can assign a probability to it. However, he may plan to use the car after the known things have been fixed without ever using probabilities in any conscious way. Maybe none of the nonmonotonic formalizations discussed in AI actually assign probabilities, because they can be treated either as infinitesimal or near 1.

However, suppose we want to formalize a domain where nontrivial numerical probabilities are relevant. Suppose also that the propositions to which probabilities are usefully assigned are not given in advance, i.e. that there is nothing else wrong with the car. Then it will be necessary to combine nonmonotonic logical formalisms with probabilities, and if a computer program is to do the job by itself then it will have to combine the formalisms.

Actually, humans do nonmonotonic reasoning all the time in forming the propositions to which they later attach probabilities. However, as long as this part of the problem is done by people and not by computers, it can be treated informally.

(5) Some of the most confused people about formalized nonmonotonic reasoning and the problems for which AI people use it have been philosophers. This seems to come from trying to fit it into categories that philosophers have previously studied.

References

[1] D.W. Etherington, S. Kraus and D. Perlis, Nonmonotonicity and the scope of reasoning, *Artif. Intell.* **52** (1991) 221–261.
[2] G. Frege, *Begriffsschrift* (1879).
[3] S. Hanks and D. McDermott, Nonmonotonic logic and temporal projection, *Artif. Intell.* **33** (3) (1987) 379–412.
[4] Kolaitis and Papadimitriou (198x).
[5] D. Lehmann and M. Magidor, Rational logic and their models: a study in cumulative logic, Tech. Rept. TR 88-16, Leibniz Center for Computer Science, Department of Computer Science, Hebrew University, Jerusalem (1988).

[6] J. McCarthy, Programs with common sense, in: *Proceedings Teddington Conference on the Mechanization of Thought Processes* (Her Majesty's Stationery Office, London, 1959).

[7] J. McCarthy, Epistemological problems of artificial intelligence, in: *Proceedings IJCAI-77*, Cambridge, MA (1977).

[8] J. McCarthy, Circumscription—a form of non-monotonic reasoning, *Artif. Intell.* **13** (1–2) (1980) 27–39.

[9] J. McCarthy, Applications of circumscription to formalizing common sense knowledge, *Artif. Intell.* **28** (1986) 89–116.

[10] M. Minsky, A framework for representing knowlege, in: P.H. Winston, ed., *Psychology of Computer Vision* (McGraw-Hill, New York, 1975).

Artificial Intelligence 59 (1993) 27–30
Elsevier

ARTINT 984

Autoepistemic logic revisited

Robert C. Moore

Artificial Intelligence Center, SRI International, 333 Ravenswood, Menlo Park, CA 94025, USA

"Semantical considerations on nonmonotonic logic" [10] started off to be a short commentary of a methodological/philosophical character on McDermott and Doyle's work on nonmonotonic logics [7,8]. When I started writing the paper, I didn't understand the technical details of McDermott and Doyle's logics very well, but I knew that they had some peculiar and unintuitive properties, and I believed that these might be related to what I saw as some methodological problems in their approach. The principal problem I saw was in trying to model jumping to conclusions by default with a logic whose notion of inference is guaranteed by its semantics to be truth-preserving. To drive home the point, I tried to distinguish between default reasoning and what I called "autoepistemic reasoning", or reasoning about one's own beliefs. (To be linguistically pure, I should have called it "autodoxastic reasoning", but in all honesty, that just didn't have the same ring to it.) I won't go any further into the details here, because that short methodological commentary survives as Section 2 of what turned out to be a work of much broader scope. As I studied McDermott and Doyle's papers in more detail, I discovered that the problematical features of their logics had technical remedies that could be motivated within a framework based on autoepistemic reasoning. Therefore, I called my reconstruction of nonmonotonic logic "autoepistemic logic". The result was a simple and elegant logic that both explained and eliminated many of the unintuitive properties of McDermott and Doyle's logics, and that also turned out to provide a foundation for a substantial amount of further work.

This material was first presented at the 1983 International Joint Conference on Artificial Intelligence (although it was not published in *Artifical Intelligence* until 1985). In 1984, I presented a second paper [9], providing a possible-world semantics for autoepistemic logic. The original work had

Correspondence to: R.C. Moore, Artificial Intelligence Center, SRI International, 333 Ravenswood, Menlo Park, CA 94025, USA.

been based on a syntactic notion of belief: The beliefs of an agent were characterized simply by an arbitrary list of formulas. The original paper went on to develop a theory of an ideal autoepistemic reasoner, but the basic framework could be applied to any reasoner, ideal or not. By confining its scope to ideal reasoners, the second paper is able to develop a more structured model theory that makes concrete examples much easier to present. In particular, in the original framework, the characterization of an ideal reasoner required an infinite number of formulas in the syntactic model, since an ideal reasoner always has an infinite number of beliefs. With the possible-world framework, however, the beliefs of an ideal reasoner based on simple premises can be characterized by a simple, finite model, which makes it easy to rigorously demonstrate the existence of autoepistemic theories having particular properties.

The publication of these two papers was followed by considerable activity by other researchers. The majority of this work attempts to relate autoepistemic logic to other formalisms. This literature has become far too extensive to catalogue here, but some of the more interesting papers include Konolige's [3] and Marek and Truszczynski's [6] studies of the relationship between autoepistemic logic and default logic, Gelfond's [1] and Gelfond and Lifschitz's [2] work on the relation of autoepistemic logic to negation-as-failure in logic programming, and Przymusinski's [11] grand unification of three-valued forms of all the major formalisms for nonmonotonic reasoning using the "well-founded semantics" for logic programming. In addition Shvarts [12] has gone back to look more closely at the relationship between autoepistemic logic and McDermott's [7] nonmonotonic modal logic. Shvarts has shown that autoepistemic logic does, in fact, fall within McDermott's framework and would be nonmonotonic K45, or nonmonotonic weak S5, to use the terminology of "Semantical considerations" [10]. McDermott, however, looked only at nonmonotonic T, S4, and S5, and so missed out on the appropriate logic for the autoepistemic interpretation of the modal operators.

To me, the most interesting open problems connected with autoepistemic logic concern its extension from propositional logic to first-order logic and the computational properties of the resulting systems. The original papers on autoepistemic logic concerned only the propositional version of the logic. With the possible-world semantics, it is easy to show that any propositional autoepistemic theory is decidable, as long as there are only finitely many proposition letters. For each such theory, there are only finitely many possible-world models, which are themselves finite structures. So any questions of validity, satisfiability, or consequence can be answered simply by enumerating and checking all the models.

If autoepistemic logic is extended to first-order logic, but "quantifying-in" is dissallowed—that is, if autoepistemic modal operators are never applied to formulas with free variables—then all the important syntactic and semantic properties of the logic seem to carry over, but the computational properties change because the models are no longer guaranteed to be finite, and there may be infinitely many of them. In fact, it is easy to see that an autoepistemic version of an essentially undecidable theory would not even be recursively enumerable. The reason is that formulas of the form $\neg LP$ will mean "P is not provable". So if we could enumerate the formulas of the autoepistemic theory, we would have a way to decide the formulas of (perhaps an extension of) the original theory. But if the original theory is essentially undecidable (e.g., Peano arithmetic), this is known to be impossible.

The interesting question then, is what happens with an autoepistemic version of a *decidable* theory. If no extra axioms are added, then it is easy to show that the theory remains decidable. If a finite number of extra axioms are added, the theory remains decidable, as long as quantifying-in is not allowed. This might seem to give us a lot, but in fact such theories are not very expressive. Without quantifying-in, the only way to express a generalization such as "my only brothers are the ones I know about", is to use an axiom schema, which amounts to adding an infinite number of axioms. If we allow axiom schemata or other infinite sets of axioms, it is an open question whether the theory remains decidable.

Finally, the extension of first-order autoepistemic logic to allow quantifying-in remains unsettled. This is a conceptually difficult area, because it is not completely clear what such formulas mean. There is a long and unresolved debate in the philosophy of language about the difference between "it is believed that something has the property P", and "there is something that is believed to have the property P". Yet that is exactly the distinction that would be marked in autoepistemic logic by the difference between $L\exists x P(x)$ and $\exists x LP(x)$. Levesque [5] has proposed a logic containing an operator whose intuitive interpretation is meant to be "all that I know", which could be thought of as a metatheory for autoepistemic logic and which does allow quantifying-in. However, Levesque has been unable to prove that his logic is semantically complete.

In any case, at this writing, I am unaware of any published attempts to allow quantifying-in directly in autoepistemic logic, although a paper by Konolige [4] on the subject is in press. It will be interesting to see whether a concensus can be reached on the right approach to this problem.

References

[1] M. Gelfond, On stratified autoepistemic theories, in: *Proceedings AAAI-87*, Seattle, WA (1987) 207–211.
[2] M. Gelfond and V. Lifschitz, The stable model semantics for logic programming, in: R. Kowalski and K. Bowen, eds., *Proceedings Fifth Logic Programming Symposium*

(MIT Press, Cambridge, MA, 1988) 1070–1080.

[3] K. Konolige, On the relation between default logic and autoepistemic theories, *Artif. Intell.* **35** (3) (1988) 343–382.

[4] K. Konolige, Quantification in autoepistemic logic, *Fundamenta Informaticae* (to appear).

[5] H.J. Levesque, All I know: a study in autoepistemic logic, *Artif. Intell.* **42** (2–3) (1990) 263–309.

[6] W. Marek and M. Truszczynski, Relating autoepistemic and default logic, in: *Proceedings First International Conference on Principles of Knowledge Representation and Reasoning,* Toronto, Ont. (1989) 276–288.

[7] D. McDermott, Nonmonotonic logic II: Nonmonotonic modal theories, *J. ACM* **29** (1) (1982) 33–57.

[8] D. McDermott and J. Doyle, Non-monotonic logic I, *Artif. Intell.* **13** (1–2) (1980) 41–72.

[9] R.C. Moore, Possible-world semantics for autoepistemic logic, in: *Proceedings Non-Monotonic Reasoning Workshop,* New Paltz, NY (1984) 344-354.

[10] R.C. Moore, Semantical considerations on nonmonotonic logic, *Artif. Intell.* **25** (1) (1985) 75–94.

[11] T.C. Przymusinski, Three-valued nonmonotonic formalisms and semantics of logic programs, *Artif. Intell.* **49** (1–3) (1991) 309–343.

[12] G. Shvarts, Autoepistemic modal logics, in: *Theoretical Aspects of Reasoning about Knowledge: Proceedings of the Third Conference,* Pacific Grove, CA (1990) 97–109.

Artificial Intelligence 59 (1993) 31–38
Elsevier

ARTINT 986

Reflections on the knowledge level

Allen Newell

School of Computer Science, Carnegie Mellon University, Pittsburgh, PA 15213, USA

"The knowledge level" [9] describes the nature of *knowledge* as the medium of a system level that lies above the *symbol* or *program level* in the hierarchy of levels of computational systems. The unique character of the knowledge level is that its central law of behavior, the principle that the system will take whatever actions attain its *goals* given its knowledge, can be computed without positing any internal structure of the system. Put another way, the knowledge level abstracts completely from representation, structure, and process. That this is possible—that a system's behavior can be predicted based only on the *content* of its representations plus its knowledge of its goals—is the essence of being an *intelligent* system. The knowledge level finds its most common use in designing systems, where the designer specifies a component by positing its function (i.e., its goal) and the knowledge available to it.

Systems can be described at many levels. A system described at the knowledge level can also be described at the symbol level, which is to say in terms of representations, data structures, and processes. The symbol-level description shows how the knowledge-level behavior is attained, just as the register-transfer description shows how the symbol-level system is realized by architectural mechanisms, and so on down to descriptions in terms of physical concepts.

The paper claims these concepts of knowledge and knowledge-level system are used in practice by the AI and computer science community, hence understood implicitly. The paper itself is just making explicit to the community what it already knows in practice.

The genesis of the knowledge level

"The knowledge level" officially came about as a presidential address to the AAAI at their first scientific conference, which was held at Stanford University in the summer of 1979. The paper, published simultaneously in both *Artificial Intelligence* and the *AI Magazine*, is essentially a written version of the talk, and I always think of the two of them together.

The occasion of a presidential address, especially an initial one, has the potential to be precedent-setting in a variety of ways and I gave considerable thought to what I wanted to do. Chief among these was to set the course for presidential addresses to be about our science and not about our society or the state of applications or any of the other myriad things that presidents of societies find interesting to talk about.

Giving a contentful talk on a ceremonial occasion would seem to add some strong constraints. But I had already developed a strategy of using ceremonial talks to present general views of the science, where the material was contentful but not highly technical. Herb Simon and I had employed this strategy in our Turing Award lecture [12], where we talked about symbols and search as the two great pillars of artificial intelligence. I had used the strategy in my talk on physical symbol systems, at the inaugural meeting of the Cognitive Science Society at La Jolla [8]. Talking about the knowledge level fit this strategy exactly, it seemed to me.

This still might appear strange—the knowledge level was a new technical concept, which needed to be introduced to the scientific community in technical terms before it could be summarized or discussed in high-level terms. But that wasn't the way I saw it. Knowledge was, like two or three other fundamental concepts in computer science and AI, a concept that everyone had, and had largely correctly, but a concept that had not been discovered or invented by any specific scientist—certainly not myself. Two other important examples are symbol systems and architectures. What I was doing in talking about the knowledge level, I believed, was simply giving voice to a scientific concept that we all had. Whether the knowledge level was exactly the right way to cast our common understanding of knowledge was perhaps a little problematic, but not the main understanding of the nature of knowledge.

There was a final ingredient in my orientation to the talk, and hence the paper. Although I believed that all of us in AI and computer science had an essentially correct concept of knowledge, I was acutely aware that knowledge had not been conceptualized explicitly in the literature. The concept was used entirely implicitly in our practice. Indeed, the explicit use of the term *knowledge* still resided with the philosophers—who, from my perspective, didn't understand at all what knowledge was. In accordance with my own belief that I was not giving a scientific talk, only talking about scientific matters, I was not about to provide in my talk (and paper) a fully technical treatment of the knowledge level. So I viewed the talk (and paper) as launching a not-yet-robust explicit formulation, with the hope that others would pick it up, find out how to use it in technical ways, and thus begin the evolutionary process of creating a useful technical concept.

These are the four main ingredients that existed for me at the the the time of creation of the knowledge-level talk—the honor of the first AAAI presidential address, the attempt to establish its culture to be scientific, the presentation of another noninvented but fundamental scientific concept, and the attempt to bring to the surface the concept of knowledge and launch its life as a technical notion. All of these ingredients were quite explicit, not only in my thinking, but in the talk, and some of them even survived into the published paper. There was, by the way, no prior work by me on the subject of knowledge, before being invited to be president and facing the challenge of what to do for the initial presidential address. After all, I had understood the concept since the late 1950s [7] and felt no need to put its study on my scientific agenda.

What has happened?

On the style of the AAAI presidential address, the results have been decidedly mixed. The presidential address has certainly not developed a tradition of dealing with science. There have been some such presidential addresses, but also many that dealt with more general matters—though no less presidential for that. Of course, it was naive of me to believe I could influence the successive leaders in AI, who, of all people, are independent agents.

On the other hand, I was quite successful in the strategy of using ceremonial talks to convey general scientific results without benefit of the hard research that should be there to back them up. "The knowledge level" has joined "Symbols and search" and "Physical symbol systems" as some of my more well-known papers. However, some people have told me that "The knowledge level" is rather hard to understand, so these papers may be more technical than I realize (or just badly written—always a real possibility).

On the third hand, no one has taken seriously—or even been intrigued with—the proposition that the knowledge level was not invented or discovered by me (or anyone else). As well, this has not happened for Herb Simon and myself on the physical symbol system. In both cases, we are cited according to standard practice as the progenitors of these ideas.

Let me be clear, once again, about what is going on (although with no hope of communicating to anyone). The standard realist conception of science has it that nature is the way it is. Scientists, in attempting to understand nature, engage in deliberate activities of observation, measurement, and theorizing. They discover facts and regularities about nature, and their theories sometimes successfully predict these facts and regularities. Science gives credit (and sometimes glory) to the scientists who make these discoveries. The social structure of science is such that the only way additions to the body of science get made is through the agency of human scientists.

But with computer science and AI, an alternate path has emerged. These fields build artifacts—computers, architectures, languages, software systems—which can embody scientific truths about the domain of information processing. The creators of these systems need not be aware of all that they put into these artifacts. They can construct an artifact under one mental model that suffices to get the artifact built. But this same artifact can embody additional truths, which can be learned by the people that use it. Just as in mathematics, in computing there are many implications of a computing system that can emerge with investigation and use. It is obvious, for instance, that the engineers who designed and built the Rand Johnniac and the IBM704 did not envision list processing as something their machines could do. To this potential for learning must be added that AI and computer scientists spend great amounts of time using computers and programming systems, thereby learning from them. Someone who learns to use Lisp assimilates many of the essential concepts of physical symbol systems. It is irrelevant whether John McCarthy was thinking about physical symbol systems at the time he created Lisp. In fact, he wasn't quite. He was close in a number of ways, but conceptualized it somewhat differently.

People learn about the knowledge level because they must specify systems to be programmed. They do not specify these in terms of just inputs and outputs, but also in terms of what the program knows that it can use to compute the outputs from the inputs. So they induce from their practice a working notion of what it means for a system to have knowledge and what it means to supply the symbol-level mechanisms that encode that knowledge and extract it to make the program behave as desired. It does not require a Newton to conceive of the knowledge level, all that is required was to build general-purpose computers which were large enough so that large and complex programs could be built for them. So we all read out of computers an essentially correct operational notion of knowledge, without having any particular person conceptualize computers in these terms. Thus, no scientist discovered either knowledge or the knowledge level in the sense of discovery that science uses and honors.

Now we turn to what has happened to the concept of the knowledge level since I gave the talk in 1979. The story here is very mixed and varies by community.

The knowledge-based systems community has picked up the concept and uses it extensively. They have not refined it much nor do they use it in a highly technical way. But it serves them well as a way of talking about what knowledge a system must have without regard to how it is to be represented. It is not clear that they need much more than this.

The logicist community will have nothing to do with the concept. It is not that they disagree with it or think it is wrong—at least so far as I can detect. It is that it doesn't help them in what they want to do and it doesn't interest them as a concept to be pursued. Hector Levesque was intrigued enough by the notion to use it to recast his thesis work [6], but it has played no continuing role in his research, as far as I can see.

The logicist community would seem to be a natural group to take up the nature of knowledge and the knowledge level. They do deal with knowledge, but in their own way. Two factors seem to me to have worked against the knowledge level becoming a topic for logicist research. First, and most important, the vehicle for research within the logicist community is a logic. There are dozens of logics—monotonic, nonmonotonic, temporal, and otherwise. A logic is a particular symbol-level representational system. No matter how general a logic is, it is not at the knowledge level. The knowledge level is, in a certain sense, formless and it is not clear what to do with it. Second, the logicists pay attention to the philosophy of epistemology and take seriously its orientation on knowledge and what the proper questions are. Neither of these lead to taking the knowledge level seriously. Interestingly, there exists a well-developed axiomatic formulation of knowledge (Hintikka [5]), but as far as I know it has never caught the attention of the AI logicist community either, except for the small foray by Levesque mentioned above.

The machine-learning community picked up the concept through an important article of Dietterich, "Learning at the knowledge level" [4]. *Knowledge-level learning* is where the system acquires new knowledge. In contrast, *symbol-level learning* is where the system learns only to evoke the knowledge it already has faster and more reliably. Systems that take in information from the outside world are engaged in knowledge-level learning. Systems that cache are engaged in symbol-level learning—they run faster after caching but they don't know anything they didn't before. It is a nice distinction and very useful, and established the use of the knowledge level in the machine-learning community. The work is limited by its restriction that the knowledge of a knowledge-level system must be representable as the deductive closure of a set of statements in a logic. This probably reinforced a common error in understanding the knowledge level, since there are many other ways to represent the knowledge in a system.

For the main stream AI community, concerned with constructing intelligent systems (which includes the machine-learning community), a key implication of the knowledge level is its provision of a definition of *intelligence* [11, Chapter 2]. The knowledge-level description of a system is the ideal point—any system that can be fully described at the knowledge level is a system of perfect intelligence, for its symbol-level mechanisms bring to bear all that can be brought to bear to solve its problems. Systems that cannot be so described (which are most systems) are intelligent to the degree that they approximate a knowledge-level system—which is to say, to the degree that they can bring the knowledge in the system to bear on the system's goals. I detect very little interest in this definition of intelligence within the AI community and, in fact, very little interest at all in defining intelligence. I think this arises because a definition of intelligence does not seem to play any operational role in their research. I can tie this to my original assessment that the knowledge level had not yet been developed into an appropriate technical concept. That is still missing here. There is no way, given the current formulation, to assess the degree of approximation, hence to be able to get some leverage on how systems could be made more intelligent or any number of other questions. Dietterich's effort, described above, started this process for machine learning. No one has done it for the nature of intelligence. Until then, I can't blame the AI community for ignoring the concept.

The cognitive-science philosophy community does not pay the concept of the knowledge level any attention. There are two good reasons for this. First, philosophy essentially owned the concept of knowledge for all history up to the coming of computer science. So they believe they already have a line on the notion. Its focus was and remains on questions of certainty, and its style is epitomized by trying to establish by argument that "knowledge is justified true belief". Second, a concept of *intentional stance* and *intentional system* was introduced by Dan Dennett [1,2], which is in most ways identical to the knowledge level. I believe that it puts the emphasis in the wrong place, namely on the outside observer who takes the intentional stance vis a vis an agent. Thus the concept conveys the view that whether an agent can be described as an intentional system (i.e., at the knowledge level) is in the eye of the beholder—which is false without a fine capability of hallucination. But my attempts to convince Dennett have proved futile [3,10]. In any event, the intentional stance serves to keep the knowledge level alive within philosophy. My impression is that it plays an extremely minor role there—something that Dennett introduced that has to be acknowledged on occasion.

The last community is a very small one, namely, the Soar community, a collection of about a hundred scientists around the world who use the Soar architecture [14]. Here the knowledge level has been deeply integrated into the research on Soar. We take the nature of intelligence to be how well a system delivers the knowledge that can be ascribed to it, and find this a very useful formulation [15].

The most interesting thing we have done with the knowledge level is to use it in formulating the *problem-space computational model*. Gradually it has become apparent that between the knowledge-level description of a Soar system and the symbol-level description (the one that talks about recognition memory, working memory, the decide process, impasses, and chunking) there is an organization in terms of problem spaces which in many ways is like another computational model. One need only talk about operators, states, desired states, selection knowledge for operators, etc. This must be a symbol-level organization (we know of no way to have a genuine system level between the symbol level and the knowledge level), but different from the one we call Soar5.2 (the recognition memory, etc.). In searching for the nature of this independent-appearing organization, we have formulated a recursive structure in which knowledge-level systems fill in the details of the problem spaces (such as selecting operators and implementing operators), and problem spaces are the symbol-level organizations that realize the knowledge-level systems. Finally, of course, there is immediately available knowledge to realize a knowledge-level system for some aspect of a problem space, and no further decomposition into subproblem spaces is required [13]. Thus the knowledge level is beginning to play a technical role in our attempts to define Soar as having a problem-space computational model as an intermediate level.

What will happen?

Nothing has changed my mind about the existence of the knowledge level or the nature of knowledge in the decade since the paper was written. After all, nothing has happened in the meantime to change the way the computational community uses the concept of knowledge, which is the grounding of the paper. I think the acceptance of the concept will rise very gradually. The logicists will never give it a thought, no matter what. For the rest of us, everything will depend on some scientists turning the concept to specific technical uses, such as the assessment of the intelligence of a system, which will lock the concept into the technical fabric of our field. This, of course, is the same thought which ended the original paper.

References

[1] D.C. Dennett, *Content and Consciousness* (Routlege and Kegan Paul, London, 1969).
[2] D.C. Dennett, *The Intentional Stance* (Bradford Books/MIT Press, Cambridge, MA, 1988).
[3] D.C. Dennett, Precis of *The Intentional Stance, Behav. Brain Sci.* **11** (3) (1988) 495–546. (Commentary by 25 authors and final response by Dennett.)
[4] T.G. Dietterich, Learning at the knowledge level, *Mach. Learn.* **1** (1986) 287–316.
[5] J. Hintikka, *Knowledge and Belief* (Cornell University Press, Ithaca, NY, 1962).
[6] H.J. Levesque, Foundations of a functional approach to knowledge level representation, *Artif. Intell.* **23** (1984) 155–212.

[7] A. Newell, Some problems of basic organization in problem-solving programs, in: M.C. Yovits, G.T. Jacobi and G.D. Goldstein, eds., *Self Organizing Systems* (Spartan, Washington, DC, 1962).

[8] A. Newell, Physical symbol systems, *Cogn. Sci.* **4** (1980) 135–183.

[9] A. Newell, The knowledge level, *Artif. Intell.* **18** (1982) 87–127; also: *AI Mag.* **2** (Summer 1981) 1–20; also: CMU CSD Tech. Report, Carnegie Mellon University, Pittsburgh, PA (1981).

[10] A. Newell, The intentional stance and the knowledge level: Comments on Daniel Dennett, *The Intentional Stance, Behav. Brain Sci.* **11** (3) (1988) 520–522.

[11] A. Newell, *Unified Theories of Cognition* (Harvard University Press, Cambridge, MA, 1990).

[12] A. Newell and H.A. Simon, Computer science as empirical inquiry: symbols and search, *Commun. ACM* **19** (3) (1976) 113–126.

[13] A. Newell, G. Yost, J.E. Laird, P.S. Rosenbloom and E. Altmann, Formulating the problem space computational model, in: R.F. Rashid, ed., *Carnegie-Mellon Computer Science: A 25-Year Commemorative* (ACM Press/Addison-Wesley, Reading, MA, 1991).

[14] P.S. Rosenbloom, J.E. Laird, A. Newell and R. McCarl, A preliminary analysis of the Soar architecture as a basis for general intelligence, *Artif. Intell.* **47** (1991) 289–325.

[15] P.S. Rosenbloom, A. Newell and J.E. Laird, Towards the knowledge level in Soar: the role of the architecture in the use of knowledge, in: K. VanLehn, ed., *Architectures for Intelligence* (Erlbaum, Hillsdale, NJ, 1991).

Artificial Intelligence 59 (1993) 39–42
Elsevier

ARTINT 985

Probabilistic logic revisited

Nils J. Nilsson

Robotics Laboratory, Department of Computer Science, Stanford University, Stanford, CA 94305, USA

1. Origins

Before beginning the research that led to "Probabilistic logic" [11], I had participated with Richard Duda, Peter Hart, and Georgia Sutherland on the PROSPECTOR project [3]. There, we used Bayes' rule (with some assumptions about conditional independence) to deduce the probabilities of hypotheses about ore deposits given (sometimes uncertain) geologic evidence collected in the field [4]. At that time, I was also familiar with the use of "certainty factors" by Shortliffe [18], the use of "fuzzy logic" by Zadeh [20], and the Dempster/Shafer formalism [16]. All of these methods made (sometimes implicit and unacknowledged) assumptions about underlying joint probability distributions, and I wanted to know how the mathematics would work out if no such assumptions were made. I began by asking how *modus ponens* would generalize when one assigned probabilities (instead of binary truth values) to P and $P \supset Q$. As can be verified by simple calculations using a Venn diagram, the probability of Q is under-determined in this case but can be bounded as follows:

$$p(P) + p(P \supset Q) - 1 \leqslant p(Q) \leqslant p(P \supset Q).$$

The techniques that I developed in the paper for calculating bounds on probabilities can be understood as a kind of generalization of the Venn diagram method. While I was working out the ideas in "Probabilistic logic", I was unaware of similar work by Good [7], Smith [19], and de Finetti [2].

Given probabilities on sentences, one can do no better than calculate bounds on derived sentences because the probabilities of the given sentences

Correspondence to: N.J. Nilsson, Robotics Laboratory, Department of Computer Science, Stanford University, Stanford, CA 94305, USA. E-mail: nilsson@cs.stanford.edu.

do not, in general, completely determine the underlying joint distribution. However, it is of interest to ask about the minimum-entropy joint distribution because, perhaps unlike some of the other methods for reasoning with uncertain information, the minimum-entropy distribution assumes minimal additional information. For this reason, I included in the paper Cheeseman's technique for minimum entropy [1].

My primary aim in writing "Probabilistic logic" was to present an intuitively reasonable but foundational account of the problem of uncertain reasoning. The complete impracticability of calculating the bounds prescribed in the paper was of little concern to me because I imagined that approximate methods might later be devised, and I even suggested an approximate method in the paper. Pearl [12, p. 463] mentions that a mechanism in Quinlan's INFERNO [14] can be regarded as a local approximation to probabilistic logic.

2. Main contribution

The key intellectual contribution of "Probabilistic logic" was a formal procedure for calculating the bounds on the probability of a sentence in the predicate calculus given the probabilities (or the bounds on the probabilities) of other sentences. I called this process "probabilistic entailment" because it is based on models of the sentences. The contribution served mainly to elucidate the foundations of probabilistic reasoning even though it is in general, intractable. I hoped that it would set the stage for possible approximate methods and for comparison with other methods.

3. Open issues

A major omission from the paper was any discussion of proof-theoretic methods for making probabilistic deductions. The paper stimulated some attempts to develop deductive techniques; see, for example, recent work by Haddawy and Frisch who have found a complete set of inference rules for a subset of probabilistic logic [9].

Devising good approximate methods for probabilistic entailment is still an important area for future work. It would seem that assumptions about conditional independence (as might be represented by influence diagrams or belief networks) could be used to simplify the bounds calculations in probabilistic entailment. In that connection, see a recent paper by Fertig and Breese [6].

Judea Pearl [13] has persuaded me that I should have shown more explicitly how probabilistic logic should handle assignments of conditional rather than absolute probabilities. For example, a more natural generalization of *modus ponens* emerges if we specify $p(P)$ and, then, $p(Q|P)$ instead of $p(P \supset Q)$. The probability of Q is then bounded by

$$p(Q|P)p(P) \leqslant p(Q) \leqslant 1.$$

Pearl [12, p. 459] argues that the probability $p(P \supset Q)$ does not properly reflect what we normally mean by the certainty of the rule "if P then Q". For example, if we want to say that some rare event P has a likely consequence Q, and we write $p(P) = 0.01$ and $p(P \supset Q) = 0.9$, we find that the two sentences are inconsistent. Writing $p(P) = 0.01$ and $p(Q|P) = 0.9$ gives the bound $0.09 \leqslant p(Q) \leqslant 1$, which is more reasonable.

4. Subsequent work

Work on probabilistic reasoning exploded after the mid-1980s. Several "Workshops on Uncertainty in Artificial Intelligence" have been held, and their proceedings have been published. The volume edited by Shafer and Pearl contains many important papers as well as illuminating perspectives by the editors about various aspects of uncertain reasoning [17]. Pearl has also written an indispensable text on the subject [12], now available in a revised and updated second printing.

Fagin and Halpern have presented a more formal and general analysis than that contained in my paper [5].

Two other important developments have occurred. One is the use of belief networks and influence diagrams to represent causal relations that allow simplifying assumptions to be made about the conditional independence of propositions (see [12, Chapters 2–4] and [15]). Another development involves analyses by Heckerman [10] and by Grosof [8] that establish important connections among techniques that use (slightly modified) certainty factors, the Dempster/Shafer formalism, and special cases of Bayes' rule.

5. Conclusions

Since my foray into probabilistic reasoning was brief, and because I have not acquainted myself with the extensive and growing literature in this field, I will refrain from attempting any sage remarks about how my work might relate to that of others. The reader might want to consult a few paragraphs by Pearl, however, on the circumstances under which one might want to use probabilistic logic [12, pp. 461–462]. I am also indebted to Judea Pearl for his comments and suggestions about the present note.

References

[1] P.Cheeseman, A method of computing generalized Bayesian probability values for expert systems, in: *Proceedings IJCAI-83*, Karlsruhe, Germany (1983)

[2] B. de Finetti, *Theory of Probability* (Wiley, New York, 1974).

[3] R.O. Duda, The PROSPECTOR system for mineral exploration, Final Report to the U.S. Geological Survey, Contract No. 14-08-0001-17296, SRI International, Menlo Park, CA (1980).

[4] R.O. Duda, P.E. Hart and N.J. Nilsson, Subjective Bayesian methods for rule-base inference systems, in: *Proceedings 1976 National Computer Conference*, AFIPS **45** (1976) 1075–1082; also in: B.W. Webber and N.J. Nilsson, eds., *Readings in Artificial Intelligence* (Morgan Kaufmann, San Mateo, CA, 1981).

[5] R. Fagin and J. Halpern, Uncertainty, belief, and probability, in: *Proceedings IJCAI-89*, Detroit, MI (1989) 1161–1167.

[6] K.W. Fertig and J.S. Breese, Interval influence diagrams, in: M. Henrion, R.D. Shachter, T.S. Levitt, L.N. Kanal and J.F. Lemmer, eds., *Uncertainty in Artificial Intelligence* **5** (Elsevier Science Publishers B.V., Amsterdam, 1990) 149–161.

[7] I.J. Good, *Probability and the Weighing of Evidence* (Griffin, London, 1950).

[8] B. Grosof, Evidential confirmation as transformed probability, in: L.N. Kanal and J.F. Lemmer, eds., *Uncertainty in Artificial Intelligence* (North-Holland, Amsterdam, 1986).

[9] P. Haddawy and A. Frisch, Anytime deduction for probabilistic logic, Unpublished Manuscript (submitted for publication).

[10] D. Heckerman, Probabilistic interpretations for MYCIN's certainty factors, in: L.N. Kanal and J.F. Lemmer, eds., *Uncertainty in Artificial Intelligence* (North-Holland, Amsterdam, 1986) 167–196; also in: G.A. Shafer and J. Pearl, *Readings in Uncertain Reasoning* (Morgan Kaufmann, San Mateo, CA, 1990) 298–312.

[11] N.J. Nilsson, Probabilistic logic, *Artif. Intell.* **28** (1986) 71–87.

[12] J. Pearl, *Probabilistic Reasoning in Intelligent Systems: Networks of Plausible Inference* (Morgan Kaufmann, San Mateo, CA, 1988; revised and updated second printing, 1991).

[13] J. Pearl, Private communication (1992).

[14] J.R. Quinlan, INFERNO: a cautious approach to uncertain inference, *Comput. J.* **26** (1983) 255–269.

[15] R.D. Shachter, Evaluating influence diagrams, *Oper. Res.* **33** (6) (1986); also in: G.A. Shafer and J. Pearl, *Readings in Uncertain Reasoning* (Morgan Kaufmann, San Mateo, CA, 1990) 79–90.

[16] G.A. Shafer, *Mathematical Theory of Evidence* (Princeton University Press, Princeton, NJ, 1979).

[17] G.A. Shafer and J. Pearl, *Readings in Uncertain Reasoning* (Morgan Kaufmann, San Mateo, CA, 1990).

[18] E.H. Shortliffe, *Computer-Based Medical Consultations: MYCIN* (American Elsevier, New York, 1976).

[19] C.A.B. Smith, Consistency in statistical inference and decision, *J. R. Stat. Soc. Ser. B* **23** (1961) 218–258.

[20] L.A. Zadeh, Fuzzy logic and approximate reasoning, *Synthese* **30** (1975) 407–428.

Artificial Intelligence 59 (1993) 43–47
Elsevier

ARTINT 996

A method for managing evidential reasoning in a hierarchical hypothesis space: a retrospective

Jean Gordon and Edward H. Shortliffe

*Section on Medical Informatics, Departments of Medicine and of Computer Science,
MSOB X-215, Stanford University School of Medicine, Stanford, CA 94305-5479, USA*

A central issue in the design of expert systems is the representation and manipulation of uncertain and incomplete knowledge. "A method for managing evidential reasoning in a hierarchical hypothesis space" [4] was an attempt to apply a rigorous mathematical theory of evidence, the Dempster–Shafer (DS) theory, to this problem. In the 1970s, the application of artificial intelligence (AI) to the field of medicine had necessitated the development of ad hoc techniques for the management of uncertainty. Classical probability theory had been rejected due to difficulties in the assessment of conditional probabilities, to the complexity of calculations involved, and to the perceived need to assume conditional independence. Various ad hoc models were thus developed to handle uncertainty—for example, MYCIN's CF model [18], Internist's evoking-strength/frequency-weight model [12] and Casnet's causal-weighting model [20]. The ad hoc basis of these models, their lack of generality, and their inability to deal with the observed tendency of experts to reason about abstract entities before focusing on single hypotheses led us to explore the DS theory.

The appeal of this theory lay in its mathematical rigor and in its ability to model the narrowing of the hypothesis set with the gathering of evidence, a process characterizing expert reasoning. Since an expert uses evidence relevant to sets of hypotheses as well as to single hypotheses, the ability of

Correspondence to: E.H. Shortliffe, Section on Medical Informatics, Departments of Medicine and of Computer Science, MSOB X-215, Stanford University School of Medicine, Stanford, CA 94305-5479, USA. Telephone: (415) 723-6979. Fax: (415) 725-7944. E-mail: ehs@camis.stanford.edu.

the DS theory to represent hierarchical relationships was very attractive. We felt it important to explicate and motivate this theory for the AI research community.

We had three major goals. We wished to present the DS theory in a simple and concise manner, avoiding the excessive mathematical notation which had perhaps deterred many from an appreciation of the theory. We then demonstrated its relevance to a familiar expert system, MYCIN. Finally, we derived a computationally efficient algorithm for utilizing the DS theory in a hierarchical hypothesis space.

We feel the paper made two very different intellectual contributions. The first was its use of formal combinatorial analysis to derive the algorithm. The second was to bring to the attention of the AI community a mathematical model which captured the essence of the medical and general expert evidence-gathering process. Thus, we attempted to reach a broad and not necessarily mathematically sophisticated audience. Much of our paper focused on detailed examples drawn from medical reasoning in an effort to motivate the DS theory.

Our paper spawned an almost immediate sequel by Shafer and Logan [16]. They proposed an algorithm which, like ours, was computationally efficient but which did not require the approximation employed in our method. Shafer and Logan found our approximation to be close in most cases but gave examples of non-intuitive results in others. Their algorithm also applied to slightly more general types of evidence—bearing on hypotheses outside the hierarchical hypothesis space—and computed degrees of belief for these hypotheses.

The DS approach was subsequently challenged in a research note by Pearl [13]. He argued that evidential reasoning in a hierarchical space could be conducted using a Bayesian approach. His key assumption was to identify belief in a hypothesis with the probability that the hypothesis was true given all previous evidence. To calculate the impact of new evidence on the belief of every hypothesis in the hierarchy, he proposed the following. Given a piece of evidence, e, bearing on a set of hypotheses, S, assign to each hypothesis in S the likelihood ratio of S, an estimation of the degree to which the evidence confirms or disconfirms S. The ratio is that of the conditional probabilities, $P(e|S)/P(e|\text{not}S)$. Belief in each single hypothesis of S is updated by multiplying the original belief by this likelihood ratio and by a normalizing factor. A set of hypotheses, i.e., an intermediate-level hypothesis, is assigned the sum of the beliefs of its individual hypotheses. This process can be applied recursively, where the updated beliefs serve as prior beliefs for new evidence. Pearl also proposed an alternative process avoiding normalization and propagating beliefs up and down the hypothesis hierarchy tree to neighboring nodes.

Fundamental to Pearl's approach was the following probabilistic interpretation of the statement whose essence we tried to capture (namely, "*e* bears directly on *S* but says nothing about the individual hypotheses in *S*"): the conditional probability of the evidence given *S* is independent of the identity of a single element in *S*, i.e., $P(e|S, h) = P(e|S)$ for every hypothesis *h* in *S*. Thus, evidence bearing on a set contributes no information about the relative likelihood of individual hypotheses in the set. This assumption, together with Bayes' rule, allows the computation of belief in every subset, *T*, of the hierarchy given *e*, i.e., $P(T|e)$.

The appeal of this probabilistic interpretation lay in its clearly stated assumptions, distinction between partial confirmation and disconfirmation, and easily understood meaning and definition of the likelihood ratio. Experts were required to assess only one number, this ratio, which could possibly be taken from actual data. Experts also appeared to be more comfortable assessing the probability that a finding is present in a given disease, $P(e|S)$, versus the probability that a disease is present given a particular finding, $P(S|e)$. Finally, a Bayesian approach easily adapted itself to methods for converting beliefs to decisions about cost–benefit and utility questions.

Recent and current research in our group at Stanford reflects Pearl's point of view in a return to the formal axioms of probability and decision theory in the representation and manipulation of uncertainty. Most successful has been the theory of probabilistic belief networks, developed by Howard and Matheson [7] and Pearl [14], which makes unnecessary the restriction of conditional independence among variables. A belief network is a graphical knowledge representation of probabilistic relationships which facilitates communication between the expert and the model. Formally, it is a directed, acyclic graph whose nodes represent variables such as diseases and features of diseases and whose arcs reflect conditional dependencies. Probabilities are attached to nodes: each node without predecessors is assigned an unconditional probability distribution and each node with predecessors is assigned a conditional probability distribution for each instance (possible value) of the conditioning nodes.

Heckerman and others utilized belief networks in Pathfinder, an expert system in the domain of lymph node pathology [6]. Instrumental to the success of this approach has been the similarity network, developed as a tool to elicit subjective probabilities from experts. This representation was developed to overcome difficulties they experienced due to conditional dependencies among some features of diseases. Heckerman proved formally that similarity networks enable the construction of large belief networks from subproblems comparing two diseases and their distinguishing features [5]. Another key contribution was that of partitions. This representation is a generalization of Pearl's Bayesian method for representing evidence relevant to sets of hypotheses, a major asset of DS theory.

Another application of belief networks has been made in Nestor, a hypercalcemia expert system developed by Cooper [2]. The system utilizes belief networks to represent the pathophysiology of diseases causing hypercalcemia. Causal rules were acquired from medical texts and augmented with the subjective probabilities of an expert. Nestor has been mostly a research, rather than a clinical, tool as opposed to Pathfinder, which has undergone extensive clinical evaluation. Other medical expert systems utilizing probabilistic and decision-theoretic inference include the Glasgow Dyspepsia system for gastroenterology [19], the Neurex system for neurologic diagnosis [15], and the MUNIN system for diagnosis of muscular problems [1].

Several other researchers associated with our group have explored other aspects of uncertainty management for medical decision support [17]. For example, Lehmann's program, Thomas, helps physicians determine the clinical significance of a study from the clinical trials literature [11]. It incorporates the user's prior beliefs and methodological concerns in generating a statistical model with updated probability distributions on the likely outcomes for the competing interventions. Thus, Thomas attempts a normative representation of the clinical trials literature problem [10].

Klein has developed a method, "interpretative value analysis", for representing hierarchically organized value models for realms involving frequent tradeoffs between objectives [8]. This method has been implemented in Virtus, a modeling tool based on formal decision theory. In Virtus, multi-attribute models enable a dialogue with the user wishing to understand the basis of the program's advice or to adapt the value model to his own preference structures. Virtus has been used to develop RCTE (Randomized Clinical Trials Evaluator), a decision tool which assesses the strengths and weaknesses of a clinical trial and provides a net evaluation of its credibility [9]. Klein is currently exploring extensions of his methodology to multi-attribute decision making under uncertainty.

In conclusion, it appears that our paper spawned renewed interest in developing formal normative models of reasoning with uncertainty. Clearly, an axiomatic approach is appealing in its explicit formulation of the assumptions being made in a particular system or in the system's computational methods. We feel that the exposition of the DS theory was an important first step in this return to formal models based on probability and decision theory. For as Dempster writes: "[Such] 'beliefs' are intended for interpretation as subjective probabilities and the formal manipulations of the subjective theory are embedded in the theory of belief functions" [3].

References

[1] S. Andreassen, M. Woldbye, B. Falck and S. Andersen, MUNIN: a causal probabilistic network for interpretation for electromyographic findings, in: *Proceedings IJCAI-87*, Milan, Italy (1987) 366–372.

[2] G.F. Cooper, NESTOR: a computer-based medical diagnostic aid that integrates causal and probabilistic knowledge, Ph.D. Thesis, Medical Information Sciences, Stanford University, Stanford, CA (1986).

[3] A. Dempster, Commentary on papers by Lane and Cooper, *Appl. Stoch. Models Data Anal.* **5** (1989) 77–81.

[4] J. Gordon and E.H. Shortliffe, A method for managing evidential reasoning in a hierarchical hypothesis space, *Artif. Intell.* **26** (1985) 323–357.

[5] D. Heckerman, Probabilistic similarity networks, *Networks* **20** (1990) 607–636.

[6] D. Heckerman, E. Horvitz and B. Nathwani, Toward normative expert systems, Part I: the Pathfinder project, *Methods Inf. Med.* **31** (1992) 90–105.

[7] R.A. Howard and J.E. Matheson, Influence diagrams, in: R.A. Howard and J.E. Matheson, eds., *Readings on the Principles and Applications of Decision Analysis*, Vol. II (Strategic Decision Group, Menlo Park, CA, 1981) 721–762,

[8] D. Klein, Interpretive value analysis, IBM Tech. Rept. RC 15278 (#68173), Ph.D. Dissertation, Computer and Information Sciences, University of Pennsylvania, Philadelphia, PA (1989).

[9] D. Klein, H. Lehmann and E.H. Shortliffe, A value-theoretic expert system for evaluating randomized clinical trials, in: *Proceedings Fourteenth Annual Symposium on Computer Applications in Medical Care*, Washington, DC (1990) 810-814.

[10] H. Lehmann, A Bayesian computer-based approach to the physician's use of the clinical research literature, Ph.D. Dissertation, Medical Information Sciences, Stanford University, Stanford, CA (1991).

[11] H. Lehmann and E.H. Shortliffe, THOMAS: building Bayesian statistical expert systems to aid in clinical decision making, in: *Proceedings Fourteenth Annual Symposium on Computer Applications in Medical Care*, Washington, DC (1990) 58–64.

[12] R. Miller, H. Pople and J. Myers, INTERNIST-1: an experimental computer-based diagnostic consultant for general internal medicine, *New England J. Med.* **307** (1982) 468–476.

[13] J. Pearl, On evidential reasoning in a hierarchy of hypotheses (Research Note), *Artif. Intell.* **28** (1986) 9–15.

[14] J. Pearl, Fusion, propagation, and structuring in belief networks, *Artif. Intell.* **29** (1986) 241–288.

[15] J. Reggia and B. Perricone, Answer justification in medical decision support systems based on Bayesian classification, *Comput. Biol. Med.* **15** (1985) 161–167.

[16] G. Shafer and R. Logan, Implementing Dempster's rule for hierarchical evidence, *Artif. Intell.* **33** (1987) 271–298.

[17] E.H. Shortliffe, Medical informatics and clinical decision making: the science and the pragmatics, *Med. Decision Making* **11** (1991) S2–S14.

[18] E.H. Shortliffe and B. Buchanan, A model of inexact reasoning in medicine, *Math. Biosci.* **23** (1975) 351–379.

[19] D.J. Spiegelhalter, Probabilistic reasoning in predictive expert systems, in: L.N. Kanal and J.F. Lemmer, eds., *Uncertainty in Artificial Intelligence* (North-Holland, Amsterdam, 1986) 47–67.

[20] S. Weiss, C. Kulikowski, S. Amarel and A. Safir, A model-based method for computer-aided medical decision making, *Artif. Intell.* **11** (1978) 145–172.

Artificial Intelligence 59 (1993) 49–56
Elsevier

ARTINT 997

Belief networks revisited *

Judea Pearl

Cognitive Systems Laboratory, Computer Science Department, University of California, Los Angeles, CA 90024, USA

1. Introduction

The article "Fusion, propagation and structuring in belief networks" [18] (hereafter *Fusion*) was the culmination of a series of papers (e.g., Pearl [16], Kim and Pearl [13], Pearl [17]) in which I advocated the restoration of probabilistic methods in AI systems and explored the possibility of representing and manipulating probabilistic knowledge in graphical forms, later called *belief networks* (also known as *Bayesian networks* and *causal diagrams*). In recent years, belief networks have become a tool of great versatility and power and are now considered the most common representation scheme for probabilistic knowledge. They have been used to aid diagnosis of medical patients and malfunctioning systems, to understand stories, to interpret pictures, to perform filtering, smoothing and prediction, to facilitate planning in uncertain environments, and to study causation, nonmonotonicity, action, change, and attention. [1]

The following is a brief personal account of the development of belief networks, both before and after the publication of *Fusion*, although space permits but a sketchy account of the wealth of recent developments in this area. [2]

Correspondence to: J. Pearl, Cognitive Systems Laboratory, Computer Science Department, University of California, Los Angeles, CA 90024, USA. E-mail: judea@cs.ucla.edu.

*This work was supported in part by NSF grant IRI-9157936, AFOSR grant 900136, and by State of California MICRO grants 91-124 and 91-125.

[1] Some of these applications are described in a recent tutorial article by Charniak [1].

[2] A more complete account and an updated bibliography are provided in the revised second printing of my book *Probabilistic Reasoning in Intelligence Systems* [20].

2. Origins

The idea of studying distributed probabilistic computations on graphical models began brewing in my mind in the late 1970s, after I read Rumelhart's paper on reading comprehension [24]. In this paper, Rumelhart presented compelling evidence that text comprehension must be a distributed process that combines both top-down and bottom-up inferences. Strangely, this dual mode of inference, so characteristic of Bayesian analysis, did not match the capabilities of either the "certainty factors" calculus or the inference networks of PROSPECTOR—the two major contenders for uncertainty management in the 1970s. I thus began to explore the possibility of achieving distributed computation in a "pure" Bayesian framework, so as not to compromise its basic capacity to combine bi-directional inferences (i.e., predictive and abductive). Not caring much about generality at that point, I picked the simplest structure I could think of (i.e., a tree) and tried to see if anything useful can be computed by assigning each variable a simple processor, forced to communicate only with its neighbors. This gave rise to the tree-propagation algorithm reported in [16] and, a year later, the Kim–Pearl algorithm [13], which supported not only bi-directional inferences but also intercausal interactions, such as "explaining away". These two algorithms were described in Section 2 of *Fusion*.

In the course of developing these algorithms, it became clear that *conditional independence* is the most fundamental relation behind the organization of probabilistic knowledge and the most crucial factor facilitating distributed computations. I therefore decided to investigate systematically how directed and undirected graphs could be used as a language for encoding, decoding, and reasoning with such independencies. At about the same time, Howard and Matheson were studying the properties of influence diagrams [11] and were asking similar questions about graphs and dependencies, albeit from a somewhat different perspective: the links in the diagrams were treated as pointers to the information that a person finds convenient to consider while assessing probabilities.

The myriad of questions left unanswered in Howard and Matheson's report jolted me into trying a different approach, in which the links are designated specifically to *causal* associations. However, having found no satisfactory definition of causality in the literature, I decided to search for one myself by asking what mathematical relationships exist between probabilities and directed acyclic graphs. I asked how a directed acyclic graph (dag) can be extracted from a given probability distribution, whether the extracted dag is unique, what kind of distributions can be specified by a given dag, how we can read off the independencies that are embedded in the dag, and whether they match those associated with causal organizations. This line of inquiry resulted in Section 1 of *Fusion*, in which the construction, consistency, and completeness of belief networks were demonstrated and the d-separation criterion was presented. Eventually, this inquiry developed into the axiomatic theory of *graphoids* (Pearl and Paz [22], Pearl [20], Geiger [5]), in which directed and undirected graphs are treated as representations of abstract mathematical objects, called *dependency models*, and are interpreted and manipulated by the logic of conditional independence.[3]

3. Motivations and speculations

Fusion was motivated by a busy mixture of observations and speculations, some of which I recall quite vividly:

(1) The failure of rule-based systems to exhibit certain plausible patterns of reasoning is symptomatic of fundamental limitations, and these limitations can be overcome only by grounding automated reasoning in some safe and friendly calculus of uncertainty.

(2) The consistent agreement between plausible reasoning and probability calculus could not be coincidental, but strongly suggests that human intuition invokes some crude form of probabilistic computation.

(3) In light of the speed and effectiveness of human reasoning, the computational difficulties that plagued earlier probabilistic systems could not be very fundamental and should be overcome by making the right choice of simplifying assumptions.

(4) No reasoning can take place unless our knowledge embodies many (conditional) independence assumptions, and graphical forms are the only plausible way in which these assumptions could be represented.

(5) If a graphical knowledge representation could be found, then it should be possible to use the links as message-passing channels, and we could then update beliefs by parallel distributed computations, reminiscent of neural architectures.

(6) If belief updating could be achieved by such distributed mechanisms, then the update would be easier to explain, since the flow of information would transverse conceptually meaningful paths.

(7) If distributed updating were feasible, then probabilistic inference would be as easy to program and execute (even on a serial machine) as rule-based systems, since no timing information, hence only simple control mechanisms, would be required.

---

[3] *Fusion* has been criticized for "substituting mathematics for clarity" (e.g., R.E. Barlow, in [15, p. 117]). In my judgment, it was precisely this conversion of networks and diagrams to mathematically defined objects that led to their current acceptance in practical reasoning systems.

In hindsight, some of these speculations were rather naive. For example, fully distributed updating turned out to be feasible only in singly connected networks, and some conditional independence relationships were shown to defy graphical representation altogether. Nevertheless, many of these speculations have survived the test of time, as the following section reflects.

4. The main contributions

The key contribution of *Fusion* was the formulation and demonstration of some of the basic properties and capabilities of belief networks:

(1) Graphical methods make it easy to maintain consistency and completeness in probabilistic knowledge bases. They also define modular procedures of knowledge acquisition that reduce significantly the number of probability assessments required,[4] and they guard the model builder from assigning numerical values that lead to unintended dependencies.

(2) Independencies can be dealt with explicitly. They can be articulated by an expert, encoded graphically, read off the network, and reasoned about, yet they forever remain robust to numerical imprecision. Every conditional independency embedded in the network can be recognized in linear time (using the d-separation rule).

(3) Graphical representations uncover opportunities for efficient computation. Distributed updating is feasible in knowledge structures rich enough to exhibit intercausal interactions (e.g., "explaining away"), and, when extended by clustering or conditioning, tree-propagation algorithms are capable of updating networks of arbitrary topology.

(4) The combination of predictive and abductive inferences has resolved many problems encountered by first generation expert systems and has rendered belief networks a viable model for cognitive functions requiring both top-down and bottom-up inferences.

(5) Causal utterances such as "X is a direct cause of Y" were given a probabilistic interpretation as distinctive patterns of conditional independence relationships that can be verified empirically. "Hidden causes" were given operational definition and, under certain conditions, were shown to be identifiable by efficient algorithms.

---

[4]A further reduction has been achieved by Heckerman's *similarity networks* [9].

5. Recent progress

5.1. d-separation and graphoids

In retrospect, perhaps *Fusion* made its greatest immediate impact through the introduction of the d-separation criterion. *d-separation* (the "d" denoting "directional") is a simple graphical test for deciding which conditional independence relations are implied by a given network's topology. It provides, therefore, the semantics needed for defining and characterizing belief networks. Technically, the d-separation criterion has facilitated immediate solutions to three practical problems (see [21, Section 4.4.]):[5]

(1) how to characterize precisely the set of graphical transformations (e.g., arc reversals, node removals, node collapsing) that can legitimately be performed on a network,

(2) how to test whether one network is entailed by or is equivalent to another, and

(3) how to delineate the minimum information needed for answering a given query.

On the conceptual side, by identifying the independencies embedded in directed acyclic graphs, the d-separation criterion has also identified special patterns of independencies that are characteristics of causal organizations. These patterns have since been used to define causation in default reasoning (Goldszmidt and Pearl [8]) and relational databases (Dechter and Pearl [4]), and to uncover causal relationships in data (Pearl and Verma [23]) (see also last paragraph in this section).

Verma [29] has proved the soundness of the d-separation criterion using the semi-graphoid axioms (Pearl and Paz [22]), thus rendering the criterion valid for a wide class of informational dependencies, including probabilistic, graphical, correlational, and database dependencies. Geiger [5] has shown that the criterion cannot be improved; namely, d-separation reveals *all* the independencies that can be inferred from the information provided by the network builder. A more comprehensive separation criterion, applicable to networks containing deterministic nodes, was developed by Geiger, Verma, and Pearl [6] and has been shown to be testable in time proportional to the number of edges in the network.

The relation of conditional independence has received an axiomatic characterization using the theory of graphoids [22] (see also [20, Chapter 3]), which provides symbolic machinery for deciding whether one independency

[5]Specific aspects of these problems (e.g., Shachter's arc reversals [25]) had been worked out in the literature on influence diagrams, but the general problems remained unsettled until quite recently (Smith [26]).

follows from others and whether we can capture such independencies by graphs. Representations using undirected graphs (also known as Markov fields) are discussed in [20, Chapter 3], and [5]; representations using multi-graphs and annotated graphs have been developed by Geva and Paz [7].

5.2. Network updating techniques

Since the publication of *Fusion*, many techniques for updating belief networks have been developed and refined. Among the most popular are Shachter's method of node elimination [25], Lauritzen and Spiegelhalter's method of graph-triangulation and clique-tree propagation [14], and the method of loop-cut conditioning [18, Section 2.4]. While the task of computing probabilities in general networks is NP-hard (Cooper [2]), the complexity of the first two methods is exponential in the size of the largest clique found in some triangulation of the network. The third method might yield a higher complexity in some networks, but it is convenient in networks with a few long loops. It is fortunate that these complexities may be estimated prior to actual processing, because, when the estimates exceed reasonable bounds, we can switch to an approximation method such as stochastic simulation (Henrion [10], Pearl [19]). Statistical techniques have also been developed for systematic updating of the conditional probabilities annotating the network so as to achieve a better match with past empirical data (Spiegelhalter and Lauritzen [27]). The preprocessing method of tree decomposition with hidden variables [18, Section 3] is still not well developed.

5.3. Causal discovery

One of the most exciting prospects in recent years has been the possibility of using belief networks to discover causal relationships in raw statistical data. Technically, the probabilistic semantics that belief networks attribute to the links and their orientations has rendered this prospect feasible, and several systems have been developed for this purpose.

Pearl and Verma [23] have developed a probabilistic account of causation based on minimal-model semantics.[6] This theory provides criteria for identifying genuine and spurious causes, with and without temporal information, and yields algorithms for recovering causal networks with hidden variables from statistical data. A fast algorithm for recovering sparse networks is described by Spirtes and Glymour [28], and Bayesian methods of computing the "probability that X is a cause for Y" were developed by Cooper and Herskovits [3]. In addition to their likely impact on the

---

[6] In this semantics, a variable X is said to have a causal influence on a variable Y if there is a directed path from X to Y in all minimal causal networks (dags) consistent with the data.

practice of building knowledge systems, these developments also promise finally to give causation a purely empirical semantics—the illusive goal of many philosophers and statisticians since the time of Hume.

6. Regrets and near misses

One regrettable step in *Fusion* was my betting on what turned out to be the less attractive way of extending tree propagation to multiply connected networks. I speculated that the loop-cut conditioning method would be more efficient than the one I labeled "compounding", that is, forming clusters of compound variables that are tree-structured and applying the tree-propagation algorithm to the resulting tree. Lauritzen and Spiegelhalter [14], and later Jensen et al. [12], have perfected this tree-clustering method to the point that it is now the most widely used algorithm in practical applications. The popularity of the tree-clustering method stems from its inheriting the distributed character, and hence robustness and versatility of the basic tree-propagation algorithm, as described in *Fusion* (Section 2.1). [7] Thus, my regrets are somewhat mitigated by the realization that concentrating my initial efforts on trees and polytrees did yield some useful insights.

Finally, to the many readers intrigued by the lengthy review process for *Fusion* (*Received January 1982; revised version received February 1986*): Yes, it indeed took four years to get the article accepted, but the reviewers were not at fault. The article simply got lost (literally!) twice, which was not entirely without virtue; each time the editor asked me to replace a lost copy, I would seize the opportunity and send an improved version. I hope the final outcome was worth the wait.

References

[1] E. Charniak, Bayesian networks without tears, *AI Mag.* **12** (4) (1991) 50–63.
[2] G.F. Cooper, Computational complexity of probabilistic inference using Bayesian belief networks (Research Note), *Artif. Intell.* **42** (2) (1990) 393–405.
[3] G.F. Cooper and E. Herskovits, A Bayesian method for constructing Bayesian belief networks from databases, in: *Proceedings Sixth Conference on Uncertainty in AI*, Cambridge, MA (1990) 86–94.
[4] R. Dechter and J. Pearl, Directed constraint networks: a relational framework for causal modeling, in: *Proceedings IJCAI-91*, Sydney, Australia (1991) 1164–1170.
[5] D. Geiger, Graphoids: a qualitative framework for probabilistic inference, Ph.D. Dissertation, University of California, Los Angeles, CA (1990).

[7]Structurally, the two algorithms are essentially the same; the one described in *Fusion* propagates messages in a tree of singletons, whereas Lauritzen and Spiegelhalter's algorithm propagates these messages in a tree of compound variables known as a *join tree* (Pearl [20, pp. 111–113]) or *junction tree* (Jensen et al. [12]).

[6] D. Geiger, T.S. Verma and J. Pearl, Identifying independence in Bayesian networks, *Networks* **20** (5) (1990) 507–534.

[7] R.Y. Geva and A. Paz, Towards complete representation of graphoids in graphs, in: *Proceedings 15th International Workshop on Graph Theoretic Concepts in Computer Sciences*, Rolduc (Springer, New York, 1989) 41–62.

[8] M. Goldszmidt and J. Pearl, Rank-based systems: a simple approach to belief revision, belief update, and reasoning about evidence and actions, in: B. Nebel, C. Rich and W. Swartout, eds., *Principles of Knowledge Representation and Reasoning: Proceedings of the Third International Conference* (Morgan Kaufmann, San Mateo, CA, 1992) 661–672.

[9] D. Heckerman, Probabilistic similarity networks, *Networks* **20** (5) (1990) 607–636.

[10] M. Henrion, Propagation of uncertainty by probabilistic logic sampling in Bayes' networks, in: J.F. Lemmer and L.N. Kanal, eds., *Uncertainty in Artificial Intelligence* **2** (Elsevier Science Publishers/North-Holland, Amsterdam, Netherlands, 1988) 149–164.

[11] R.A. Howard and J.E. Matheson, Influence diagrams, in: R.A. Howard and J.E. Matheson, eds., *The Principles and Applications of Decision Analysis*, Vol. 2 (Strategic Decisions Group, Menlo Park, CA, 1984) 721–762.

[12] F.V. Jensen, K.G. Olsen and S.K. Andersen, An algebra of Bayesian belief universes for knowledge-based systems, *Networks* **20** (5) (1990) 637–660.

[13] J.H. Kim and J. Pearl, A computational model for combined causal and diagnostic reasoning in inference systems, in: *Proceedings IJCAI-83*, Karlsruhe, Germany (1983) 190–193.

[14] S.L. Lauritzen and D.J. Spiegelhalter, Local computations with probabilities on graphical structures and their application to expert systems (with discussion), *J. Roy. Stat. Soc. Ser. B* **50** (2) (1988) 157–224.

[15] R.M. Oliver and J.Q. Smith, eds., *Influence Diagrams, Belief Nets and Decision Analysis* (Wiley, Rexdale, Ont., 1990).

[16] J. Pearl, Reverend Bayes on inference engines: a distributed hierarchical approach, in: *Proceedings AAAI-82*, Pittsburgh, PA (1982) 133–136.

[17] J. Pearl, How to do with probabilities what people say you can't, in: *Proceedings Second IEEE Conference on AI Applications*, Miami, FL (1985) 6–12.

[18] J. Pearl, Fusion, propagation, and structuring in belief networks, *Artif. Intell.* **29** (1986) 241–288.

[19] J. Pearl, Evidential reasoning using stochastic simulation of causal models, *Artif. Intell.* **32** (2) (1987) 245–258.

[20] J. Pearl, *Probabilistic Reasoning in Intelligent Systems*, (Morgan Kaufmann, Palo Alto, CA, 1988; revised second printing, 1991).

[21] J. Pearl, D. Geiger and T.S. Verma, The logic of influence diagrams, in: [15] 67–88.

[22] J. Pearl and A. Paz, On the logic of representing dependencies by graphs, in: *Proceedings Canadian AI Conference*, Montreal, Que. (1986) 94–98.

[23] J. Pearl and T. Verma, A theory of inferred causation, in: J.A. Allen, R. Fikes and E. Sandewall, eds., *Principles of Knowledge Representation and Reasoning: Proceeding of the Second International Conference* (Morgan Kaufmann, San Mateo, CA, 1991) 441–452.

[24] D.E. Rumelhart, Toward an interactive model of reading, Tech. Rept. #CHIP-56, University of California, La Jolla, CA (1976).

[25] R.D. Shachter, Evaluating influence diagrams, *Oper. Res.* **34** (6) (1986) 871–882.

[26] J.Q. Smith, Influence diagrams for statistical modelling, *Ann. Stat.* **17** (2) (1989) 564–572.

[27] D.J. Spiegelhalter and S.L. Lauritzen, Sequential updating of conditional probabilities on directed graphical structures, *Networks* **20** (5) (1990) 579–605.

[28] P. Spirtes and C. Glymour, An algorithm for fast recovery of sparse causal graphs, *Social Sci. Comput. Rev.* **9** (1) (1991) 62–72.

[29] T. Verma, Causal networks: semantics and expressiveness, Tech. Rept. #R-65, Cognitive Systems Laboratory, University of California, Los Angeles, CA (1986); also in: *Proceedings Fourth Workshop on Uncertainty in Artificial Intelligence*, Minneapolis, MN (Advanced Decision Systems, Mountain View, CA, 1988) 352–359.

Artificial Intelligence 59 (1993) 57–62
Elsevier

ARTINT 988

The complexity of constraint satisfaction revisited

Alan K. Mackworth

Department of Computer Science, University of British Columbia, Vancouver, BC, Canada V6T 1W5

Eugene C. Freuder

Department of Computer Science, University of New Hampshire, Durham, NH 03824, USA

Abstract

Mackworth, A.K. and E.C. Freuder, The complexity of constraint satisfaction revisited, Artificial Intelligence 59 (1993) 57–62.

This paper is a retrospective account of some of the developments leading up to, and ensuing from, the analysis of the complexity of some polynomial network consistency algorithms for constraint satisfaction problems.

1. Historical context

In 1970 one of us (AKM) worked on an implementation of Huffman–Clowes labeling of line drawings [1]. This exploited the consequences of a deceptively simple constraint on the visual world of planar objects: the three-dimensional interpretation of a line as an edge must be the same at both ends. Unfortunately, he observed that standard breadth-first and depth-first search techniques suffered from severe combinatorial explosions. About the same time the other one of us (ECF) shared a graduate student office in the MIT AI Lab with David Waltz, who was also working on a program to interpret line drawings. Waltz designed a *filtering* process to remove inconsistent interpretations during the analysis of a scene [21], making the

Correspondence to: A.K. Mackworth, Department of Computer Science, University of British Columbia, Vancouver, BC, Canada V6T 1W5. E-mail: mack@cs.ubc.ca.

combinatorial explosion manageable. Waltz observed experimentally that the effort required for this filtering process was "roughly" linear in the size of the scene. A heuristic argument based on the semantics of his domain supported the plausibility of this behavior.

Since this technique appeared to have promise, AKM described a class of network consistency algorithms [10], abstracted away from the applications, which contains, amongst others, the algorithms described by Waltz [21] and Ugo Montanari [16]. Incidentally, one of the referees of [10] suggested further complexity analysis of the problems and the algorithms could be done. Bernard Meltzer, the founding editor of *Artificial Intelligence*, agreed but did not require it for publication. He suggested it as a topic for a sequel as, indeed, it became. John Gaschnig subsequently raised some doubt about the linear behavior of filtering [8]; however, he was careful not to draw any firm conclusions from the limited data, and the complexity of the process remained an open issue.

Both of us solved this problem, independently, in 1981. Raimund Seidel, a student in AKM's graduate course, had achieved a nice new algorithm [18]. In the course of discussion with ECF, Seidel realized we (AKM and ECF) each had the same result. We joined forces and eventually the paper appeared [11].

2. Complexity and network consistency

One outcome of our 1985 paper [11] was a resolution of the open issue. Heuristic intuition and experimental data could not, by their nature, hope to achieve a complete resolution of the question. We used formal analytical techniques to prove that the filtering process could be carried out in linear time for any application.

The proof relied on our analysis of an abstraction of the visual filtering process called *arc consistency*. Arc consistency is a basic tool in what has come to be called *constraint-based reasoning*. Constraint-based reasoning has been widely used in artificial intelligence: in vision, language, planning, diagnosis, scheduling, configuration, design, temporal reasoning, defeasible reasoning, truth maintenance, qualitative physics, logic programming, and expert systems. The analysis of techniques like arc consistency can thus lead to tractability results in many areas of artificial intelligence.

A *constraint satisfaction problem* (CSP) involves finding values for a set of problem variables which simultaneously satisfy a set of restrictions (*constraints*) on which combinations of variables are acceptable (*consistent*). The Huffman–Clowes–Waltz scene labeling problem is a Finite CSP (FCSP) since the variable domains are discrete and finite. Our complexity results were for FCSPs.

One of the key insights of arc consistency for FCSPs can be found in Fikes' paper in the very first issue of *Artificial Intelligence* [6]; in particular, if a value, c, for one problem variable is inconsistent with all values for some other problem variable, then c will never participate in a complete solution to the problem and can be eliminated from all further consideration. The obvious algorithm for removing all such inconsistencies, AC-1, has an $O(n^3 d^3)$ complexity bound for an FCSP with n variables each with d possible values. AC-3, a simpler and more general version of the Waltz filtering algorithm AC-2, was shown in our paper to have an $O(n^2 d^3)$ bound.

That bound can be expressed as $O(ed^3)$, where e is the number of constraints, or edges in a *constraint graph*, whose vertices correspond to variables and whose edges correspond to constraints between variables. (We will restrict our attention here to binary constraints, which involve only two variables; analogous methods are available for dealing with higher-order constraints.) Since scene labeling problems have planar constraint graphs, and for planar graphs the number of edges is linear in the number of vertices, we were able to show that arc consistency for the scene labeling problem is linear in the number of problem variables. We also showed that path consistency, a generalization of arc consistency, could be achieved in time cubic in the number of variables.

The complexity of arc consistency has since been refined further. Mohr and Henderson [15] found an arc consistency algorithm, AC-4, which has a theoretically optimal $O(ed^2)$ bound. (In retrospect, we regret that this did not fall out in our paper; optimality was within our grasp—only a factor of d away!) This brought the complexity of scene labeling filtering down to $O(nd^2)$. However, better bounds have been found for arc consistency for restricted classes of problems. In particular, Perlin [17] has identified a class of problems that includes scene labeling for which arc consistency can be obtained in time linear in d. Thus arc consistency can, in fact, be obtained for scene labeling in time that is linear in both the number of variables and the number of values per variable. There are even cases where it can be obtained in $O(e \log d)$ [12]. This may be the end of that story, but there are other stories to tell, too many for this short note.

3. Tractable problem classes

It is important to realize that the varying forms of consistency algorithms can be seen as *approximation* algorithms, in that they impose *necessary* but not always *sufficient* conditions for the existence of a solution on a CSP. Each of them can be thought of as a low-order polynomial algorithm for exactly solving a relaxed version of an FCSP whose solution set contains the set of solutions to the FCSP. The more effort one puts into finding the approximation the smaller the discrepancy between the approximating solution set and the exact solution set.

Since FCSPs are so hard (NP-complete) as a general class, it became important to identify specific classes of problems which admit tractable solution techniques. Tradeoffs can be made between representational and computational complexity, trading representational complexity to remain within the comfortable computational confines of a tractable problem class. These tractable classes can also be used to assist in the solution of more general problems. One way to identify these classes is to look for restricted FCSP classes where the approximation algorithms are *exact*, namely, where the consistency conditions are necessary *and* sufficient. These classes can be characterized by restrictions on the topology of the constraint graph, on the size of the domains or on the nature of the constraints. We pointed out this possibility, giving one concrete example and leaving it as an open issue to identify others.

FCSPs with tree-structured constraint graphs were the first such tractable class to be identified, and provide a good illustration of these issues. Our paper provided an $O(nd^3)$ bound on the complexity of tree-structured problems (improved to an optimal $O(nd^2)$ in [3]). Tambe and Rosenbloom used these results to bound the complexity of production rule pattern matching by restricting to tree structures [19]. Dechter, Pearl and Meiri have demonstrated how tree-structured substructure or superstructure can assist in the solution of non-tree-structured problems [2–4,14]. Complexity bounds have been obtained for "higher-level" tree structures, where each level trades increased representational power for increased complexity [7].

One of the practical consequences of our results was that the designers and implementers of constraint-based programming languages could feel comfortable including consistency algorithms as primitives in the language [6,10]. Ideally, a language primitive should require constant time; but, failing that, it is comforting to know that it will terminate in linear time. The constraint logic programming language CHIP [20] was the first to exploit this potential fully by providing an arc-consistency-based inference engine.

Progress continues to be made on finding efficient ways to solve important classes of problems, e.g. Deville and Van Hentenryck's $O(ed)$ algorithm for a successor to CHIP [5], and on identifying the tradeoffs between representational adequacy and computational complexity, e.g. Meiri's clarification of the effort required to answer consistency questions for classes of temporal reasoning problems [13].

Another interesting follow-on result was that although arc consistency is achievable in linear sequential time there is apparently no polylogarithmic time parallel algorithm in the general case: it is log-space complete for P [9] and, hence, unlikely to be in NC. (There are, though, well-behaved parallel and distributed algorithms for some special cases [22].) This negative result struck some as counter-intuitive. Algorithm AC-1, which has poor sequential complexity, has a high degree of intrinsic parallelism (but potential serial data dependencies); whereas each AC-p ($p > 1$) has been optimized for a single processor. In fact, various generalizations of AC-1 have been proposed for neural networks. But the gloomy theoretical result has not deterred the designers of AC VLSI chips or other intrepid experimentalists.

4. Conclusion

The development of constraint satisfaction algorithms was originally motivated by concerns for efficiency. The subsequent analysis of the complexity of both the problems and the algorithms further stimulated the development of practical tools and the identification of significant tractable problem classes. So the history of the topic is a tale of intimate interaction amongst theory, implementation, experiment, and application characteristic of artificial intelligence research.

Acknowledgement

This material is based, in part, upon work supported by the National Science Foundation under Grant No. IRI-8913040 to Eugene Freuder. The United States Government has certain rights in part of this material. Alan Mackworth is supported by the Shell Canada Fellowship of the Canadian Institute for Advanced Research, by the Institute for Robotics and Intelligent Systems Network of Centres of Excellence and by the Natural Sciences and Engineering Research Council of Canada.

References

[1] M.B. Clowes, On seeing things, *Artif. Intell.* **2** (1971) 79–116.
[2] R. Dechter, Enhancement schemes for constraint processing: backjumping, learning and cutset decomposition, *Artif. Intell.* **41** (1990) 273–312.
[3] R. Dechter and J. Pearl, Network-based heuristics for constraint-satisfaction problems, *Artif. Intell.* **34** (1988) 1–38.
[4] R. Dechter and J. Pearl, Tree clustering for constraint networks, *Artif. Intell.* **38** (1989) 353–366.
[5] Y. Deville and P. Van Hentenryck, An efficient arc consistency algorithm for a class of CSP problems, in: *Proceedings IJCAI-91*, Detroit, MI (1991) 325–330.
[6] R.E. Fikes, REF-ARF: a system for solving problems stated as procedures, *Artif. Intell.* **1** (1970) 27–120.

[7] E.C. Freuder, Complexity of k-tree structured constraint satisfaction problems, in: *Proceedings AAAI-90*, Boston, MA (1990) 4–9.

[8] J. Gaschnig, Performance measurement and analysis of certain search algorithms, Thesis CMU-CS-79-124, Department of Computer Science, Carnegie-Mellon University, Pittsburgh, PA (1979).

[9] S. Kasif, On the parallel complexity of discrete relaxation in constraint satisfaction networks, *Artif. Intell.* **45** (1990) 275–286.

[10] A.K. Mackworth, Consistency in networks of relations, *Artif. Intell.* **8** (1977) 99–118.

[11] A.K. Mackworth and E.C. Freuder, The complexity of some polynomial network consistency algorithms for constraint satisfaction problems, *Artif. Intell.* **25** (1985) 65–74.

[12] A.K. Mackworth, J.A. Mulder and W.S. Havens, Hierarchical arc consistency: exploiting structured domains in constraint satisfaction problems, *Comput. Intell.* **1** (1985) 118–126.

[13] I. Meiri, Combining qualitative and quantitative constraints in temporal reasoning, in: *Proceedings AAAI-91*, Anaheim, CA (1991) 260–267.

[14] I. Meiri, R. Dechter and J. Pearl, Tree decomposition with applications to constraint processing, in: *Proceedings AAAI-90*, Boston, MA (1990) 10–16.

[15] R. Mohr and T.C. Henderson, Arc and path consistency revisited, *Artif. Intell.* **28** (1986) 225–233.

[16] U. Montanari, Networks of constraints: fundamental properties and applications to picture processing, *Inf. Sci.* **7** (1974) 95–132.

[17] M. Perlin, Arc consistency for factorable relations, *Artif. Intell.* (to appear).

[18] R. Seidel, A new method for solving constraint satisfaction problems, in: *Proceedings IJCAI-81*, Vancouver, BC (1981) 338–342.

[19] M. Tambe and P. Rosenbloom, A framework for investigating production system formulations with polynomially bounded match, in: *Proceedings AAAI-90*, Boston, MA (1990) 693–700.

[20] P. Van Hentenryck, *Constraint Satisfaction in Logic Programming* (MIT Press, Cambridge, MA, 1989).

[21] D. Waltz, Understanding line drawings of scenes with shadows, in: P.H. Winston, ed., *The Psychology of Computer Vision* (McGraw-Hill, New York, 1975) 19–91.

[22] Y. Zhang and A.K. Mackworth, Parallel and distributed algorithms for finite constraint satisfaction problems, in: *Proceedings 3rd IEEE Symposium on Parallel and Distributed Processing*, Dallas, TX (1991) 394–397.

Artificial Intelligence 59 (1993) 63–67
Elsevier

ARTINT 987

A perspective on assumption-based truth maintenance

Johan de Kleer

Xerox Palo Alto Research Center, 3333 Coyote Hill Road, Palo Alto, CA 94304, USA

1. Prehistory: LOCAL and SOPHIE

One of the key capabilities of an assumption-based truth maintenance system (ATMS) is that it allows a problem solver to keep track of multiple contexts at once. It was this capability that motivated the invention of a precursor of the ATMS for use in LOCAL [3,13] (and later in SOPHIE [1,13]). LOCAL performed model-based diagnosis on an analog circuit. LOCAL started with observations of the circuit and propagated these through individual components to identify inconsistencies. With each propagated value, LOCAL stored both a justification [16] and a set of assumptions (the components which must function correctly to produce the propagated value). LOCAL records each propagation of a value through a component by constructing a justification and adding the component to the union of the sets of assumptions underlying the values propagating into the component.

Although the set of assumptions associated with a propagation could always be computed from the justification network, it was far more efficient to maintain these assumptions explicitly with the values because:

(1) LOCAL could determine the components underlying an inconsistency directly instead of searching the justification network,
(2) LOCAL could directly determine whether the propagation path was circular causing infinite loops—as would otherwise occur in analyzing analog systems,

Correspondence to: J. de Kleer. E-mail: dekleer@parc.xerox.com.

(3) LOCAL could directly compare diagnoses and analyze the utility of making a particular measurement by examining the assumption sets underlying the possible outcomes,

(4) the propagation could be restricted to the logically strongest ones—those with fewest assumptions.

Analogs to these four properties also motivate the use of the ATMS in more modern problem solvers.

One of the main conclusions of the LOCAL/SOPHIE project was that local analysis based on the propagation of numerical ranges through constraint models was inadequate to fully diagnose analog circuits. We observed that human diagnosticians often draw on qualitative causal models of device behavior to successfully diagnose complex circuits. This motivated me to study qualitative reasoning of circuit behavior and its role in diagnosis. Unfortunately, ambiguity is everywhere in qualitative reasoning. The loss of precision often makes it impossible, especially locally, to determine which of two influences on a circuit quantity dominates. Therefore, the qualitative reasoning system QUAL [4,6] continually introduced assumptions as it reasoned hoping that these would be discharged at the conclusion of a qualitative analysis. Although most assumptions were discharged at the end of analysis, often a few remained, as a device might have several possible global behaviors. In order to manage all these different alternatives I re-implemented as a separate module the simple proto-ATMS of LOCAL.

2. Development of the ATMS

This is the first point at which the proto-ATMS existed as a separate distinct module. Unfortunately, the computational demands of qualitative physics were far more severe than that of LOCAL and SOPHIE (the reason for this is that when signals are represented as numerical ranges, the ranges quickly become so large that the propagation is not worth continuing and hence a combinatorial explosion is avoided). Therefore, during this time I devised special bit-vector representations of assumption sets as well as special data structures for representing nogoods (inconsistent sets of assumptions).

The first attempt at writing up this ATMS was the AAAI-84 paper "Choices without backtracking" [5]. At this point I also made the final innovation which resulted in the current-day conception of an ATMS. Until this time, if the same node (result, datum, or value) was produced under two sets of assumptions, the node would have to be duplicated. The ATMS described in [5] associated a set of sets of assumptions with each node. Therefore, the potential combinatorial explosion in number of nodes is avoided. The response to [5] clearly indicated the widespread interest and utility of an ATMS. A couple of years of further exploration and development led to the papers in the *Artificial Intelligence Journal* [7–9].

3. QPE and GDE

Ken Forbus who had been developing a qualitative physics based on process theory [19] had become very frustrated with the computational properties of the TMSs he had been using. After the ATMS became available he quickly saw its advantages for his form of qualitative reasoning as well. His experiences with the ATMS helped significantly improve both the ATMS implementation and its interface. The combined result was dramatically improved functionality and performance for QPE [20].

The original inspirations for the ATMS idea came from diagnostic tasks. Therefore, once the idea had been fleshed out, it was very natural to re-examine using the ATMS for diagnosis. The result was the General Diagnostic Engine [15] which is a general domain-independent probabilistic approach for diagnosing systems which can contain multiple faults. GDE was remarkably easy to implement as the ATMS provided exactly the functionality needed to easily diagnose multiple faults (see [22]). In addition, it was very easy to introduce probabilities into the ATMS.

4. The future

The ATMS has become a widely used tool in artificial intelligence research. Its use has been explored in the full spectrum of AI—from diagnosis and qualitative physics to natural language and vision. In hindsight we can now see that the ATMS is actually extremely simple. In addition, the functionality of the ATMS is implementable in only a few pages of Lisp code [22]. How can something so simple have become so useful? Some of the reasons for this are:

- Perhaps the most important, for a large number of tasks the division of the problem solver into an inference engine and an ATMS provides just the right natural partitioning of concerns necessary to enable a designer to build problem solvers relatively easily.
- The ATMS is a very generic facility. On the one hand it can be viewed as a general-purpose TMS and on the other hand as a general-purpose abduction engine.

- The ATMS is very simple—but that makes it easy to implement, use, and exploit.
- The ATMS was and remains available via anonymous FTP.[1]

As the ATMS is of such widespread use it was quickly generalized and analyzed from many different perspectives. The original ATMS used only Horn clauses. It has been extended to function with arbitrary clauses [10,24]. Dressler extended it to function with nonmonotonic justifications [17]. Raiman and de Kleer extended the ATMS to function with circumscribed theories [25]. Also, Reiter and de Kleer showed how the ATMS could be viewed as computing prime implicates, thereby providing it a formal foundation [24]. This paper also formally pointed out the connection to abduction which is further elaborated in papers such as [23,26]. At this point there are over a 100 different papers which analyze or generalize the ATMS in some way and the flow of ideas shows no sign of stopping.

We have now had almost a decade of experience with ATMS-based problem solvers. Unfortunately, it appears that some of the properties which led to its initial success are now the very properties which are causing problems as we try to scale up to larger tasks. The ATMS is so simple that it doesn't have enough information available to prevent combinatorial explosions [2,11,26]. Therefore, one of the more active areas of current ATMS research is the investigation of additional mechanisms to control the combinatorial explosion without sacrificing its inherent advantages (usually known as focusing techniques). In order to completely control the combinatorics of the problem one must focus both on the rule execution in the inference engine [14,21] as well as on the ATMS itself [12,18]). (See [11] for a diagnostic problem solver which utilizes both types of focusing to do model-based diagnosis efficiently.)

References

[1] J.S. Brown, R.R. Burton and J. de Kleer, Pedagogical, natural language and knowledge engineering techniques in SOPHIE I, II and III, in: D. Sleeman and J.S. Brown, eds., *Intelligent Tutoring Systems* (Academic Press, New York, 1982) 227–282.

[2] T. Bylander, D. Allemang, M.C. Tanner and J.R. Josephson, The computational complexity of abduction, *Artif. Intell.* **49** (1–3) (1991) 25–60.

[3] J. de Kleer, Local methods of localizing faults in electronic circuits, AI Memo 394, Artificial Intelligence Laboratory, MIT, Cambridge, MA (1976).

[4] J. de Kleer, Causal and teleological reasoning in circuit recognition, Tech. Report TR-529, Artificial Intelligence Laboratory, MIT, Cambridge, MA (1979).

[5] J. de Kleer, Choices without backtracking, in: *Proceedings AAAI-84*, Austin, TX (1984) 79–85.

---

[1] Although there is limited documentation.

[6] J. de Kleer, How circuits work, *Artif. Intell.* **24** (1984) 205–280; also in: D.G. Bobrow, ed., *Qualitative Reasoning about Physical Systems* (North-Holland, Amsterdam, 1984/MIT Press, Cambridge, MA, 1985) 205–280.

[7] J. de Kleer, An assumption-based TMS, *Artif. Intell.* **28** (1986) 127–162.

[8] J. de Kleer, Extending the ATMS, *Artif. Intell.* **28** (1986) 163–196.

[9] J. de Kleer, Problem solving with the ATMS, *Artif. Intell.* **28** (1986) 197–224.

[10] J. de Kleer, A practical clause management system, SSL Paper P88-00140, Xerox PARC, Palo Alto, CA (1988).

[11] J. de Kleer, Focusing on probable diagnoses, in: *Proceedings AAAI-91*, Anaheim, CA (1991) 842–848.

[12] J. de Kleer, A hybrid truth maintenance system, submitted for publication.

[13] J. de Kleer and J.S. Brown, Model-based diagnosis in SOPHIE III, in: W. Hamscher, J. de Kleer and L. Console, eds., *Readings in Model-Based Diagnosis* (Morgan Kaufmann, San Mateo, CA, 1992).

[14] J. de Kleer and B.C. Williams, Back to backtracking: controlling the ATMS, in: *Proceedings AAAI-86*, Philadelphia, PA (1986) 910–917.

[15] J. de Kleer and B.C. Williams, Diagnosing multiple faults, *Artif. Intell.* **32** (1987) 97–130; also in: M.L. Ginsberg, ed., *Readings in Nonmonotonic Reasoning* (Morgan Kaufmann, San Mateo, CA, 1987) 372–388.

[16] J. Doyle, A truth maintenance system, *Artif. Intell.* **12** (1979) 231–272.

[17] O. Dressler, Extending the basic ATMS, in: *Proceedings European Conference on Artificial Intelligence*, Munich, Germany (1988) 535–540.

[18] O. Dressler and A. Farquhar, Putting the problem solver back in the driver's seat: contextual control of the ATMS, in: *Proceedings Second AAAI Workshop on Model Based Reasoning*, Boston, MA (1990) 106–112.

[19] K.D. Forbus, Qualitative process theory, *Artif. Intell.* **24** (1984) 85–168; also in: D.S. Weld and J. de Kleer, eds., *Readings in Qualitative Reasoning about Physical Systems* (Morgan Kaufmann, San Mateo, CA, 1990) 178–219.

[20] K.D. Forbus, The qualitative process engine, Tech. Rept. No. UIUCDCS-R-86-1288, University of Illinois, Urbana-Champaign, IL (1986); also in: D.S. Weld and J. de Kleer, eds., *Readings in Qualitative Reasoning about Physical Systems* (Morgan Kaufmann, San Mateo, CA, 1990) 220–235.

[21] K.D. Forbus and J. de Kleer, Focusing the ATMS, in: *Proceedings AAAI-88*, Saint Paul, MN (1988) 193–198.

[22] K.D. Forbus and J. de Kleer, *Building Problem Solvers* (MIT Press, Cambridge, MA, 1992).

[23] H.J. Levesque, A knowledge-level account of abduction, in: *Proceedings IJCAI-89*, Detroit, MI (1989) 1061–1067.

[24] R. Reiter and J. de Kleer, Foundations of assumption-based truth maintenance systems: preliminary report, in: *Proceedings AAAI-87*, Seattle, WA (1987) 183–188.

[25] O. Raiman and J. de Kleer, A minimality maintenance system, in: *Proceedings Third International Conference on Principles of Knowledge Representation and Reasoning*, Cambridge, MA (1992) 532–538.

[26] B. Selman and H.J. Levesque, Abductive and default reasoning: a computational core, in: *Proceedings AAAI-90*, Boston, MA (1990) 343–348.

Vision

Artificial Intelligence 59 (1993) 71–80
Elsevier

ARTINT 999

Retrospective on "Interpreting line drawings as three-dimensional surfaces"

Harry G. Barrow

School of Cognitive and Computing Sciences, University of Sussex, Brighton, BN1 9QH, England, UK

J.M. Tenenbaum

Enterprise Integration Technologies, 459 Hamilton Avenue, Palo Alto, CA 94301, USA

1. Context

In 1977 we proposed a computational model of visual perception which focused our own work and influenced that of a number of others (Barrow and Tenenbaum [4]). A key feature was the simultaneous recovery of retinotopic arrays of characteristics intrinsic to the scene, such as surface color, depth, and orientation. Such a representation appeared useful in its own right (e.g., for obstacle avoidance and grasping) and as a facilitator for later stages of vision, such as finding surfaces and their boundaries, or recognizing objects. We were encouraged that humans seem able to estimate intrinsic scene characteristics reliably under a wide range of conditions. Moreover, algorithms (based on very particular assumptions) had been developed for finding surface shape from shading (Horn [13]), or stereo (Marr and Poggio [23]), or for finding reflectance or color from brightness gradients (Horn [12]).

The central problem in recovery is the confounding of intrinsic scene characteristics in the image data. The brightness measured at each point in an image depends upon several independent characteristics of the corresponding scene point, primarily the intensity of incident illumination, the

Correspondence to: H.G. Barrow, School of Cognitive and Computing Sciences, University of Sussex, Brighton, BN1 9QH, England, UK. E-mail: harryb@cogs.susx.ac.uk.

reflectance of the surface, and the local surface orientation. To separate these confounded characteristics with mutual consistency, it is necessary to recover them all simultaneously. Moreover, data from neighboring points must be combined using some regularizing assumptions about the scene, such as continuity of surfaces, as well as some explicit boundary conditions. Essential sources of information about such boundary conditions and constraints are the image intensity discontinuities commonly depicted in line drawings.

The key to making the recovery process work lies in determining what assumptions can be made about the physical nature of an intensity edge. The pattern of brightness on either side can give clues to the appropriate interpretation, and the interpretation provides boundary conditions and constraints for the recovery process. Reflectance determination, for example, relies on continuity of illumination across the region, so that abrupt brightness changes can be assumed to be due to changes in reflectance rather than illumination, depth, or orientation. Clearly, it is an important first step to detect boundaries in the image and interpret them, as a reflectance or shadow edge, a discontinuity in surface orientation, or an occlusion.

The approach can be summarized as follows:

(1) detect boundaries in the image;
(2) interpret boundaries, using local brightness variations;
(3) impose boundary conditions and constraints on recovery;
(4) estimate locally the scene characteristics consistent with the boundary conditions, continuity constraints, and photometric evidence;
(5) use the recovered intrinsic scene data to refine the boundaries.

We envisaged this recovery process as a set of interacting parallel local computations, more like solving a system of simultaneous equations by relaxation than like a feed forward sequence of stages. More than a decade of experience had shown that simple feed forward processing of an image cannot produce reliably an ideal line drawing of the scene.

Our work on line drawing interpretation was undertaken in this context to help elucidate some aspects of the intrinsic image paradigm. We were particularly interested in understanding further how the 2-D geometry and topology of image boundaries could be used in forming 3-D interpretations. We therefore began by assuming an ideal line drawing (despite the difficulty of obtaining one from a real image), and focused on the problem of deriving 3-D curve and surface shapes from it. There were two additional reasons for this purely geometric approach. Firstly, photometric data from the image cannot always be used quantitatively, especially if incident illumination or surface reflectance cannot be simply modeled. Geometry and topology then become the prime sources of information about the scene. Secondly, humans are able to interpret line drawings, even though the only available information is boundary geometry. To build computational models of vision we need to understand how this information is exploited.

In our "line drawing" paper, then, we concentrated on stages (2), (3), and (4) of the intrinsic image model, considering what might be done in the absence of photometric data. We sought answers to five specific questions: What different classes of boundary are there? How might one classify a boundary by its shape? What constraints does each provide on the surfaces on either side? How may 3-D boundary geometry be inferred from 2-D image geometry? And how may surface geometry be inferred from boundary geometry?

In exploring this problem we felt it was important to look to other disciplines for hints and inspiration. Neuroscience, at that time, did not seem to provide much evidence beyond the existence of cells in primary visual cortex tuned to particular image features resembling edges or bars (Hubel and Wiesel [16]). The role of these "feature detectors" was not clear: they might be detecting edges, computing local Fourier transforms, or simply computing first and second derivatives of brightness. Experimental psychology seemed more promising. Although it dealt with visual perception as a black box, there seemed to be a wealth of data concerning various phenomena, limitations, constancies, and illusions. We very much enjoyed talking to psychologists like Al Yonas and Richard Gregory, with whom we speculated about elucidating the architecture of the human visual system from the observations. A third contributing discipline was that of computational vision, from which most of our ideas and algorithms came. Like David Marr, who contributed so much and popularized the methodology [24], we were interested in discovering the principles of vision, independent of their implementation, and in understanding how human vision worked in the real world.

2. Contributions

Our paper was an initial exploration of the problem of interpreting curves in images as three-dimensional structures, and we made an attempt at being systematic. We identified the different varieties of 3-D curve in a scene: wires, edges of sheets, edges of solids, extrema of surfaces. For each category, we determined some plausible constraints on three-dimensional curve shape, such as uniformity of curvature, and planarity, plus some constraints on the surfaces in which the boundary lay. We then implemented algorithms which used the constraints in boundary and surface reconstruction. We discovered limitations of our implementations and we reported them. Although we investigated several distinct shape recovery techniques, we had very much in mind the idea that they must be integrated eventually into a single coherent vision system.

Our paper should be viewed as a beginning. Its main value, in retrospect, is not in any particular conclusion or algorithm, but rather in simply opening up a new area a little, highlighting some principles and some phenomena, and suggesting some possible approaches. We certainly felt that we had not yet found all the answers to our questions. Like many others before us, we also discovered that a piece of vision is more complex than we had thought previously. Perhaps the paper has been cited frequently because others felt they could readily improve on its contents!

3. Developments

During the 1980s, a main theme of research in computer vision was the recovery of low-level scene characteristics (but mainly surface shape) from images. Volume 17 of *Artificial Intelligence*, in which our "line drawing" paper appeared, contains papers on recovering shape from texture (Witkin [33]), shading (Woodham [35]), stereo (Mayhew and Frisby [25]), and optic flow (Horn [14]). It also contains other papers dealing with the interpretation of boundaries (Stevens [27]) and line drawings (Binford [6], Kanade [19], Draper [10]).

Over the past decade, there has been steady progress on the general problem of "visual recovery", which is well documented by Aloimonos and Rosenfeld [1].

Early recovery programs concentrated on a single mechanism, and were typically comprised of a method for propagating derived characteristics and a method for handling boundary conditions (Horn [12,13]). More recently, the problem of integrating mechanisms has received a little attention. Ikeuchi and Horn [18] experimented with a parallel iterative system for recovering reflectance and surface orientation simultaneously, with boundary conditions provided by occluding boundaries. Sugihara [28] attempted to provide a consistent framework for "shape-from-image" problems involving polyhedral objects. In principle, Sugihara's approach can deal with multiple sources of evidence (shading, texture, etc.) but in practice he only dealt with one at a time. Terzopoulos [29] also considered a general approach to recovery, using multigrid relaxation methods to speed convergence to solution. He applied his approach to recovery of reflectance, surface shape from shading, optic flow, and sparse stereo data.

One important line of research has been concerned with simultaneously fitting smooth surfaces to data and breaking surfaces at boundaries. Geman and Geman [11] used a stochastic relaxation algorithm to find regions of uniform brightness and region boundaries in noisy images. Terzopoulos [29] and Blake and Zisserman [7] used similar approaches, modeling physical surfaces with thin plates, bending them to fit the image data and breaking them at points of excessive stress and strain.

Research into three-dimensional interpretation of line drawings has generally focused on individual methods with limited integration. Brady and Yuille [8], for example, described an algorithm for determining the three-dimensional shape of a planar contour, choosing the plane orientation that maximized the overall compactness (area/perimeter squared) of the resulting 3-D shape. It was claimed that this algorithm was superior in the presence of noisy images or wiggly contours to our approach, which required higher-order derivatives to minimize local curvature and torsion, although no experimental validation was offered. Kube [20] has explored more recently similar ideas for determining local shape from contour.

The line of work on relaxation labeling of line drawings originating with Huffman [17], Clowes [9], and Waltz [32] has also been further developed. Turner [31] first developed a large catalog of labels for interpreting drawings of scenes with curved objects. Shapira and Freeman [26] subsequently formulated a greatly simplified catalog of the boundaries and junctions of bodies bounded by quadric surfaces, excluding such refinements as cracks and shadows. It was the Shapira–Freeman catalog that was suggested for line labeling in our paper. Malik and Maydan [21] integrated line drawing labeling with shape from shading in a single system which both qualitatively interpreted boundaries in the drawing, using a catalog, and recovered 3-D shapes of surfaces. Their system is very much in line with what we had in mind. In a very recent paper, Marill [22] proposed a scheme for interpreting drawings of polyhedra which also has some close similarities with our polyhedra reconstruction algorithms.

4. Open issues

Ten years after publication of our paper, many issues remain open.

(i) Perhaps the most direct issue is, simply, can the recovery process be made to work either for line drawings or for real world images? Algorithms do indeed exist for recovering particular characteristics under specific conditions, but their competence generally remains limited and they cannot cope with all the richness of our visual world. For example, the iterative technique we proposed for inferring the 3-D conformation of a space curve is unstable and slow, requiring between fifty and a hundred iterations to converge. This is probably unacceptable for a biological system that must operate with computing elements with a basic cycle time of many milliseconds. Moreover, no one has yet implemented a complete, integrated system, for either line drawing interpretation or full Intrinsic Image recovery. It still remains to be demonstrated that such systems are possible, even for a restricted domain such as line drawings. For instance, our algorithms for recovering the 3-D conformation of smooth space curves and the straight edges of polyhedra use different minimization criteria. A comprehensive theory of line drawing understanding must reconcile these, either by handling polyhedra as a limiting case of curved objects, or as a special purpose model with an appropriate invocation criterion.

(ii) There are fundamental questions to be answered about the architecture of a visual system. For nearly two decades the field has assumed that the visual system can be decomposed into independent modules, each performing a well-defined function, like estimating color, and that their outputs are integrated at a later stage. Is this a valid hypothesis? There is some evidence from psychophysics (Triesman [30]) and from anatomy and physiology (Hubel [15]) for modularity. Different cortical areas seem to specialize in processing color, motion, and form, but they have direct and reciprocal connections among them. If they do correspond to modules, the modules do not seem to be independent, but interacting. What is more, natural visual systems are not simply feed forward. Wherever a forward path exists, there seems to be a direct feedback path also.

(iii) We have been discussing recovery of values for characteristics at each point in an image. Is it necessary to do so explicitly, or can we make do with sparse representations in visual tasks? In our research, we concentrated on full and explicit recovery, partly to ensure that the information needed was really present in the data and that recovery was really possible. Natural vision may not explicitly represent scene characteristic values, but perhaps their derivatives, or combinations of values, just as receptor responses are not themselves transmitted directly up the optic nerve.

(iv) In our models of vision, we hypothesized a transition from image brightness and image features to scene values and scene features as soon as possible. Our approach is to find boundary elements and immediately attempt to interpret them. Perhaps this is premature. There may well be a role for much more two-dimensional perceptual organization, perhaps implementing something like the Gestalt laws. The resulting global structures could greatly simplify 3-D interpretation, for example, by helping to delimit suitable boundary fragments for applying planarity constraints, or suitable regions for applying continuity constraints. Our interest in recovering scene characteristics arose in part through a belief that it was not possible to segment an image reliably into meaningful regions and boundaries on the basis of raw brightness: a better job could be done if scene charac-teristics were available. However, the baby may have been thrown out with the bathwater, and should perhaps be rescued: perceptual organization may play a much more important role (Witkin and Tenenbaum [34]).

5. Hindsight

Shortly after writing this paper, we left SRI and took a sabbatical from research on vision.

Marty Tenenbaum pursued a computational theory of sound understand-ing, in the belief that the same confounding problems and solutions might apply to the auditory stream and the representation of three-dimensional auditory space. He also became interested in perceptual organization and came to regard it as a primary process in early perception, a prerequisite for recovery [34].

Harry Barrow became concerned with the methodology underlying the computational approach to vision. When a perceptual problem is specified, we can explore computational solutions to the problem under particular assumptions: However, we cannot be certain we have correctly formulated the specification and assumptions which apply to a real visual system in the real world. Accordingly, he took a different research direction and began building neural level models of the early visual pathway and its development. The models are adaptive and develop simple-cell receptive fields, topographic maps, and orientation and ocular dominance columns, like those found in primary visual cortex [2,3].

We have independently come to question the modular approach to vision. In proposing the intrinsic image and line drawing interpretation models, we always felt that the different mechanisms had to be tightly integrated. We wonder now to what extent a real visual system can be decomposed in the ways we have imagined, or even whether it is decomposable at all. Certainly, information flows top-down as well as bottom-up, but it also seems likely that it may skip stages and violate the stage-by-stage view of processing.

It may also be the case that we have placed too much emphasis on analytical recovery models and exact recovery (although our intent was partly to see how far the ideas could be pushed). Perhaps greater attention should be paid to qualitative methods which can still function when faced with the range of situations encountered in the real world. For example, photometric information might be most useful as a qualitative switch (e.g., to determine boundary and surface type, and hence what constraints to apply), or to refine shape locally (i.e., to find bumps and dents). In any event, we are convinced that it is very important to use images of real scenes, to reduce the risk of developing techniques which are not robust or versatile enough.

After ten years, certainly, progress has been made in understanding visual perception. A large number of papers on computational vision are published each year in a range of specialist journals, with a certain amount of reinventing of wheels. These are perhaps signs of the maturity of the field. It is evident, however, that there is plenty of scope for further research and new ideas.

Ten years ago there was excitement in the air. We all felt that we were making great strides in understanding vision through the computational approach. There is something of the same excitement abroad now, but particularly among those who are exploring the neurobiological approach. Since the early experiments of Hubel and Wiesel very significant advances have been made in neuroscience. New techniques have been developed which allow simultaneous recording from multiple cells, recording from cells in vitro, and visualization of neural activity on both small and large scales. Much more is known about the neural wiring diagrams and about the behaviour of the components. More than thirty cortical areas involved in visual processing have been identified, some of which have been found to process particular types of information, such as color or movement. Cells have been found which respond to structured objects (like faces), which depend on attention in visual tasks, and which anticipate eye movements. The neural basis of learning is under active investigation. The cortex has be found to be more adaptive than previously thought, and so general-purpose that auditory areas can adapt to processing visual input. Serious attempts are under way in several laboratories to build neural-level models of early vision, with active collaboration between experimental neuroscientists and modelers. The theory of neural circuits is being gradually worked out. We now have a reasonably good understanding of how and why the "oriented-feature-detectors" develop, how retinotopic maps are formed, and a little about the role of feedback.

Despite the maturity of computational vision and the rapid developments in neural systems, we still have a long way to go before we can come close to our goal of understanding visual perception. To do so we will need to draw upon what we have learned in many fields, including neuroscience, neural networks, experimental psychology and computational vision. One thing is clear: the next decade will be every bit as exciting and productive as the last.

Acknowledgement

We would like to thank Marty Fischler and Alan Yuille for helpful communications during preparation of this note.

References

[1] J. Aloimonos and A. Rosenfeld, Visual recovery, CS-TR 2580, University of Maryland, College Park, MD (1991).

[2] H.G. Barrow, Learning receptive fields, in: *Proceedings First International Conference on Neural Networks*, San Diego, CA (1987) 115–122.

[3] H.G. Barrow and A. Bray, A computational model of orientation map development, in preparation.

[4] H.G. Barrow and J.M. Tenenbaum, Recovering intrinsic scene characteristics from images, in: A. Hanson and E. Riseman, eds., *Computer Vision Systems* (Academic Press, New York, 1978) 3–26.

[5] H.G. Barrow and J.M. Tenenbaum, Interpreting line drawings as three-dimensional surfaces, *Artif. Intell.* **17** (1981) 75–116.

[6] T.O. Binford, Inferring surfaces from images, *Artif. Intell.* **17** (1981) 205–244.

[7] A. Blake and A. Zisserman, *Visual Reconstruction* (MIT Press, Cambridge, MA, 1987).

[8] J.M. Brady and A.L. Yuille, An extremum principle for shape from contour, *IEEE Patt. Anal. Mach. Intell.* **6** (1984) 288–301.

[9] M.B. Clowes, On seeing things, *Artif. Intell.* **2** (1) (1971) 79–112.

[10] S.W. Draper, The use of gradient and dual space in line-drawing interpretation, *Artif. Intell.* **17** (1981) 461–508.

[11] S. Geman and D. Geman, Stochastic relaxation, Gibbs distributions, and the Bayesian restoration of images, *IEEE Patt. Anal. Mach. Intell.* **6** (1984) 721–741.

[12] B.K.P Horn, Determining lightness from an image, *Comput. Graph. Image Process.* **3** (1974) 277–299.

[13] B.K.P. Horn, Obtaining shape from shading information, in: P.H. Winston, ed., *The Psychology of Computer Vision* (McGraw-Hill, New York, 1975) 115–155.

[14] B.K.P Horn and B.G. Schunck, Determining optical flow, *Artif. Intell.* **17** (1981) 185–204.

[15] D.H. Hubel, *Eye and Brain* (Scientific American Library, New York, 1988).

[16] D.H Hubel and T.N. Wiesel, Receptive fields and functional architecture of monkey striate cortex, *J. Physiology* **195** (1968) 215–243.

[17] D.A. Huffman, Impossible objects as nonsense sentences, in: B. Meltzer and D. Michie, eds., *Machine Intelligence* **6** (Edinburgh University Press, Edinburgh, England, 1971).

[18] K. Ikeuchi and B.K.P. Horn, Numerical shape from shading and occluding boundaries, *Artif. Intell.* **17** (1981) 141–184.

[19] T. Kanade, Recovery of the three-dimensional shape of an object from a single view, *Artif. Intell.* **17** (1981) 409–460.

[20] P. Kube, Likely local shape, in: *Proceedings CVPR* (1989).

[21] J. Malik and D. Maydan, Recovering three-dimensional shape from a single image of curved objects, *IEEE Patt. Anal. Mach. Intell.* **11** (1989) 555–566.

[22] T. Marill, Emulating the human interpretation of line-drawings as three-dimensional objects, *Int. J. Comput. Vis.* **6** (2) (1991) 147–161.

[23] D. Marr and T. Poggio, Cooperative computation of of stereo disparity, *Science* **194** (1977) 441–475.

[24] D. Marr, *Vision* (Freeman, San Francisco, CA, 1982).

[25] J.E.W. Mayhew and J.P. Frisby, Psychophysical and computational studies towards a theory of human stereopsis, *Artif. Intell.* **17** (1981) 349–386.

[26] R. Shapira and H. Freeman, Computer descriptions of bodies bounded by quadric surfaces from a set of imperfect projections, *IEEE Trans. Comput.* **9** (1978).

[27] K.A. Stevens, The visual interpretation of surface contours, *Artif. Intell.* **17** (1981) 47–74.

[28] K. Sugihara, An algebraic approach to shape-from-image problems, *Artif. Intell.* **23** (1984) 59–95.

[29] D. Terzopoulos, Image analysis using multigrid relaxation methods, *IEEE Patt. Anal. Mach. Intell.* **8** (1986) 129–139.

[30] A. Triesman, Properties, parts, and objects, in: K.R. Boff, L. Kaufman and J.P. Thomas, eds., *Handbook of Perception and Human Performance* (Wiley-Interscience, New York, 1986).

[31] K.J. Turner, Computer perception of curved objects using a television camera, Ph.D. Dissertation, Edinburgh University, Edinburgh, Scotland (1974).

[32] D.L. Waltz, Generating semantic descriptions from drawings of scenes with shadows, Tech. Rept. AI-TR-271, MIT, Cambridge, MA (1972).

[33] A.P. Witkin, Recovering surface shape and orientation from texture, *Artif. Intell.* **17** (1981) 17–45.

[34] A.P. Witkin and J.M. Tenenbaum, What is perceptual organization for? in: *Proceedings IJCAI-83*, Karlsruhe, Germany (1983) 1019–1022.

[35] R.J. Woodham, Analysing images of curved objects, *Artif. Intell.* **17** (1981) 117–140.

Artificial Intelligence 59 (1993) 81–87
Elsevier

ARTINT 1000

"Determining optical flow": a retrospective

Berthold K.P. Horn

MIT, Artificial Intelligence Laboratory, 545 Technology Square, Cambridge, MA 02139, USA

B.G. Schunck

Artificial Intelligence Laboratory, University of Michigan, 144 ATL, 1101 Beal Avenue, Ann Arbor, MI 48109-2110, USA

1. Overview

Our work on estimating optical flow [8] was important not because it solved (in some limited way) the problem of estimating optical flow, but because it represented the start of the variational approach to machine vision. The variational approach to machine vision problems was applied to shape-from-shading soon afterwards (Ikeuchi and Horn [10]), and has since found its way into many areas of machine vision. The variational approach lends itself particularly well to methods that are not feature-based. It provides a way of taking into account contributions from all parts of the image rather than just special isolated points, and it makes it possible to incorporate prior knowledge about what may be expected in particular imaging situations. It can also suggest methods for solving vision problems using nonlinear analog networks (Horn [6]), and it may lead to new ways of integrating multiple cues in images (Thompson [15]).

2. Origins

The idea behind the "optical flow" paper took form in the summer of 1978 when I was invited to the Motion Vision Laboratory established by

Correspondence to: B.K.P. Horn, MIT, Artificial Intelligence Laboratory, 545 Technology Square, Cambridge, MA 02139, USA. E-mail: bkph@ai.mit.edu.

Hans-Helmut Nagel at the University of Hamburg. I had no real exposure to motion vision problems before this. My interest was heightened by a paper presented by Clocksin that summer at a conference in Hamburg [3] that irritated me for some reason.

I was struck right away by the local ambiguity in recovering "optical flow", which I formulated as a linear constraint between the two components of the optical flow, with the derivatives of brightness as coefficients. This "brightness change constraint" can be conveniently exhibited as a line in velocity space. The local ambiguity inherent in this constraint was later termed the "aperture problem" (Marr [11]). An aside: this illustrates (a) how important it is to give an evocative name to an idea, and (b) how the simplest ideas are the ones that stick in peoples minds—not the ones that *you* think are important.

In attempting to deal with the local ambiguity it occurred to me that, in many cases, flow at nearby places in the image will be similar. But this is not a hard constraint that could be easily exploited. And the "constraint-propagation" methods popular in the field in the early seventies did not appeal to me. I started instead to think of the problem in least-squares terms, where there would be penalties for violating the basic brightness change constraint equation, and also penalties for having a flow that varied "too quickly" from place to place—the latter needed simply because the first "constraint" was not enough to provide a unique solution.

It took a bit of time, however, before I realized that this was really a problem in the calculus of variation (not too surprising, given that I knew nothing about the calculus of variation). While trying to read the work of Courant and Hilbert [4], I discretized the problem so that I could make some progress using traditional least-squares methods. After solving the discrete version, I would grovel over the local weighted sums that appeared, in order to try and guess what partial derivative operators were being approximated by these "computational molecules"!

Even-order partial differential equations of similar form to those arising in this variational problem were not entirely foreign to me, since we had used Poisson's equation (thin membrane) and the biharmonic equation (thin plate) earlier for interpolation of digital terrain models (DTMs) from contours (topographic maps) in our work for DARPA on image understanding—hill shading in particular [5].

Upon my return from Hamburg to MIT, I had Anni Bruss summarize the calculus of variations for me, and handed the problem over to Brian Schunck, who later did his Ph.D. thesis on this topic. We checked the basic ideas mostly on synthetic data, using various shapes with sinusoidal kinds of "textures". The images were created using a ray-tracing approach—as usual, this "forward optics" part was much simpler than the "inverse optics" part.

3. Variational approach to machine vision problems

The interesting part of this work was, in my opinion, the realization that tasks in machine vision can be posed as variational problems. A number of other tasks were later tackled in this way, starting with the shape-from-shading problem, which Katsushi Ikeuchi and I worked on using a penalty function containing the error in image brightness and again a "lack-of-smoothness" term [10].

There are several things to say about the variational approach to machine vision. First of all, it typically is not feature-based. Marvin Minsky told me, when Patrick Winston, Gene Freuder and I completed the "copy demo" in December 1970, that the time had come to leave the blocks world behind. To me this meant forgetting about edges. Most of my work has focused on image cues other than edges, since "edge detection" is only really a well-defined problem in a world of polyhedral shapes. (Note that I said "well-defined", not "well-posed".)

Another aspect of the variational approach is that it permits one to introduce information about how imaging works, as well as prior information about what is likely to happen in the scene. One part of the error being minimized is invariably some measure of how much the image actually observed differs from an image predicted from the computed solution. This seems like an eminently reasonable term to have in the penalty function!

Another aspect of the variational approach is that it leads to methods that use information from all over the image, *not* just isolated points. This provides for more robust results, since there is the opportunity for many small errors to more or less cancel out—an error at one pixel is not usually catastrophic. True, information from some areas, where brightness changes rapidly, may be more important than that from others, but why draw a line and say that some of this information should be thrown out altogether. Instead, just weight it in such a way that contributions from "important" areas have a stronger influence. The least-squares approach allows one to formalize this notion, and actually get the optimal weighting automatically.

4. False leads

There were several attempts to analyze our method and to improve upon it. Not all were productive. One notion was to note that "edges" provide strong constraint in one direction ("grey-level corners" provide strong constraint in two directions). So the propagation of velocities should perhaps be anisotropic—favored in certain directions. But the original formulation already took care of that, what looks like an isotropic "smoothing" interpolation is actually distinctly directional, and in just the right way—and how could it be otherwise? After all, the method is solving the least-squares problem by finding the optical flow that gives the best fit.

Some efforts to replicate our results, particularly on real data, failed because of lack of attention to basic numerical analysis. For example, it is important that the brightness derivatives be estimated so as to refer to the same point in time and space, and that the estimator do some smoothing, yet not lose locality. The estimator we used was described in detail in the paper, but some people simply used forward differences. Also, there are serious aliasing effects that may occur when the images moves more than a fraction of the wavelength of the dominant components of the scene "texture". Estimating derivatives from aliased data is not a productive activity. Not unexpectedly, there is a certain range of velocities over which these types of method work well. For large disparities between successive images one has to resort to a feature matching method.

5. Unfortunate side-effects

A few years after the birth of the variational approach to machine vision, Tomaso Poggio noticed that some of the variational methods used could be viewed as regularization of ill-posed problems. This has led to at least two mistaken ideas:

(1) that the variational approach *is* regularization, and
(2) that all vision problems are ill-posed.

To some extent the second error was fueled by the approach that Ikeuchi and I took in the paper "Numerical shape from shading and occluding boundaries" [10] where we abandoned the integrability constraint—because we couldn't find a convergent iterative scheme based on it—and instead used a departure-from-smoothness penalty term—quite analogous to that appearing in the optical flow method. This is basically the approach one would take if shape-from-shading was an ill-posed problem. But it is not, as has been forcefully pointed out by John Oliensis [12], Bror Saxberg [13], and Mike Brooks (and as should actually also be apparent from the original solution involving characteristic strips).

6. What was left out

Perhaps the main omission in the approach taken to optical flow at that time was the neglect of boundaries between different regions moving differently. The variational approach chosen was based on the idea that flow at neighboring places in the image is similar—without exception. Not surprisingly, large errors can occur at occluding boundaries in the image of rigid body motion—as illustrated in the original paper. Independently moving objects will lead to errors where one obscures another.

The reason the segmentation problem was not addressed in the original paper is that we had no reasonable ideas about how to solve it, other than simply omitting contributions to the departure-from-smoothness penalty term in places where there appeared to be rapid changes in the estimated optical flow. But this was neither a principled approach nor particularly effective in practice (although several papers have been written since then that basically pursue this heuristic).

Recently a number of approaches to the flow segmentation have arisen that look more promising. Starting with the idea of a line process and simulated annealing—which is not computationally reasonable—Andrew Blake, Christof Koch, John Harris, Tomaso Poggio and others (see [1]) have developed approximations thereof that are computationally tractable.

Another thing we did not do enough of in the paper is an analysis of what the sources of errors might be and what circumstances contributed to successful recovery of optical flow. We obviously knew something about this, since we chose experimental image sequences that worked! But we did not say enough about when the algorithm would not produce useful output. And in the tradition of machine vision programs based on single cues, there are plenty of situations that confuse this algorithm.

7. Optical flow and the motion field

One thing that I regret now in looking back at the paper is that we did not draw a clear distinction between what I would now call the "motion field" and the "optical flow". The optical flow is a velocity field in the image that transforms one image into the next image in a sequence. As such, it is not uniquely determined. One needs to add additional constraint to obtain a particular "optical flow". The motion field, on the other hand, is a purely geometric concept, without any ambiguity—it is the projection into the image of three-dimensional motion vectors. One endeavours to recover an optical flow that is close to the motion field—which is what one would really like in order to estimate shapes and motions. Much confusion has resulted from a lack of distinction between these two quite distinct concepts.

8. Where did the work go from there

There are really two "directions" to discuss. The first is in work on motion vision *per se*. Here my own work with Anni Bruss [2], Shariar

Negahdaripour [7] and Ned Weldon [9] focused on introducing the rigid body constraint. This is such a powerful constraint, reducing the "number of unknowns" from two at every picture cell (components of flow) to roughly one at every picture cell (depth alone), that it would be silly not to exploit it when it applies. With rigid body motion, the problems are no longer variational, but instead "ordinary" (albeit complex and nonlinear) least-squares problems. And in several special cases (such as pure rotation, pure translation, motion with respect to a planar surface), closed form solutions exist. Again, the problem of segmentation was not addressed in our work, because it throws a real spanner in the works. Yet in many practical situations, depth discontinuities and independently moving objects require that the scene be segmented before the methods we developed can be applied to the regions therein.

The second "direction" is broader, that of variational methods for machine vision in general. Variational methods have now been brought to bear on a variety of problems, including optical flow, shape-from-shading, interpolation from sparse data and yes, even edge detection and segmentation.

9. What can be built more easily as a result of the paper?

The optical flow method described in the paper allows the flow velocity to vary from place to place in the image—albeit slowly. An even simpler situation is one where the flow is the same everywhere—as might be a reasonable assumption if we consider a small enough patch of an image. This problem has a simple closed form solution involving two linear equations in two unknowns, which is variously attributed to Ned Weldon or Hans-Helmut Nagel, although it was also a long-standing homework problem in my course on machine vision here at MIT.

John Tanner and Carver Mead at Caltech built an analog VLSI circuit that solves this simplified optical flow problem [14]. They did it using a feedback scheme quite analogous to gradient descent, rather than by working with the closed form solution directly. This is particularly nice, since a simple extension (replacing a global bus with a resistive network) would solve the variational problem, where flow *is* allowed to vary from place to place. A circuit for doing this has not been built, to my knowledge, but is well within the state of the art.

More interesting perhaps than computation of optical flow itself is the recovery of rigid body motion and a depth map, if possible. Work on "direct" methods (that is, based on derivatives of brightness at all picture cells) for motion vision has led to some schemes that lend themselves to implementation in analog VLSI hardware. The pure rotation case is so simple (and has so little application in practice) that nobody has bothered to built a chip for it. Pure translation is much harder, and Ignacio Sean McQuirk is now building an analog chip here at MIT to find the focus of expansion.

Such efforts may lead to more complex chips that find both translation and rotation of a camera in a fixed environment. These should be useful in robotics and guidance of vehicles.

References

[1] A. Blake and A. Zisserman, *Visual Reconstruction* (MIT Press, Cambridge, MA, 1987).

[2] A.R. Bruss and B.K.P. Horn, Passive navigation, AI Memo 662, MIT, Cambridge, MA (1981).

[3] W.F. Clocksin, Determining the orientation of surfaces from optical flow, in: *Proceedings AISB Conference*, Hamburg, Germany (1978).

[4] R. Courant and D. Hilbert, *Methods of Mathematical Physics* (Interscience, New York, 1937/1953).

[5] B.K.P. Horn, Hill shading and the reflectance map, *Proc. IEEE* **69** (1) (1981).

[6] B.K.P. Horn, Parallel analog networks for machine vision, AI Memo 1071, MIT, Cambridge, MA (1988).

[7] B.K.P. Horn and S. Negahdaripour, Direct passive navigation: analytical solution for planes, *IEEE Trans. Pattern Anal. Mach. Intell.* **9** (1) (1987) 168–176.

[8] B.K.P. Horn and B.G. Schunck, Determining optical flow, *Artif. Intell.* **17** (1981) 185–203.

[9] B.K.P. Horn and E.J. Weldon Jr, Direct methods for recovering motion, *Int. J. Comput. Vis.* **2** (1) (1988) 51–76.

[10] K. Ikeuchi and B.K.P. Horn, Numerical shape from shading and occluding boundaries, *Artif. Intell.* **17** (1981) 141–184.

[11] D. Marr, *Vision* (Freeman, San Francisco, CA, 1982).

[12] J. Oliensis, Existence and uniqueness in shape form shading, Ph.D. Thesis, University of Massachusetts, Amherst, MA (1989).

[13] B.V.H. Saxberg, A modern differential geometry approach to shape from shading, Ph.D. Thesis, Electrical Engineering and Computer Science Department, MIT, Cambridge, MA (1989).

[14] J.E. Tanner and C.A. Mead, An integrated optical motion sensor, *VLSI Signal Processing II* (Proceedings of the ASSP Conference on VLSI Signal Processing), Los Angeles, CA (1986) 59–76.

[15] C.M. Thompson, Robust photo-topography by fusing shape-from-shading and stereo, Ph.D. Thesis, Mechanical Engineering Department, MIT, Cambridge, MA (1993).

Artificial Intelligence 59 (1993) 89–94
Elsevier

ARTINT 1001

Comment on "Numerical shape from shading and occluding boundaries"

K. Ikeuchi

School of Computer Science, Carnegie Mellon University, Pittsburgh, PA 15213, USA

Abstract

Ikeuchi, K., Comment on "Numerical shape from shading and occluding boundaries", Artificial Intelligence 59 (1993) 89–94.

The paper "Numerical shape from shading and occluding boundaries" [10] proposed a method to determine the 3D shape of an object from a single brightness image using the smoothness constraint on surface orientations, and the orientations of the surface given along an occluding boundary. This paper contributed both a specific algorithm for solving a specific problem, and a general approach that could be applied in other low-level vision problems.

1. Research background

It has long been known that the human visual system is capable of determining the 3D structure (relative depth or surface orientations) of a scene, given only 2D information. For example, a black-and-white photograph of an object is only 2D, yet can be used by a human to determine the 3D shape of the object. The human visual system uses a variety of cues to determine 3D shape. One such cue is shading information: the way in which brightness varies along the surface of an object is used by the human visual system to determine the underlying 3D shape of the object; the process is known as shape-from-shading.

Correspondence to: K. Ikeuchi, School of Computer Science, Carnegie Mellon University, Pittsburgh, PA 15213, USA.

In the late 1970s and early 1980s, at the Artificial Intelligence Laboratory of the Massachusetts Institute of Technology, several projects were conducted to investigate computational algorithms to emulate on computers these modules of the human visual system that determine (relative) depth from images. Such projects investigated shape-from-shading (Horn, Woodham, Ikeuchi, Pentland), shape-from-texture (Richard, Witkin, Stevens), optical flow (Horn, Marr, Schunk, Hildreth), and binocular stereo (Marr, Poggio, Grimson).

Shape-from-shading research, originally suggested as a thesis topic by Minsky, was initiated by Horn as his Ph.D. thesis in 1970 [7]. Horn formalized the shape-from-shading problem using the nonlinear partial differential *image irradiance equation*,

$$E(x,y) = R(p,q), \tag{1}$$

where $R(p,q)$ is a known reflectance function of an object surface, represented using the standard (p,q) gradient space coordinate system to define unknown orientations and assuming orthographic projection down the z axis onto the (x,y) plane for image formation, and $E(x,y)$ is a given input brightness distribution at each image point, (x,y).

Horn solved the equation using the characteristic strip expansion method. The method draws characteristic strips—special strips which satisfy a certain condition—in a shaded image and determines orientations iteratively along the characteristic strips from a point whose orientation is known. As the starting point, Horn used the point which provides the maximum brightness, $R(p,q) = 1$. (In particular, on a Lambertian surface, the point of the maximum brightness is oriented toward the light source.) The method demonstrated was able to determine the shape of 3D objects such as a human nose from its black/white shaded image.

Horn's original method, however, has two main defects.

- Direct integration of the characteristic equations to find the characteristic strips suffers from noise sensitivity in practical implementations. As the solution proceeds along constructed strips from the initial points, these strips, as well as the computed orientations, can deviate from the actual strip positions and orientations as a result of quantization errors and other noise influences.
- The method starts characteristic strips from a point with a known orientation. The method employs the point of maximum brightness for the starting point. However, at such points the partial derivatives of R vanish, so the strips cannot be uniquely constructed. To overcome this problem, the original method uses the points on a circumscribing circle to approximate the starting points.

2. Technical contents

In 1979 [1] we (Ikeuchi and Horn) solved these problems by introducing the *smoothness constraint* and by utilizing the information given along *occluding boundaries*:

- *Noise sensitivity*: Horn's original method can only determine surface orientations along the characteristic strips. Thus, a single noisy point on a strip could throw off all of the following computations. Our method introduced the smoothness constraint, which required neighboring points to have similar surface orientations:

$$p_x^2 + p_y^2 + q_x^2 + q_y^2 = 0. \tag{2}$$

  By using this constraint, our method propagated, combined, and averaged orientations over neighboring grid points to determine the orientation at the central point. By averaging the information in a neighborhood, sensitivity to noise was greatly reduced.

- *Singular point*: Horn's original method can only use the orientation at a singular point. Our method uses more widely available orientations along an occluding boundary. (Horn's method cannot use these orientations due to its parameterization.)

  At the points along occluding boundaries of objects, orientations are perpendicular to the lines of sight. From the shape of the silhouette, which is the projection of an occluding boundary onto the image plane, we can determine the tangential direction of the occluding boundary parallel to the image plane, and thus, the orientation there. Our method uses these orientations as the initial conditions for the algorithm.

The image irradiance equation, $E(x, y) - R(p, q) = 0$, only provides one constraint at each image point. The surface orientation of the point has two degrees of freedom (p, q). We used the smoothness constraint, $p_x^2 + p_y^2 + q_x^2 + q_y^2 = 0$, as an additional constraint. (Horn's method uses a weak smoothness constraint given by the continuity of the characteristics strips.)

We formalized the shape-from-shading problem as a minimization problem of the difference between the observed brightness and the expected brightness given through the image irradiance equation from the expected surface orientation, while maintaining the smoothness constraint.

$$\iint_A (E(x, y) - R(p, q))^2 + \lambda(p_x^2 + p_y^2 + q_x^2 + q_y^2) \, \mathrm{d}x \, \mathrm{d}y. \tag{3}$$

---

[1] The original working memo was published November 1979, the revised AI memo published February 1980, and the revised journal article was published in August 1981.

The minimization is performed over the region, A, enclosed by an occluding boundary, ∂A; the aim is to obtain a distribution of (p,q)s which minimize the equations over the region, A.

Using the calculus of variations, we formulated an iterative scheme to obtain the (p,q) which minimizes the equation. Since the iterative scheme requires a boundary condition, we used the orientations along the occluding boundary, ∂A. The method was demonstrated to determine orientations over the region, A, from the shading information over the region, A, and the orientation along the boundary, ∂A.

3. Contributions

One of the main intellectual contributions of the paper came from reporting the effectiveness of the smoothness constraint on low-level vision modules. The smoothness constraint forces neighboring points to have similar surface orientations. Later this constraint was generalized into the *regularization term* by Poggio. The paper predicted that the smoothness constraint would be effective with other low-level vision modules. (See the discussion in [10, p. 181].)

The paper also demonstrated the effectiveness of the variational approach for low-level vision problems. Using this method, various low-level vision problems can be solved in a uniform manner.

4. Open issues

The following are research issues that were left out of the original paper but are still open. Some of the recent representative research toward the issues are also discussed:

The smoothness constraint

Though robust, the method based on the smoothness constraint does deviate from the real solution. That is, the algorithm converges to shapes that are slightly different from the real shapes. Another problem of the smoothness constraint is that it does not guarantee that the solution obtained is integrable because our method determines p and q independently. Several researchers (Horn and Brooks [5,6] and Frankot and Chelappa [4]) pointed out these two effects and proposed new algorithms by introducing integrability constraints. However, I (Ikeuchi) believe that the smoothness constraint is still interesting enough as a mechanism to emulate modules of the human visual system.

(1) The smoothness constraint can be applied to a wide variety of low-level vision modules regardless of parameterizations. Some of the proposed constraints are only valid for a certain parameterization. The notion of smoothness should be independent of parameterizations. It is quite likely that the human visual system imposes such smoothness constraints (nearby points have similar characteristics) to its default interpretation of a scene.

(2) The method based on the smoothness constraint has the preferred default shape. In the absence of any shading information, the method applied to the boundary condition yields the default shape. When shading information is present, this shape is modified so as to satisfy the image irradiance equation. It seems to me that this mechanism is quite reasonable as the behavior of the human visual system. Namely, the mechanism has an underlying default shape and outputs such a default shape when no input information is available. When some input is available, it modifies the output accordingly.

From these two points, I conjecture that some sort of smoothness constraint mechanism exists in the human visual system. Research on the similarities and differences between human and machine shape-from-shading algorithms is an interesting topic. Such comparisons are reported by Mingolla and Todd [11].

Occluding boundary

The method requires surface orientations along a closed occluding boundary. We can observe a whole occluding boundary only when a viewer and a light source are located at the same position. Under general conditions, an illuminated region is partly enclosed by an occluding boundary and partly by a self-shadowed boundary. Along a self-shadowed boundary, no orientation information is available. Thus, under general conditions, our method cannot be applied to the shape-from-shading problem. It is necessary to remedy this point (see Pentland [14]).

Binocular stereo provides depth information along a boundary, ∂A. In order to obtain depth information over the region A, it is necessary to interpolate depth information from that along the boundary ∂A. Shape-from-shading provides (relative) depth information over the region A, from those along the boundary ∂A. Both modules are complementary in nature, and thus combining the methods is an interesting research goal (Ikeuchi [8,9], Blake et al. [1]).

Known reflectance map

Our shape-from-shading algorithm requires a known exact reflectance map, that is, known reflectance characteristics, and a known light source direction.

It is rather unusual to know the exact reflectance characteristics of an object and the exact direction of the light source. A method for determining the shape using a rough reflectance map is necessary (Brooks and Horn [2], Nayar et al. [12]).

Interreflection

Finally, the method assumes that one light source directly illuminates a surface. However, it often occurs that several light sources illuminate a surface simultaneously, and interreflections occur among nearby surfaces. Research on shape-from-shading under complicated illumination conditions should be explored (Forsyth [3], Nayar et al. [13]).

References

[1] A. Blake, A. Zisserman and G. Knowles, Surface descriptions from stereo and shading, *Image Vis. Comput.* **3** (4) (1985) 183–191.

[2] M.J. Brooks and B.K.P. Horn, Shape and source from shading, in: *Proceedings IJCAI-85*, Los Angeles, CA (1985) 932–936.

[3] D. Forsyth and A. Zisserman, Reflections on shading, *IEEE Trans. Pattern Anal. Mach. Intell.* **13** (7) (1991) 671–679.

[4] R.T. Frankot and R. Chellappa, A method for enforcing integrability in shape from shading algorithm, *IEEE Trans. Pattern Anal. Mach. Intell.* **10** (4) (1988) 439–451.

[5] B.K.P. Horn, Height and gradient from shading, *Int. J. Comput. Vis.* **5** (1) (1990) 37–74.

[6] B.K.P. Horn and M.J. Brooks, The variational approach to shape from shading, *Comput. Vis. Graph. Image Process.* **33** (2) (1986) 174–208.

[7] B.K.P. Horn, Shape from shading: a method for obtaining the shape of a smooth opaque object from one view, Tech. Rept. MAC-TR-79, MIT, Cambridge, MA (1970).

[8] K. Ikeuchi, Reconstructing a depth map from intensity map, in: *Proceedings International Conference on Pattern Recognition* (1984) 736–738.

[9] K. Ikeuchi, Determining a depth map using a dual photometric stereo, *Int. J. Rob. Res.* **6** (1) (1987) 15–31.

[10] K. Ikeuchi and B.K.P. Horn, Numerical shape from shading and occluding boundaries, *Artif. Intell.* **17** (1981) 141–184.

[11] E. Mingolla and J.T. Todd, Perception of solid shape from shading, *Biol. Cybern.* **53** (1986) 137–151.

[12] S.K. Nayar, K. Ikeuchi and T. Kanade, Determining shape and reflectance of hybrid surfaces by photometric sampling, *IEEE Trans. Rob. Autom.* **6** (4) (1990) 418–431.

[13] S.K. Nayar, K. Ikeuchi and T. Kanade, Shape from interreflections, *Int. J. Comput. Vis.* **6** (3) (1991) 173–195.

[14] A.P. Pentland, Linear shape from shading, *Int. J. Comput. Vis.* **4** (1990) 153–162.

Artificial Intelligence 59 (1993) 95–101
Elsevier

ARTINT 1002

From a real chair to a negative chair

Takeo Kanade

School of Computer Science, Carnegie Mellon University, Pittsburgh, PA 15213, USA

1. How it started

In the fall of 1977, I was invited by Raj Reddy to spend a year at the Computer Science Department of Carnegie Mellon University as a visiting scientist from Kyoto University in Japan. My plan for research during the stay was to develop a model-based object recognition program. Upon arrival, I chose an image of an office scene (Fig. 1) as an example image; the image was one of a set that Ron Ohlander had used in his research on color image segmentation. The task I set for my program was to recognize the chair in this image.

I began to write a "knowledge-based" program for chair recognition by creating a set of heuristic rules for the task. It seemed that in addition to geometric relationships, a good source of constraints was color information, such as "the back and the seat of a chair have the same color". The effort of creating heuristic rules one after another, however, was not a satisfying game, since every time I came up with a reasonably functioning program, I could also find a chair that was an exception to the rules.

2. The Origami world

Ohlander's color segmentation program, which was quite famous at the time, could segment the image of Fig. 1 into regions as shown in Fig. 2. As I stared at the results, not only could I still see a chair without using color information, but I could also perceive the shape of the object without

Correspondence to: T. Kanade, School of Computer Science, Carnegie Mellon University, Pittsburgh, PA 15213, USA. E-mail: kanade@cs.cmu.edu.

Fig. 1. An office scene—one of Ohlander's image set.

Fig. 2. Ohlander's segmentation result.

knowing it was a chair. In other words, I realized that there must exist geometrical constraints which enable us to recover shape from a single image.

To make the problem simpler, I turned Fig. 2 into a more stylized line drawing of a chair as shown in Fig. 3, and again started to develop heuristic rules for shape recovery, this time using geometric constraints only. Being heuristic, this effort did not lead me to a satisfactory systematic solution, either. Six months had passed since I arrived at CMU, and I was beginning to feel frustrated.

One day, Allen Newell asked me to come to his office and talk about my research. I felt embarrassed about not having achieved much yet. When I finished explaining what I had been doing, Newell asked what the difference is between my method and Waltz's line labeling method [6]. I gave a very vague answer, "Waltz's method cannot handle this image, and mine will be more flexible". When I returned to my office, I quickly found the exact reason why Waltz's labeling method did not work with Fig. 3. Its trihedral world assumption (i.e., at each vertex three planes meet) implies solid objects, and while the chair is a solid object, pictures like Fig. 3 typically fail to depict the width of thin objects, such as legs, and thus become "illegal" drawings. The two drawings of a box in Fig. 4 are good illustrations of the effect.

So, to generalize beyond the trihedral world, I constructed a shape labeling theory for the world consisting of planar surfaces which may be folded, cut, or glued together only along straight lines. From the metaphor of the Japanese art of paper folding, I named it a theory of the Origami world [1].

3. Multiple interpretations and qualitative shapes

The labeling procedure for the Origami world could interpret line drawings like Fig. 3 and Fig. 4(b) as well as Fig. 4(a), but revealed two interesting

Fig. 3. A "chair" line drawing.

Fig. 4. (a) A box in the trihedral world and (b) a box in the Origami world.

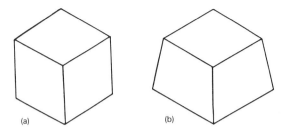

Fig. 5. (a) A "cube" line drawing and (b) a "trapezoid" line drawing.

issues, both of which are obvious upon afterthought. The first phenomenon
was that it generated many legal interpretations. For example, Fig. 4(b)
was given eight interpretations. For the chair scene in Fig. 3, my program
generated several hundred interpretations after spending two hours of a
DEC-10's CPU time, but it was far less than halfway through enumerating
all the possible interpretations. Though many of these interpretations appear
strange to us, all of them are correct and *physically possible* shapes that can
correspond to the drawings. I used to say, "If you bet that this drawing is
of a chair, your bet is one to at least several hundred or against two CPU
hours of DEC-10, so most likely you will lose".[1]

Generating multiple interpretations for a single drawing is certainly counter-intuitive, since humans don't usually do so. Mathematically, however,
it is obvious that a drawing cannot determine a unique shape, since a
2D picture is only a projection of a 3D scene, and many 3D shapes can
produce the same projection. The trihedral world of Waltz and others was
so constrained that it had not needed to face multiple interpretations often.
The Origami world is bigger than the trihedral world, and thus began to
reveal the issue.

The second issue that the Origami world revealed was the realization
that the labeling does not really specify the shape. Till then, people talked
as if the Waltz labeling procedure had recovered the shape. Actually, line
labels can only analyze and recover a qualitative characterization of the
shape. This is clear from Figs. 5(a) and 5(b): each figure can have the
same labeling or qualitative shape (convex corner), but the figures suggest
different quantitative shapes (cube and trapezoid). While the POLY system
of Mackworth [5] used the gradient space as a quantitative tool, it did so
only for the purpose of *analyzing* the feasibility of shapes, not for *recovering*
the quantitative shape.

---

[1] When I told this to my current students, their response was "DEC-10 must have been a
slow machine".

4. Quantitative recovery of plausible shapes

It became clear that we cannot avoid multiple interpretations, and that we cannot recover "the" shape that a drawing depicts. Still, however, the problem remained as to why certain shape interpretations appear more plausible than others. To say "a certain shape is more familiar" or "I learned it over the years", though not incorrect, simply ducks the question and does not really answer it, since most of us, in fact, *cannot* think of multiple interpretations. We do not select a particular interpretation after we think of all the possibilities; rather we think of *only* a certain shape. Thus, additional shape constraints must be used at a relatively early stage of the interpretation process.

My goal became the development of a quantitative geometrical theory to shed light on this problem. The two drawings in Fig. 5 turned out to be the simplest example that illustrated the problem: they have exactly the same set of three qualitatively different interpretations, they each have only three quadrilateral regions one of which (the top region) is exactly the same in each, but the seemingly most plausible quantitative interpretations are different, i.e., cube versus trapezoid. Thus, the two side regions must be responsible for the difference.

The idea I came up with was a principle of non-accidental regularity. That is, regular image properties, such as collinearity, parallelism, and regular spacing, occur for a good reason, not by accident. John Kender, who was working on his thesis on texture, phrased it as the "seeming so is actually so" principle [4]. I devised a method to convert the non-accidental regularities into shape constraints.

One of the most interesting new classes of the non-accidental regularity I defined was skew symmetry. Real symmetry in 2D has an axis for which the opposite sides are reflective; in other words the symmetry is found along lines perpendicular to the symmetrical axis. The concept of skew symmetry relaxes this condition, such that symmetry is found along lines not necessarily perpendicular to the axis, but at a fixed angle to it. Figures like a leaf and a parallel quadrilateral have skew symmetry. Non-accidentalness of skew symmetry implies "A skewed symmetry depicts a real symmetry viewed from some (unknown) viewing direction" [2, p. 424]. This results in quantitative constraints on surface orientations that include a skew symmetry, and the constraints can be represented very neatly in gradient space. Using the similar idea, I found that various regular image properties, including parallelism, regular spacing, and affine-transformable texture patterns, can be mapped to constraints on plausible shapes.

Once we combine these quantitative constraints with the qualitative shape characterizations given by labeling, we can compute the particular plausible shapes that a drawing can depict. The principle of non-accidental regularity and its mathematical embodiment in the skew symmetry heuristic, together with a method to compute the quantitative shape, constituted the main part of the *AI Journal* paper that is included in the set of the most influential works [2].

Using the theory, it turned out that the "normal" interpretations of many drawings (a box for Fig. 4(b), a cube for Fig. 5(a) and a trapezoid for Fig. 5(b), respectively) could be proven to be the most plausible. For the chair scene of Fig. 3, however, my program found two "most plausible" interpretations. One of them was a "normal" chair, and the other was a strange shape which I called a "negative" chair.

Although it looks odd, a negative chair is physically realizable, satisfies the non-accidental regularity principle, and, of course, its picture can look the same as the normal one. Interestingly, when we construct a negative chair and swing it a little in the air, it appears as if a normal chair is flexing its arms back and forth. This effect awaits a psychophysical explanation.

5. Computer vision as a physical science

One of the main contributions of the paper "Recovery of the three-dimensional shape of an object from a single view" is that it demonstrated a simple fact in vision: there are a multiplicity of possible image interpretations, and if we want to obtain a unique interpretation, we must use some assumptions, constraints, or heuristics. Since humans usually think of only a single interpretation, many vision researchers accepted the requirement that a computer vision program also generate only a single interpretation. In fact, when I submitted the Origami world paper [1] to the *Artificial Intelligence Journal*, one of the reviewers gave a comment like, "This paper is wrong since it does not give the interpretation 'box' to the drawing of a box". Early researchers attempted to meet this requirement by hastily incorporating domain heuristics, often, implicitly, without understanding their effects, limitations, or implications. In contrast, the paper "Recovery of the three-dimensional shape of an object from a single view" showed how far one could go purely with geometrical principles, and what exact specification was for the set of possible interpretations by that method.

A series of works appeared in the last decade which formalized many of the geometrical constraints which relate properties in the image domain to three-dimensional shape constraints. Some of these constraints may have been conceived from observations of human perception, and they may be heuristic in the sense that they do not always hold. The implications were clearly defined, however, and therefore it was possible to predict the consequences when rules did not apply. In this sense they are not *ad hoc*. This is in direct contrast to the purely heuristic methods, ranging from various line drawing interpretation methods in the early 1970s, to the use of global minimization of arbitrarily created energy functions in the 1980s. In these cases, the implications are neither clearly defined nor predictable in terms of physical reality.

Systematic formulation of constraints in vision need not be limited to geometric constraints. Recent attention has turned to putting other physical properties, such as the optical and statistical processes which underlie vision, into a quantitative, computational framework. That is, the emphasis is on developing *physical* models for computer vision. Vision is the process of using images (data) taken about the real (physical) world. Therefore, as with any physical science, a clear technical understanding of the physical nature of the data (i.e., images) is required for formulating a solution. Such modeling reveals the structure of visual information: the exact information that is contained in an image, the limits of processing algorithms, and the heuristic knowledge required to resolve any remaining ambiguity. Hence, I advocate computer vision is a physical science as well as a cognitive science [3].

References

[1] T. Kanade, A theory of Origami world, *Artif. Intell.* **13** (1980) 279–311.

[2] T. Kanade, Recovery of the three-dimensional shape of an object from a single view, *Artif. Intell.* **17** (1981) 409–460.

[3] T. Kanade, Computer vision as a physical science, in: R. Rashid, ed., *Carnegie Mellon Computer Science: A 25-Year Commemorative* (Addison-Wesley, Reading, MA, 1991) 345–369.

[4] J.R. Kender, Shape from texture, Ph.D. Thesis, Carnegie Mellon University, Pittsburgh, PA (1980).

[5] A.K. Mackworth, Interpreting pictures of polyhedral scenes, *Artif. Intell.* **4** (2) (1973) 121–137.

[6] D. Waltz, Generating semantic descriptions from drawings of scenes with shadows, in: P.H. Winston, ed., *The Psychology of Computer Vision* (McGraw-Hill, New York, 1975).

Qualitative reasoning

Artificial Intelligence 59 (1993) 105–114
Elsevier

ARTINT 990

A view on qualitative physics

Johan de Kleer

Xerox Palo Alto Research Center, 3333 Coyote Hill Road, Palo Alto, CA 94304, USA

1. Introduction

The paper "A qualitative physics based on confluences" [18] by John Seely Brown and myself was one of the first papers in what is today a large and active area of artificial intelligence. As John Seely Brown has become the Chief Scientist of Xerox Corporation and is therefore somewhat distracted, this brief note represents my (Johan) personal views.[1] I will focus on some of the events and experiences which motivated me to become interested in qualitative physics and where it should be going.

When I was first exposed to the notions of symbolic computation and reasoning, these notions appeared as the ideal tools for the enterprise of understanding the physical world around us. Computers were already in widespread use in science and engineering for data analysis and simulation. However, even with the AI technologies of the 1970s, it was clear we could exploit computers in a far grander way. In particular, it became thinkable that we might be able to build systems that would be capable of reasoning about the physical world much as we ourselves, as engineers and scientists, do. I found this challenge enormously exciting because I saw (and still see) this as probably the only way that we will be able to build intelligences that can function successfully in the real world. Therefore, with the hubris characteristic of researchers in artificial intelligence, I set myself on a research programme with the goal of constructing what could best be described as an "artificial engineer" or "artificial scientist".

Correspondence to: J. de Kleer. E-mail: dekleer@parc.xerox.com
[1] Some of this material is extracted from the section "Qualitative physics: a personal view" in [33].

2. The confusion seminar

In 1974 I participated in a seminar run by Seymour Papert that was nick-
named "the confusion seminar". This half-year seminar proceeded through
a sequence of confounding physical puzzles, sometimes spending weeks on
a single example. These concerned commonsense questions about familiar
topics such as bouncing balls, roller coasters, pulleys, rockets, strings, see-
saws, swings, and juggling—as can be found in [7,32] and analyzed in [20].
The purpose of the seminar was to study thinking, the maxim at the time being, "You can't think about thinking without thinking about thinking about
something." Examining the kind of mistakes one commonly makes while
reasoning about the physical world serves as insight into how one thinks. I
came away from the seminar with a completely different lesson. For almost
all the examples we considered, the conventional mathematical formulation
of physics was useless or unnecessary. It became apparent that most of the
problems could be solved by simple qualitative reasoning alone. For most
puzzles, it was eventually possible to resolve them to everyone's satisfaction
by writing down at most one or two extremely simple equations. Invariably,
writing down the full equations was the wrong tactic because either

(1) the equations were intractable because we couldn't figure out the
    right idealization or approximation,
(2) people weren't convinced unless the answers predicted by the equa-
    tions were substantiated by intuition, or
(3) more often than not the seminar participants would write down the
    wrong equations and get the wrong answers.

3. Qualitative reasoning for solving physics problems

Although it was clear that qualitative reasoning of some sort is central for
solving the kinds of puzzles that arose in the confusion seminar, I wondered
if this would be true for more standard physics tasks, and therefore I started
thinking about what knowledge was required to solve classical physical
problems and how to build a system that could solve them. There had
been two previous such problem solvers built: STUDENT (Bobrow [1])
and CARPS (Charniak [5]) (there have been many subsequent ones, for
example, by Bundy et al. [3,4], Novak [24,25], and Skorstad and Forbus
[28]). However, these two programs solved only an extremely narrow range
of problem types. STUDENT, and to a large extent CARPS, primarily
exploited the standard ways in which textbook problems are stated and
incorporated essentially no knowledge about the physical world. The systems
would produce nonsensical solutions for problems stated in nonstandard

ways or which required even a rudimentary model of the physical world (e.g., that objects fall, boats are constrained to move on the surface of lakes, and masses are positive).

My research focused on a class of problems studied in the confusion seminar: roller coasters, or the movement of a cart (under gravity) on a track. The motion of the cart is governed by the laws of kinematics and Newton's laws, so it seemed like a simple place to start. The experience of building NEWTON [10], a system which could solve such problems, made the case for qualitative reasoning all the more compelling. For example, the research showed that qualitative reasoning is critical for comprehending the problem in the first place, formulating a plan for solving the problem, identifying which quantitative laws apply to the problem, and interpreting the results of quantitative analysis. In fact, the so-called physics knowledge of kinematics and Newton's laws are only a small fraction of the knowledge needed to solve problems. Most of the knowledge is "pre-physics", and considerable effort is required to codify it.

Physicists typically have a hard time understanding the goals of qualitative physics. When we present them some theory of qualitative reasoning (e.g., carts on roller coaster tracks), their first reaction is that they already knew that and see no point to developing a theory of such. When we answer by saying that we have explicitly codified this knowledge (e.g., about concavity) in such a way that a program can perform this reasoning, they remain unconvinced because they say the FORTRAN program they just built to analyze their data incorporated the same sort of knowledge. Under closer analysis, what they mean is that when *they* wrote the program to interpret a particular set of experimental data, they exploited this knowledge of their own. It is impossible to identify the location of this knowledge in the FORTRAN program, and a different program needs to be written for the next experiment. Typically, the program has no way to detect that it is producing nonsense results when the implicit assumptions under which it was written are violated. Qualitative physics aims to lay bare the underlying intuitions and make them sufficiently explicit that they are directly reasoned with and about. Only in this way can AI reasoners approach the rich and diverse capabilities of human problem solvers.

4. Qualitative and causal reasoning for circuit diagnosis

In 1974 I joined the SOPHIE project (summarized in [2]) at BBN led by John Seely Brown. SOPHIE was an Intelligent Computer Aided Instructional (ICAI) tool for teaching students diagnostic skills. One part of the task consisted of developing an AI-based diagnostician capable of expert-level diagnosis of an electronic power supply (and giving explanations for its conclusions). This diagnostician is faced with the formidable task of drawing diagnostic inferences from whatever measurements the student made. The project developed a system capable of diagnosing an electronic circuit from first principles alone. This subsystem, called LOCAL (de Kleer [9]), incorporated many ideas now included within model-based diagnosis (Davis [8]). It used knowledge about the known good and faulty behaviors of device components to detect inconsistencies between actual and predicted behaviors, which it then used to pinpoint the circuit fault.

Unfortunately, LOCAL suffered a very serious shortcoming: Although it was very good at pinpointing faulty components once two or three circuit measurements had been made, it was poor at drawing diagnostic inferences from initial measurements. It turned out that simple, first-principles reasoning about currents and voltages was insufficient to start diagnosing even fairly simple circuits, such as a six-transistor (and 31 other components) series-regulated power supply. This posed both pragmatic and theoretical difficulties: SOPHIE needed an automated expert-level diagnostician to pursue the instructional aspects of the research. To achieve this pragmatic goal, LOCAL was augmented with conventional expert-system rules to guide the initial phase of troubleshooting. These rules were tuned by trying hundreds of different circuit faults, comparing LOCAL's conclusions to those of a human expert, and adding rules to achieve what model-based reasoning missed. In the end, this was accomplished by augmenting LOCAL with only 39 circuit-specific rules.

LOCAL faced a difficult task:

(1) there were 37 potentially failing components;
(2) being an analog circuit, each component could fail in an infinite number of ways; and
(3) the student, not LOCAL, was in control of which measurements were made, so LOCAL had to make its inferences from any set of measurements whatsoever (there were 80 possible current measurements and 601 potential voltage measurements).

Thus it was extremely surprising that LOCAL, augmented with only 39 rules, would be able to localize the same set of faulty components as a human expert would.

Subsequently, we analyzed each of the rules to understand what model-based reasoning was missing. Consider one such rule: "If transistor Q5 is off, then the external symptom cannot be caused by the voltage reference being low." The rationale behind this rule is as follows: (Notice the qualitative form of the argument, not the content.)

> The power supply outputs a voltage and current limited by the minimum of its two control settings. This minimum is computed

through a feedback path in which transistor Q5 is a central part. If the voltage reference were low enough to cause a symptom, then Q5 would be on, so there is no way that a low voltage reference could be contributing to the power supply's faulty behavior if Q5 was off. If Q5 were off, then the output might be high, but the output could not be too low because the reference was too low.

Notice that this argument is both qualitative (e.g., too high and too low) and reliant on an underlying causal model of the feedback operation of the power supply. Most of SOPHIE's 39 rules arise from a qualitative causal understanding of the power supply's functioning. Again, this made it convincingly clear that qualitative and causal reasoning were central for diagnostic tasks.

5. Qualitative and causal reasoning for design

The first phase of Sussman's engineering-problem-solving project made significant progress toward using AI techniques (in particular truth maintenance and constraint propagation techniques) for electronic circuit analysis [29,31]. Based on these successes, Sussman and I attempted to exploit the same underlying technologies for electronic circuit design. The program SYN [19] was based on the observation that as the previous analysis programs were based on constraint propagation, the usual process of determining circuit behavior from circuit parameters could be inverted to determine circuit parameters from desired circuit outputs.

SYN could successfully choose circuit parameters for simple one- and two-transistor circuits. However, somewhat to our surprise, even slightly more complex circuits quickly overwhelmed the memory available on the computers of the day. This difficulty manifested itself by the algebraic expressions among circuit parameters growing without bound. But even (successful) second-year electrical engineering students have little difficulty at the same tasks for more complex circuits. Closer examination revealed the following:

- Students know how components are functioning in the circuit and choose the least detailed model that produces a good enough answer.
- Students make (appropriate) algebraic approximations that simplify the algebra enormously without significantly changing the answer. Typically these involve feedback loops whose effect could be partially ignored.
- For any component, there are usually a set of equivalent models (because of circuit equivalences). Students know the one to pick which best simplifies the algebra. (See [30] for some examples.)
- Students know where to break feedback loops to make analysis simpler.

- Students are familiar with common component configurations and their models.

Even neophyte engineering students do not begin a symbolic analysis of even the simplest circuit without first understanding how the circuit functions qualitatively and the roles of the components within it. Armed with that understanding, the students select component models, variables, and approximations to perform the necessary symbolic computation and to interpret the results in terms of their commonsense understanding of how the circuit works.

This experience parallels the one with NEWTON: To perform what initially seems to be a simple analysis requires an extensive qualitative pre-analysis of the situation. Although qualitative reasoning is critical to succeeding at even simple engineering tasks, it is usually tacit and rarely taught explicitly—making it all the harder to formalize in an AI system. The observation that qualitative causal analysis was critical to engineers' thinking was brought home by two other personal experiences during this time.

The first involved an electrical engineering design course I was taking. The course consisted solely of designing new circuits. A typical lecture would consist of the professor presenting a design and spending an hour analyzing it. He would pick models, variables, and approximations that simplified his analysis such that it seemed almost trivial. (Of course, students often found it difficult to replicate this performance on homework sets.) In one of the later lectures a student asked a simple question about a variation of the design being presented, which stumped the professor (a famous electrical engineer). For the remaining fifteen minutes of the class the professor stood close to the blackboard with his back to us to obscure his scribblings. I was sitting close enough so I could half follow what was going on. The professor was qualitatively simulating the effects of an input perturbation through the circuit with the goal of determining what role the components were playing. I could hear him: "If this voltage difference drops, then the forward bias on this transistor drops causing the collector current to drop ...." Toward the end of the class the professor quickly erased all his scribbles, stated the (correct) answer, and gave a very simple (and correct) rationale. This example illustrated two important things: (1) When a world class engineer was confronted with a novel variation he used qualitative analysis; (2) although he was unwilling to communicate that he actually used any kind of qualitative reasoning to obtain his conclusion.

The second experience involved a seminar series to which we invited analog VLSI designers from industry to visit and explain how they designed circuits. The practicing designers were much more up front about how they reasoned about circuits. When asked about how a particular circuit functioned or how they thought of adding such-and-such innovation, they would invariably launch into a qualitative and intuitive argument.

Motivated by these many examples of the use of qualitative knowledge for reasoning about electrical circuits, I developed a qualitative reasoner capable of doing some of the qualitative and causal analysis engineers perform. This program is called EQUAL [11–13]. Many of the issues that arise in electrical circuits are no different from those faced in other disciplines (e.g., fluid, thermal, mechanical). Indeed, the techniques used by EQUAL apply to all disciplines in which the lumped-parameter modeling assumptions apply (i.e., the classes of devices considered by Cochin [6] and Shearer et al. [27]). The paper "A qualitative physics based on confluences" [18] describes ENVISION which could do a qualitative and causal analysis with the standard lumped-parameter models and therefore analyze devices such as pressure regulators and spring-mass oscillators as well as complex circuits.

6. Whither qualitative physics?

Since the publication of "A qualitative physics based on confluences" research progress has been extremely exciting but at the same time a bit disappointing. Great strides forward have been made in understanding qualitative mathematics, time, shape, and function, etc. In addition, the requirements of qualitative physics have caused significant progress on topics as diverse as explicit control of reasoning, constraint propagation, truth maintenance systems, and knowledge representation.

Much AI research falls into the trap of examining issues for their own sake, losing sight of the overall objective, and thereby effectively building bridges over dry land. Whether or not one is interested in the ultimate goals of qualitative physics, focusing on reasoning about the physical world constantly brings fundamental issues to attention. Significant AI progress can be made only by applying AI ideas to tasks. Otherwise, we tend to spin our wheels.

Unfortunately, codifying qualitative knowledge about the physical world has proven to be surprisingly difficult. Just getting the qualitative version of the calculus (used to express qualitative knowledge) roughly right took many years of work by a large number of people. In retrospect it seems obvious what qualitative integration, differentiation, and continuity mean and what role they play—but these were not at all obvious at the beginning of 1980s.

It is disappointing that for most of the 1980s the tasks that originally motivated the development of qualitative physics were set aside. Too much of the research in qualitative physics loses sight of the original tasks by investigating some non-central issue raised by the exploration of some subtask. A mature field can afford to dissipate its energies in this way, indeed this is often a sign of maturity; but it is too soon for qualitative physics to lose that much vision of its original goals.

If qualitative physics is to have a significant impact on our science, we must seriously focus on the tasks that originally motivated its inception. For example, in exploring diagnosis we must develop theories of qualitative simulation and causality to enable pinpointing faulty components; in exploring design we must develop modeling techniques to support matching structures to functions.

Piecemeal steps toward these goals are not going to get us there. Qualitative physics must make larger steps toward its goals and set aside concern on the fine details until it becomes clear which details are worth carefully analyzing. Much more work is required such as Williams' [34], which develops a theory of innovative design using qualitative physics. The qualitative physics of engineered artifacts begs for a better language for describing device purpose. Even at this point qualitative physics is far from being able to construct anything like the cause–effect diagrams of Rieger and Grinberg [26], although de Kleer and Brown [16] describe some rudimentary ideas. Insufficient progress has been made using qualitative physics for diagnostic tasks or for integrating qualitative and quantitative knowledge. Currently the physical theories incorporated in most qualitative physics programs are developed painstakingly by hand. We have to find some way to accelerate this process (see Falkenhainer et al. [21]). Most qualitative physics researchers use their own individualized representations and reasoning methods. However, there is great commonality among the ideas. Perhaps qualitative physics should begin a CYC-like project to develop a common language for describing the physical world to be used throughout the qualitative physics research community (Lenat et al. [23]). Ironically, this brings us back to the central point of the naive physics manifesto (Hayes [22]), one decade earlier.

References

[1] D.G. Bobrow, Natural language input for a computer problem-solving system, in: M. Minsky, ed., *Semantic Information Processing* (MIT Press, Cambridge, MA, 1968) 146–226.

[2] J.S. Brown, R.R. Burton and J. de Kleer, Pedagogical, natural language and knowledge engineering techniques in SOPHIE I, II and III, in: D. Sleeman and J.S. Brown, eds., *Intelligent Tutoring Systems* (Academic Press, New York, 1982) 227—282.

[3] A. Bundy, G. Luger, M. Stone and R. Welham, MECHO: year one, in: *Proceedings Second AISB Conference*, Edinburgh, Scotland (1976) 94–103.

[4] A. Bundy, L. Byrd, G. Luger, C. Mellish, R. Milne and M. Palmer, MECHO: a program to solve mechanics problems, Working Paper 50, Department of Artificial Intelligence, Edinburgh, Scotland (1979).

[5] E. Charniak, CARPS, a program which solves calculus word problems, MAC-TR-51, Project MAC, MIT, Cambridge, MA (1968).

[6] I. Cochin, *Analysis and Design of Dynamic Systems* (Harper and Row, New York, 1980).

[7] H. Cohen, The art of snaring dragons, AIM-338, AI Lab., MIT, Cambridge, MA (1974).

[8] R. Davis and W. Hamscher, Model-based reasoning: troubleshooting, in: H.E. Shrobe and the American Association for Artificial Intelligence, eds., *Exploring Artificial Intelligence* (Morgan Kaufmann, San Mateo, CA, 1988) 297–346.

[9] J. de Kleer, Local methods of localizing faults in electronic circuits, AIM-394, AI Lab., MIT, Cambridge, MA (1976).

[10] J. de Kleer, Multiple representations of knowledge in a mechanics problem-solver, in: *Proceedings IJCAI-77*, Cambridge, MA (1977) 299–304.

[11] J. de Kleer, The origin and resolution of ambiguities in causal arguments, in: *Proceedings IJCAI-79*, Tokyo, Japan (1979) 197–204.

[12] J. de Kleer, Causal and teleological reasoning in circuit recognition, AI-TR-529, AI Lab., MIT, Cambridge, MA (1979).

[13] J. de Kleer, How circuits work, *Artif. Intell.* **24** (1984) 205–280; also in: D.G. Bobrow, ed., *Reasoning about Physical Systems* (North-Holland, Amsterdam, 1984/MIT Press, Cambridge, MA, 1985) 205–280.

[14] J. de Kleer and D.G. Bobrow, Higher-order qualitative derivatives, in: *Proceedings AAAI-84*, Austin, TX (1984) 86–91.

[15] J. de Kleer and J.S. Brown, Foundations of envisioning, in: *Proceedings AAAI-82*, Pittsburgh, PA (1982) 434–437.

[16] J. de Kleer and J.S. Brown, Assumptions and ambiguities in mechanistic mental models, in: D. Gentner and A.L. Stevens, eds., *Mental Models* (Erlbaum, Hillsdale, NJ, 1983) 155–190.

[17] J. de Kleer and J.S. Brown, The origin, form and logic of qualitative physical laws, in: *Proceedings IJCAI-83*, Karlsruhe, Germany (1983) 1158–1169.

[18] J. de Kleer and J.S. Brown, A qualitative physics based on confluences, *Artif. Intell.* **24** (1984) 7–83.

[19] J. de Kleer and G.J. Sussman, Propagation of constraints applied to circuit synthesis, *Circuit Theory Appl.* **8** (1980) 127–144.

[20] A.A. diSessa, Phenomenology and the evolution of intuition, in: D. Gentner and A.L. Stevens, eds., *Mental Models* (Erlbaum, Hillsdale, NJ, 1983) 15–190.

[21] B. Falkenhainer, K.D. Forbus and D. Gentner, The structure-mapping engine: algorithm and examples, *Artif. Intell.* **41** (1990) 1–63.

[22] P.J. Hayes, The second naive physics manifesto, in: J.R. Hobbs and R. Moore, eds., *Formal Theories of the Commonsense World* (Ablex, Norwood, NJ, 1985) 1–36.

[23] D.B. Lenat, M. Prakash and M. Shepherd, CYC: using commonsense knowledge to overcome brittleness and knowledge acquisition bottlenecks, MCC Tech. Rept. AI-055-85, MCC, Austin, TX (1985).

[24] G. Novak, Computer understanding of physics problems stated in natural language, Ph.D. Thesis, Department of Computer Science, University of Texas, Austin, TX (1976).

[25] G. Novak, Representations of knowledge in a program for solving physics problems, in: *Proceedings IJCAI-77*, Cambridge, MA (1977) 286–291.

[26] C. Rieger and M. Grinberg, The declarative representation and procedural simulation of causality in physical mechanisms, in: *Proceedings IJCAI-77*, Cambridge, MA (1977) 250–256.

[27] J. Shearer, A. Murphy and H. Richardson, *Introduction to System Dynamics* (Addison-Wesley, Reading, MA, 1971).

[28] G. Skorstad and K.D. Forbus, Qualitative and quantitative reasoning about thermodynamics, in: *Proceedings Eleventh Annual Conference of the Cognitive Science Society*, Ann Arbor, MI (1989).

[29] R.M. Stallman and G.J. Sussman, Forward reasoning and dependency-directed backtracking in a system for computer-aided circuit analysis, *Artif. Intell.* **9** (1977) 135–196.

[30] G.J. Sussman, SLICES: at the boundary between analysis and synthesis, AIM-433, AI Lab., MIT, Cambridge, MA (1977).

[31] G.J. Sussman, Electrical design: a problem for artificial intelligence research, in: *Proceedings IJCAI-77*, Cambridge, MA (1977) 894–900.

[32] J. Walker, *The Flying Circus of Physics with Answers* (Wiley, New York, 1977).

[33] D.S. Weld and J. de Kleer, eds., *Readings in Qualitative Reasoning about Physical Systems* (Morgan Kaufmann, San Mateo, CA, 1990).

[34] B.C. Williams, Invention from first principles: an overview, in: P.H. Winston and S. Shellard, eds., *Artificial Intelligence at MIT: Expanding Frontiers* (MIT Press, Cambridge, MA, 1990) 430–463.

[35] B.C. Williams, A theory of invention from fundamental principles of physics based on topologies of interaction, AI-TR-1127, AI Lab., MIT, Cambridge, MA (1989).

Artificial Intelligence 59 (1993) 115–123
Elsevier

ARTINT 991

Qualitative process theory: twelve years after

Kenneth D. Forbus

Qualitative Reasoning Group, The Institute for the Learning Sciences, Northwestern University, 1890 Maple Avenue, Evanston, IL 60201, USA

1. Introduction

The scientific goal of artificial intelligence is to understand minds by trying to build them. To make progress towards this goal requires careful decomposition. An especially productive strategy has been to focus on the knowledge and reasoning required for a particular class of domains or tasks. Some domains or tasks have special features which make them tractable, while still providing generalizable insights. If the domains and tasks have practical value then so much the better, for then scientific progress and economic benefits can go hand-in-hand. Qualitative physics is such an area. Reasoning about the physical world is clearly central to intelligences (human or machine). Moreover, it encompasses a variety of tasks and skills, thus providing a range of interesting problems. Physics and mathematics provide us with clues about what special constraints might help make such reasoning tractable. And the potential economic impact of intelligent computer-aided engineering systems is clearly enormous. Indeed, qualitative physics is one of the most exciting areas in AI today.

An important event in the growth of qualitative physics was the 1984 special issue of *Artificial Intelligence* edited by Bobrow. My paper in that issue, "Qualitative process theory", was one-half of my Ph.D. thesis; the other half described algorithms for implementing QP theory and results obtained with them. This essay summarizes the context of that work and the main contributions of QP theory. A cautionary point about basic research

Correspondence to: K.D. Forbus, Qualitative Reasoning Group, The Institute for the Learning Sciences, Northwestern University, 1890 Maple Avenue, Evanston, IL 60201, USA. E-mail: forbus@ils.nwu.edu.

is made, and the essay ends by describing some current directions this work is taking.

2. Context

Johan de Kleer got me interested in qualitative physics when I was an undergraduate at MIT. I had been working at the AI Lab since 1973 with David Marr on vision, but had always wanted to tackle more central issues of cognition. Seeing SOPHIE in action was a revelation; building systems that smart seemed on a clear path towards the goal of building a humanlike intelligence. When I started graduate work at MIT in 1977 I joined Sussman's engineering problem solving group. I began to work on spatial reasoning, since it was clearly a rich, deep problem, and my earlier work on vision might provide a useful perspective on it. In 1978 draft copies of Pat Hayes' "Naive physics manifesto" [19] and liquids paper [20] galvanized me further: The notion of histories seemed crucial, for it decomposed reasoning about change into dynamics (to evolve possible behaviors) and spatio-temporal problem solving (to determine interactions). Ultimately this work led to a model of qualitative spatial reasoning, demonstrated by FROB, a system which used a diagram to reason about motion of point masses through space [8,10]. For my Ph.D. thesis I originally intended to extend this work into a system that could flexibly reason about a variety of more complex mechanical systems, including clocks. However, circumstances soon led me in a different direction.[1]

To help make ends meet I started working part-time at BBN with Al Stevens and Bruce Roberts on the STEAMER project [22,31]. The goal of STEAMER was to produce an intelligent tutoring system for training operators of oil-fired steam propulsion plants. Its core was a numerical simulation program, originally written to drive the steamship equivalent of a flight simulator, itself a warehouse-sized replica replete with gauges, noisy pumps, pipes, and so on. Such high-fidelity simulators are very useful for drilling students in operating procedures, but are very expensive. Our plan was to develop complementary desktop systems that could help trainees come to a global understanding of the system, including explanations of how physical and engineering principles applied to the safe operation of the plant. In the end, most of STEAMER's power came from providing a flexible, extensible graphical interface to the numerical simulator that a computer-naive trainee or instructor could use to explore the behavior of the steam plant. Today

---

[1]My work on spatial reasoning continued later, and the work of Faltings [7] and Nielsen [25] finally culminated in a system which could understand mechanical clocks (as well as other fixed-axis mechanical systems) in 1988 [16].

such interfaces are taken for granted, but in 1980 they were rather new, and in fact STEAMER was a major catalyst for the idea of direct manipulation interfaces [23].

My role in the project was to use ideas of qualitative physics to provide humanlike reasoning about the plant's principles and operation, in order to produce understandable explanations. The best qualitative physics available at the time (1979) was in de Kleer's Ph.D. thesis [2]. He had developed a device-centered ontology and the idea of incremental qualitative analysis, in which quantities were represented by the sign of their change from equilibrium in response to a disturbance. I used that physics in a demonstration system for teaching about feedback, using a spring-loaded reducing valve as an example. [2]

The Reducing Valve Demo was a great success [17]. It propagated a disturbance through a constraint network to construct a qualitative description of behavior. The resulting values and dependency structure were then used to automatically generate explanations, interleaving English with color animations of changes propagating through the system. Inspired by this initial success, I tried modeling other steam plant components and subsystems in the same way. These efforts were mostly failures. Several of the reasons were quite interesting:

(1) The notion of quantity used in incremental qualitative analysis was too weak. Often a quantity needed to be compared with several others, and knowledge about relative rates was often important. At minimum, ordinal information about amounts and derivatives seemed to be required.

(2) Identifying causality with the path of propagation in a constraint network sometimes led to unintuitive causal arguments. For example, the arguments *"The increased heat causes the temperature to rise."* and *"The increased heat causes the amount of stuff to drop."* can both be generated via propagation from a constraint defining the relationship between heat, temperature, and mass. The first is a legitimate causal argument but the second is not, and a qualitative physics that tries to capture human intuitions about causality should explain why.

(3) The device ontology which was so suitable for electronics seemed unnatural for steam plants. Explanations of phenomena in engineering thermodynamics typically included *physical processes*, which cut across component boundaries.

---

[2] The popular pressure-regulator example is actually a simplification of this valve: The original contains two stages, since the input stream is 1200 psi steam and would rip apart a single-stage regulator.

This analysis of the limitations of de Kleer's 1979 qualitative physics when applied to engineering thermodynamics led directly to the creation of QP theory.

The first paper about QP theory appeared in 1981 [9], with several other conference papers (AAAI [8] and Cognitive Science Society [17]) leading up to the paper in *Artificial Intelligence*. During this period (1980–1984) QP theory evolved considerably, thanks in part to a variety of stimulating interactions. While Johan de Kleer and John Seely Brown had since moved to Xerox PARC, our discussions continued electronically. QP theory's decidedly cognitive leaning, as well as my interest in cognitive modeling and simulation, grew out of working at BBN with Al Stevens, Dedre Gentner, and Allan Collins. And of course the MIT AI Lab remained a hotbed of engineering problem solving research, ranging from the work of Sussman's VLSI group to the work of Davis' Hardware Troubleshooting Group.

3. Contributions

QP theory introduced some key ideas of qualitative physics:

Physical processes as organizing principle

Ontology plays a central role in the organization of knowledge. A crucial observation in formulating QP theory was that concepts of physical processes (e.g., flows, motion, phase changes) seemed to play an important role in human reasoning about physical systems. Therefore it makes sense to organize theories of physical domains around a formalization of this intuitive notion of physical process.

Representing numerical values via ordinal relationships

Important qualitative distinctions are often tied to comparisons between parameters: Flows occur when pressures or temperatures differ, for instance, and phase changes occur when temperatures reach certain thresholds. If a parameter participates in only one comparison, sign values provide a satisfactory qualitative representations. However, for many circumstances representing values by a set of ordinal relationships (formalized in QP theory as the *quantity space* representation) is more natural.

Sole mechanism assumption

Physical processes are viewed as the mechanisms by which changes occur (excluding the actions of agents). Thus any changes must be explainable by the direct or indirect effects of some collection of physical processes. Causality in QP theory is thus grounded in ontology, rather than in constraint propagation as in de Kleer's account.

For instance, consider again the proposed causal arguments concerning heat, temperature, and mass above. In any reasonable model, heat and mass can each be directly affected by physical processes (e.g., mass or heat flows). Temperature is a causally dependent parameter, determined in terms of heat and mass. Thus the causal argument "*The increased heat causes the temperature to rise.*" is legitimate, since it follows the causality imposed by the physical processes in the domain. On the other hand, the argument "*The increased heat causes the amount of stuff to drop.*" is not legitimate since it reverses the direction of causality imposed by the physical processes.

Compositional qualitative mathematics

A missing ingredient in early attempts to formalize physical reasoning (cf. [20,21,29]) was the idea of *compositionality*. That is, a major factor in the flexibility of human reasoning about complex physical systems comes from the ability to use partial information and combine it as available.

The idea of *qualitative proportionality* captures one aspect of this productive use of partial information. For example, in modeling fluid resistance we might know that it depends on the area and the length of the path, i.e.,

$$\texttt{resistance(path22)} \propto_{Q+} \texttt{length(path22)},$$

$$\texttt{resistance(path22)} \propto_{Q-} \texttt{area(path22)}.$$

These qualitative relationships tell us that two potential ways to increase the resistance of `path22` is to increase its length or decrease its area.

Explicit representation and reasoning about modeling assumptions

De Kleer and Brown's notion of *class-wide assumptions* [3] was a valuable contribution in thinking about how knowledge about physical systems should be organized. However, their focus on electronics did not drive them to fully explore its consequences since the mapping from a circuit schematic to abstract electronic components is fairly direct. In thermodynamics the task of setting up a model is more difficult, and that factor, along with the goal of trying to capture different states of student knowledge, led me to focus on the task of model building as central to QP theory.

QP theory was the first system of qualitative physics to explicitly represent the conditions under which particular pieces of knowledge were applicable, and to make constructing the model of a specific system from a domain theory a central part of its computational account. QP theory can be viewed as a partial specification of a space of modeling languages for domains where physical processes are the appropriate ontology.

4. A cautionary note

The relationship between basic research and applied work is being debated strongly in the U.S. right now, with a strong tendency to push researchers towards applied work. I believe science progresses best when basic researchers remain connected to real problems, but are not obliged to solve them on any short-range timetable. The development of QP theory provides an illustration of this point.

In the summer of 1980 I tried to apply the existing theories of qualitative physics to the problems confronting us in the STEAMER project. The Reducing Valve Demo took two weeks to build. The next two months were spent mostly producing failures. The third month was spent reflecting on what was going wrong. Completing the first paper on QP theory [9] took roughly six months. In 1982 the *AI Journal* version was submitted, it appeared in 1984, the same year I received my Ph.D. Since then, my students and I have done basic research, motivated in part by the problems I could not solve then. Only now, ten years later, do we think we have enough ideas and technology to try developing some useful applications again.

I believe that we (and the field as a whole) have made substantial progress during those ten years. I also believe that our progress would have been impossible if we had been forced to field a new demo or working application every year. This lesson is of course an old one, deeply ingrained in the very division between basic and applied work. However, in today's troubled economic climate many seem to have forgotten it. Clearly practical problems and examples are crucial sources of inspiration and motivation—for instance, my group draws on engineering problems arising in space station design, civilian aviation, and propulsion plants in our research. However, the "demo or die" strategy often touted today seems to me to be a prescription for "demo *and* die", at least with respect to scientific progress.

5. Towards tutor compilers and learning machines

Research in qualitative physics is progressing well these days, and the future looks extremely bright. There is so much activity in qualitative physics these days that any brief summary cannot do it justice, so I will focus on my group's efforts.

One important problem is the need for intelligent tutoring systems and learning environments for science and engineering education and training. The kind of system that STEAMER was supposed to be, where a numerical simulation is integrated with an intuitive understanding of the artifact, is clearly an important component for such computer-based teaching systems. Developing a solid theoretical foundation for such systems has been a major motivation for our qualitative physics work. For example, what STEAMER should have been is what we now call a *self-explanatory simulator* [13,14], that is, a numerical simulation with an integrated qualitative understanding of the plant. Self-explanatory simulators can explain as well as reproduce the behavior of what they are modeling, and thus provide a basis for deeper reasoning about behavior. The qualitative model provides the information needed to compile such simulators automatically: It identifies what equations are appropriate under different conditions, and the causal account provides an order of computation in the numerical aspect of the simulation.

One of our medium-term goals is to develop a *tutor compiler* that can produce self-explanatory simulators that can be used either as stand-alone training systems or as modules in multimedia learning environments. In addition to self-explanatory simulators, two other ideas are key pieces to the puzzle of how qualitative physics can help build intelligent tutoring systems and learning environments. Reasoning about a complex system often requires formulating a model tuned towards that specific task, which in turn requires reasoning about modeling assumptions. This problem is especially acute in training situations, since the learner cannot be expected to know what models are appropriate. The *compositional modeling* strategy Falkenhainer and I developed [5] extends the modeling capabilities of QP theory to orchestrate the construction and use of domain theories that describe phenomena at multiple grain sizes and from different, often conflicting, perspectives. The other problem is that teaching correct operation of a system (or understanding how the operation of a system might be impaired by malfunctions) requires understanding the interaction of actions taken by an agent with the physical world. The idea of *action-augmented envisionments* [12] provides a simple conceptual framework for integrating action with dynamics, which should support the generation, verification, and teaching of operating procedures.

The tutor compiler work, like our work on monitoring [1,11], engineering analysis [30], and design, is heavily motivated by classes of applications. The perceived applications potential seems in fact to be a major reason for the popularity of qualitative physics. However, a side of the field which is just as important, but has been relatively neglected, is cognitive modeling. Certainly building engineering problem solvers under the sole constraint of optimum performance will reveal interesting properties of complex reasoning in complicated domains. However, providing a formalism for investigating human mental models of complex systems was, and should continue to be, another motivation for qualitative physics.[3]

---

[3]Even from an applications perspective such research should be interesting: Evidence suggests that qualitative physics representations provide a good conceptual account of human mental models, making qualitative physics a valuable tool for human/computer interaction.

So far the use of qualitative physics for modeling scientific discovery has been one of the few uses of qualitative physics in other parts of AI and Cognitive Science (cf. [4,26–28]). We believe there is a variety of exciting, productive possibilities for such research (cf. [15]). One approach we are exploring is integrating QP theory with other common-sense theories to see if we can develop programs that learn in a humanlike way from science books. We are focusing especially on analogical learning, based on Gentner's Structure-Mapping theory [6,18]. To provide the domain knowledge for analogizing we are implementing QP theory in CYC [24]. This is a long-term enterprise, but we hope to learn much on the way about how qualitative reasoning can be used in a much broader context.

References

[1] D. DeCoste, Dynamic across-time measurement interpretation, *Artif. Intell.* **51** (1991) 273–341.

[2] J. de Kleer, Causal and teleological reasoning in circuit recognition, MIT AI Lab, Tech. Report No. 529, Cambridge, MA (1979).

[3] J. de Kleer and J.S. Brown, Assumptions and ambiguities in mechanistic mental models, in: D. Gentner and A. Stevens, eds., *Mental Models* (Lawrence Erlbaum, Hillsdale, NJ, 1983).

[4] B. Falkenhainer, A unified approach to explanation and theory formation, in: J. Shrager and P. Langley, eds., *Computational Models of Scientific Discovery and Theory Formation* (Morgan Kaufmann, San Mateo, CA, 1990).

[5] B. Falkenhainer and K.D. Forbus, Compositional modeling: finding the right model for the job, *Artif. Intell.* **51** (1991) 95–143.

[6] B. Falkenhainer, K.D. Forbus and D. Gentner, The structure-mapping engine: algorithm and examples, *Artif. Intell.* **41** (1990) 1–63.

[7] B. Faltings, Qualitative kinematics in mechanisms, *Artif. Intell.* **44** (1990) 41–87.

[8] K.D. Forbus, Spatial and qualitative aspects of reasoning about motion, in: *Proceedings AAAI-80*, Stanford, CA (1980).

[9] K.D. Forbus, Qualitative reasoning about physical processes, in: *Proceedings IJCAI-81*, Vancouver, BC (1981).

[10] K.D. Forbus, Qualitative reasoning about space and motion, in: D. Gentner and A. Stevens, eds., *Mental Models* (Lawrence Erlbaum, Hillsdale, NJ, 1983).

[11] K.D. Forbus, Interpreting observations of physical systems, *IEEE Trans. Syst. Man Cybern.* **17** (3) (1987).

[12] K.D. Forbus, Introducing actions into qualitative simulation, in: *Proceedings IJCAI-89*, Detoit, MI (1989) 1273–1278.

[13] K.D. Forbus and B. Falkenhainer, Self-explanatory simulations: an integration of qualitative and quantitative knowledge, in: *Proceedings AAAI-90*, Boston, MA (1990).

[14] K.D. Forbus and B. Falkenhainer, Self-explanatory simulations: scaling up to large models, in: *Proceedings AAAI-92*, San Jose, CA (1992).

[15] K.D. Forbus and D. Gentner, Learning physical domains: towards a theoretical framework, in: R.S. Michalski, J.G. Carbonell and T.M. Mitchell, *Machine Learning: An Artificial Intelligence Approach*, Vol. 2 (Tioga Press, Palo Alto, CA, 1986).

[16] K.D. Forbus, P. Nielsen and B. Faltings, Qualitative spatial reasoning: the CLOCK project, *Artif. Intell.* **51** (1991) 417–471.

[17] K.D. Forbus and A. Stevens, Using qualitative simulation to generate explanations, in: *Proceedings Third Annual Conference of the Cognitive Science Society*, Berkeley, CA (1981).

[18] D. Gentner, Structure-mapping: a theoretical framework for analogy, *Cogn. Sci.* **7** (2) (1983).

[19] P.J. Hayes, The naive physics manifesto, in: D. Michie, ed., *Expert Systems in the Micro-Electronic Age* (Edinburgh University Press, Edinburgh, Scotland, 1979).

[20] P.J. Hayes, Naive physics 1: ontology for liquids, in: J.R. Hobbs and R. Moore, eds., *Formal Theories of the Commonsense World* (Ablex, Norwood, NJ, 1985).

[21] G.G. Hendrix, Modeling simultaneous actions and continuous processes, *Artif. Intell.* **4** (1973) 145–180.

[22] J.D. Hollan, E.L. Hutchins and L. Weitzman, STEAMER: an interactive inspectable simulation-based training system, *AI Mag.* **5** (2) (1984) 15–27.

[23] E.L. Hutchins, J.D. Hollan and D.A. Norman, Direct manipulation interfaces, *Human–Comput. Interaction* **1** (1985) 311–338.

[24] D.B. Lenat and R.V. Guha, *Building Large Knowledge-Based Systems* (Addison-Wesley, Reading, MA, 1990).

[25] P. Nielsen, A qualitative approach to mechanical constraint, in: *Proceedings AAAI-88*, St. Paul, MN (1988); also in: D.S. Weld and J. de Kleer, eds., *Qualitative Reasoning about Physical Systems* (Morgan Kaufman, San Mateo, CA, 1990).

[26] B. Nordhausen and P. Langley, An integrated approach to empirical discovery, in: J. Shrager and P. Langley, eds., *Computational Models of Scientific Discovery and Theory Formation* (Morgan Kaufmann, San Mateo, CA, 1990).

[27] P. O'Rorke, S. Morris and D. Schulenberg, Theory formation by abduction: a case study based on the chemical revolution, in: J. Shrager and P. Langley, eds., *Computational Models of Scientific Discovery and Theory Formation* (Morgan Kaufmann, San Mateo, CA, 1990).

[28] S. Rajamoney, A computational approach to theory revision, in: J. Shrager and P. Langley, eds., *Computational Models of Scientific Discovery and Theory Formation* (Morgan Kaufmann, San Mateo, CA, 1990).

[29] C. Rieger and M. Grinberg, The declarative representation and procedural simulation of causality in physical mechanisms, in: *Proceedings IJCAI-77*, Cambridge, MA (1977).

[30] G. Skorstad and K.D. Forbus, Qualitative and quantitative reasoning about thermodynamics, in: *Proceedings Eleventh Annual Conference of the Cognitive Science Society*, Ann Arbor, MI (1989).

[31] A. Stevens, B. Roberts, L. Stead, K.D. Forbus, C. Steinberg and B. Smith, STEAMER: advanced computer-aided instruction in propulsion engineering, BBN Tech. Report, Cambridge, MA (1981).

Artificial Intelligence 59 (1993) 125–132
Elsevier

ARTINT 994

Reasoning with qualitative models *

Benjamin J. Kuipers

Computer Sciences Department, University of Texas at Austin, Austin, TX 78712, USA

1. Introduction

Qualitative reasoning about physical systems has become one of the most productive areas in AI in recent years, due in part to the 1984 special issue of *Artificial Intelligence* on that topic. My contribution to that issue was a paper entitled "Commonsense reasoning about causality: deriving behavior from structure" [9]. From my perspective, that paper laid out a research program that has continued to be productive to this day, and promises to continue well into the future.

After establishing a framework for qualitative reasoning, the primary technical contribution of the paper was a simple, clear representation for qualitative structure and behavior, abstracted from ordinary differential equations. My subsequent *Artificial Intelligence* paper, "Qualitative simulation" [10], made that abstraction relation precise, presented the vastly improved QSIM algorithm for qualitative simulation, and used the abstraction relation to prove the soundness and incompleteness of QSIM. I will discuss developments in qualitative simulation in my retrospective on that paper [12], and concentrate here on the larger issue of reasoning with qualitative models.

Correspondence to: B.J. Kuipers, Computer Sciences Department, University of Texas at Austin, Austin, TX 78712, USA. E-mail: kuipers@cs.utexas.edu.

*This work has taken place in the Qualitative Reasoning Group at the Artificial Intelligence Laboratory, The University of Texas at Austin. Research of the Qualitative Reasoning Group is supported in part by NSF grants IRI-8905494 and IRI-8904454, by NASA grant NAG 2-507, and by the Texas Advanced Research Program under grant no. 003658-175.

2. Context

In 1978, thanks to Peter Szolovits, I started working on the problem of causal reasoning about physiological mechanisms by expert physicians. I was initially attracted to Rieger and Grinberg's causal link models, presented at IJCAI-77 [14], and I began working with Jerome P. Kassirer, an eminent nephrologist at Tufts Medical School. We applied Newell and Simon's protocol analysis methods to interviews with expert physicians, to extract clues about the cognitive representation of physiological mechanisms. This protocol analysis provided one of two essential constraints on the design of the qualitative representation: empirically, it should account for the behavior of the human subjects, and computationally, it should be capable of deriving the observed conclusions.

From analyzing the protocols, it quickly became clear that there was a cognitively meaningful distinction between the time-independent *structure* of a mechanism, and its time-dependent *behavior*. This distinction did not seem to map clearly onto causal networks, but fit better with Johan de Kleer's work on qualitative envisionment. Starting with this foundation, my applications and my intuitions led me away from the quasi-static equilibrium assumption, and toward monotonic function constraints and nonzero landmarks: essentially the QSIM representation, although the name came later. Kassirer and I published our protocol analysis and its explanation in terms of the qualitative representation in *Cognitive Science* [13], where it appeared at about the same time as the *Artificial Intelligence* special issue.

Meanwhile, Johan de Kleer, Ken Forbus, Dan Weld, Brian Williams and others were also developing and extending methods and applications for qualitative reasoning. While there were many fruitful discussions among the early participants in this research community, differences in outlook, assumptions, and notation often made it difficult for us to communicate clearly. Although it is sometimes said that differences in notation have acted as a barrier to unifying the different perspectives in qualitative reasoning, it now seems clear that the notational differences reflect genuine semantic distinctions among types of knowledge used in different types of reasoning: for example, model building versus model simulation, and dynamic simulation versus comparative statics.

3. Contributions and applications

An enormous amount of subsequent work has been inspired by the papers in the 1984 special issue, including international workshops on qualitative reasoning, model-based reasoning, and the principles of diagnosis. I will discuss developments specifically related to the qualitative simulation and

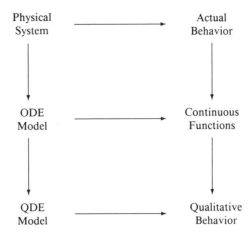

Fig. 1. All models are abstractions of the world. Qualitative models are related to ordinary differential equations, but are more expressive of incomplete knowledge.

the QDE representation in the retrospective [12] on the paper "Qualitative simulation", and focus here on applications of qualitative reasoning to diagnosis, monitoring, and design, and on several conceptual schemes that have been helpful to me in clarifying and factoring the problems and applications of qualitative reasoning.

3.1. Abstraction relations

Qualitative structure and behavior can be most clearly understood and analyzed as abstractions of ordinary differential equations and their solutions (Fig. 1). (Both types of models are, of course, abstractions of the physical world.) This abstraction relation (hypothesized in this paper, and proved rigorously in [10]) has been critical to making qualitative simulation mathematically tractable, and to communicating it successfully with the engineering and mathematics communities. It legitimizes the term *qualitative differential equation* or QDE for the qualitative structural description.

3.2. Structure, behavior, function, and design

There is an important distinction between three types of descriptions of a mechanism, and how they depend on each other:

$$structure \rightarrow behavior \rightarrow function.$$

A clear distinction among these is particularly important because function and behavior are often confused. The essence of a functional description is teleology or purpose, and hence the relation of the structure and behavior of a mechanism to its larger context. Now that the roles of structural and

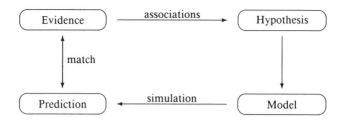

Fig. 2. Diagnosis viewed as a generate-and-test process, proposing models capable of explaining observations.

behavioral descriptions are better understood (Fig. 1), it has become clearer how to represent and reason with *functional* description of a device.

A motivating example from the 1984 paper is the assertion, "The function of the pressure release valve is to prevent explosions." Semantic analysis reveals that the verb *prevent* represents a relation between an element of structure (the pressure release valve) and a possible behavior (an explosion). However, simulation of the working device model does not include an explosion among its possible behaviors. The explosion referred to appears "upstream" in the *design process* for the device, prior to the addition of the pressure release valve.

David Franke [6,7] has defined a precise semantics for teleological relations such as *guarantee* and *prevent*, in terms of the incremental transformations to the device model that take place during design and a branching-time temporal logic over the set of behaviors predicted from each qualitative model. His system is associated with a CAD system, in order to acquire teleological descriptions when they are most available: during the design process. The teleological descriptions are then used to index design transformations for reuse, and to propose plausible candidates during diagnosis.

3.3. Diagnosis and monitoring

Diagnosis can be defined in several ways. The modeling and simulation perspective makes it natural to view diagnosis as an instance of the more general problem of causal explanation: a set of observations are explained by a set of general laws and specific initial conditions such that the observations can be predicted as consequences of the laws and initial conditions (Kuipers [11], Simmons and Davis [15]) (Fig. 2).

According to this view, the goal of diagnostic reasoning is to find a useful predictive model of a possibly faulty device, given a description of the working device and knowledge of possible fault modes, either of components or of the device as a whole. The task thus blends smoothly into monitoring, where the task is to maintain an accurate model of a mechanism and its state, even while faults occur and are repaired. This position contrasts with the "constraint suspension" view of diagnosis, where the task is to identify minimal sets of components whose correct behavior is inconsistent with observations. Constraint suspension seems most appropriate for devices where faults are relatively isolated, and where it is practical to shut the system down to replace components. Large-scale systems such as chemical plants, space vehicles, and the human body have many self-regulatory systems, and are expected to continue functioning even in the presence of numerous faults. These intuitions have led to the development of the MIMIC approach to monitoring and diagnosis (Dvorak and Kuipers [3,4]).

The basic idea behind MIMIC is very simple: track the observed state of a system against predictions derived from one or more models; discrepancies are used to refute some current models and suggest new ones. However, the success of this approach depends critically on the ability to cover a realistically large set of hypotheses with a tractably finite set of models. Traditional ODE models contain many assumptions of specific functional forms and numerical parameter values, often going beyond the knowledge available, particularly for fault models. Qualitative models can cover a wide range of possible ODEs with a single QDE, and can refine the qualitative predictions using numerical information when it is available.

3.4. Modeling and simulation

There is an important distinction between the tasks of model building and model simulation:

- *Model building*: starts with a description of a physical situation and builds an appropriate simplified model, in this case a QDE.
- *Model simulation*: starts with a model and predicts the possible behaviors consistent with the model.

The research issues involved in model building and model simulation are quite distinct, and the two tasks interact via the QDE representation. Therefore, as a research strategy, this factoring of the problem makes it possible for a qualitative reasoner to benefit from independent advances in the two areas.

Much of the work that my students and I have done within this framework has concentrated on the representation and tractable simulation of QDE models, with the view that QDE models could be constructed by a variety of different methods, including those pioneered in the work of de Kleer and Brown [2] and Forbus [5]. It has seemed to me that both of these pieces of work are clarified by separating their contributions to model building and model simulation. Accordingly, we have built two compilers that produce QDE models for simulation by QSIM.

- *CC* (Franke and Dvorak [8]) builds a QDE from a description of a physical system in terms of explicit connections among instances of components defined in a component library.
- *QPC* (Crawford et al. [1]) builds QDE models after the manner of qualitative process theory by identifying sets of active views and processes in a view library, and applying the Closed World Assumption to transform influences into constraints.

The two approaches to model building differ in the nature of the knowledge supplied by the modeler, and in the way the Closed World Assumption is applied. Specifically, by describing a device with a component-connection (CC) model, the *modeler* asserts that all relevant interactions between the components take place via explicit connections. In QPC, by contrast, the *system* is responsible for determining the set of relevant interactions and deciding when to apply the Closed World Assumption.

In the simplest, linear view, the modeler builds a model which the simulator uses to predict behaviors. More realistically, the process iterates, with the model builder responding to feedback from the simulator about the implications of the model and from the world about the success of the model to explain the physical phenomenon of interest.

Figure 3 illustrates the main linear path through model building and model simulation, separating the process into weakly interacting modules. Each module draws on certain information (e.g., the component library or asserted quantitative bounds), may make certain assumptions as needed (e.g., smoothness of monotonic functions or the CWA), and provides certain guarantees (i.e., that its conclusion follows soundly from its premises). One perspective on the field of qualitative reasoning is that its goal is to specify the modules and their intermediate representations so as to make this framework real.

4. Open problems

There are several "paths not taken" whose beginnings were visible in the 1984 paper, and which still seem very fruitful.

- The title of the 1984 paper refers to "causal" reasoning about physical mechanisms. In fact, we developed modeling and simulation methods based on constraint propagation and satisfaction. Any causality in these models is imposed from the outside by the viewer. The problem of describing and reasoning about causality seems important and has received a great deal of attention, but on careful examination both its content and its value are surprisingly hard to pin down, at least with the tools now available.

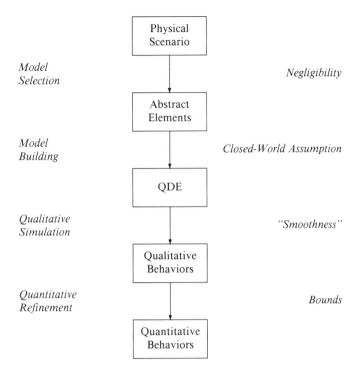

Fig. 3. Each step in modeling a physical system and predicting its behavior requires particular types of assumptions. Using qualitative models makes this set of assumptions tractable.

- A qualitative differential equation is a set of constraints, from which other constraints and equations can be derived by algebraic manipulation. One point of the 1984 paper was that certain conclusions that were intractable in the given model could be derived easily from an algebraically simplified abstraction of the model, automatically derived using the set of algebraic transformation rules in Appendix D. A good general-purpose algebraic manipulation utility applicable to QDE models would make it possible to search for Lyapunov functions or to symbolically evaluate the sign of a discriminant expression, and thus improve the power of qualitative simulation. Williams [16] made progress toward this goal, by clarifying the relationship between qualitative and real algebras, and demonstrating the use of MINIMA, an algebraic reasoner for qualitative models based on Macsyma.

References

[1] J.M. Crawford, A. Farquhar and B.J. Kuipers, QPC: a compiler from physical models into qualitative differential equations, in: *Proceedings AAAI-90*, Boston, MA (1990).

[2] J. de Kleer and J.S. Brown, A qualitative physics based on confluences, *Artif. Intell.* **24** (1984) 7–83.

[3] D. Dvorak and B.J. Kuipers, Model-based monitoring of dynamic systems, in: *Proceedings IJCAI-89*, Detroit, MI (1989).

[4] D. Dvorak and B.J. Kuipers, Process monitoring and diagnosis: a model-based approach, *IEEE Expert* **6** (3) (1991) 67–74.

[5] K.D. Forbus, Qualitative process theory, *Artif. Intell.* **24** (1984) 85–168.

[6] D.W. Franke, Representing and acquiring teleological descriptions, in: *Proceedings IJCAI-89, Model-Based Reasoning Workshop*, Detroit, MI (1989).

[7] D.W. Franke, Deriving and using descriptions of purpose, *IEEE Expert* **6** (1991) 41–47.

[8] D.W. Franke and D. Dvorak, Component-connection models, in: *Proceedings IJCAI-89, Model-Based Reasoning Workshop*, Detroit, MI (1989).

[9] B.J. Kuipers, Commonsense reasoning about causality: deriving behavior from structure, *Artif. Intell.* **24** (1984) 169–203.

[10] B.J. Kuipers, Qualitative simulation, *Artif. Intell.* **29** (1986) 289–338.

[11] B.J. Kuipers, Qualitative simulation as causal explanation, *IEEE Trans. Syst. Man Cybern.* **17** (3) (1987) 432–444.

[12] B.J. Kuipers, Qualitative simulation: then and now, *Artif. Intell.* **59** (1993) 133–140 (this volume).

[13] B.J. Kuipers and J.P. Kassirer, Causal reasoning in medicine: analysis of a protocol, *Cogn. Sci.* **8** (1984) 363–385.

[14] C. Rieger and M. Grinberg, The declarative representation and procedural simulation of causality in physical mechanisms, in: *Proceedings IJCAI-77*, Cambridge, MA (1977) 250–256.

[15] R. Simmons and R. Davis, Generate, test and debug: combining associational rules and causal models, in: *Proceedings IJCAI-87*, Milan, Italy (1987).

[16] B.C. Williams, MINIMA: a symbolic approach to qualitative algebraic reasoning, in: *Proceedings AAAI-88*, St. Paul, MN (1988) 264–269.

Artificial Intelligence 59 (1993) 133–140
Elsevier

ARTINT 995

Qualitative simulation:
then and now *

Benjamin J. Kuipers

Computer Sciences Department, University of Texas at Austin, Austin TX 78712, USA

Qualitative reasoning about physical systems has become one of the most active and productive areas in AI in recent years. While there are many different kinds of qualitative reasoning, the central role is played by *qualitative simulation*: prediction of the possible behaviors consistent with incomplete knowledge of the structure of physical system.

In the retrospective [8] on my 1984 paper, "Commonsense reasoning about causality: deriving behavior from structure", I describe the framework for qualitative reasoning that has motivated this work, and the applications that have come out of that framework. That paper [5] includes the conjecture that the structural and behavioral representations for qualitative simulation could be rigorously shown to be abstractions of ordinary differential equations and their solutions. My 1986 paper, "Qualitative simulation", established that conjecture and legitimized the term *qualitative differential equation* or QDE. It also presented the clear and efficient QSIM algorithm. In this retrospective, I describe aspects of the body of work on qualitative simulation that has developed from there.

1. Background

Three motivating insights led to the development of the QSIM algorithm. First, the design for the QDE representation for qualitative models, presented

Correspondence to: Computer Sciences Department, University of Texas at Austin, Austin TX 78712, USA. E-mail: kuipers@cs.utexas.edu.

*This work has taken place in the Qualitative Reasoning Group at the Artificial Intelligence Laboratory, The University of Texas at Austin. Research of the Qualitative Reasoning Group is supported in part by NSF grants IRI-8905494 and IRI-8904454, by NASA grant NAG 2-507, and by the Texas Advanced Research Program under grant no. 003658-175.

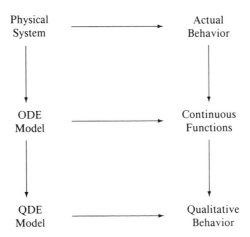

Fig. 1. All models are abstractions of the world. Qualitative models are related to ordinary differential equations, but are more expressive of incomplete knowledge.

in the 1984 *Artificial Intelligence Journal* paper, had been inspired both by observations of human experts (Kuipers and Kassirer [13]) and by the language of ordinary differential equations, so it was natural to ask how the mathematical similarity could be proved to be a true abstraction relation (Fig. 1).

Second, my previous ENV algorithm and its implementation had become unwieldy both in theory and in practice, so it was time to redesign the algorithm and reimplement the simulator. My research assistant at the time, Christopher Eliot, suggested the approach of proposing transitions and filtering inconsistent combinations. We were both inspired by David Waltz' compelling animation of his constraint filtering algorithm in the classic MIT AI Lab film, "The Eye of the Robot". Rather later, it became clear that the QSIM algorithm was almost a textbook application of Mackworth's node, arc, and path consistency algorithms for constraint satisfaction, but our inspiration came from the film, not the theory.

The third insight came from attempting to do a qualitative simulation, by hand, of the simple undamped oscillator: $x'' = -M^+(x)$. At the end of the first complete cycle, the simulation branches three ways according to whether the oscillation was increasing, steady, or decreasing, although only the steady case is consistent with this equation. After some confusion, it became clear that this apparent bug in the algorithm reflected a fundamental and revealing limitation in the mathematics of qualitative simulation.

2. Abstraction, soundness, and incompleteness

Once the abstraction relations from ODEs to QDEs, and from continuously differentiable functions to qualitative behaviors, are carefully defined,[1] the mathematical results are relatively straightforward.

We can view an ordinary differential equation solver as a theorem-prover for theorems of a special form:

$$DiffEqs \vdash ODE \wedge State(t_0) \rightarrow Beh. \tag{1}$$

A qualitative simulation algorithm can also be viewed as a special-purpose theorem-prover:

$$QSIM \vdash QDE \wedge QState(t_0) \rightarrow or(QBeh_1, \ldots, QBeh_n). \tag{2}$$

The soundness theorem says that when QSIM proves a theorem of form (2), it is true: that is, for any ODE described by the QDE, and $State(t_0)$ described by $QState(t_0)$, the solution Beh to the ODE is described by one of the qualitative behaviors, $QBeh_1, \ldots, QBeh_n$. The constraint filtering algorithm makes the proof very simple: all possible real transitions from one qualitative state to the next are proposed, and only impossible ones are filtered out, so all the real ones must remain.

The incompleteness theorem says that some qualitative behaviors in the disjunct may be *spurious*: that is, not abstracting any real solution to an ODE corresponding to the QDE. In the simple oscillator example, the increasing and decreasing behaviors are spurious. This situation is properly considered incompleteness, since QSIM has failed to prove the stronger theorem with fewer disjuncts.

3. Progress in qualitative simulation

The constraint filtering architecture of the QSIM algorithm lends itself to natural extension with a set of global filters[2] on complete qualitative states or behaviors. The goal of each filter is to make certain consequences of the qualitative description explicit, and to detect inconsistencies so the behavior

---

[1] A QDE is a description of a set of ODEs, with two essential abstractions. First, a *quantity space* is an abstraction of the real number line to an ordered set of *landmark values*, symbolic names for qualitatively significant values. Second, the arithmetic and differential constraints in the ODE are augmented by a *monotonic function* constraint describing a fixed but unknown function in terms of its direction of change.

[2] These filters are "global" in the sense that they apply to complete qualitative state descriptions, not just to individual assignments of values to variables, or tuples of assignments. The filters also vary according to whether their scope is an individual state or an entire behavior.

can be filtered out. The creation of a suitable set of global filters has been an ongoing and productive line of research.

3.1. State-based filters

- *Infinite values and infinite times.* The QSIM abstraction is defined over the extended number line, so $+\infty$ and $-\infty$ are represented by landmark values in each quantity space. There are useful constraints on the possible combinations of finite and infinite values, times, and rates of change (Kuipers [6]).

- *Higher-order derivatives.* Certain unconstrained or "chattering" sets of qualitative behaviors can be pruned by deriving and applying expressions for higher-order derivatives of key variables in the QDE (Kuipers and Chiu [11], Kuipers et al. [12], building on earlier work by Williams [19] and by de Kleer and Bobrow [2]). The derivation may require additional assumptions about the behavior of unspecified monotonic functions.

- *Ignoring direction of change.* Chattering behaviors can also be collapsed into a single description without an additional assumption by ignoring certain qualitative features, at the cost of additional possible spurious behaviors (Kuipers and Chiu [11], Kuipers et al. [12]).

3.2. History-based filters

- *Non-intersection of trajectories in qualitative phase space.* The solution to a differential equation can be viewed as a trajectory in phase space. These trajectories cannot intersect themselves or each other at finite times. Methods for testing for self-intersection, applicable even under the qualitative behavior description, were developed independently by Lee and Kuipers [14] and by Struss [18].

- *Kinetic energy theorem.* Under very general circumstances, a QDE can be viewed as representing motion in response to a force, which in turn can be decomposed into a conservative and a non-conservative component. Then, over any segment of behavior, the change in kinetic energy of the system must be equal to the sum of conservative and non-conservative work. This equation can often be evaluated qualitatively, and eliminates an important source of spurious behaviors (Fouché and Kuipers [3]).

3.3. Quantitative constraints

Methods for adding quantitative information to qualitative behaviors can be used both to exploit additional *a priori* knowledge, and to interpret quantitative observations by unifying them with a qualitative behavior.

- *Q2: bounds on landmarks and monotonic functions.* A qualitative behavior predicted by QSIM can serve as a framework for representing quantitative information by annotating landmark values with real intervals and monotonic function constraints with real-valued functions serving as bounding envelopes. The quantitative bounds can be propagated across constraints to derive tighter bounds, or to detect a contradiction and filter out the behavior (Kuipers and Berleant [9,10]).

- *Q3: adaptive discretization.* The quantitative precision of the prediction from Q2 is drastically limited by the coarse grain-size of the qualitative behavior. The grain-size can be adaptively refined by inserting additional qualitative states, to converge to a real-valued function as uncertainty goes to zero (Berleant and Kuipers [1]).

3.4. Operating region transitions

A given QDE model has a region of applicability. When a behavior is about to cross the boundary of that region, simulation stops within the current region. If a model exists for the region on the other side of the boundary, a transition is created to a new state defined with respect to that model. In QSIM this is done by an explicit transition function that specifies which values are inherited, asserted, or inferred in the new state. The two states linked by a region transition are both considered time-points, and refer to the "same" point in time. This has two different interpretations:

- The two regions may have different constraints, but have identical descriptions of the state on their shared boundary. Therefore, the two transition states are alternate descriptions of the same physical state in time.
- The transition may represent the two sides of a "discontinuous" change: really a continuous but fast process whose extent is abstracted to zero for the purposes of the current model (Nishida and Doshita [16]).

This distinction can be illustrated with two models of a bouncing ball (provided as examples with the distributed version of QSIM): one models the bounce as a continuous transition between a gravity model and a spring model, and the other models the bounce as a discontinuous reflection of the velocity when the ball strikes the floor.

3.5. Time-scale abstraction

Time-scale abstraction allows us to decompose a model of a complex system into a hierarchy of simpler models of the system operating at different time-scales. A process in the midst of a time-scale hierarchy can view slower processes as constant and faster processes as acting instantaneously. That is, it can take a quasi-equilibrium view of the faster process, and abstract its behavior to a monotonic function (Kuipers [7]). There is much more to be done in this area, particularly drawing on traditional mathematical work on time-scales.

4. Open problems

There are many important open problems that naturally arise from the QDE representation and the QSIM algorithm. I list three interesting ones.

- *Qualitative phase portrait analysis.* Derive the set of all possible qualitative phase portraits of a given second-order QDE.

A phase portrait captures the set of all possible behaviors of a dynamical system, for all initial states. It thus fills the same role as the "total envisionment", but with a more expressive language for qualitative features. Sacks [17] and Yip [20] have demonstrated important results in the intelligent control of numerical experiments to map phase portraits of dynamical systems, given numerically specific equations.

It is known that the phase portraits of all second-order systems can be described in terms of a simple qualitative language (Hirsch and Smale [4]). Preliminary experiments suggest that these terms can be inferred from intelligently guided *qualitative* simulation of a QDE model. This project would require automated algebraic analysis of the QDE to search for Lyapunov functions and other derived qualitative properties of the QDE. The resulting qualitative phase portrait would depend on fewer assumptions and thus have wider applicability than the corresponding numerically-based description.

- *Automatic formulation of numerical problems.* Use the tree of qualitative behaviors to formulate problems for a numerical equation-solver, for example an optimizer.

Each predicted qualitative behavior represents a qualitatively equivalent set of continuous behaviors. The qualitative behavior description can be mapped naturally onto a set of equations over landmark values and other symbolic terms (Kuipers and Berleant [10]). It should be possible to transform that set of equations into the appropriate forms for input to a variety of numerical equation-solving algorithms. For example, an optimizer could be used to find the numerical values for certain landmarks that optimize the value of some objective function.

The set of continuous behaviors corresponding to a single qualitative behavior provides useful assumptions to the equation-solver. Where there are several qualitative behaviors, the numerical solutions found along each branch can be combined, in the case of an optimizer by searching for the maximum value.

- *Completeness.* Is the problem of spurious behaviors a fundamental limitation of qualitative reasoning, or is the QDE language sufficiently limited that sound *and* complete qualitative simulation is possible?

On the one hand, recently developed methods are capable of detecting and filtering out many of the previously-troublesome sources of spurious behaviors. On the other hand, algebraic equivalence to zero is recursively unsolvable for a language rich enough to include the transcendental functions (Moses [15]). Either outcome to this question would be of considerable interest to the QR community.

References

[1] D. Berleant and B.J. Kuipers, Qualitative-numeric simulation with Q3, in: B. Faltings and P. Struss, eds., *Recent Advances in Qualitative Physics* (MIT Press, Cambridge, MA, 1992) 3–16.

[2] J. de Kleer and D.G. Bobrow, Qualitative reasoning with higher-order derivatives, in: *Proceedings AAAI-84*, Austin, TX (1984).

[3] P. Fouché and B.J. Kuipers, Reasoning about energy in qualitative simulation, *IEEE Trans. Syst. Man Cybern.* **22** (1) (1992) 47–63.

[4] M.W. Hirsch and S. Smale, *Differential Equations, Dynamical Systems, and Linear Algebra* (Academic Press, New York, 1974).

[5] B.J. Kuipers, Commonsense reasoning about causality: deriving behavior from structure, *Artif. Intell.* **24** (1984) 169–203.

[6] B.J. Kuipers, Qualitative simulation, *Artif. Intell.* **29** (1986) 289–338.

[7] B.J. Kuipers, Abstraction by time-scale in qualitative simulation, in: *Proceedings AAAI-87*, Seattle, WA (1987).

[8] B.J. Kuipers, Reasoning with qualitative models, *Artif. Intell.* **59** (1993) 125–132 (this volume).

[9] B.J. Kuipers and D. Berleant, Using incomplete quantitative knowledge in qualitative reasoning, in: *Proceedings AAAI-88*, St. Paul, MN (1988).

[10] B.J. Kuipers and D. Berleant, A smooth integration of incomplete quantitative knowledge into qualitative simulation, Artificial Intelligence Lab TR AI 90-122, University of Texas at Austin (1990).

[11] B.J. Kuipers and C. Chiu, Taming intractible branching in qualitative simulation, in: *Proceedings IJCAI-87*, Milan, Italy (1987).

[12] B.J. Kuipers, C. Chiu, D.T. Dalle Molle and D.R. Throop, Higher-order derivative constraints in qualitative simulation, *Artif. Intell.* **51** (1991) 343–379.

[13] B.J. Kuipers and J.P. Kassirer, Causal reasoning in medicine: analysis of a protocol, *Cogn. Sci.* **8** (1984) 363–385.

[14] W.W. Lee and B.J. Kuipers, Non-intersection of trajectories in qualitative phase space: a global constraint for qualitative simulation, in: *Proceedings AAAI-88*, St. Paul, MN (1988).

[15] J. Moses, Algebraic simplification: a guide for the perplexed, *Commun. ACM* **14** (8) (1971) 527–537.

[16] T. Nishida and S. Doshita, Reasoning about discontinuous change, in: *Proceedings AAAI-87*, Seattle, WA (1987).

[17] E.P. Sacks, Automatic qualitative analysis of dynamic systems using piecewise linear approximations, *Artif. Intell.* **41** (1990) 313–364.

[18] P. Struss, Global filters for qualitative behaviors, in: *Proceedings AAAI-88*, St. Paul, MN (1988).

[19] B.C. Williams, The use of continuity in a qualitative physics, in: *Proceedings AAAI-84*, Austin, TX (1984) 350–354.

[20] K.M.-K. Yip, *KAM: A System for Intelligently Guiding Numerical Experimentation by Computer* (MIT Press, Cambridge, MA, 1991).

Artificial Intelligence 59 (1993) 141–146
Elsevier

ARTINT 993

Retrospective on "Causality in device behavior"

Yumi Iwasaki

Knowledge Systems Laboratory, Department of Computer Science, Stanford University, Stanford, CA 94305, USA

Herbert A. Simon

Departments of Computer Science and Psychology, Carnegie Mellon University, Pittsburgh, PA 15213, USA

Since the interests of the two of us that led up to our joint paper have quite different origins, we will first comment individually, then offer some additional joint comments on recent and future developments.

Simon:

I first encountered causality in the late 1940s, while seeking to formalize the concept of political power (causation of the behavior of one person by another). This concept turned out to be closely related to the concept of identification in simultaneous equation models, then being investigated by the Cowles Commission for Research in Economics. I published in 1952–54 several papers [13,14] introducing a definition of causal ordering and exploring both the mathematical properties and the underlying semantics of the formalism.

When, years later, I read the early papers on qualitative reasoning in AI, it seemed to me that causal ordering, and related ideas for applying the method of comparative statics (with which I had also had experience in my work in economics) provided a more powerful method than those being proposed.

Correspondence to: H.A. Simon, Department of Psychology, Carnegie Mellon University, Pittsburgh, PA 15213, USA. E-mail: has@cs.cmu.edu.

The decision of Yumi Iwasaki to write a dissertation on qualitative modeling allowed me to collaborate with her in exploring the relation between the AI approaches and the earlier work. In her research, Yumi carried the analysis much further than I had, developing and clarifying the analysis for systems that included both dynamic and static components. Our paper in *Artificial Intelligence* was written to demonstrate the advantages of the causal ordering and comparative statics frameworks for handling qualitative reasoning in artificial intelligence.

Iwasaki:

As a computer science graduate student in 1984, I wanted to study AI not so much from a desire to create intelligence on a machine but rather to understand the nature of human intelligence through such attempts. I became interested in qualitative reasoning about physical systems, because the ability to reason about the physical world is obviously a significant part of intelligence, essential for survival. The concept of causality seems to play a central role in this type of intelligence in humans, and has intrigued philosophers for many centuries. Human beings seem to have an innate need to understand and explain everything which happens in the world in terms of causes and effects. Formally, we describe physical phenomena using physics and mathematics. Modern physics sees no need for causality. Mathematics sees no reason to formalize it. Yet, we talk and think about physical phenomena in terms of causal relations all the time. We consider numerical computations carried out by a computer program to simulate the weather system as mindless, mechanical chores. However, as soon as the computer starts to provide not only numbers but a causal account of how and why the weather changes, the program all of a sudden puts on the air of somehow "understanding" the weather. Causation is a cornerstone of human intelligence about physical phenomena.

The concept of causation is difficult to define precisely. In AI, almost every work that deals with reasoning about the behavior of systems has something to say about causality. Yet, the concept is rarely defined explicitly. Causality is one of those things that everybody intuitively knows (or thinks he/she knows) and, therefore, is usually left undefined. However, once one tries to pin down exactly what a statement such as "drought caused the trees to die" means, one finds it difficult to come up with a precise logical definition. The statement does not mean that trees will necessarily die when drought happens, nor that only drought can kill trees. Another person observing the same event may come to a completely different conclusion about the cause of the trees' death, for instance, someone having forgotten to water them. Moreover, the language of causation is used in many different situations.

One may say "my earning poor grades caused the class average to drop" as well as "heat caused the ice to melt". Both seem to be reasonable uses of the word *cause*; yet the sense of causation in each case seems slightly different. To summarize, causality is a highly intuitive concept and as such, an ill-defined one. But it is crucial for understanding human ability to reason about the world.

It was fortunate for me that Professor Simon, who was then my advisor, had previously done significant research into this subject of causation [13,14]. The theory of causal ordering he advanced seemed to capture the essential intuition behind people's perception of causal relation in an elegant and general manner. Professor Simon and I started re-examining the concept of causality in several pieces of work in qualitative physics in light of his theory. We found that the theory allowed us to demystify the notions of causality in these works by explicating the underlying intuition. This is what led us to write the paper, "Causality in device behavior" [10].

Iwasaki and Simon:

The main contributions of the paper were:

(1) to introduce the theory of causal ordering to the artificial intelligence community,
(2) to demonstrate its application to physical domains, and
(3) to interpret, in light of the theory, the concept of causal relations suggested by de Kleer and Brown [2].

The paper developed into Iwasaki's thesis [6], in which she expanded the scope of the causal ordering theory to cover systems having a mixture of dynamic and equilibrium equations [5]. She also examined techniques of aggregation by model abstraction and their relations to causal ordering [7].

In retrospect, we see two problems that were ignored in the paper and another topic that was not sufficiently developed:

(1) equations cannot be interpreted in all possible causal directions,
(2) in certain physical phenomena the perceived direction of causation does not seem to agree with the theory's definition of causation in dynamic systems, and
(3) the theory does not show how to formulate an equation model.

The last topic has turned out to be the significant open issue that has dictated much of Iwasaki's research interest in the last several years.

The theory of causal ordering is based on the idea that equations by themselves are inherently acausal and can give rise to different causal interpretations depending on the context (i.e. the set of equations and exogenous variables) of an equation. However, as Washio pointed out [15], there are some equations that are never interpreted in certain directions.

For example, the equations $pv = nrt$ and $v = ir$ should not, by themselves, disallow such causal interpretations as "n (or r) causally depends on p, v, and t" or "v and i causally determine r", but we never interpret them in these ways. These examples do not invalidate the idea that individual equations are inherently acausal since it is not the equations themselves that inhibit such interpretations. The examples show that other types of knowledge about physical phenomena, besides knowledge about the functional relations, make people view causality in these relations only in certain directions. Examination of examples of this type would shed more light on the knowledge underlying equation models.

The second issue has to do with the causal relations in dynamic systems. The present theory of causal ordering requires the differential equations in the model to be in canonical form and defines the direction of causality (e.g., in $dv/dt = f(v_1, \ldots, v_n)$) to be from the variables on the right-hand side to the derivative on the left. For example, in the heat flow equation, $dH/dt = c(T_1 - T_2)$, where H, T_1, and T_2 are the rate of heat transfer, and the temperatures of the heat source and the sink, the rate is causally dependent on the temperatures. This seems to agree with our intuitive notion of causality in most cases.

However, there are cases in physics where a *change* in a quantity is perceived as the cause of some other quantity. An example is Faraday's law of induction, $E = -d\Phi_B/dt$, where a change in magnetic flux ($d\Phi_B/dt$) produces electromagnetic force (E) but not vice versa. In light of this exception, one may want to generalize the definition of causal ordering by removing the requirement that all differential equations must be in canonical form. That requirement could actually make it impossible for each equation to represent a distinct mechanism in the system .

The third problem, which actually subsumes the first two, is how to formulate a model. In our paper, the causal ordering theory was presented in two parts: the procedural definition of causal ordering among variables and the discussion of the semantics of a model—what each equation in the model must represent—that underlie the procedure. Even though it was the discussion of de Kleer and Brown's mythical causality that stirred up the subsequent debate, we think in retrospect that the consideration of what models represent and where they come from is the most important open area of investigation of causality.

Our paper contained some discussion of how to formulate a model in the context of causal ordering theory. For the theory successfully to produce relations that reflect our intuitive perception of causality, the equations must be structural, that is, must represent conceptually distinct mechanisms in the system being modeled. Deciding what equations are structural in a given situation is essentially the problem of model formulation. Once a set of equations and exogenous variables is given, the theory allows one to uncover the causal relations implicit in the set through a mechanical procedure. Thus, it appears that the "real" work lies in coming up with the set of equations.

The choice of equations depends not only on the physical scope of the problem but also on such factors as the temporal scope, the level of abstraction, the appropriate perspective, the amount of available computational resources, etc. We mentioned some of these issues in the paper. One of them, the issue of abstraction was further explored in Iwasaki's thesis [6]. However, the model abstraction techniques explored there also start from a given mathematical model, and do not address directly the issue of where the model comes from. How to formulate the model in the first place is the biggest present challenge, and we have barely scratched the surface.

Other researchers in qualitative physics also seem to have come to the conclusion that model formulation is the key issue. Many papers that address this problem appeared both before and after the publication of our paper (Forbus [4], Addanki et al. [1], Falkenhainer and Forbus [3], Weld [16], Nayak et al. [12]). Iwasaki's recent work also has pursued the problem of model formulation based on a QPT-style compositional modeling paradigm, combining modeling of continuous and discrete phenomena (Iwasaki and Low [9]). She has also been experimenting with a general framework for reasoning about relevance of knowledge for model formulation (Levy and Iwasaki [11]).

Another problem that an interest in causation has led Iwasaki to investigate is verification of causal accounts of behavior. "Causality in device behavior" was concerned exclusively with determining the causal dependency relations among *variables*. In a causal explanation of how things work, references to causal relations among *events* are also very common. One example is "turning on the switch causes the current to flow, which causes the lamp to light up". What does "to cause" mean in the context of a real behavior? Given some description of what actually happened, when can we say that this causal account correctly describes the event?

This is an important question in design verification. Given a causal explanation of how a device is supposed to work, and an account of what actually happens, when can we say that the device is working as intended? Is it enough that those events—current flow, lamp lighting up, etc.—actually take place? It seems that the assertion of a causal relation among the events requires more than that they simply occur. Iwasaki is exploring this issue with Chandrasekaran to produce a formal definition of matching between an actual behavior of a device and a causal account of how it is supposed to work [8].

Our initial inquiry into the issue of causality has led to interesting new problems. But have we made any progress towards deeper understanding of this important area of human intelligence? We hope so even if the progress may be small. We certainly have miles to go before we can rest in confidence that we have understood the part of our intelligence that allows us to cope with causality in the complex real physical world.

Acknowledgement

Pandu Nayak provided helpful comments on a draft of this article.

References

[1] S. Addanki, R. Cremonini and J.S. Penberthy, Reasoning about assumptions in graphs of models, in: *Proceedings IJCAI-89*, Detroit, MI (1989).

[2] J. de Kleer and J.S. Brown, A qualitative physics based on confluences, *Artif. Intell.* **24** (1984) 7–83.

[3] B. Falkenhainer and K.D. Forbus, Compositional modeling: finding the right model for the job, Tech. Rept. SSL-90-85, Palo Alto Research Center, XEROX Corporation, Palo Alto, CA (1990); also: *Artif. Intell.* **51** (1991) 95–143.

[4] K.D. Forbus, Qualitative process theory, *Artif. Intell.* **24** (1984) 85–168.

[5] Y. Iwasaki, Causal ordering in a mixed structure, in: *Proceedings AAAI-88*, St. Paul, MN (1988).

[6] Y. Iwasaki, Model-based reasoning of device behavior with causal ordering, Ph.D. Thesis, Department of Computer Science, Carnegie Mellon University, Pittsburgh, PA (1988).

[7] Y. Iwasaki and I. Bhandari, Formal basis for commonsense abstraction of dynamic systems, in: *Proceedings AAAI-88*, St. Paul, MN (1988).

[8] Y. Iwasaki and B. Chandrasekaran, Design verification through function- and behavior-oriented representations: bridging the gap between function and behavior, *Artificial Intelligence in Design '92 Conference* (submitted).

[9] Y. Iwasaki and Chee Meng Low, Device modeling environment: an interactive environment for modeling physical device behavior, Tech. Rept., Knowledge Systems Laboratory, Department of Computer Science, Stanford University, Stanford, CA (1990).

[10] Y. Iwasaki and H.A. Simon, Causality in device behavior, *Artif. Intell.* **29** (1986) 3–32.

[11] A. Levy and Y. Iwasaki, Relevance reasoning to guide compositional modeling, Tech. Rept., Knowledge Systems Laboratory, Stanford University, Stanford, CA (1991).

[12] P. Nayak, S. Addanki and L. Joskowicz, Modeling with context-dependent behaviors, in: *Proceedings Fifth International Workshop on Qualitative Reasoning about Physical Systems*, Austin, TX (1991).

[13] H.A. Simon, On the definition of the causal relation, *J. Philos.* **49** (1952).

[14] H.A. Simon, Causal ordering and identifiability, in: W.C. Hood and T.C. Koopmans, eds., *Studies in Econometric Methods* (Wiley, New York, 1953).

[15] T. Washio, Causal ordering methods based on physical laws of plant systems, Rept. No. MITNRL-033, Nuclear Reactor Laboratory, MIT, Cambridge, MA (1989).

[16] D.S. Weld, Approximation reformulations, in: *Proceedings AAAI-90*, Boston, MA (1990) 407–412.

Diagnosis

Artificial Intelligence 59 (1993) 149–157
Elsevier

ARTINT 989

Retrospective on "Diagnostic reasoning based on structure and behavior"

Randall Davis

Artificial Intelligence Laboratory, Massachusetts Institute of Technology, Cambridge, MA 02139, USA

1. Origins

Interest in model-based reasoning arose out of the desire to capture reasoning based on an understanding (i.e., a model) of how a device works. Consider, for example, an automobile that presents the following symptoms: nothing happens when you turn the ignition key to start it, but the radio works. Even without ever having encountered that particular set of symptoms before, most people can quickly infer that the starter might be broken but the battery is ok, by reasoning from a very simple model of the structure (e.g., there is only one battery) and behavior (e.g., batteries supply power) of the device. Knowing how something is supposed to work provides a strong foundation on which to build diagnostic engines, as well as supporting test generation, design, and design for testability.

The intellectual foundation for the paper "Diagnostic reasoning based on structure and behavior" [4] was provided by a significant body of prior work in AI, including Sussman's early work on constraints [17], de Kleer's work on troubleshooting using local propagation [6], Rieger's causal models [14], and the work of Brown et al. on CAI and troubleshooting in SOPHIE [2].

The report in [3] provides a contemporary and more detailed view of the early context for this body of work. The paper on diagnostic reasoning was motivated by having a program reason successfully about a fault that

Correspondence to: R. Davis, Artificial Intelligence Laboratory, Massachusetts Institute of Technology, Cambridge, MA 02139, USA. E-mail: davis@ai.mit.edu.

introduces an unexpected interconnection in a digital circuit. Such faults pose a particularly interesting challenge for model-based reasoning, because one of the technique's central virtues is that it works from a description of structure and behavior (i.e., from the schematic), and with an unexpected connection the schematic is not an accurate description of the pathways of causality in the device.

2. Key intellectual contributions

The highlighted items in Sections 1 and 2 of the paper [4], while occasionally redundant, still stand the test of time reasonably well. Among the most significant are the following.

- Languages used in model-based reasoning should distinguish carefully between structure and behavior, and should provide multiple descriptions of structure, organizing it both functionally and physically.
- Diagnosis can be accomplished via the interaction of simulation and inference (later termed prediction and observation).
- *Constraint suspension* is a new tool for troubleshooting, capable of determining which components can be responsible for a set of observed symptoms.
- The concept of the *paths of causal interaction*—the mechanisms and pathways by which one component can affect another—is a primary component of the knowledge needed to do reasoning from structure and behavior.
- Model-based diagnosis is faced with an inescapable tradeoff of completeness and specificity: if all possible paths of causal interaction are considered, diagnosis becomes indiscriminant, but omitting any one pathway means that an entire class of faults will be out of reach.
- The tradeoff can be managed by layering the paths of causal interaction considered during the diagnostic process.
- An enumeration of the different kinds of pathways of interaction can in turn be produced by examining the assumptions underlying the representation.
- This layering provides a novel way to view troubleshooting, casting it as the methodical enumeration and relaxation of assumptions about the device. A system working in this way can focus its efforts initially for the sake of efficiency and diagnostic power, yet will methodically expand its focus to include a broad range of faults.
- The concept of *adjacency* helps in understanding why some faults are especially difficult, what it means to have a good representation, and why multiple representations are useful.

3. What was misunderstood?

3.1. What kind of model?

"Model" is sufficiently vague that the term has been used subsequently to describe a variety of different kinds of model-based systems. The models used here have several distinctive properties: they are models of structure and behavior; they are capable of both simulation and inference; they are organized around components and connections; and they are often hierarchical. As Sections 3 and 4 of the paper [4] note, structure includes both the functional and physical organization of components, while behavior is the standard black-box notion. To support model-based diagnosis, the model should be capable of both simulation (predicting outputs from inputs) and inference (inferring inputs from observations).

The model is component-oriented in the sense that it explicitly represents the components of which the device itself is composed, and interconnects them in the same way that they are interconnected in the device. In the world of digital devices, for example, a 32-bit ripple-carry adder is made up of 32 individual bit slices connected in a particular pattern. The model we build would similarly be composed of 32 subcomponents connected in the same pattern (Fig. 2 of [4] shows a 4-bit example). The nodes of this sort of model represent device components, while links represent pathways of interaction (e.g., wires) between components.[1] The models are hierarchical for all the standard reasons of efficiency that hierarchical descriptions offer.

Given the numerous other ways in which the term "model" can be used, many other systems can properly be called model-based. But as the title of the paper [4] purposely emphasized, it was talking about reasoning from one particular variety of model, viz., a model of structure and behavior. Some subsequent work appears to have misunderstood the source of power in this approach, apparently ascribing the power to reasoning from any model, rather than to reasoning from the specific kind of model used here.

3.2. Distinguishing logical and physical possibility of candidates

As the paper notes in Section 6.2, constraint suspension in particular and model-based reasoning in general distinguish between the logical possibility of a candidate and its physical possibility, a distinction that has subsequently at times been overlooked and then rediscovered. Logical possibility tells us whether there is *any* set of values a component might display that could

---

[1]A contrasting alternative is provided by state-oriented causal models, which represent the progression of states through which a device can pass. In this case nodes indicate states and links indicate transitions from one state to another. Note that in this variety of model neither the nodes nor the links have any correspondence to physical objects.

account for the observations, where physical possibility tells us whether a particular component is observed to fail in real use in a way that would produce the symptoms observed. For example, it might be logically possible to account for observed symptoms by hypothesizing that a wire on a circuit board is misbehaving by turning 1's into 0's and vice versa, even though there is in fact no common physical fault mode that causes a wire to start acting as an inverter.

This distinction was made initially in order to see what could be gained by reasoning only from how the device is supposed to work (i.e., reasoning only from knowledge about its correct behavior). In this view a device is a candidate if it displays anything other than its correct behavior. There are, by contrast, approaches based solely on fault models; these systems select as candidates any component with a known fault mode that would produce the observed symptom. As Section 6.2 explains, one virtue of reasoning from correct behavior is the breadth of diagnostic power it supplies: among other things, it can deal gracefully with symptoms that have never been encountered previously (e.g., those that arise from a new variety of failures).

Reasoning solely from correct behavior, however, ignores the useful constraint and focusing provided by fault models. Section 6.2 indicates one simple way in which model-based reasoning can make use of fault models: the list of candidates is pruned (perhaps during candidate generation itself) by checking to determine whether each logically possible candidate is known to fail in real use in a way that would produce the symptoms inferred for it.

The distinction between logical and physical possibility and the capacity of model-based reasoning to use fault models has at times been overlooked. As one example, the basic technique of model-based reasoning has subsequently been claimed (e.g., [11,18]) to produce conclusions of the form "light bulb B_3 is faulted: it is lit although there is no voltage [across it]".

In fact the actual conclusion in that case would be that "light bulb B_3 is *not behaving as expected*: it is lit although there is no voltage". This second phrasing is an accurate expression of what model-based reasoning actually indicates, exhibiting the care it takes in distinguishing between "not behaving as expected" and "faulted". Not behaving as expected often means that the component is faulted, but the two are not synonymous: there are many other reasons why the component might not behave as expected (e.g., it is not wired up in the way the schematic indicates). Hence the distinction matters and has been a part of the model-based reasoning approach from early on.

3.3. Distinguishing fault modes and physical failures

A fault mode is the behavior produced by some variety of physical failure. One common fault mode in digital electronics, for example, is "stuck at 0", in which a wire always carries a zero, no matter what we attempt to put on it. This behavior can arise from a variety of different physical events: the wire may be shorted to ground; it may be cut (and hence disconnected from any driving signal), which in some digital technologies produces a zero, etc. In the paper being reviewed here, the interesting physical failure was the inadvertent wiring together of two adjacent pins on a chip by a pool of solder (called a bridge fault); the fault mode produced is the and-gate behavior shown in Fig. 19 of the paper.

The paper thus distinguishes between the physical event and its behavioral consequences. The distinction matters for several reasons, one of which arises when probabilities are used to guide diagnosis: the probability of a physical event is a reasonably well-defined concept, but the probability of a behavior is considerably less obvious. Subsequent work using probabilities has at times glossed over this distinction.

3.4. Models and rules

Some work has investigated the notion of "turning models into rules", often on the grounds that model-based reasoning is supposedly slow, while rule-based systems are allegedly faster. As noted at some length elsewhere [5], this appears to be a confusion of form and content, apparently assuming that the power in a representation arises primarily from its form (e.g., a conditional statement) rather than its content (empirical association versus a description of structure and behavior). Rule-based systems capture one form of knowledge, while model-based systems represent a different kind of knowledge and use it in a correspondingly different way. Re-writing model-based reasoning as conditional statements is neither surprising (Post productions have long been known to be Turing equivalent) nor particularly useful (because speed and power arise primarily from the content, not the form of the knowledge).

3.5. Diagnosis as a process

AI work on model-based diagnosis, and indeed diagnosis in general, has attempted to capture the diagnostic process. That is, we not only want to determine what experts know and what answers that leads to (i.e., the epistemology of diagnosis), but also want to understand the process by which they arrive at that result. This emphasis on process is important for several reasons: It provides insight into one important form of human reasoning; it makes automated reasoners more transparent (and easier to build and hence more acceptable to users); and it is a source of significant reasoning power (expert diagnosticians are considerably better than any program on complex circuits or systems).

Hence efforts to recast model-based reasoning in logic, while useful as a way of studying issues of the epistemology and semantics of the task, also have the nontrivial problem of losing almost all contact with the *process* of diagnosis. Work attempting to view diagnosis as nonmonotonic inference may be an interesting challenge to logic and may offer some insight about the problem, but it often obscures distinctions that are important in understanding the diagnostic reasoning process.

4. Open issues

A number of the open issues mentioned in the paper remain subjects of active work, including: scaling up to realistically large devices, facilitating model construction, doing model selection, and handling analog devices.

4.1. Model construction

Perhaps the most significant pragmatic barrier to the routine industrial use of this technology is the difficulty of building a device model. Several factors make the task is daunting for many real devices:

(i) it requires an exhaustive, explicit reconstruction of the design of the entire device, often needing information not contained in available documentation,

(ii) there is often a large volume of information to be captured, and

(iii) the information is often described in numerous informal languages (e.g., the precision of schematics soon gives way to informal block diagrams with many, ill-defined sorts of arrows).

Hence even for devices as apparently simple as a personal computer, the modeling task is a challenging one of intellectual archeology (reconstructing the design details) and translation (from informal to more precise descriptions).

We need to make this process both easier and more intuitive. At the purely pragmatic level, simply being able to read and translate existing CAD files reduces the amount of manual work involved. More importantly, we need a better understanding of both the nature of the end-product (the model) and the process by which informal descriptions are translated into such a model.

4.2. Model selection

Given a basic knowledge of how to use models of structure and behavior in diagnosis, it is intriguing to push the process back one step: How are models selected to begin with? Since all devices can be viewed from multiple perspectives, how do we decide which view is appropriate in any given circumstance? The is the sort of reasoning that goes on in the heads of engineers before the equations or block diagrams ever hit the page. Interesting starts on this problem have been made (e.g., [1,9,19], and others), but much remains to be done.

4.3. Scaling

Scaling model-based reasoning techniques to deal with realistic devices involves handling increases in both the number of components and the complexity of their behavior. Of the two, structure appears somewhat easier: some early work reported diagnosing a system of 2000 very simple components [10], while more recent work [7] handles multiple faults in devices with up to 5000 gates by doing most-probable-first generation of diagnoses.

Difficult problems arise from attempts to deal with complex behavior. The work in [12] for instance, describes the development of a vocabulary of coarse temporal abstractions that enables troubleshooting of devices whose behavior extends over many thousands of clock cycles. This set of abstractions reduces what would have been an untenable amount of detail to a level that can be handled with existing machinery. There appears to be considerable power in such abstractions and some evidence that one of the best sources for them is the vocabulary used by people who routinely solve the same task. The intuition here is that cognitive limitations force human experts to invent vocabularies that make problems tractable and that our systems can benefit significantly from adopting the same vocabularies. In the area of device behavior description, as with many others, we have only begun to accumulate the appropriate vocabulary.

4.4. Reasoning about analog devices

In some ways modeling the digital world is particularly easy: Considerable computational simplicity arises from reasoning with the discrete, finite set of values needed, and from the inherent directionality (i.e., distinguished inputs and outputs) of the devices. Conversely, a number of known difficulties arise in dealing with analog devices, because of the infinite set of continuous real numbers needed to model them and the non-directional nature of their behavior.

Problems in modeling include dealing with inexactness (e.g., components good to $\pm 10\%$), the necessity of propagating intervals instead of integers (and of doing interval arithmetic), and the large number of predictions generated (e.g., at nodes with multiple wires attached). Non-directional behavior of devices means that there is no notion of focusing on only those components causally "upstream" of a symptom. In principle, any component in an analog circuit can be responsible for any symptom. Circuits are designed with stages in order to localize the effect of components, but little use is currently made of this information.

5. The future of the work

Numerous papers can be seen as reflecting the future of this line of work, many arising from independent efforts at other laboratories pursuing similar interests. A few examples illustrate various threads of work.

Work on GDE [8] offered the ability to diagnose multiple faults in ways that minimized the inherent exponential nature of the problem. It also displayed the use of probabilities of component failure, both to focus candidate generation and to select good probe points. Later work in this vein (e.g., [7]) showed that a probability-based search could allow the system to use correct behavior and fault mode information and still keep the combinatorics manageable.

The diagnostic problem was recast in formal terms in [13], where it was viewed as nonmonotonic inference in which the goal was to find the minimal set of abnormal components.

Work in [15] demonstrated that setting test generation in the context of model-based reasoning offered significant power, while [20] showed how design for testability could be similarly enhanced.

Work on XDE [12] offered the notion of coarse temporal abstractions as one illustration of the need for good abstractions as a means of dealing with complex behavior.

Finally, the GORDIUS program [16] offered the notion of generate, test, and debug as a problem solving paradigm, based in part on an understanding of the different kinds of knowledge embodied in empirical associations on one hand and models of structure and behavior on the other, and an understanding of how each form of knowledge could be used to support the other.

References

[1] S. Addanki, R. Cremonini and J.S. Penberthy, Graphs of models, *Artif. Intell.* **51** (1–3) (1991) 145–177.
[2] J.S. Brown, R. Burton and J. de Kleer, Knowledge engineering and pedagogical techniques in SOPHIE I, II, and III, in: D.H. Sleeman and J.S. Brown, eds., *Intelligent Tutoring Systems* (Academic Press, New York, 1982).
[3] R. Davis, Expert systems—Where are we? And where do we go from here? *AI Mag.* **3** (2) (1982) 3–22.
[4] R. Davis, Diagnostic reasoning based on structure and behavior, *Artif. Intell.* **24** (1984) 347–410.

[5] R. Davis, Form and content in model-based reasoning, in: *Proceedings IJCAI-89 Workshop on Model-Based Reasoning*, Detroit, MI (1989).

[6] J. de Kleer, Local methods of localizing faults in electronic circuits, AI Memo 394, MIT, Cambridge, MA (1976).

[7] J. de Kleer, Focusing on probable diagnoses, in: *Proceedings AAAI-91*, Anaheim, CA (1991) 842–848.

[8] J. de Kleer and B.C. Williams, Diagnosing multiple faults, *Artif. Intell.* **32** (1987) 97–130.

[9] B. Falkenhainer and K.D. Forbus, Compositional modeling: finding the right model for the job, *Artif. Intell.* **51** (1–3) (1991) 95–143.

[10] M.B. First, B.J. Weimer, S. McLinden and R.A. Miller, LOCALIZE: computer-assisted localization of peripheral nervous system lesions, *Comput. Biomed. Res.* **15** (6) (1982) 525–543.

[11] G. Friedrich, G. Gottlob and W. Nejdl, Physical impossibility instead of fault models, *Proceedings AAAI-90*, Boston, MA (1990) 331–336.

[12] W.C. Hamscher, Modeling digital circuits for troubleshooting, *Artif. Intell.* **51** (1991) 223–271.

[13] R. Reiter, A theory of diagnosis from first principles, *Artif. Intell.* **32** (1987) 57–95.

[14] C. Rieger and M. Grinberg, The declarative representation and procedural simulation of causality in physical mechanisms, Tech. Rept. TR-512, University of Maryland, College Park, MD (1977).

[15] M. Shirley, Generating tests by exploiting designed behavior, in: *Proceedings AAAI-86*, Philadelphia, PA (1986) 884–890.

[16] R. Simmons and R. Davis, Generate, test and debug: combining associational rules and causal models, in: *Proceedings IJCAI-87*, Milan, Italy (1987) 1071–1078.

[17] R.M. Stallman and G.J. Sussman, Forward reasoning and dependency-directed backtracking in a system for computer-aided circuit analysis, *Artif. Intell.* **9** (1977) 135–196.

[18] O. Struss and O. Dressler, "Physical negation" integrating fault models into the general diagnostic engine, in: *Proceedings IJCAI-89*, Detroit, MI (1989) 1318–1324.

[19] D.S. Weld, Automated model switching, in: *Proceedings Third Workshop on Qualitative Physics* (1989).

[20] P. Wu, Design for testability, in: *Proceedings AAAI-88*, St. Paul, MN (1988) 358–363.

Artificial Intelligence 59 (1993) 159–165
Elsevier

ARTINT 992

From Dart to Designworld: a chronicle of research on automated engineering in the Stanford Logic Group

Michael R. Genesereth

Knowledge Systems Lab., Department of Computer Science, Stanford University, Stanford, CA 94305-2095, USA

1. Background

For those of us in the Stanford Logic Group, the Dart project marks the beginning of a long-term commitment to research on the use of computers in the service of engineering. Oddly enough, the project began not in engineering, but in medicine; and it was originally concerned with explanation, not diagnosis.

When I arrived at Stanford in 1979, I assembled a small research group with financial support from a research contract belonging to Bruce Buchanan and Ed Feigenbaum. I asked Bruce how we might earn our keep, and he suggested that we look into ways of improving Mycin's explanation capability. Mycin was already world-renowned for its ability to explain its conclusions by citing the data and rules used to make those conclusions. The problem was that it was unable to explain why its rules were correct.

We knew that physicians could supply rationale for many of Mycin's rules by reference to underlying physiological principles. So, our idea was to capture this physiological knowledge and produce a program that could use it to verify Mycin's rules. A trace of the verification could then be used to explain the rules.

Correspondence to: M.R. Genesereth, Knowledge Systems Lab., Department of Computer Science, Stanford University, Stanford, CA 94305-2095, USA. E-mail: mrg@cs.stanford.edu.

Not being totally witless, we realized that, if our program could explain Mycin's rules, it could also generate them; in fact, it could skip that step and perform the diagnosis directly, albeit with some degradation in runtime efficiency. (A couple of years later, with the help of Ted Shortliffe, we produced a simple physiological model of the human endocrine system and showed how Dart could be used to predict and recognize various endocrine disorders.)

Returning from his sabbatical in mid-1980, Ed Feigenbaum took a look at our work, suggested that we shift our focus from medicine to engineering, and lined up some funding from IBM.

We took a two-pronged approach. First, we developed a traditional rule-based program for diagnosing a portion of the IBM 4331. In parallel, we developed a *model-based* version. (In a public relations blunder, both programs were called Dart, though the name eventually came to be associated with the model-based approach.) A comparison of these two efforts showed up the real advantages of the model-based approach, viz. "programming" efficiency and a guarantee of correctness and completeness.

While the rule-based approach works, it is extremely labor-intensive. This is okay for medical problems, since it has to be done only once—after all there is really only one model of human being (with slight variations). However, for the world of computer hardware, with new designs being introduced every year, this is simply too expensive. In the model-based approach, the cost is paid by the computer.

The second advantage of the model-based approach is correctness and completeness. In the rule-based approach, all rules are written by a human being, who may fail to see a possible interaction and thereby create an incorrect rule or even omit an important rule altogether. By contrast, with the model-based approach, we have a guarantee of soundness and completeness.

Our first attempt at building a model-based diagnostician was based on justification analysis. The idea was for the diagnostician to simulate the malfunctioning device to determine the expected outputs and, along the way, to record justifications for its conclusions. A comparison of the observed symptoms to the expected outputs would then lead the program to the suspect components via the recorded justifications. We expected to use an ad hoc technique to generate tests to discriminate the computed suspects.

Ironically, no sooner had we developed the approach than we dropped it in favor of a simpler and much prettier algorithm called *resolution residue* (a kind of abduction using the resolution principle). We were able to use this algorithm to compute suspects, as with the justification-based algorithm. Furthermore, we could use the same algorithm to generate tests to discriminate among suspects (a task which few other diagnostic programs have tackled, even those developed since 1980).

By the end of 1980, we had worked out the details of the algorithm and produced an implementation. I spent the Christmas break writing the first draft of the Dart paper. After some further work on performance improvement, the paper was presented at AAAI-82. It was finally published in *Artificial Intelligence* in 1984 [1].

2. Dart

The Dart program was intended for use in conjunction with a tester (human or robotic) that could manipulate and observe the malfunctioning device. It took as input a design description for the device under test. It queried its user for observations and symptoms about the device; it prescribed tests (inputs to set and outputs to observe) and accepted the results; and ultimately it returned as value a list of possibly faulty components.

The answer returned by Dart was a conflict set, not a complete diagnosis—at least one of the components on the list was guaranteed to be malfunctioning, but there was no guarantee that all faulty components were on the list. If the program was interrupted, the current list could be used as answer, though it might include spurious entries (components that could be shown to be working properly). On the other hand, if the program was allowed to run to completion, the list was guaranteed to be minimal, i.e. no test could further discriminate the possibilities.

One of the distinctive features of Dart was its generality. Unlike previous programs, Dart was designed to operate on arbitrary discrete devices. It was not, as many believe, restricted to digital circuits. In fact, to stress this generality, we applied it to the diagnosis of several non-digital devices and even some non-electronic devices (e.g. the cooling system for a nuclear reactor, modeled as a discrete device).

Although generality is usually associated with inefficiency, Dart's generality was in some cases a source of enhanced efficiency. Since the program could be applied at multiple levels of abstraction, it could do diagnosis in a hierarchical fashion, first finding the major component within which the fault lies, then moving to a detailed description of that component to find the failing subcomponent, and so forth, thereby decreasing combinatorial cost.

Another distinctive (though, to some, dubious) feature of the program was its use of logic-based technology. The use of first-order predicate calculus gave designers a very expressive language within which to characterize their designs. The use of general symbolic reasoning techniques allowed the program to be applied even to incompletely specified designs.

With regard to efficiency, this feature was a mixed blessing. On the negative side, this approach had substantial (though constant) overhead. On the positive side, the generality of the techniques made it possible to use various constraint propagation techniques and thereby avoid unnecessary combinatorics.

While Dart was faster than single-abstraction diagnostic methods (such as the d-algorithm), computational cost remained a problem. One way we tried to deal with inefficiency was to invent smarter inference procedures. David Smith, Richard Treitel, and Jeff Finger devoted their doctoral theses to finding improved search control strategies to alleviate this problem. Another avenue we explored was automatic reformulation of design descriptions into more efficient forms. Following up on this idea led Narinder Singh and Devika Subramanian to their doctoral theses. A final approach to dealing with inefficiency was to compile design descriptions into Mycin-like symptom–fault rules. As we knew from our work on improving Mycin's explanation capability, it was possible to generate a set of diagnostic rules automatically. The disadvantage of this approach was that the generation cost was extremely large, since the compiler had to take into account all possible failures and combinations of failures.

3. Helios

The implementation of Dart left us with one additional worry – where do we get the design information it needs? Our original idea was to get the information from design workstations used by designers in creating their products. The problem was that most design workstations in those days were awkward to use, and few top designers were inclined to use them. Rather than waiting for CAD vendors to improve their products sufficiently to remedy this situation, we decided to tackle the problem ourselves. This led to the creation of Helios.

Helios was a successor to a CAD program called Palladio, developed by Harold Brown and Gordon Foyster of Stanford in collaboration with Danny Bobrow and Mark Stefik from Xerox Palo Alto Research Center. Helios was written over a number of years by many people, with early contributions (ca. 1985) by Narinder Singh, Terry Barnes, and Glenn Kramer of Stanford and later contributions (ca. 1988) by Jon Schlossberg and Brian Livesey of Lockheed.

Like Dart, Helios was broad enough to handle the design of arbitrary discrete devices. It included a graphical editor that allowed its user to enter information about the structure and behavior of a device and the rationale for various design decisions. This interface provided different graphical languages for different types of information, such as schematics, tables, and free-form constraints. Once the design description was entered, the system was able to perform a variety of services, including automated simulation, semi-automated design debugging, automated testability analysis, automated test pattern generation, and automated diagnosis.

In designing Helios, we took advantage of three key ideas to make the program as desirable as possible. The first idea was the capture of extensive information about a design. The program provided a way for the user to describe a device at any level of abstraction from block diagrams to detailed schematics. It allowed the user to supply information about the structure and behavior of the device but also design alternatives and the rationale for selecting among these alternatives. The second idea was timely feedback on design decisions, an idea that even then was being developed in other communities under the heading *design for manufacturability* and *design for testability*. Helios provided automatic analysis of testability. The third idea was extensive automation, i.e. all those services the system was able to provide.

Helios was used by two different design groups affiliated with the Logic Group—one at the Knowledge Systems Laboratory and the other at Schlumberger Palo Alto Research Center. It was also transferred to Boeing, Grumman, Lockheed, and various other organizations.

Although the program's interface was a hit with these groups, the rest of the program was less popular. Few used any of the capabilities other than the simulator, and many found the simulator to be too slow. Although we had planned to produce a compiler for our simulator to enhance efficiency and eliminate this need, the compiler was not then available.

The concept of Helios enjoyed much greater success than the implementation. Some of the basic ideas were picked up by vendors like Applicon, and the concept of integrated engineering services was used in the implementation of succeeding programs like NVisage at Lockheed and Tenenbaum's MKS. We in the Logic Group also incorporated those concepts into Designworld.

4. Designworld

Designworld is the current focus of application work in the Logic Group. As implemented, it is an automated prototyping system for digital circuits built from standard parts (TTL chips, prototyping boards, and connectors).

The distinguishing feature of Designworld is that it provides support for all aspects in the life cycle of the prototype—from early design, through manufacture, to maintenance. The designers enter information about the prototype using Helios-like workstations. The system automatically lays out the circuit, plans the assembly, and executes its plan using a robotic assembly cell. If the prototype malfunctions in use, it can be returned to the robotic assembly cell for automated diagnosis and repair (using an updated version of Dart).

The concept of Designworld is similar to that of desktop publishing. The user of a desktop publishing system typically interacts with a "what-you-see-is-what-you-get" editor to create the desired document on the computer screen and then uses a laser printer to produce the hardcopy. In Designworld, the robot assembly cell is the printer, and the CAD workstation is the editor. The user creates his design on the screen, and the robotic cell "prints" the hardware.

Although it is not really relevant to the users of Designworld, the architecture of the system is an important part of the Designworld for AI researchers. In its current form, the system consists of eighteen different programs, written by eight programmers in two languages, running in ten processes on six machines.

In building the system, we dealt with this complexity through the use of the techniques of *agent-based software engineering*. In this approach, programs are written as modules called *software agents*. These programs can use whatever data structures and algorithms their programmers like so long as they are able to communicate with their peers in a particular implementation-independent language. The collaboration of these agents is assisted through the use of an application-independent program called a *facilitator*.

The value of agent-based software engineering is that the burden of interoperability is placed on the system rather than the programmers or users. Individual programmers can write their programs without knowledge of the data structures and algorithms of other programs, without knowledge of the hardware configuration in which those programs are going to be run. Computer users can avail themselves of the services of different programs by asking their systems to coordinate their interaction. For these reasons, it appears that this approach to software engineering may have applicability in the future that reaches far beyond its origin in the engineering world.

Since the implementation of Designworld, this approach has been used to integrate programs on an even larger scale (most notably in the Palo Alto Collaborative Testbed (PACT), which incorporates Designworld, NVisage, MKS, and DME). There are also plans to expand this effort to a nationwide experiment in the coming years.

5. Conclusion

The progress of technology in this century has brought about products of unprecedented complexity. Devices like VLSI chips, nuclear power plants, and jet aircraft are among the most complex physical devices ever created by man. Unfortunately, with increased complexity has come increased difficulty in all aspects of product engineering. Dart and Helios and Designworld are three steps on the road to dealing with this difficulty.

Designworld represents an especially significant point on this road—the point at which the balance of responsibility for a product shifts from the human engineer to the computer engineer. It is the point at which we switch from computer-*aided* engineering to computer-*based* engineering (or, as Reed Letsinger has called it, *human-aided engineering*).

Although Designworld is intended primarily for use within engineering environments, we expect that it will someday be possible to create popular versions of Designworld, which would allow consumers to specify custom products, produce them, and obtain service, with minimal knowledge of the underlying technology. In this event, there is likely to be a shift of balance from mass production to custom design (in which products are ordered by feature rather than by stock number).

The exact nature of engineering technology in the future is uncertain. However, it is a good bet that that future holds a greater degree of automation than anything we have seen thus far. It is also a good bet that the ideas developed in the AI community will be essential in creating that technology. We have spent the last decade developing these ideas, and we plan to spend the next decade continuing this work.

Reference

[1] M.R. Genesereth, The use of design descriptions in automated diagnosis, *Artif. Intell.* **24** (1984) 411–436.

Artificial Intelligence 59 (1993) 167–180
Elsevier

ARTINT 998

Categorical and probabilistic reasoning in medicine revisited *

Peter Szolovits

MIT, Laboratory for Computer Science, 545 Technology Square, Cambridge, MA 02139, USA

Stephen G. Pauker

Division of Clinical Decision Making, Department of Medicine, New England Medical Center, Tufts University School of Medicine, 750 Washington Street, Boston, MA 02111, USA

1. Introduction

Our 1978 paper [27] reviewed the artificial intelligence-based medical (AIM) diagnostic systems. Medical diagnosis is one of the earliest difficult intellectual domains to which AI applications were suggested, and one where success could (and still can) lead to benefit for society. The early 1970s brought Schwartz's clarion call to adopt computers to augment human reasoning in medicine [24], Gorry's rejection of older flowchart and probabilistic methods [11], and the first demonstrations of "expert systems" that could indeed achieve human expert-level performance on bounded but challenging intellectual tasks that were important to practicing professionals, such as symbolic mathematics and the determination of chemical structure. By the mid-1970s, a handful of first-generation medical AI systems had been developed, demonstrated, and at least partially evaluated. Although the methods employed appeared on the surface to be very different, we identified the underlying knowledge on which each operated and classified the general methods they used. We emphasized the distinction between the "categorical" or structural knowledge of the programs and the particular

Correspondence to: P. Szolovits, MIT, Laboratory for Computer Science, 545 Technology Square, Cambridge, MA, USA. E-mail: psz@medg.lcs.mit.edu.

*Supported in part by grants R01 LM 04493 from the National Library of Medicine and HS 6503 and HS 6665 from the agency for Health Care Policy and Research.

calculi they employed to approximate some form of probabilistic reasoning. Our analysis also suggested that alternative combinations of these methods could be equally well applied to solve diagnostic problems.

In this note, we explore several research themes concerning medical expert systems that have emerged during the past fifteen years, review the roles of diagnosis and therapy in medicine, and make some observations on the future of medical AI tools in the changing context of clinical care. This paper is discursive; for a more complete treatment of these issues, please refer to the paper, "The third decade of artificial intelligence in medicine: challenges and prospects in a new medical era" [28].

2. Reasoning about multiple diagnoses

One difficulty encountered by most of the initial AIM programs was how to deal with the simultaneous presence of multiple disorders. The AIM programs we described in 1978 each took a different, and not altogether satisfactory, approach. Basically, CASNET/Glaucoma concerned only a single disease. MYCIN worked in a domain in which any strongly suspected disease must be treated because the risk of not treating a serious infection typically far outweighs the risk of the treatment. Thus, whether two suspected infections might actually both be present or might really represent an ambiguous presentation of a single infection, MYCIN proposed treatment for both. PIP considered all disorders to be competitors to explain all findings unless the disorders were connected by causal or associational links. PIP therefore tended to produce many alternative explanations for a case, each centered on a likely actual disorder but with no indication that some combinations of disorders were more suitable diagnostic conclusions. INTERNIST had a clever partitioning heuristic that helped sort out and allocate specific findings to particular disorders and worked well when asked to identify co-occurring disorders whose findings neither overlapped significantly nor interfered with each other; it was weak, however, at identifying clusters of related diseases, such as might arise in the multiple facets of a systemic disorder.

Although Pople [20] suggested interesting heuristics for dealing with multiple disorders and reformulated diagnosis as a search problem, Reggia [21], Reiter [22], and de Kleer and Williams [6] best formalized and solved at least a simplified version of the multiple-diagnosis problem. These efforts consider the simplified case where the knowledge base consists of a bipartite graph of diseases (each unrelated to the other) and findings (also unrelated to each other), interconnected so that each disease is linked to each finding that it may cause. Reggia's insight was that for such a knowledge base, an adequate diagnosis consisted of a minimal set of diseases whose associated findings covered the set of observed findings. Normally, there is no unique minimal set, and additional criteria (e.g., likelihood) could be used to select among alternative minimal candidate sets. This process is, in general, combinatorial, and careful guidance is needed to achieve practical performance. Wu [32,33] has recently shown that a heuristic but robust symptom clustering method dramatically improves search performance by introducing the equivalent of "planning islands" in the overall diagnostic process: it first partitions the symptoms into sets in which all symptoms must have a common explanation; then it performs differential diagnosis among the possible causes of each set. The overall diagnosis will identify a single disorder as the cause of each set of symptoms. An efficient factored representation cuts down combinatorial growth of the search space. The simple bipartite model is not entirely satisfactory, however. It does not deal well with situations in which the absence of a particular observation is key, nor with keeping clear the distinction between a finding that is unknown because its presence has yet to be investigated and one that is known to be absent.

3. Reasoning at multiple levels of detail

Each of the programs we surveyed in 1978 based its reasoning on associations among diseases or abnormal states and their manifestations, without any explicit representation of the mechanisms whereby the diseases caused their symptoms. In cases where two or more disorders interact, such associational methods either require explicit encoding of the effects of all possible combinations of disorders (prohibitive for sizable domains) or some generative theory that allows the program to predict their joint effects. Such a generative theory must typically be based on a much more causal and possibly quantitative description of the domain than what would serve to diagnose isolated disorders. An easy illustration is the case of two diseases, one of which raises the blood concentration of some ion, the other of which lowers it. In this case, a measurement of that ion in the blood can indicate only the relative severity and duration of the two disorders, and may take on virtually any value. In particular, it could be perfectly normal if the two disorders happen to cancel out in this dimension. Yet it would be odd for an associational diagnostician to link both disorders with a normal level of that ion!

This problem is far more common in contemporary medicine than one might at first imagine, because almost any identifiable disease normally elicits medical treatment. One goal of treatment is to eliminate the underlying disturbance, but another common one is to compensate for abnormalities caused by the disease, to keep the patient in some stable state, even if not perfectly healthy. But each instance of this leads precisely (and deliberately) to just the sorts of interactions that make associational diagnosis difficult. Furthermore, even when a diagnosis is not firmly established, empiric treatments or therapeutic trials often produce partially treated (and often partially obscured) diseases. Although it is tempting therefore to adopt a diagnostic strategy based on reasoning from first principles about the possible consequences of any combinations of diseases and their treatments, this turns out to be impractical for several reasons. First, much of medicine remains a sufficient mystery that even moderately accurate models are beyond our knowledge. Second, even in domains where such models have been developed (e.g., circulatory dynamics), the models require a level of detail and consistency of global analysis that is clinically not achievable.

Ideally, a program should reason simply about simple cases and resort to a more complex generative theory only when the actual complexity of the case requires it. Human experts appear to have this skill—to recognize simple cases as simple, to recognize minor discrepancies as minor, and, after a cursory ruling out of potentially serious alternatives, to treat the cases as adequately solved. With this skill, intensive investigation is reserved for cases (or aspects of cases) that actually involve complicated interactions or serious discrepancies and require deeper thought. How is a program to recognize, however, that a case thought to be simple really is not? And how is it to do so without concluding that every case is complex?

Patil's ABEL program for diagnosing acid–base and electrolyte disorders [18] employed a five-level pathophysiological model in which the top level contained associational links among clinically significant states and lower levels introduced successively more physiological detail, until the lowest layer represented our most detailed biochemical understanding of the mechanisms of acid–base physiology (at least as clinicians think of it). ABEL would begin by trying to construct a consistent explanation at the highest level, and then would use discrepancies between that model's predictions and subsequently gathered data as the clue that more detailed investigation was needed. Although this insight is valuable, the technique suffered some important deficiencies: As soon as any unexpected finding arose, its control strategy would tend to "dive" down to the deepest model layer because that is the one at which quantitative measurements could best resolve questions of interaction among multiple disturbances. In its narrow domain, this was tolerable, but more generally it leads to a very detailed and costly analysis of any case that departs from the textbook norm. Furthermore, a discrepancy detected in a hypothesis at some level could actually mean either that a more detailed analysis will lead to an incrementally augmented successful hypothesis, or that this hypothesis should be abandoned in favor of one of its competitors.

A few other successful programs in non-medical domains (e.g., Hamscher's program for diagnosing faulty circuit boards by considering their aggregate temporal behavior [13]) have also demonstrated the value of more abstract or aggregate levels of representation in diagnostic problem solving, but a clear exposition and formal analysis of this approach remains in the future.

4. Doing probabilities "right"

Medical diagnosis is innately an uncertain business, due to our imperfect understanding of medicine, variations among individual patients, measurement and observational errors, etc. Numerical measures, such as probabilities, are a convenient and conventional way to summarize uncertainty and are an essential part of medical diagnosis programs. Programs in the mid-1970s used a variety of metrics and mechanisms for propagation, inspired by classical probability theory, fuzzy set theory, Dempster–Shafer belief functions, and other formalisms. Bayesian probabilities were often taken as the norm, but were thought to be impractical. Our paper argued, for example, that a full accounting for non-independence would require vast numbers of estimated joint probabilities for even a small diagnostic problem. The alternative, assuming global independence, was clearly wrong. CASNET/Glaucoma used a causal–associational network that could be interpreted to represent probabilistic dependence, but it was overloaded because it also attempted to represent temporal progression of disease. Weiss' formulas for propagating numerical estimates of certainty, therefore, were a combination of probabilistic, fuzzy set, and heuristic approaches, and did not easily lend themselves to systematic analysis. INTERNIST used crudely quantized scores that seemed somewhat like log odds. MYCIN presented an idiosyncratic system of certainty factors that had to be revised in response to empirical inadequacies. We considered interpreting the causal and associational links in PIP as probabilistic influences, but our attempts to assign both prior probabilities to every node in the graph and conditional probabilities along links led to an over-constrained model that we failed to solve by relaxation methods. Duda and Hart [7] had presented an uncertainty scheme based on propagation of likelihood ratios, but required fudge factors to make the estimated values non-contradictory.

The early 1980s finally saw insightful analyses of networks of probabilistic dependence by Cooper and Pearl, and Pearl's formulation [19] has had a revolutionary impact on much of AI. (It is interesting to note, by the way, that equivalent techniques had been published by geneticists interested in the analysis of pedigrees with inbreeding in 1975, but were unknown to the general computer science community until very recently.) The critical insight here is that in even large networks of interrelated nodes (representing, say, diseases and symptoms), most nodes are not directly related to most others; indeed, it is only a very small subset of all the possible links that need be present to represent the important structure of the domain. When such a network is singly-connected, efficient methods can propagate the probabilistic consequences of hypotheses and observations. When there are multiple connections among portions of the network, exact evaluation is combinatorial, but may still be practical for networks with few multiple connections. Approximation methods based on sampling are relatively fast, but cannot guarantee the accuracy of their estimates. With these new powerful probabilistic propagation methods, it has become possible to build medical expert systems that obey a correct Bayesian probabilistic model. Cooper's program [5] for diagnosing hypercalcemic disorders has been followed by MUNIN [1] (for diagnosing muscle diseases), PATHFINDER [14] (for pathology diagnosis), and BUNYAN [31] (for critiquing clinically oriented decision trees). Several other programs now use these techniques, in domains ranging from physiological monitoring to trying to recast the INTERNIST (now QMR) knowledge base in strictly probabilistic terms. Eddy [8] has been developing a related basis for supporting and quantifying the uncertainty in inferences based on partial data from separate studies.

5. Reasoning about therapy

Although it is tempting to view medical management as a sequential process consisting first of diagnosis and then of therapy, the separation of those two phases, with an expert system focusing primarily on one or the other, is too simplistic. In 1978 our descriptions of first generation AIM programs presented an iterative diagnostic process that included context formation, information gathering, information interpretation, hypothesis generation, and hypothesis revision. A second module, in programs that contained it, was invoked to select therapy, typically from a rather straightforward table or list, but only when the diagnosis had been established. The probabilistic threshold or categorical rule by which a diagnosis is established must be explicitly specified so that the diagnostic program has clearly defined "stopping criteria". In some programs those thresholds and rules were based on information content alone (either how certain the leading diagnosis is or how unlikely the next leading contending hypothesis is), whereas in others those cutoff points included explicit consideration of the risks and benefits of errors of omission and commission. In programs whose focus was purely diagnostic, like PIP and INTERNIST, such criteria were either arbitrary or altogether absent.

In medical practice, the management process is far more complex, with diagnostic reasoning and therapeutic action belonging to a spectrum of options that are presented and manipulated iteratively. First, the patient's presenting or chief complaint allows the clinician to form a context for further management. Of course, context revision occurs as additional information is acquired and processed. As Kassirer and Kopelman [15] and Elstein have noted, the physician gathers and then interprets information, typically in discrete chunks. It would seem only reasonable for the clinician to process all available information before electing either to gather more information, to perform an additional test that carries some risk or cost, to undertake a therapeutic maneuver (be it administering a drug or submitting the patient to surgery), or to announce a diagnosis. In actual practice, though, physicians will often take an action before all the available information has been processed. Because the "complete" interpretation of all available information can be costly in terms of time and processing effort, the physician sometimes feels compelled to deal with either seemingly urgent or important hypotheses even while additional information remains in the input list. Of course, some preprocessing and ranking of the list usually occurs to identify critical findings that require immediate attention.

Actions to be taken may be clearly therapeutic, clearly diagnostic, or more likely may represent a mixture of goals. When a therapy is given, the patient's response often provides important information that allows refinement or modification of diagnostic hypotheses. Silverman's Digitalis Therapy Advisor [12] and its progeny (Long's Heart Failure Program [16] and Russ' approach to diabetic ketoacidosis [23]), as well as ONCOCIN [25], VM [9], and T-HELPER [29] utilize such responses in either simple rules or a complex network to improve diagnostic certainty. Even diagnostic maneuvers often affect patient outcomes. Tests can produce complications that introduce either entirely new diseases, that make the existing disease more severe, or that preclude certain therapeutic options.

Expert system-based decision support can address many phases of patient management, but as yet, no integrated system has addressed the entire problem, even in rather limited domains. In our 1978 paper, we applied the terms probabilistic and categorical reasoning exclusively to medical diagnosis. We now believe that such a classification scheme should be applied to therapeutic problems as well. Although therapy selection might be considered to be largely a categorical process (e.g., given a diagnosis and perhaps a set of complicating factors, optimal therapy can be defined by a simple table, algorithm, or heuristic), it need not be. Quantitative and probabilistic information is available about the benefits and risks of alternative therapies (even at different stages of an evolving disease), and the risks, benefits, costs, and efficiencies of different strategies must be weighed. In the 1990s, it is no longer sufficient to say that pneumocystis pneumonia in a patient with AIDS is treated in the hospital. One must ask whether therapy can be delivered on an out-patient basis and what patient characteristics should dictate the choice and setting of therapy. Analogously, thrombolytic therapy has become the standard therapy for patients with acute myocardial infarction, but we must consider whether or not it should be administered to patients with suspected infarction as well. Although such therapeutic tradeoffs can and perhaps should be approached quantitatively and explicitly, they are now prey to implicit clinical judgment because the explicit process is often too cumbersome and inadequately explicated for the practicing physician. Perhaps expert systems can help.

6. Machinable data

Perhaps the greatest limitation to providing medical decision support is the absence of clinical data that can be conveniently accessed by such programs and the inability to incorporate either computer or paper-based decision support into the physician's daily routine in an efficient manner. Although decision support has been included in hospital information systems such as Pryor and Warner's HELP [30] and although new information systems have been designed for some AIM projects like ONCOCIN, the total absence—or certainly the lack of uniformity—of credible hospital and office practice information systems means that the clinician must manually enter her patients' clinical information, typically in a somewhat different format and with a different syntax and vocabulary for each program she might want to use. Although this problem will eventually be ameliorated by the standardization that MacDonald proposes [17] and by unification of medical terminology (such as Lindberg's UMLS), it will remain problematic for most practice settings at least for the next decade.

The importance of having slick and efficient "front ends" to make any system acceptable is particularly important in dealing with medical professionals who are often pressed simultaneously by the double burdens of limited time and enhanced responsibility. We believe, however, that an efficient and perhaps invisible "back end" connection to both the patient's clinical data and to a variety of knowledge bases is even more important. In system development and maintenance, the medical informatician must have access to large clinical datasets, to create appropriate interfaces and to develop knowledge from the clinical data elements. In the past, such access has been either developed manually in a single institution or has used a registry (local or national) of relevant cases (e.g., ARAMIS [10], Duke Cardiovascular Database [4]). Given the expense and administrative problems of collecting such special datasets for a broad spectrum of disease, we believe that expert system developers will need to rely increasingly on general hospital information systems, hoping to merge data from a variety of such sources. One additional information source is readily available, although as yet of only limited utility: the large administrative datasets, such as those maintained by HCFA and private insurers. Although the primary motivation for maintaining such datasets is financial and although the clinical information in them is often sparse, they have revealed important lessons about variations and patterns of care and complications. The routine inclusion of some clinical information in those datasets will surely increase. The AIM community should have at least two lines of interest in these datasets. First, they may provide useful machinable information for expert system development. Second, the adaptation of such administrative data to provide clinical insights about clinical practice is complex but will occur increasingly. Expertise in this process is, however, limited to a few groups and poorly distributed. The development of expert systems to manage, query, and interpret responses from such datasets may be an important new domain for system development.

In providing expert system-based decision support for clinicians, the AIM community must rely on developers of medical information systems to support AIM projects, both by supplying machinable data and by presenting decision support to the clinician in a timely and efficient manner. For decision support to be relevant, it must be provided at the time that choices must be made. The clinician must not need to interrupt her flow of activity either to enter information to the expert system or to review the suggestions of the system. When the clinician is making a choice among therapies and writing the relevant orders, she must have access to any advice the system provides, whether that advice is individualized to the specifics of the patient at hand or is generic, suggesting something that should apply to all patients with that problem.

Substantial effort is being devoted to developing guidelines and algorithms for clinical care. To the extent that such paper-based decision support is read by the clinician and perhaps even filed in a notebook over her desk, its implementation will be limited by the clinician's ability to remember the details of the often complex guideline. Much as a logistic regression equation or its daughter, a clinical decision rule, can be quite misleading if certain terms are omitted, even the most carefully crafted guideline can produce grossly inadequate care if it is not followed in its entirety. If critical loops and checks are omitted because they are not remembered, then the guided care may be misguided. A related problem arises if the guideline is applied in an inappropriate context or to the wrong patient. Similarly, expert system developers must be cognizant of the environment in which their decision support tool will be placed so its database is as complete as necessary and so its advice can be followed as completely as possible. Developers must also be careful to include surface or common sense checks to detect situations in which the system is applied inappropriately in a setting for which it was not intended and must anticipate that the system's advice may not be followed completely. Given the limitations of the clinical environment, we believe that all such implementations must include a feedback and iteration phase so that errors, mistranslations, and omissions can be detected and corrected in a timely fashion, not only for the patient at hand but for future applications of the guideline, rule, or tool.

7. Problem breadth

Expert systems in medicine have always represented a mix of domains—broad (e.g., the general diagnostic problem in medicine as evidenced by INTERNIST, and now DxPLAIN [3] and QMR [2]) and narrow (e.g., CASNET/Glaucoma, MYCIN, ABEL, ONCOCIN). The attraction of the broad domain has always been to provide a critical mass of expertise in one system, such that it was applicable to many patients and physicians. Yet if one examines critically the successes of expert systems outside of medicine, the importance of a narrow focus becomes clear. The general diagnostic problem is just too hard and covers too much territory both for knowledge capture and knowledge-base maintenance and for the efficient application of reasoning algorithms. Although both QMR and DxPlain have interesting behaviors which clinicians find fascinating and initially helpful, the problem of inappropriate context and false positives ("false drops" in the vernacular of the medical library science) may become sufficiently annoying to limit continuing use. These programs serve to jog the clinician's memory and suggest unconsidered possibilities (often unusual ones) but do not tend to replace consultation by an experienced clinician. Narrower, more specialized systems may have a more compelling, if limited impact. However, a proliferation of specialized systems, each relying on its idiosyncratic interface, database, forms of explanation, and medical knowledge base, cannot offer a satisfactory systematic solution to the broad needs of clinical medicine. Much remains to be done in creating common frameworks in which specialized systems can work effectively together to produce a usable and useful whole.

8. New themes in medicine

Medicine is changing. The past quarter century has been called the golden years of medicine. But knowledge and technology, exploding at breakneck pace, have run headlong into the wall of resource limitation. Fueled by the need to constrain the unchecked expansion of medical resource use, which even now consumes some 10% of our gross national product (contributing more to the cost of Detroit's now non-competitive behemoths than does their steel), the clinician is for the first time beset by the need to consider the resources that her care consumes, to explain and justify her care, to be accountable for both the cost of care and any adverse outcomes that may occur, and to explain variations in the kind and intensity of care she provides, especially if those variations increase cost or the number of procedures performed. Unfortunately, by both education and temperament most clinicians are ill-equipped to prosper or even to survive professionally on the new playing field.

When medicine first provided a fertile playground for computer scientists developing artificial intelligence approaches to problem solving, the primary concern was the distribution of expertise to medically underserved areas. Physicians were increasingly less able to capture knowledge and update their personal knowledge bases because the exponential expansion of medical information was producing an unmanageable tide. Thus, programs focused on making a correct diagnosis and demonstrating expertise similar to that of experienced clinicians. These programs also addressed the variability of patients' presentations and the optimization of therapy based on such variations. The goal was not to minimize variation but rather to maximize flexibility.

In the third decade of AIM, the goals of a relevant expert system have changed and additional attributes must be considered. The use of health care resources must be made more efficient. For hospitalized patients, length of stay must be minimized, within the constraints of not compromising therapeutic efficacy or increasing the rate of complications. The process of care can no longer run without feedback or oversight. Health outcomes and resource use must be accurately quantified and monitored.

The new goals redefine both relevant expertise for medical practice and decision support. The expert system developer may no longer be able just to simulate the behavior of experienced clinicians. The environment and its rules are new and evolving rapidly. Some experienced clinicians will adapt effectively to these additional concerns while others may be unable to alter their styles sufficiently. Expert systems may be able to provide important services in this environment but will likely need to be driven more directly by the new multi-attribute goal structure.

9. Conclusions

In this brief note, we have surveyed the major technical advances in medical reasoning systems since our 1978 paper, described the shift from purely diagnostic programs to those whose concern is more with therapeutic management, reviewed changing needs and opportunities that are coming into play as medical data are becoming more routinely computerized, and outlined some dramatic changes in the practice of medicine itself that will have profound impacts on medical AI research in the coming years. We continue to be optimistic, although the dissemination and use of AIM systems has remained minuscule.

Physicians and other health care personnel seem unlikely to reject computer technology which has become ubiquitous in our society. It is already cheaper to maintain electronic rather than paper records, and pressures for accountability and cost containment will undoubtedly bring about the availability of machinable data that we had anticipated long ago.

Dramatic advances in genetics and molecular biology that will surely result from the Human Genome Project will fuel both clinicians' information overload and create further technological imperatives for diagnosis and therapy. So long as constraints of cost, laboratory capacity, and human cognition remain, however, difficult diagnostic and therapeutic choices in clinical care will be necessary. The methods of model-based reasoning being developed by AIM researchers may take a more prominent role in clinical informatics as more detailed models become available. Constraining the use of such models to appropriate contexts, getting multiple models to interact in the absence of an overarching model, and developing abstract models for reasoning when detailed data are unavailable will continue to pose formidable and exciting technical challenges.

Changes in medicine call into question some of AIM's original goals while providing new challenges. Twenty years ago, an anticipated severe shortage of well-trained physicians motivated, in large part, the development of AIM systems. Today we speak of a doctor glut; the proliferation of physicians appears to generate a proliferation of medical services. Early efforts focused on improving the quality of care for all patients to that provided by the world's foremost experts. Today society values more highly uniform, accessible care at prices we can all afford. These factors suggest that AIM programs should be an integral part of a broader system to support all aspects of health care delivery, evaluation, and policy.

References

[1] S. Andreassen, M. Woldbye, B. Falck and S. Andersen, MUNIN: a causal probabilistic network for interpretation for electromyographic findings, in: *Proceedings IJCAI-87*, Milan, Italy (1987) 366–372.
[2] R.A. Bankowitz, M.A. McNeil, S.M. Challinor, R.C. Parker, W.N. Kapoor and R.A. Miller, A computer-assisted medical diagnostic consultation service, *Ann. Internal Med.* **110** (10) (1989) 824–832.
[3] G.O. Barnett, J.J. Cimino, J.A. Hupp and E.P. Hoffer, DXplain: an evolving diagnostic decision-support system, *J. Am. Med. Assoc.* **258** (1987) 67–74.
[4] R.M. Califf, D.B. Pryor and J.C. Greenfield, Beyond randomized clinical trials: applying clinical experience in the treatment of patients with coronary artery disease, *Circulation* **74** (1986) 1191–1194.

[5] G.F. Cooper, NESTOR: a computer-based medical diagnostic aid that integrates causal and probabilistic knowledge, Ph.D. Thesis, Medical Information Sciences, Stanford, CA (1986).

[6] J. de Kleer and B.C. Williams, Diagnosing multiple faults, *Artif. Intell.* **32** (1987) 97–130.

[7] R.O. Duda, P.E. Hart and N.J. Nilsson, Subjective Bayesian methods for rule-based inference systems, in: *AFIPS Conference Proceedings* **45** (1976) 1075–1082.

[8] D.M. Eddy, V. Hasselblad and R. Shachter, *Meta-analysis by the Confidence Profile Method: The Statistical Synthesis of Evidence* (Academic Press, Boston, MA, 1992).

[9] L.M. Fagan, VM: representing time-dependent relations in a medical setting, Ph.D. Thesis, Stanford University, Stanford, CA (1980).

[10] J.F. Fries, Time-oriented patient records and a computer databank, *J. Am. Med. Assoc.* **222** (1972) 1536.

[11] G.A. Gorry, Computer-assisted clinical decision making, *Methods Inf. Med.* **12** (1973) 45–51.

[12] G.A. Gorry, H. Silverman and S.G. Pauker, Capturing clinical expertise: a computer program that considers clinical responses to digitalis, *Am. J. Med.* **64** (1978) 452–460.

[13] W.C. Hamscher, Modeling digital circuits for troubleshooting, *Artif. Intell.* **51** (1991) 223–271.

[14] D. Heckerman, E. Horvitz and B. Nathwani, Toward normative expert systems, Part I: the Pathfinder project, *Methods Inf. Med.* **31** (1992) 90–105.

[15] J.P. Kassirer and R.I. Kopelman, *Learning Clinical Reasoning* (Williams and Wilkins, Baltimore, MD, 1991).

[16] W.J. Long, Medical diagnosis using a probabilistic causal network, *Appl. Artif. Intell.* **3** (2–3) (1989) 367–384.

[17] C.J. McDonald, Standards for the electronic transfer of clinical data: progress, promises, and the conductor's wand, in: *Proceedings Fourteenth Annual Symposium on Computer Applications in Medical Care* (1990) 9–14.

[18] R.S. Patil, P. Szolovits and W.B. Schwartz, Causal understanding of patient illness in medical diagnosis, in: *Proceedings IJCAI-81*, Vancouver, BC (1981) 893–899.

[19] J. Pearl, Fusion, propagation, and structuring in belief networks, *Artif. Intell.* **29** (1986) 241–288.

[20] H.E. Pople Jr, Heuristic methods for imposing structure on ill-structured problems: the structuring of medical diagnostics, in: P. Szolovits, ed., *Artificial Intelligence in Medicine* (Westview Press, Boulder, CO, 1982) 119–190.

[21] J.A. Reggia, D.S. Nau and P.Y. Wang, Diagnostic expert systems based on a set covering model, *Int. J. Man Mach. Stud.* **19** (1983) 437–460.

[22] R. Reiter, A theory of diagnosis from first principles, *Artif. Intell.* **32** (1987) 57–95.

[23] T.A. Russ, Reasoning with time dependent data, Ph.D. Thesis, Department of Electrical Engineering and Computer Science, Massachusetts Institute of Technology, Cambridge, MA (1991).

[24] W.B. Schwartz, Medicine and the computer: the promise and problems of change, *New England J. Med.* **283** (1970) 1257–1264.

[25] E.H. Shortliffe, A.C. Scott, M.B. Bischoff, A.B. Campbell, W. van Melle and C.D. Jacobs, ONCOCIN: an expert system for oncology protocol management, in: *Proceedings IJCAI-81*, Vancouver, BC (1981) 876–881.

[26] H. Silverman, A Digitalis Therapy Advisor, Project MAC, MIT Tech. Rept. TR-143, Cambridge, MA (1975).

[27] P. Szolovits and S.G. Pauker, Categorical and probabilistic reasoning in medical diagnosis, *Artif. Intell.* **11** (1978) 115–144.

[28] P. Szolovits and S.G. Pauker, The third decade of artificial intelligence in medicine: challenges and prospects in a new medical era, in preparation.

[29] S. Tu, Y. Shahar, J. Dawes, J. Winkles, A. Puerta and M. Musen, A problem-solving model for episodic skeletal-plan refinement, *Knowledge Acquisition* **4** (1992) 197–216.

[30] H.R. Warner, *Computer Assisted Medical Decision-Making* (Academic Press, New York, 1979).

[31] M.P. Wellman, M.H. Eckman, C. Fleming, S.L. Marshall, F.A. Sonnenberg and
     S.G. Pauker, Automated critiquing of medical decision trees, *Med. Decision Making*
     9 (4) (1989) 272–284.
[32] T.D. Wu, Efficient diagnosis of multiple disorders based on a symptom clustering
     approach, in: *Proceedings AAAI-90*, Boston, MA (1990) 357–364.
[33] T.D. Wu, Domain structure and the complexity of diagnostic problem solving, in:
     Proceedings AAAI-91, Anaheim, CA (1991) 855–861.

Artificial Intelligence 59 (1993) 181–189
Elsevier

ARTINT 978

Retrospective on "Production rules as a representation for a knowledge-based consultation program"

Randall Davis

Artificial Intelligence Laboratory, Massachusetts Institute of Technology, Cambridge, MA 02139, USA

Bruce G. Buchanan

Computer Science Department, University of Pittsburgh, Pittsburgh, PA 15260, USA

Edward H. Shortliffe

Section on Medical Informatics, Department of Medicine, Stanford University School of Medicine, Stanford, CA 94305-5479, USA

Origins

Work at the Stanford Medical Center in the early 1970s had produced a successful system called Mediphor, which monitored prescriptions sent to the pharmacy and issued warnings of interactions among the multiple drugs prescribed for a patient. The original conception of MYCIN was as a follow-on: where Mediphor had checked for inappropriate combinations of drugs, MYCIN was to send warnings about inappropriate selection of a single antibiotic for a particular patient.

It was intended to gather data from the clinical lab, the pharmacy, and the microbiology lab, then evaluate that data against a set of criteria for

Correspondence to: R. Davis, Artificial Intelligence Laboratory, Massachusetts Institute of Technology, Cambridge, MA 02139, USA. E-mail: davis@ai.mit.edu.

determining whether an antibiotic prescription was appropriate (e.g., data from the microbiology lab might indicate that the organism was known to be insensitive to the drug chosen).

Two major difficulties soon forced changes in this original conception. The first problem was data gathering: In the early 1970s networking three different computers was a research project by itself. Second, the breadth and complexity of the knowledge required for the task seemed to far exceed what had been required for the drug interaction problem.

In response to these difficulties, MYCIN was reconceived as both a stand-alone system (with a nurse or physician entering data), and one whose fundamental task was diagnosis and therapy selection (since determining whether a drug was appropriate had as a subgoal arriving at a diagnosis). We saw therapy recommendation as a feature distinguishing this project from other contemporary AI in medicine projects that generally focussed on only the diagnosis component.

The necessity of collecting data from the physician and the difficulty of dealing with natural language together led to the requirement that the program would have to ask questions, rather than allowing the physician to volunteer information. That in turn led to the choice of a goal-directed inference engine, which has in some ways become a hallmark of MYCIN-style systems in the years since.

The paper itself [6] was motivated by the recognition that the system had been described several times for medical audiences, but no comprehensive article had appeared in the AI literature. The authors shared the feeling that the fundamental mechanism that had evolved was not specific to medicine, and might be of considerable interest to a wider audience.

Key intellectual contributions

MYCIN seems to have served variously as a proof of existence, proof of adequacy, and proof of utility:

- Early work on production systems by Newell had introduced to AI the notion of a rule-based system, i.e., the idea that a program might consist almost solely of a collection of simple conditional statements. MYCIN showed that this could be employed on tasks of pragmatic significance and that it could be used at the "knowledge level", i.e., to capture what the expert knew, as well as at the symbol processing level, to model the details of how he thought (as used by Newell and others interested in cognitive modeling).
- MYCIN demonstrated that handling the uncertainty present in most real-world tasks was important and that an adequate empirical solution to the problem was available with relatively modest machinery.

- It was a demonstration that a few hundred rules could be adequate for tasks of intellectual and economic significance, helping to calibrate what it took to be good at a nontrivial task.

- It was an existence proof that, in one domain at least, knowledge really was modular enough to be captured as a set of mostly independent inferences.

- It was, like DENDRAL and MACSYMA before it, and like many programs since, an existence proof that knowledge can obviate search and complex control. Simply put, a surprising degree of performance can emerge with even trivial control, if you know enough. This was particularly notable in its time: the early 1970s was a period of intense interest in complex control structures as a foundation for intelligence (e.g., dependency-directed backtracking, PLANNER and CONNIVER's catch-and-throw mechanism, etc.). As a result, few would have predicted at that time that significant expertise, even in sharply restricted domains, could result from a collection of such simple machinery.

- It was (like Winograd's work in natural language) a demonstration of the adequacy of explanations produced by simply replaying the sequence inferences that lead to a conclusion, i.e., by reviewing an audit trail of the logic. This work also made the case that an explanation ability was sufficiently significant to an intelligent consultant that the ability become a common part of the definition of the term.

- It was, like DENDRAL and MACSYMA before it, an existence proof that experts can tell you what they know, can be systematically debriefed, and their knowledge captured in a program, a notion we take as routine now, but that was hardly a given then.

- It was a demonstration of the utility of the problem solving model that would later be called heuristic classification, and the utility of even a simple "snapshot" approach that made no attempt to model change over time.

- It mentioned briefly the notion of meta-rules, (explored in detail in [8]); one of the earliest examples of what would become a burst of interest in meta-knowledge of various forms and it introduced the concept of content-directed invocation of rules.

- The program employed some simple examples of what would later be called reflection, the ability of a system to examine its own state and reasoning. The previewing mechanism described in Section 3.4.2 relies on the system's ability to examine the code it is executing, while the explanation capabilities in Section 6.2 arise in large measure from the system's ability to read its rules back to the user, and to explore and describe the state of its goal stack.

- The program was an early illustration of the notion of multiple uses of the same knowledge, a theme that was to be explored at some length in the work that followed this paper in later years. As one early example, the identical rules that were invoked by the interpreter to arrive at a diagnosis were also examined by the explanation machinery to answer questions of the sort shown in Fig. 9 in the paper.

- Finally, the paper gives an early report on work in knowledge acquisition, providing preliminary results on what would later be called the TEIRESIAS system [8]. It alludes to such notions as focusing knowledge acquisition by setting it in the context of an error by the system, an idea that would later provide useful leverage on the task of debriefing experts.

What was misunderstood or lost?

What was not well understood by the authors?

The article also displays some attitudes that, not surprisingly, seem slightly naive a decade later. The emphasis on "real-world" tasks, for instance, seems a bit over-done. But recall that in the mid-70s, AI as a field was only beginning to accept the legitimacy of studying specific application tasks, and was only beginning to appreciate that this might provide significant results of broad applicability.

A second naiveté in the article is evident in the knowledge representation vocabulary employed. Associative triples, (attribute, object, value), had been in wide use in AI, but for quite some time papers about MYCIN used the term "clinical parameter" in place of "attribute", reflecting the medical origins of the work.

While the article offers some considered thoughts on both the strengths and limitations of rules as a representation, one important claimed advantage— modularity—was not always well stated, and the limitations, while acknowledged in general terms, were not (and at that time could not be) described in particularly substantive terms. That had to wait for another five years' or so experience (see, e.g., [9]).

Finally, early descriptions of MYCIN implied that building a knowledge-based system was little more than a task of accumulating a bag of rules, i.e., a relatively unstructured collection of associations. Later work by Clancey and others (e.g., [4]) helped to make clear that there was implicit in the rules a problem solving paradigm that came to be called heuristic classification. Recognition and explicit description of that paradigm has been a substantial aid in knowledge acquisition and in construction of subsequent systems.

What was misunderstood or lost by the readers?

Several systems built in later years would demonstrate that some readers misunderstood the nature of rules as a knowledge representation. At times considerable attention was paid to the *form* of rules (conditional statements) with a corresponding lack of attention to their *content* (empirical associations). There is of course an unfortunate syntactic similarity between these rules and the conditional statement used to direct control flow in standard programming languages. This similarity led to some confusion in which MYCIN-style rules were employed as a computational mechanism rather than a means of capturing inferences. The result was often a battle in which the system builder had to resort to a wide range of tricks to get a set of rules to produce traditional control constructs (e.g., [1]), all the while overlooking one of the original motivations for using a rule-based system: human problem solving often looks nothing like traditional control constructs.

Open issues

Diagnosis as a task

One of the issues that has become markedly clearer in the years since this paper came out is the richness and complexity of the task of diagnosis, as well as the advances needed in AI programs that hope to do that task (see, for example, [15, Chapter 9]). We have yet to understand and replicate how an expert diagnostician can organize and use a very large knowledge base about hundreds of diseases, yet focus on only a very few hypotheses at any one time.

Accomodating both procedural and inferential knowledge

Some of the things we know appear to be fundamentally inferential (e.g., if the patient is a college student complaining of fever and fatigue, the disease is likely to be mononucleosis), while others have a strongly procedural character ("to change the oil in your car, first get a large disposable container, then ..."). Each of these of course has a natural representation; the difficulty arises when tasks have both sorts of knowledge. In MYCIN, for example, the diagnostic task is fundamentally inferential, but there is also an overall seven-step procedure that structures the diagnosis [4]. The difficulty of dealing with both forms of knowledge at once is displayed by MYCIN's relatively obscure solution to the problem: it produces the seven steps as a side-effect of the backward chaining process and several carefully constructed rules.

One simple reason for this implicit encoding is that rules offer no easy way to express ordering information. A deeper reason is the dearth of fundamental insights about representations that facilitate expressing both forms of knowledge and allow them to work together intimately. The issue is not simply one of providing the computational machinery to allow rules to call procedures, or vice versa, but the lack of representational machinery that can guide our understanding, expression, and use of that knowledge. Integration at the level of computational machinery is easy; the needed synergy is at the knowledge level.

Representing and reasoning with uncertainty

The certainty factor model of uncertainty used in MYCIN [13] was subsequently widely adopted in rule-based systems, including some commercial expert system shells. While functionally adequate in some circumstances, as an ad hoc model it presented difficulty to system developers, who found the approach poorly defined and confusing. There was particular discomfort with the distinction between an absolute measure of belief (widely assumed to be the nature of a CF) and a belief update (the concept that was actually used in defining certainty factors in [13]).

Later experiments suggested that the model worked well for MYCIN's particular variety of diagnosis task, in which the goal was to determine the set of organisms for which a treatment plan should be devised, rather than selecting *the* correct diagnosis.

With the introduction of graphical computing environments and more powerful processors in the last decade, research on uncertainty management in AI systems has advanced significantly. Many of the constraints that limited the options for handling uncertainty in MYCIN (in particular, the arguments against trying to adopt a classical Bayesian statistical approach) are no longer valid. For example, Bayesian networks now provide a viable approach to building large diagnostic systems without making MYCIN's coarse and inherently flawed assumptions of conditional independence and knowledge modularity (see, for example, [3,10]).

Representing and reasoning about time

MYCIN reasoned about a snapshot of the patient at a single point in time. More sophisticated handling of temporal reasoning and management of time has of course been developed in the years since, but the issue of representing and reasoning about the temporal progression of a disease remains a challenging issue. This has been a central focus of work on ONCOCIN, a descendant of MYCIN (see, for example, [16]).

Model-based reasoning

As noted above, MYCIN's rules were written as empirical associations. The program did not use any structural or behavioral models of human anatomy, infecting organisms, or drugs, largely because they were (and are) not available. In the years since then, a considerable body of work has been done in model-based reasoning (see, e.g., [7]), but the area continues to offer substantial challenges.

Common sense reasoning

MYCIN encoded some common sense implicitly, but omitted the vast body of common sense carried by humans (e.g., there are two genders, only females get pregnant, etc.). MYCIN adopted a straightforward engineering solution of writing specific rules as needed. In recent years the problem of building a common sense knowledge base has been the focus of a major effort [11].

What can we build more easily as a result?

The set of ideas MYCIN codified and reduced to practice became one of the central enabling technologies in making knowledge-based systems a tool of broad applicability and utility. The number of direct and indirect offspring is quite broad; a few of the most direct results are illustrated in the "family tree" of Fig. 1.

What would we write differently?

With the benefit of hindsight, it's clear that the story would have been better told with more emphasis on the spirit of rules as a representation and less emphasis on the underlying mechanism. Understanding and specifying that spirit of course took some time, experience, and hindsight, but it would have improved the presentation. The paper would also have been improved by more understanding of and discussion of the limits of rules as a representation, as for example the difficulty rules present in trying to express problem solving strategies like iterative refinement or reasoning by process of elimination.

The future of the work

The family tree of Fig. 1 offers one view of what lay ahead in subsequent research; the set of 36 chapters in [2] provides a thorough overview of the set of experiments in rule-based systems that spanned the decade from 1972–1982. The NEOMYCIN node of the family tree sprouted its own prolific subtree with a long sequence of systems and experiments (see, e.g., [5]). A recent text on knowledge acquisition [12] recounts the ideas and insights resulting

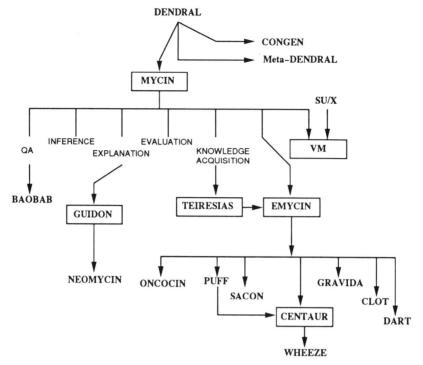

Fig. 1. HPP programs relating to MYCIN. (Program names in boxes were Ph.D. dissertation research programs.) [2, Fig. 1-3, p. 11]

from the almost twenty year's (!) worth of experience accumulated by its authors since those early experiments. Finally, ongoing work in designing medical computing environments closely matched to physician needs is described in [14].

References

[1] L. Brownston, R. Farrell, E. Kant and N. Martin, *Programming Expert Systems in OPS5* (Addison-Wesley, Reading, MA, 1985).

[2] B.G. Buchanan and E.H. Shortliffe, *Rule-Based Expert Systems: The MYCIN Experiments of the Stanford Heuristic Programming Project* (Addison-Wesley, Reading, MA, 1984).

[3] G.F. Cooper, Current research directions in the development of expert systems based on belief networks, *Appl. Stochastic Models Data Anal.* **5** (1989) 39–52.

[4] W.J. Clancey, Heuristic classification, *Artif. Intell.* **27** (1985) 289–350.

[5] W.J. Clancey, From GUIDON to NEOMYCIN to HERACLES in twenty short lessons, *AI Mag.* **7** (3) (1986) 40–50.

[6] R. Davis, B.G. Buchanan and E.H. Shortliffe, Production rules as a representation for a knowledge-based consultation program, *Artif. Intell.* **8** (1) (1977) 15–45.

[7] R. Davis and W. Hamscher, Model-Based Reasoning: Troubleshooting, in: H. Shrobe, ed., *Exploring Artificial Intelligence* (Morgan Kaufmann, Los Altos, CA, 1988)

[8] R. Davis and D.B. Lenat, *Knowledge-based Systems in Artificial Intelligence* (McGraw-Hill, New York, 1982).

 [9] D.E. Heckerman, Probabilistic similarity networks, *Networks* **20** (1990) 607–636.
[10] D.E. Heckerman and E.J. Horvitz, The myth of modularity in rule-based systems for reasoning with uncertainty, in: J.F. Lemmer and L.N. Kanal, eds., *Uncertainty in Artificial Intelligence* **2** (North-Holland, Amsterdam, 1988) 23–34.
[11] D.B. Lenat, R.V. Guha, K. Pittman, D. Pratt and M. Shepard, Cyc, toward programs with common sense, *Commun. ACM* **33** (8) (1990) 30–49.
[12] A.C. Scott, J. Clayton and E. Gibson, *A Practical Guide to Knowledge Acquisition* (Addison-Wesley, Reading, MA, 1991).
[13] E.H. Shortliffe and B.G. Buchanan, A model of inexact reasoning in medicine, *Math. Biosci.* **23** (1975) 351–379.
[14] E.H. Shortliffe, L.E. Perreault, G. Wiederhold and L.M. Fagan, *Medical Informatics: Computer Applications in Health Care* (Addison-Wesley, Reading, MA, 1990).
[15] H.E. Shrobe, ed., *Exploring AI* (Morgan Kaufmann, San Mateo, CA, 1988).
[16] S.W. Tu, M.G. Kahn, M.A. Musen, J.C. Ferguson, E.H. Shortliffe and L.M. Fagan, Episodic skeletal-plan refinement based on temporal data, *Commun. ACM* **32** (12) (1989) 1439–1455.

Artificial Intelligence 59 (1993) 191–196
Elsevier

ARTINT 976

Notes on
"Heuristic classification"

William J. Clancey

Institute for Research on Learning, 2550 Hanover Street, Palo Alto, CA 94304, USA

1. Introduction

The paper "Heuristic classification" [6] began as a memo written at Teknowledge, Inc. in late 1983, stemming from discussions with Steve Hardy and Denny Brown about how to teach knowledge engineering. We based our courses on a library of "sample knowledge systems" and looked for patterns that could be taught as design principles. Discussion raged about competing knowledge representations: rule versus frame languages, deep versus shallow systems, classification versus causal reasoning, first principles versus case-based modeling. Customers and students at Teknowledge pressed us to relate our products and terminology to our competitors' (what marketing people call "tool comparison"). Hardy and Brown wanted to relate our example systems to the "representation, inference, and control" framework, which they preferred for describing reasoning. I wanted to convince the developers of Teknowledge's S.1 and M.1 why a representation language should incorporate classification primitives.

Analyzing expert systems and articulating patterns was part of my continuing effort (with Jim Bennett) to encourage Teknowledge's programmers to develop task-specific tools [2]. We realized by 1982 that the Neomycin approach of abstracting the diagnostic inference procedure from the domain model produced a reusable shell that included not just an inference engine, but a task-specific representation language and reasoning procedure (the diagnostic metarules). The idea of reasoning patterns was therefore in the air and suggested commonalities that recurred across domains. Notably, Newell's "Knowledge-Level" AAAI Presidential Address at Stanford

Correspondence to: W.J. Clancey, Institute for Research on Learning, 2550 Hanover Street, Palo Alto, CA 94304, USA. E-mail: clancey@xerox.parc.

in August 1980 [18] impressed upon us the importance of levels of description, and the need to move our descriptions from the implementation (rules versus frames) to the conceptual level. I already had some experience in such cross-architecture comparisons (e.g., Section 7 of the "epistemology" paper [5] applied the structure–strategy–support framework to six knowledge-based systems ranging from AM to Hearsay).

2. A few clarifications

The strength of the "heuristic classification" article may be its generality, for it can be something to everyone. But there have been a few important misinterpretations:

(1) I strongly urged people not to view classification as an inherent property of problems. Classification is a *method* for constructing a situation-specific model; a given modeling *purpose*, such as diagnosis, might be accomplished in different ways, depending on the kind of model available. Problem types can be classified more usefully in terms of the purpose for constructing a model of some system in the world (i.e., the *tasks* of diagnosis, planning, control, repair, etc.).

(2) I distinguished between analytic and synthetic tasks, which I perhaps unfortunately labeled "interpret/analysis" and "construct/synthesis" (Figs. 5.1 and 5.2). A few readers confused these terms—which refer to analyzing an existing system in the world (e.g., predicting or explaining its behavior) or constructing a new system in the world (i.e., building it or repairing it)—with how the situation-specific model is *inferred*. The point of the article of course was to contrast inference by *selection* of models from a pre-enumerated classification with *construction* of models from structural and functional components related spatially, temporally, and causally. The typology of problem tasks refers to *why* the system is being modeled; the typology of inference methods refers to *how* the model is developed.

When writing the article, I was unsure how to contrast the process of constructing a line of reasoning in heuristic classification with the process of constructing a new model. Section 6.2.4 is one attempt, based on pre-enumerated versus new links between concepts. In "Model construction operators" (MCO) [11], I emphasize that construction of situation-specific model graphs is always occurring in expert systems; the distinction between Neomycin and Abel (for example) is what the nodes and links represent. For Neomycin, using heuristic classification, each node is a process description of the entire system being modeled (e.g., "there is a bacterial agent growing in the meninges of the central nervous system"). In Abel, which constructs a situation-specific model from primitives, the nodes represent physiological substances and processes *within* the system being modeled.

3. Redescribing by revisualizing

By the time I wrote MCO, I realized that many confusions about representations could be resolved if we see them as alternative perspectives on a single "virtual" formal system. In MCO, I relate node, path, subgraph, and graph views of inference [11, Section 3]. This theme plays throughout my work, as I realized that representations and reasoning processes that were commonly viewed as different could be related by a shift in visualization:

(1) Neomycin's causal-network-to-classification inference appeared in Casnet (I missed this at first because I drew horizontally what Weiss and Kulikowski drew vertically).

(2) Mycin's context tree constitutes a three-paneled blackboard (we missed this because we drew as a tree what others drew as layered boxes; we emphasized inheritance, they emphasized levels of description).

(3) Neomycin's differential (a list of diseases) can be better represented as an explanation-proof tree, which we call the *situation-specific model* (we missed this because we thought Abel was doing "deep" causal modeling while Neomycin was only doing "shallow" classification, that is, not modeling at all).

Many other examples appear in the figures of MCO (e.g., Figs. 17, 19, 27, 34, Table 5). Through this experience I developed the intuition that seemingly intractable debates about representations often stem from different visualizations or metaphors, and hence apparently incommensurable languages, not from inherent differences in the modeling methods of the programs being described. Bill Scherlis first impressed me with this possibility in 1979, when he argued that Mycin's rules could be expressed in predicate calculus, an idea that seemed sacrilegious at the time.

4. Revisualizing is reconceiving, not deriving, mapping, or compiling

Even when I realized that there were multiple perspectives for describing representations, I thought they must be derivable from each other, such as by a compilation process. For example, I had been asked by Keith Butler (at Boeing in 1984) to explain how common representational distinctions such as class/individual, type/subtype, and definition/schema relate to the heuristic classification framework. I found that these representational primitives play different roles: Definitions tend to be used for initial abstraction of data, schemas are used for heuristic association, and subtypes are used for both abstraction and refinement. Thus, we move from a concept or terminology-centered description of the knowledge base to a line-of-reasoning, data-to-solution perspective. When writing the article, I conceived of this analysis as "deriving" the horseshoe diagram from primitive relations (Section 4.4). But it is better to say that I shifted perspective from static concepts in isolation to how information about one concept is inferred from another (revealing an ordering of relations characterized as heuristic classification).

As I relate in my comments on the "epistemology" paper [12], attempting to generate patterns by reducing them to primitive representations is a powerful computational approach for constructing new and more generally useful process models. But it is also a scientific presumption about the nature of models and levels of description that is perhaps hampering our attempts to understand how people create and use representations (cf. Lave [15]). In particular, a common assumption is that there is always one "correct" description of a system and alternative representations must be logically inferable from each other (cf. Schön's [19] critique of analogical reasoning as structure mapping). This rests on the more general assumption that reality can be exhaustively modeled, with the idea that scientific laws (the "hidden truth of the matter") literally generate all the phenomena we observe. This parallels the prevalent belief of cognitive scientists that all human behavior is generated from a representational bedrock; in particular, tacit knowledge ("know how") must be compiled from representations. (Newell explicated this in his "brain as an orange" model, in which the "core" is knowledge compiled from a "rind" of production rules.) In effect, conflating knowledge, reality, and representations shaped the dilemmas of representational theory over the past few decades (Clancey [9,10]).

5. Lessons and impact

One idea in this article (Section 5) that I believe could be developed further is to integrate knowledge engineering with systems analysis. In MCO, I extend this argument to claim that AI programming should be conceived as a process-modeling technique, emphasizing qualitative or relational representations, as opposed to quantitative or numeric representations. Integrating these approaches to serve the needs of scientific and engineering modeling was at first obscured by the original emphasis that an expert system is necessarily related to how experts reason, by virtue of the knowledge "acquisition" process by which a human "transfers expertise" to the program.

For example, even though we weren't interested in strictly modeling human reasoning, we were biased against using numeric models in expert systems because we believed classification and rule-based inference to be a better model of human knowledge than equation manipulation.

Emboldened by the publication of the Winograd and Flores book [22], I first presented these ideas at the Oregon State Knowledge Compilation and Banff Knowledge Acquisition Workshops in October 1986. I argued that it is more fruitful and appropriate to characterize a knowledge base as a model of some system in the world coupled with a task-specific reasoning procedure [7], and to not equate a representation of knowledge (the knowledge base) with knowledge, a capacity to behave [10]. We should use whatever modeling techniques are useful for the problems at hand [8]. Furthermore, we should recognize that the qualitative modeling techniques of AI programming have a generality and value that extends beyond their initial development for representing human beliefs and reasoning (MCO). Framing AI research methods in this way helps us understand why numeric representations (for example, certainty factors) seem to violate the rules of the game; also this view is important for not dismissing the value of schema models as situated cognition calls assumptions about knowledge representation into question [10].

By focusing on graph manipulation operators in MCO, I aim to squarely place knowledge engineering in the realm of computer programming and operations research. Today we are less prone to confuse means (building on people's existing language and models) with goals (constructing models in order to facilitate scientific prediction and experimentation, as well as the design and maintenance of complex engineering and organizational systems). Significantly, the "information for authors" of the *Knowledge Acquisition* journal now says, "The emphasis is not on *artificial* intelligence, but on the extension of *natural* intelligence through knowledge-based systems."

The "heuristic classification" paper helped move arguments about representations from the level of programming constructs (e.g., rules versus frames) and conceptual networks (e.g., terminology classifications) to the level of *recurrent abstractions* in process modeling (e.g., kinds of taxonomies, how modeling tasks chain together). For example, the idea that causal inferences can feed into a classification, pioneered in Casnet and rediscovered in Neomycin, is now a commonplace modeling technique that can be taught explicitly to knowledge engineers and used to structure knowledge acquisition tools. Other researchers have gone beyond my promissory notes to deliver a second generation of process-modeling languages and tools (Alexander et al. [1]; Breuker and Wielinga [3]; Chandrasekaran [4]; Gruber [13]; Hayes-Roth et al. [14]; McDermott [16]; Musen [17]; Steels [20]; Stefik [21]). In many respects, the original hope behind my conversations with Steve Hardy and Denny Brown has been realized.

References

[1] J.H. Alexander, M.J. Freiling, S.J. Shulman, J.L. Staley, S. Rehfuss and M. Messick, Knowledge level engineering: ontological analysis, in: *Proceedings AAAI-86*, Philadelphia, PA (1986) 963–968.

[2] J.S. Bennett, ROGET: a knowledge-based consultant for acquiring the conceptual structure of an expert system, *J. Autom. Reasoning* **1** (1985) 49–74.

[3] J. Breuker and B. Wielinga, KADS: structured knowledge acquisition for expert systems, in: *Proceedings Second International Workshop on Expert Systems*, Avignon, France (1985).

[4] B. Chandrasekaran, Generic tasks in knowledge-based reasoning: high-level building blocks for expert system design, *IEEE Expert* **1** (3) (1986) 23–29.

[5] W.J. Clancey, Epistemology of a rule-based expert system—a framework for explanation, *Artif. Intell.* **20** (3) (1983) 215–251.

[6] W.J. Clancey, Heuristic classification, *Artif. Intell.* **27** (3) (1985) 289–350.

[7] W.J. Clancey, Viewing knowledge bases as qualitative models, *IEEE Expert* **4** (2) (1989) 9–23.

[8] W.J. Clancey, The knowledge level reinterpreted: modeling how systems interact, *Mach. Learn.* **4** (3–4) (1989) 287–293.

[9] W.J. Clancey, The frame of reference problem in the design of intelligent machines, in: K. VanLehn, ed., *Architectures for Intelligence: The Twenty-Second Carnegie Symposium on Cognition* (Lawrence Erlbaum, Hillsdale, NJ, 1991) 357–424.

[10] W.J. Clancey, Situated cognition: stepping out of representational flatland, *AI Commun.* **4** (2–3) (1991) 109–112.

[11] W.J. Clancey, Model construction operators, *Artif. Intell.* **53** (1) (1992) 1–115.

[12] W.J. Clancey, Comments on "Epistemology of a rule-based expert system", *Artif. Intell.* **59** (1993) (this volume).

[13] T. Gruber, Automated knowledge acquisition for strategic knowledge, *Mach. Learn.* **4** (3–4) (1989) 293–336.

[14] B. Hayes-Roth, M. Hewitt, M. Vaughn Johnson and A. Garvey, ACCORD: a framework for a class of design tasks, KSL Tech. Report 88-19, Computer Science Department, Stanford University, Stanford, CA (1988).

[15] J. Lave, *Cognition in Practice* (Cambridge University Press, Cambridge, England, 1988).

[16] J. McDermott, Preliminary steps toward a taxonomy of problem-solving methods, in: S. Marcus, ed., *Automating Knowledge Acquisition for Expert Systems* (Kluwer Academic Publishers, Boston, MA, 1988) 225–256.

[17] M.A. Musen, Automated support for building and extending expert models, *Mach. Learn.* **4** (3–4) (1989) 347–375.

[18] A. Newell, The knowledge level, *Artif. Intell.* **18** (1) (1982) 87–127.

[19] D.A. Schön, Generative metaphor: a perspective on problem-setting in social policy, in: A. Ortony, ed., *Metaphor and Thought* (Cambridge University Press, Cambridge, England, 1979) 254–283.

[20] L. Steels, Second generation expert systems, *Future Gen. Comput. Syst.* **1** (4) (1985) 213–221.

[21] M. Stefik, *Introduction to Knowledge Systems* (Morgan Kaufmann, San Mateo, CA, to appear).

[22] T. Winograd and F. Flores, *Understanding Computers and Cognition: A New Foundation for Design* (Ablex, Norwood, NJ, 1986).

Artificial Intelligence 59 (1993) 197–204
Elsevier

ARTINT 977

Notes on "Epistemology of a rule-based expert system"

William J. Clancey

Institute for Research on Learning, 2550 Hanover Street, Palo Alto, CA 94304, USA

1. Introduction

When I joined the Mycin project in January 1975, I was full of excitement about working with physicians and doing something "relevant to society". This excitement soon paled as I became lost by medical jargon and tedious design arguments. In April 1975, I wrote an essay, "Why is the Tetracycline rule so difficult to understand?" This simple rule presented itself as a puzzle: "If the patient is less than 7 years old, then do not prescribe Tetracycline". I knew what all the words meant, but I couldn't understand why the rule was correct. How could Mycin understand the rule? What did it mean to understand a rule? And if Mycin didn't understand the rule, how could it be said to be reasoning? Somewhat fatuously, I labeled my line-printer listing of rules "What Mycin Knows". More than a decade would pass before I realized that to have a representation in your pocket is not to be intelligent, that "having knowledge" does not mean possessing some *things*. A more accurate label for the rule listing would have been "Our representations of what Drs. Shortliffe, Blum, and Yu know".

But criticizing Mycin wasn't on my mind in 1975, before we even called Mycin an "expert system", before even the Heuristic Programming Project became the Knowledge Systems Lab. My interest was to understand the medicine and logic behind the rules. Within the AI research goals of the time, this was framed as research on explanation and teaching (Scott et al.

Correspondence to: W.J. Clancey, Institute for Research on Learning, 2550 Hanover Street, Palo Alto, CA 94304, USA. E-mail: clancey@xerox.parc.

[21], Clancey [4]). The "epistemology" article [5] was originally a chapter of my dissertation [7].

By late 1978, my interest in ordering and understanding Mycin's rules focused on the rules we (principally Victor Yu and Larry Fagan) had recently added for treating meningitis. By this time, Jim Bennett and I were influenced by Randy Davis' work on knowledge acquisition [13], and intrigued by ways in which the process could be managed and taught. From experience, we knew that building a knowledge base wasn't a matter of just generating rules and dropping them into a pot. Jim's experience in constructing Sacon [1] showed the importance of helping experts write useful rules, in particular, organizing rules conceived in isolation into lines of reasoning.

2. Structure–strategy–support design rationales

In effect, we were already moving from the programmer's view of rules as modular and independently changeable to the view that a knowledge base was designed and maintained as a coherent whole. The Mycin team was impressed by the effort in 1975–77 required to generate and test different versions of Mycin's context tree. We were attempting to represent reasoning about multiple cultures from a given body site at different points in time. Clearly, the contribution by the computer scientists was not just in developing the inference engine and attendant subsystems, but in formulating and encoding a complex reasoning network. Indeed, in formulating new concepts and causal models, we were involved in medical science.

By 1978, Bennett and I focused on the idea of *inference structure*, an outline of the dominant goal structure of a rule set. Seeing the goal structures of Mycin and Sacon on paper, we wondered, "What is the logic behind these trees?" Here I was strongly influenced by Brown, Collins, and Harris' paper, "AI and learning strategies" [3], which analyzed reasoning strategies in different domains. I noted the parallel between controlling Mycin's rules and deciding which axiom to apply in algebraic simplification [5, Fig. 12]. Until this time, the idea of strategy in the Mycin project was simply a rule that controlled other rules (a *metarule*). But here I realized that a strategy was a kind of argument. It had its own logical content, which for medical diagnosis was more like a *procedure* for focusing an extended dialogue, than isolated metarules affecting rule ordering. This was probably the most important idea in the design of Neomycin, which was already under way by the fall of 1979.

The procedural–declarative controversy also influenced my analysis. What was the relation between "explicit" and "implicit knowledge"? In what sense does clause ordering constitute implicit knowledge? For example, I can proceduralize the relation between "age of the patient" and "alcoholism" by placing the age clause before the alcoholism clause in rules. But how is this different from the "declarative representation", "If the age is less than 13, then the patient is probably not an alcoholic"? Since Mycin doesn't understand what alcoholism is anyway, in what sense is the rule's meaning more explicit? It was many years before I realized that there was no such thing as "the meaning" of a representation. And we were light years from distinguishing between "knowing a meaning" and "a representation of meaning". At the very least, the ideas of implicit and explicit knowledge encouraged me to list and study relations such as clause ordering that were crucial to the program's correct operation. Ultimately, I framed this analysis by relating it to Woods' "What's in a link?" [26] and Brachman's "What's in a concept?" [2]. Today, with more respect for simplicity, I would have called my article, "What's in a rule?".

Looking back, I believe that the "strategy–structure–support" framework holds up. The observation that an inference procedure (strategy) indexes the domain model (the knowledge base of propositions and rules) through a vocabulary of relations (structure, the domain theory) is of basic importance for understanding how changes to the theory, model, and inference procedure interrelate. Unfortunately, my misleading characterization of strategic knowledge as domain-independent (instead of domain-general) led some people to belittle the idea of representing the domain model separately from the inference and communication procedures. I believe these distinctions are central for articulating and advancing the process representation techniques of AI programming [11].

3. Knowledge bases and generative models

After constructing Neomycin and studying its metarules in the mid-1980s, I realized that removing ordering relations between rule clauses produced a special kind of model, like the relation between a grammar and a lexicon. In effect, we discover patterns in expressions (Mycin's rules) and formulate a grammar that can generate these patterns by interpreting a separate set of propositions (the domain model of propositions and rules). I believe that understanding how such process models are constructed is important for understanding the capabilities and limits of qualitative modeling.

The first idea is that general theories of processes are developed by abstracting *ordering patterns* (e.g, clause ordering, rule ordering, data-request ordering) from a collection of models written in some language [8]. We followed this approach in creating Neomycin from Mycin, and then in studying patterns in Neomycin's metarules [9]. A more general observation is that *different procedures* for interpreting a domain model (e.g., an inference procedure, a compiler, an explanation program, a student modeling program) index the model through different classifications of domain terms and relations [11].

Second, a domain-general inference procedure (general because it uses variables for domain terms) can be used like a natural language grammar to parse an expert or student's sequence of requests for data and hypothesis statements (Wilkins et al. [25]). A given sequence of expert or student behavior can be parsed in different ways, depending on different assumptions about the person's domain model [9].

Third, when we replace a representation by what appears to be its generative constituents, we specialize it (by specifying when propositions and rules should be applied), and potentially lose robustness. For example, if we replace the dictum "generalize questions" (formalized in Neomycin by a metarule) by the conditions under which this should be done (e.g., you are in a hurry and this finding is rarely present), we will require both more details to be represented (e.g., the frequency of a finding) and more information to be checked during the problem-solving context (e.g., am I in a hurry today?). That is, by making more aspects of the system being modeled and the context explicit, more reasoning (or search of triggering conditions) is required. Besides requiring more data, the program will no longer apply the rule in situations in which it might be relevant. Recent research in self-organizing and reactive architectures is partly motivated by these observations (Steels [22]).

Of course, these statements would not have been made in the 1970s, when few people acknowledged that Mycin's classification of diseases and causal relations expressed in rules constituted a model of the domain. We needed to recognize that we were constructing new models in knowledge bases before we could understand how people typically create and use models, and the capabilities of a reasoning mechanism built only out of models.

4. The role of rationalization reconsidered

We originally conceived of support knowledge as the causal and social context that justifies a rule, an objective documentation for why a rule is correct. Today we would call the justification a *design rationale*, and emphasize its use in developing better models over time. In particular, any number of rationalizations for or against a representation are possible, depending on changing circumstances in which representations are interpreted. Rather than viewing justifications as objective and pertaining to "truth", a design rationale should cite the shortcomings in the previous theory or model, relative to how it has been used (Schön [20]). Rationalization of this sort involves reconceiving the goals of the program and what constitutes a problem, not just providing "deeper" explanations for isolated rules.

Conflating knowledge and knowledge representations distorts how people create models, and leads to an inadequate conception of what tools might help us. For example, in the "epistemology" article [5] I observed that the meaning of represented concepts tends to be generalized when later additions are made to the knowledge base, which I termed *concept broadening*. I now believe that this is an inherent aspect of representational change [10], not something that can be prevented by "principled representations". Tools for maintaining and using design rationales, grounded in a case library, could take this into account.

Our conception of explanation systems was also biased by the view that knowledge bases weren't our models, but were delivered from the heads of experts. We didn't consider that users were already representing knowledge in their everyday affairs. We believed that a program's explanation would help experts improve the program (transmission from expert to program), but in the workplace we conceived of explanation as a teaching device (transmission from program to user). We viewed changes to the rules in terms of debugging a program, expecting it to be a convergent process that would be controlled by technicians, or preferably the experts themselves. After all, building a knowledge base was conceived as a process of acquiring already "known" knowledge from experts. To the extent users had knowledge, it was assumed to be unarticulated, and hence incomplete and naive.

We viewed all interactions between people and program in terms of "transfer": Experts had knowledge stored in their heads. The knowledge base was an objective inventory of expert knowledge. Users lacked knowledge. The role of consultation (and knowledge acquisition and teaching) was to transfer knowledge between experts, users, and students. Knowledge engineers are like priests; they receive "The Word" from experts above, add nothing to the content, but codify it accurately into written rules, and pass it down to ordinary folks as commandments to live by. If you are not an expert, you learn by being told. This is how knowledge engineers learn from experts and how users and students learn from the expert system. This view lacks any sense that the knowledge base could belong to a community of practitioners, the users and experts alike, and might be developed and maintained by them (but see Stefik and Conway [23]).

Similarly, apart from courtesies of the bedside manner, it was difficult to conceive what a medical student should be taught, other than Mycin's rules. We didn't realize that the complement of Neomycin—how the model relates to the unformalized world of medical practice—is an essential part of what a student needs to know. What explanations could help students and consultation users become more aware of the quality of their work, know when to question what they are doing, and generate ideas for changing what they are doing? In other words, how can we use knowledge representations to make people *reflective practitioners* [20]?

As an example, consider the disease taxonomy of Neomycin. Today we view such representations not as a *product* to be delivered to a student, but as a partial model of a practice. Besides learning the various diseases and their relations, we would want the student to learn the following:

- Why do we taxonomize diseases?
- What gets glossed? How do we know when this stereotypic view of physiological processes is misleading?
- Who knows this taxonomy; what is its origin?
- What is the nature of disagreements; how do they arise; how are they settled?
- How are taxonomies related to medical research? Are they becoming unnecessary as we develop better mechanistic models?
- What are good ways to keep a taxonomic perspective up-to-date?

By this view, knowledge is *knowing how to live* in a community, not just static facts or procedures that *represent* what people do. This is what we want the student to learn and what our computer tools could support (Lave and Wenger [17], Schön [20], Clancey [12], Greenbaum and Kyng [14]). Today we realize that "glass box design" is not an inherent property of a representational system, but a *relation* between the design and the practices of a community (Wenger [24]).

If I had this perspective in 1975, before building Guidon I would have experimented with the original Mycin program in the medical school. I would first give Mycin to the students with illustrative cases demonstrating the program's capabilities. I would then challenge them to defeat the program by selecting new cases from the clinic and explaining why Mycin fails. This would teach them something about computer models as well as the domain.

5. Subsequent research

This article helped frame explanation research in terms of content, as opposed to the goal-rule backward-chaining syntax. But given my view that the program was an omniscient expert, it is no surprise that I didn't discuss the *explanation process* as a kind of negotiation, a joint construction (cf. Moore and Swartout [18]). For example, the Pollack et al. study [19] of radio talk shows reveals how participants engage in problem framing, co-define the expert's capabilities, and evaluate the usefulness of his advice. Related work by Langlotz and Shortliffe [16] explores the relation of consultation dialogs to human involvement and responsibility; Karp and Wilkins [15] reconsider the nature of rule-based models in relation to explicit causal representations.

This article was a step in the design of Neomycin and my subsequent study of other expert systems. I was surprised to find after completing the paper "Heuristic classification" [6] that the abstraction–heuristic-association–refinement horseshoe diagram is anticipated by Fig. 8, which shows how a rule can be explained by generalizing it. In effect, I have written a trilogy of papers with expanding interests and claims about representation: The "epistemology" article [5] is a study of Mycin's rules; "Heuristic classification" [6] is a generalization to other expert systems; and "Model construction operators" [11] is a further generalization to the process modeling methodology of AI programming.

I am especially grateful to Bruce Buchanan, John Seely Brown, and Danny Bobrow for their persistent interest and direction during more than two years of rewriting this paper.

References

[1] J. Bennett, L. Creary, R. Englemore and R. Melosh, SACON: a knowledge-based consultant for structural analysis, in: *Proceedings IJCAI-79*, Tokyo (1979) 47–49.

[2] R.J. Brachman, What's in a concept: structural foundations for semantic networks, *Int. J. of Man–Mach. Stud.* 9 (1977) 127—152.

[3] J.S. Brown, A. Collins and G. Harris, Artificial intelligence and learning strategies, in: H. O'Neill, ed., *Learning Strategies* (Academic Press, New York, 1977).

[4] W.J. Clancey, An antibiotic therapy selector which provides for explanations, in: *Proceedings IJCAI-77*, Cambridge, MA (1977); expanded version in: B.G. Buchanan and E.H. Shortliffe, eds., *Rule Based Expert Systems: The MYCIN Experiments of the Stanford Heuristic Programming Project* (Addison-Wesley, Reading, MA, 1984) 133–146.

[5] W.J. Clancey, The epistemology of a rule-based expert system—a framework for explanation, *Artif. Intell.* 20 (3) (1983) 215–251.

[6] W.J. Clancey, Heuristic classification, *Artif. Intell.* 27 (1985) 289–350.

[7] W.J. Clancey, *Knowledge-Based Tutoring: The GUIDON Program* (MIT Press, Cambridge, MA, 1987).

[8] W.J. Clancey, From Guidon to Neomycin and Heracles in twenty short lessons: ONR final report, 1979–1985, in: A. van Lamsweerde, ed., *Current Issues in Expert Systems* (Academic Press, London, 1987) 79–123; also: *AI Mag.* 7 (3) (1986) 40–60.

[9] W.J. Clancey, Acquiring, representing, and evaluating a competence model of diagnosis, in: M.T.H. Chi, R. Glaser and M.J. Farr, eds., *The Nature of Expertise* (Lawrence Erlbaum, Hillsdale, NJ, 1988) 343–418.

[10] W.J. Clancey, Book Review of Rosenfield's *The Invention of Memory: A New View to the Brain, Artif. Intell.* 50 (2) (1991) 241–284.

[11] W.J. Clancey, Model construction operators, *Artif. Intell.* 53 (1) (1992) 1–115.

[12] W.J. Clancey, The knowledge level reconsidered: modeling socio-technical systems, in: K. Ford, ed., Special Issue on Knowledge Acquisition, *Int. J. Intell. Syst.* (to appear).

[13] R. Davis and D.B. Lenat, *Knowledge-Based Systems in Artificial Intelligence* (McGraw-Hill, New York, 1982).

[14] J. Greenbaum and M. Kyng, *Design at Work: Cooperative Design of Computer Systems* (Lawrence Erlbaum, Hillsdale, NJ, 1991).

[15] P.D. Karp and D.C. Wilkins, An analysis of the distinction between deep and shallow expert systems, *Int. J. Expert Syst.* 2 (1) (1989) 1–32.

[16] C.P. Langlotz and E.H. Shortliffe, Adapting a consultation system to critique user plans, *Int. J. Man–Mach. Stud.* **19** (5) (1983) 479–496.

[17] J. Lave and E. Wenger, *Situated Learning: Legitimate Peripheral Participation* (Cambridge University Press, Cambridge, England, 1991).

[18] J.D. Moore and W.R. Swartout, A reactive approach to explanation, in: *Proceedings IJCAI-89*, Detroit, MI (1989) 1504–1510.

[19] M.E. Pollack, J. Hirsherg and B.L. Webber, User participation in the reasoning processes of expert systems, in: *Proceedings AAAI-82*, Pittsburgh, PA (1982) 358–361.

[20] D.A. Schön, *Educating the Reflective Practitioner* (Jossey-Bass, San Francisco, CA, 1987).

[21] A.C. Scott, W.J. Clancey, R. Davis and E.H. Shortliffe, Explanation capabilities of knowledge-based production systems, *Am. J. Comput. Linguistics* (1977) Microfiche 62; also in: B.G. Buchanan and E.H. Shortliffe, eds., *Rule Based Expert Systems: The MYCIN Experiments of the Stanford Heuristic Programming Project* (Addison-Wesley, Reading, MA, 1984) 338–362.

[22] L. Steels, Cooperation through self-organisation, in: Y. De Mazeau and J.P. Muller, eds., *Multi-Agent Systems* (North-Holland, Amsterdam, 1989).

[23] M. Stefik and L. Conway, Towards the principled engineering of knowledge, in: R. Engelmore, ed., *Readings from the AI Magazine, Volumes 1–5, 1980–85* (AAAI Press, Menlo Park, CA, 1988) 135–147.

[24] E. Wenger, Toward a theory of cultural transparency: elements of a social discourse of the visible and the invisible, Ph.D. Dissertation, Information and Computer Science, University of California, Irvine, CA (1990).

[25] D.E. Wilkins, W.J. Clancey and B.G. Buchanan, On using and evaluating differential modeling in intelligent tutoring and apprentice learning systems, in: J. Psotka, D. Massey and S. Mutter, eds., *Intelligent Tutoring Systems: Lessons Learned* (Lawrence Erlbaum, Hillsdale, NJ, 1988).

[26] W.A. Woods, What's in a link: foundations for semantic networks, in: D.G. Bobrow and A. Collins, eds., *Representation and Understanding* (Academic Press, New York, 1975) 35–82.

Architectures

Artificial Intelligence 59 (1993) 207–211
Elsevier

ARTINT 975

Prototypical knowledge for expert systems: a retrospective analysis

Jan S. Aikins

Trinzic Corporation, 101 University, Palo Alto, CA 94301, USA

Two themes

The article, "Prototypical knowledge for expert systems" [1], published in 1983, was a summarization of my dissertation research at Stanford University in the late 1970s. This was the era of the first rule-based expert systems—MYCIN, Meta-DENDRAL, PUFF, and others from Stanford, and the early frame systems from MIT, such as PIP and NUDGE. I remember being intrigued by the simplicity of the rule-based architectures and the ease with which one could express logical heuristics that did indeed seem to be part of what an expert knew about his area of expertise. I also remember the frustration that was felt by experts and application developers alike over a lack of control in the dialog between application end users and the expert consultation system. Backward-chaining of rules was certainly efficient, but unpredictable, and resulted in dialogs that were not consistent with the way a human expert would have acquired information to solve the problem.

I realized that there was not only domain-specific knowledge that was necessary to infer new information for applications, but also control knowledge that was specific to each application, and that would direct the acquisition and application of domain knowledge. Many of the frame systems represented control knowledge in the frame structure itself, directing the flow of the consultation for each context. The knowledge representation that I devised took the best ideas from both sets of research and created what we would call today one of the first "hybrid" architectures.

Correspondence to: J.S. Aikins, Trinzic Corporation, 101 University, Palo Alto, CA 94301, USA.

The resulting system, which I named "CENTAUR", consisted of a set of frame-like structures, called prototypes, where control knowledge was explicitly represented in slots for each prototypical sutuation, plus production rules that represented the inferential knowledge for the application. The control knowledge guided the flow of the consultation and the application of production rules. There were side-benefits, too, for explanation and knowledge acquisition. The prototypes segmented rules according to the situations where they would be applied, so that experts and end users could more easily understand *why* knowledge was being applied in each situation, and where modifications were needed. The knowledge base was in many ways self-documenting. Prototypes were even used at the highest level to represent a "typical consultation".

Thus the two most significant themes that emerged from the CENTAUR work were representing control knowledge as part of each application's knowledge base, and using frames and rules together in a hybrid architecture.

Today's systems

If we jump ahead to the tools and applications of today, we see several areas in which the themes espoused in CENTAUR are realized in current products. First of all, *hybrid architectures* are standard in most of today's successful expert system tools. Systems using rules with frames, rules with objects, or even more likely, rules and objects with conventional data structures and lists are common. It seems to have become acceptable to use the "appropriate" data structure to represent domain knowledge, rather than forcing all knowledge to be represented in a single type of data structure. Most of the commercial expert system building tools on the market are hybrid architectures (e.g., Trinzic's "Aion Development System" and "KBMS", and IBM's "TIRS"), and most of these also support explicit representation of control knowledge in slots, as agendas, or as part of an object architecture.

CENTAUR's theme of *explicitly representing control knowledge* and storing it with other application knowledge is reflected in today's object-oriented tools and applications. The field of object-oriented programming was beginning to emerge during the late 1960s and 1970s, but today it has blossomed into a series of subfields, each with an ever-increasing number of commercial products, including object-oriented design and analysis tools. The concept of an object as a data structure that encapsulates both data and procedures in a single representation is consistent with the control knowledge/inferential knowledge breakdown in CENTAUR, and the notion that both types of knowledge should be placed together in the same context-specific data structure. It seems that the benefits of CENTAUR's knowledge representation concerning ease of development, maintenance, and explanation of system behaviors are realized in the object-oriented world as well.

CENTAUR's *representation of prototypical situations* as "prototypes" also has many modern-day incarnations, perhaps the most similar systems being case-based reasoning systems. Case-based reasoning has emerged from its early reseach days at Yale under Roger Schank to commercialization by companies such as Cognitive Systems and Inference Corporation. Cases, like CENTAUR's prototypes, are a more cognitive structure than rules—a set of related facts about a given context grouped together as a typical scenario. The appeal of case-based reasoning systems is that they accept raw case data as a knowledge representation and then reason about new cases by comparing them to existing, solved cases, thereby alleviating much of the knowledge acquisition bottleneck. The possibilities for using case-based reasoning systems in industry are just beginning to be realized. Corporate databases abound with "case data" that could be used both in acquiring knowledge to create initial knowledge bases, and to provide a foundation for reasoning about new cases. Some companies are embedding case-based reasoning technologies into their hybrid architectures, allowing an even richer set of knowledge representation and reasoning techniques.

So what's missing

The problem with today's hybrid, more robust, architectures is that we still lack a uniform *methodology* to tell us which structures are most appropriate to use in each situation and to guide the application of different structures in consultations. Among the questions most frequently asked in classes that offer corporate training on hybrid tools are "How do I start?", "When do I use rules, and when do I use objects?", "How long will it take to complete this application?". These questions fall into two categories: those dealing with a choice of knowledge representation structure, and those dealing with project management issues.

Answering these questions for users is complex. Part of the problem is that every tool, and thus every choice of knowledge representation structures, is different. Few vendors have taken it upon themselves to provide a methodology for determining how to use their tool. Most training courses teach proper syntax for the use of tool features, rather than a step-by-step prescription for specifying a knowledge representation. A second problem is that each application is unique, and although there are certainly common problem types, such as diagnosis and configuration, there is much variability among possible solutions. Most problems can be solved in numerous ways, and the more knowledge representation choices that are offered in a particular tool, the greater the number of possible solutions.

Ther are two directions evident from academia and industry that will help to alleviate this knowledge representation methodology problem. First are efforts to create *standards for knowledge representation* that would allow users and tool vendors alike to share knowledge across a variety of tools and platforms. Efforts from IEEE, ANSI, Object Management Group, Open Software Foundation, and others are making some progress in developing knowledge representation standards. IBM also promises help with standards in its AD/Cycle initiative.

A second direction being taken in industry to solve the knowledge representation methodology problem is to reduce the number of representation choices for a given problem type by creating more *horizontal or vertical tools* for specific problem areas such as help desks or configurators, or for specific application types, such as underwriting or insurance adjustment. By streamlining the tool so that it applies to only a very narrow set of applications, the methodology can be built into the tool design, and the tool frequently provides minimal, if any, alternate representation choices. These task-specific tools, or "task shells", enable extremely efficient development when used for the task for which they are defined. They allow little room for deviation, however, and cannot be applied to other tasks.

Questions dealing with *project management issues* are only slightly more tractable. There have been many project management methodologies in use for conventional programming systems that cover project sizing and estimating, project planning, and project tracking, among other issues. There is noticeable progress in extending these conventional methodologies to knowledge-based systems development. Even the Big Six consulting and accounting firms have recently expanded their conventional methodologies to include knowledge-based system development. However, much still remains to be done.

In hindsight ...

What would I do differently in my CENTAUR research, knowing what I know today, if I got the chance to do it over again? At the time, it seemed to me that I was taking a giant leap in combining knowledge representation structures for expert systems. Almost all of the expert systems were based on a single representation structure, generally rules. The representation was clean and simple, and the methodology for creating the systems was fairly straightforward. These simple systems did have control problems, problems that resulted from representing knowledge implicitly, and problems that resulted from trying to express contextual knowledge logically as rules. Because CENTAUR's hybrid representation seemed like such a big step, I doubt that I would have done more, or that it would have been advisable to do so. Most research proceeds, and is more readily accepted, when small advances are made at each step.

What I would change, given what I know now, is the domain in which I tested my ideas. Expert systems have evolved from being systems which exhibit human expertise for difficult, scientific or engineering tasks, to knowledge-based systems that are applied to logical components of traditional applications, and are frequently embedded in conventional sofware programs. My choice of a stand-alone medical diagnostic application proved difficult, both in gaining the expertise needed to understand the domain (I sat in on two quarters of medical classes at Stanford), and in acceptance of the final system in the medical community. The impact that artificial intelligence technologies can have in an industry such as insurance or banking, however, is staggering. Had I chosen an application such as underwriting, I believe that my results would have come more quickly and that the applicability of my ideas would have been more evident.

Fortunately, my career has followed a path that has allowed me to participate in the creation of expert systems tools that do embody the themes from CENTAUR and have been widely applied to industrial, as well as scientific and engineering applications. I truly believe that the expert systems revolution is just beginning.

Reference

[1] J.S. Aikins, Prototypical knowledge for expert systems, *Artif. Intell.* **20** (1983) 163–210.

Artificial Intelligence 59 (1993) 213–220
Elsevier

ARTINT 979

Intelligent control

Barbara Hayes-Roth

Knowledge Systems Laboratory, Department of Computer Science, Stanford University, Stanford, CA 94305, USA

1. The key ideas

How should an artificially intelligent agent decide which action to perform at each point in time?

In my 1985 paper, "A blackboard architecture for control" [7], I claimed that the control problem is fundamental to all cognitive processes and intelligent systems. At each point in time, many actions may be logically possible, given the current state of the task environment. An intelligent agent must choose among them, either implicitly or explicitly. For a given task, the agent's solution to the control problem determines what actions it performs and, therefore, what goals it achieves, what resources it uses, and what side-effects it produces. More generally, the agent's approach to control determines its potential range of behavior, its run-time flexibility, and its coherence and comprehensibility to observers.

Therefore I argued that, like human beings—and unlike conventional computer programs—an AI agent must have capabilities for intelligent control. It must use knowledge and reasoning skills to construct and modify explicit control plans for its own actions at run time. It should notice what actions are possible at each point in time and use its control plans to choose among them. Its control plans should be specific enough to select sequences of actions that achieve goals, yet general and flexible enough to accommodate unanticipated demands and opportunities for action. The agent should modify its control plans as warranted by events in the task environment.

To realize intelligent control in an AI agent, I proposed the blackboard control architecture shown schematically in Fig. 1. It comprises a set of data

Correspondence to: B. Hayes-Roth, Knowledge Systems Laboratory, Department of Computer Science, Stanford University, Stanford, CA 94305, USA. E-mail: bhr@hpp.stanford.edu.

structures (labeled boxes) in a global memory and a three-step execution cycle:

(a) an executor executes the next action, making changes to memory and producing associated events;

(b) an agenda manager triggers known actions whose conditions are satisfied by those events and puts context-specific instances on an agenda of possible actions; and

(c) a scheduler rates possible actions against the current control plan and chooses the one with the highest rating as the next action to be executed.

Control plans play a central role in the architecture. As shown in Fig. 1, the control plan is a data structure containing any number of component plans, each with its own hierarchical and temporal organization. Typical control plans are abstract and do not specify sequences of particular actions. Instead, each "step" in a plan specifies:

(a) a class of intended actions in terms of their desirable attributes (e.g., what subgoal such actions address, what kind of knowledge they apply, what resources they consume);

(b) an activation condition under which the plan step should become active;

(c) a deactivation condition under which that plan step should be deactivated; and

(d) a rating function that evaluates how well a given possible action matches the attributes of the class of intended actions.

On each cycle, the scheduler uses the rating functions in all plan leaves that are active "now" to rate possible actions on the agenda and executes the action with the highest rating. When multiple control plans are active, the scheduler gives preference to actions that have high ratings against more important plans. In Fig. 1, for example, the scheduler is using the rating function in plan P1 to choose among actions that are possible "Now". It used the functions in both P1 and subplan P2-2 to choose among actions that were possible at time t1. It will use the function in P3 to choose among actions that are possible during t2–t3. Thus, control plans do not specify in advance the particular actions an agent will execute; rather, they specify dynamic constraints it will use to choose among possible actions triggered by run-time events.

An agent constructs and modifies control plans with control actions. Like other actions, they are triggered by run-time events and placed on the agenda, where they compete for scheduling. Executing a control action can introduce a new plan, extend an existing plan in time or expand it into subplans, adapt a plan to the details of the run-time situation, or terminate

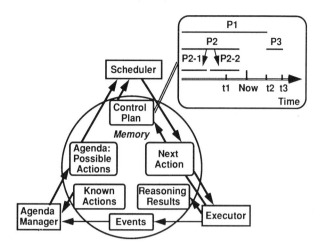

Fig. 1. Schematic of the blackboard control architecture.

a plan. For example, at "Now" in Fig. 1, the agent has terminated plan P2, but will continue to perform actions under P1 until it terminates it at time t2. It already has introduced plan P3, which it will activate for the time interval t2–t3, but has not yet expanded P3 into subplans or made any plans beyond t3. The ultimate effect of all control actions is to change the constraints the agent will use to choose among possible actions in the immediate or distant future.

In sum, the blackboard control architecture allows an agent to construct and follow plans that constrain its choices among actions triggered by run-time events, but also to depart from or change its plans in light of those events. It maintains an explicit representation of control plans that the agent can inspect, modify, describe, or transfer to new situations. It provides a uniform mechanism for all cognitive activity, including control planning.

2. Research context

I came to the idea of intelligent control from a background in cognitive science, in particular from prior research on how people plan tasks in spatial environments. In contrast to most AI planning models, people's planning behavior is very "opportunistic"; they use different planning strategies (e.g., successive refinement, backward chaining, island extension) at different times and they often depart from, modify, or switch strategies in midstream. To model this key feature of human cognition [20], my colleagues and I at the Rand Corporation (Rick Hayes-Roth, Stan Rosenschein, and Stephanie Cammarata) developed a computer program called OPM (Opportunistic Planning Model) [11, 12]. Based on the "blackboard model" [2], OPM's most important innovation was to introduce control actions that post explicit planning strategies in a specially defined data structure called the "control blackboard" for use by the scheduler. By manipulating the control actions available to OPM, we modeled people's different planning strategies and their run-time deviations from those strategies.

In 1982, Ed Feigenbaum invited me to join the Heuristic Programming Project at Stanford, specifically to continue my investigation and elaboration of the blackboard model. My first steps were to generalize and refine the architecture of OPM, as reported in the 1985 paper, and to implement it in a software system called BB1. Over the years, my students and I have taken BB1 through a series of extensions, revisions, and reimplementations, reflecting our evolving theoretical ideas about intelligent control, and used it as a platform for several experimental application systems. Thanks to the contributions of several students, but especially Mike Hewett, BB1 became an effective vehicle for distributing our ideas to colleagues outside of Stanford in a form they can run, examine, and modify.

I have been fortunate in finding interesting experimental applications for BB1 and excellent collaborators. The first experimental applications were the Protean system [9] for determining protein structures (with Bruce Buchanan, Oleg Jardetzky, and others) and the SightPlan system [23] for designing construction site layouts (with Ray Levitt and Iris Tommelein). Both systems performed instances of a class of "arrangement-assembly" tasks, in which an agent applies a series of constraints to incrementally reduce the legal positions of objects in a dimensional space. The agent's control plan (its strategy) determines the order in which it applies particular constraints to particular objects. Although many plans lead to satisfactory arrangements, they differ in computational cost—and the cost of a plan often is not known in advance. In our experiments, BB1 allowed the agent to manage computational cost and, as a result, time to complete a task by dynamically modifying its control plan at run time in light of intermediate results [17]. The computational cost of dynamic control planning itself was substantially less than the computational savings it produced for the task as a whole [5]. In addition, we discovered that explicit control plans provide a rich data structure for strategic explanation, strategy recognition, and strategy learning. On the other hand, we also learned that it is difficult to exploit BB1's capabilities for intelligent control using only architectural (task-independent) representations. To address this limitation, we extended BB1 with a framework for explicit task-level reasoning languages and a particular language called Accord for the class of arrangement-assembly tasks [13].

During the last few years, my research group has been studying a class of computer agents we call "adaptive intelligent systems". These agents must coordinate a number of reasoning tasks (e.g., fault detection, diagnosis,

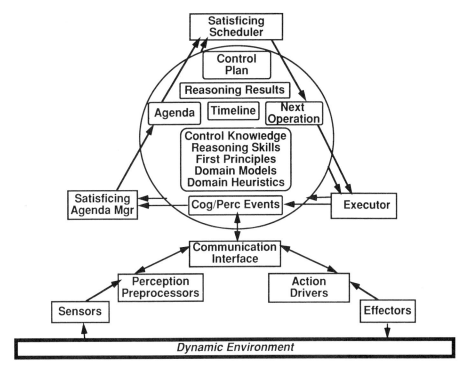

Fig. 2. Architecture for adaptive intelligent systems.

prediction, planning, explanation, learning), while perceiving and acting upon dynamic external entities, such as people, physical processes, or other computer programs. Our experimental applications are in four domains: intensive care monitoring [14, 15] (with Adam Seiver and others), semiconductor fabrication [18], power plant maintenance, and mobile robots. Adaptive intelligent systems present challenging new requirements for intelligent control: performance of diverse tasks varying in criticality and urgency; coordination of multiple interacting tasks to meet global objectives; adaptation to unanticipated demands and opportunities for action generated by dynamic external entities; and satisfaction of real-time constraints.

Figure 2 shows how we have extended the blackboard control architecture and its BB1 implementation to support adaptive intelligent systems [8]. First, a communication interface relays data between external entities and I/O buffers in the global memory. Input events trigger possible actions and output events are created by executed actions, both within the basic execution cycle. Thus, perception, reasoning, and action are concurrent and asynchronous. Second, perception preprocessors use the dynamic control plan to shield the reasoning system from sensory overload, focus its attention on important events, and protect it from distraction by unimportant events [25]. Action drivers perform similar functions in controlling effectors. Third, a "timeline" temporally organizes all observations, expectations, and intentions generated by an agent and supports temporal reasoning operations. Finally, the basic execution cycle has become a "satisficing cycle". Instead of triggering all possible actions and executing the best one, the satisficing cycle uses the current control plan to trigger a few important actions. It interrupts triggering to execute either the first one that is "good enough" or the "best available" one when a deadline occurs. Thus, BB1 can perform high-quality actions with constant-time execution cycles despite variations in data rate and knowledge base size [10]. We find it encouraging that these extensions did not require significant modifications to the architecture and, especially, that the the new functionality of the perception preprocessors and satisficing cycle further exploit the central architectural mechanism of dynamic control planning.

3. Hindsight

What do I understand about the 1985 paper now that I did not understand when I wrote it?

Like most AI researchers in the early 1980s, my thinking was oriented toward heuristic problem-solving systems operating on user-requested tasks in static environments. Intelligent control allowed such agents to adapt their problem-solving strategies to unanticipated results of their own reasoning. Both the 1985 paper and the early experimental applications of BB1 showed how this helps agents to solve problems correctly and efficiently and how explicit control plans help them to explain and learn problem-solving strategies. But this was only a weak test of the architecture's potential because it offered only internally generated demands and opportunities for run-time replanning.

In retrospect, it was a major oversight of the 1985 paper that I did not compare the proposed control architecture with "classical" planning models [3]. That comparison would have highlighted features of the architecture that anticipated important later work: its event-based ("situated") triggering of actions [1, 22]; its support for abstract control plans that constrain, but do not completely determine actions [21]; its run-time interleaving of planning, replanning, and execution [4, 6]; and its integration of deliberation and reactivity [16].

There is now a growing interest in architectures for more comprehensive autonomous agents [19, 24], including our own work on adaptive intelligent systems. In many ways, this class of applications provides the first real opportunity to exercise and evaluate the blackboard control architecture proposed in the 1985 paper.

Acknowledgement

The research and preparation of my 1985 paper were made possible by grants from ONR and DARPA.

References

[1] P.E. Agre and D. Chapman, Pengi: an implementation of a theory of activity, in: *Proceedings AAAI-87*, Seattle, WA (1987).

[2] L. Erman, F. Hayes-Roth, V. Lesser and D.R. Reddy, The Hearsay-II speech-understanding system: integrating knowledge to resolve uncertainty, *Comput. Surv.* **12** (1980) 213–253.

[3] R.E. Fikes and N.J. Nilsson, STRIPS: a new approach to the application of theorem proving to problem solving, *Artif. Intell.* **2** (1971) 189–208.

[4] J. Firby, Adaptive execution in complex dynamic worlds, Ph.D. Dissertation, Department of Computer Science, Yale University, New Haven, CT (1989).

[5] A. Garvey, C. Cornelius and B. Hayes-Roth, Computational costs versus benefits of control reasoning, in: *Proceedings AAAI-87*, Seattle, WA (1987).

[6] M.P. Georgeff and A.L. Lansky, Reactive reasoning and planning, in: *Proceedings IJCAI-87*, Milan, Italy (1987).

[7] B. Hayes-Roth, A blackboard architecture for control, *Artif. Intell.* **26** (1985) 251–321.

[8] B. Hayes-Roth, Architectural foundations for real-time performance in intelligent agents, *Real-Time Syst. Int. J. Time-Critical Comput. Syst.* **2** (1990) 99–125.

[9] B. Hayes-Roth, B.G. Buchanan, O. Lichtarge, M. Hewett, R. Altman, J. Brinkley, C. Cornelius, B. Duncan and O. Jardetzky, Protean: deriving protein structure from constraints, in: *Proceedings AAAI-86*, Philadelphia, PA (1986).

[10] B. Hayes-Roth and A. Collinot, A satisficing cycle for real-time reasoning in intelligent agents, *Expert Syst. Appl.* (to appear).

[11] B. Hayes-Roth and F. Hayes-Roth, A cognitive model of planning, *Cogn. Sci.* **3** (1979) 275–310; reprinted in: A. Collins and E.E. Smith, eds., *Readings in Cognitive Science: A Psychological and Artificial Intelligence Perspective* (Morgan Kaufmann, San Mateo, CA, 1988).

[12] B. Hayes-Roth, F. Hayes-Roth, S. Rosenschein and S. Cammarata, Modelling planning as an incremental, opportunistic process, in: *Proceedings IJCAI-79*, Tokyo (1979).

[13] B. Hayes-Roth, M.V. Johnson, A. Garvey and M. Hewett, Applications of BB1 to arrangement-assembly tasks, *J. Artif. Intell. Eng.* **1** (1986) 85–94.

[14] B. Hayes-Roth, R. Washington, D. Ash, R. Hewett, A. Collinot, A. Vina and A. Seiver, Guardian: A prototype intelligent agent for intensive-care monitoring, *J. Artif. Intell. Med.* **4** (1992) 165–185.

[15] B. Hayes-Roth, R. Washington, R. Hewett, M. Hewett and A. Seiver, Intelligent monitoring and control, in: *Proceedings IJCAI-89*, Detroit, MI (1989).

[16] J. Hendler and J. Sanborn, Planning and reaction in dynamic domains, in: *Proceedings DARPA Planning Workshop* (1987).

[17] M.V. Johnson and B. Hayes-Roth, Integrating diverse reasoning methods in BB1, in: *Proceedings AAAI-87*, Seattle, WA (1987).

[18] J. Murdock and B. Hayes-Roth, Intelligent monitoring of semiconductor manufacturing, *IEEE Expert* **6** (1991) 19–31.

[19] A. Newell, *Unified Theories of Cognition* (Harvard University Press, Cambridge, MA, 1992).

[20] A. Newell and H.A. Simon, *Human Problem Solving* (Prentice-Hall, Englewood Cliffs, NJ, 1972).

[21] M. Pollack, The uses of plans, Computers and Thought Lecture, IJCAI-91, Sydney, Australia (1991); also: *Artif. Intell.* **57** (1) (1992) 43–68.

[22] S.J. Rosenschein and L.P. Kaelbling, The synthesis of digital machines with provable epistemic properties, in: *Proceedings Conference on Theoretical Aspects of Reasoning about Knowledge*, Monterey, CA (1986) 83–98.

[23] I. Tommelein, R. Levitt, B. Hayes-Roth and A. Confrey, SightPlan experiments: alternate strategies for site layout design, *J. Comput. Civil Eng.* **5** (1991) 42–63.

[24] K. VanLehn, ed., *Architectures for Intelligence* (Lawrence Erlbaum, Hillsdale, NJ, 1991).

[25] R. Washington and B. Hayes-Roth, Input data management in real-time AI systems, in: *Proceedings IJCAI-89*, Detroit, MI (1989).

Artificial Intelligence 59 (1993) 221–224
Elsevier

ARTINT 982

Retrospective on "The organization of expert systems, a tutorial"

Mark Stefik

Xerox Corporation, Palo Alto Research Center, 3333 Coyote Hill Road, Palo Alto, CA 94304, USA

Jan S. Aikins

Trinzic Corporation, 101 University, Palo Alto, CA 94301, USA

Robert Balzer

USC, Information Sciences Institute, Marina del Rey, CA, USA

John Benoit

The MITRE Corporation, McLean, VA, USA

Lawrence Birnbaum

The Institute for the Learning Sciences and Department of Electrical Engineering and Computer Science, Northwestern University, Evanston, IL 60201, USA

Frederick Hayes-Roth

Cimflex Teknowledge Corp., 1810 Embarcadero Road, Palo Alto, CA, USA

Earl D. Sacerdoti

Machine Intelligence Corporation, Palo Alto, CA, USA

The context

In August 1980, the first meeting of the American Association of Artificial Intelligence was held at Stanford University. In contrast to earlier AI

Correspondence to: M. Stefik, Xerox Corporation, Palo Alto Research Center, 3333 Coyote Hill Road, Palo Alto, CA 94304, USA. E-mail: stefik@parc.xerox.com.

conferences, there was a new and very visible presence of people with strong commercial interests in AI—as venture capitalists, representatives of large corporations, and AI'ers turned entrepreneurs. There was a pervasive sense that AI was beginning to leave the confines of research laboratories and to take root in many different and practical settings.

A week or so after the conference, the National Science Foundation and the Defense Advanced Research Projects Agency co-sponsored a workshop on expert systems in San Diego. The conference organizers were Frederick Hayes-Roth, Don Waterman, and Douglas Lenat. The purpose of the workshop was to organize the writing of an edited book about expert systems. Workshop participants believed that expert systems were becoming a hot topic. The topic did not have clear boundaries. Defining those boundaries and articulating the practice of the field was the purpose of the workshop.

The participants were organized in groups corresponding to book chapters. The authors of this paper were the members of the "architecture" committee with Mark Stefik as its chair. During the conference the committee worked intensively for three days to organize its ideas. Two large tablets of flip charts were filled out, critiqued by members, ordered and collected. Over the next few months we turned these notes into a more finished work.

Ultimately, the work was published in three forms. In the book *Building Expert Systems* [1], the work was split into two chapters. The first chapter was a brief introduction to vocabulary and basic concepts about symbols, search, and symbolic reasoning. The second chapter included a sampling of roughly characterized tasks for which expert systems were being built and a "pedagogical tour" of organizational prescriptions for increasingly difficult cases. The material in the second chapter appeared in print first as the tutorial in *Artificial Intelligence* [3]. To help meet the demand for reprints, the complete work was also distributed as a Xerox PARC technical report.

Contributions of the work

The tutorial offered a way of thinking about a familiy of representation and problem solving approaches. For the more complex examples, this amounted to a selection from what we considered to be the "big ideas" of AI, described in a context of their application.

The first case on the pedagogical tour was the simplest. We characterized it as having a small search space, with reliable and unchanging data describing the problem, and with reliable knowledge for guiding the search. These characteristics precluded the need to adjust for errorful or noisy data. They precluded the need to represent the search hierarchically or to use nonmonotonic reasoning.

The rest of the cases were organized in a tree in which the constraints on problem characteristics were progressively relaxed, admitting more difficult problems and requiring more sophisticated approaches for representation and reasoning. Concepts introduced in the tour included Bayesian approaches to probabilistic reasoning, fuzzy logic, approaches for representing time-varying data, hierarchical generate-and-test, match methods, hierarchical planning, representations for interacting goals in planning problems, nonmonotonic reasoning, use of multiple lines of reasoning, and use of multiple cooperating models as in many blackboard systems.

The tutorial projected an engineering attitude in describing techniques and approaches used in AI systems of the time. Although the techniques and approaches were not new to the paper, they were explained in a unified context to make them more comparable for people in AI and more accessible to people who were entering the field. It was a selected introduction to the literature of AI bearing on architectural choices of expert system design.

Side-effects

Our tutorial provided an entry point to AI and expert systems. The collecting of citation index counts in this issue are the first attempt we know of to measure the influence of this and other AI papers. The only other information we had is that we received several hundred requests for reprints. We had also heard testimonials from many people who found that they could classify their problems and systems along the dimensions we suggested and build systems following the guidance.

The area of expert system architecture has not advanced significantly in the last decade. Most commercial systems that were built correspond to architectures early within our tour. Most of that effort necessarily has gone into simple, high leverage applications. Most of the system building was involved in integration with conventional programming and databases.

Retrospecting and prospecting

During the last decade, research has taken a swing toward analysis. General frameworks of understanding are being replaced by specialized studies. It is no longer unusual to model problem solving as search, to use heuristic knowledge to reduce the time complexity of search from exponential to linear, or to use different kinds of symbolic models for different kinds of problems. Rather, the field has specialized toward doing detailed comparisons of alternative models. We are better able to characterize the structural richness of search spaces. Substantially more powerful mathematical tools are employed to analyze performance, especially at what we now call the symbol level.

Knowledge level issues, however, are still less well defined. Current commercial efforts in the creation of task-specific shells are taking place in pragmatic settings, without much coordinated support from research. In this context, the area of expert systems—now more-often called knowledge systems—is again attracting students from outside of computer science.

Today in universities, interest in building expert systems is shifting to engineering and science departments where the creation and study of particular computational models is seen as advancing its subject matter. Within a department of (say) civil engineering, chemistry, or business, building an expert system is not "just an application of AI". Rather it is a way of expressing knowledge in a computational medium. People in these fields are engaged in building increasingly competent and complex models.

The perspective of a knowledge medium raises new kinds of questions about the creation, encoding, and reuse of knowledge. There is a growing interest in the sharing of computational models. Projects for building large, knowledge bases for experimental reuse are being advocated and in some cases are underway.

One of the questions we were asked to answer in this retrospective is what we would do differently given what we know today. One member of the original architecture group—Mark Stefik—has been writing a textbook, *Introduction to Knowledge Systems* [2], that is in many ways a follow-on to the original paper. The book is for model builders who want to understand how a computational medium can represent knowledge, reason with it, and create it. It is for those who want to automate some knowledge-intensive task and who expect to use knowledge systems. Persons interested in finding out more about that or in course testing draft versions of the text are invited to contact the publisher, Morgan Kaufmann.

References

[1] F. Hayes-Roth, D.A. Waterman and D.B. Lenat, eds., *Building Expert Systems* (Addison-Wesley, Reading, MA, 1983).
[2] M.J. Stefik, *Introduction to Knowledge Systems* (Morgan Kaufmann, San Mateo, CA, in preparation).
[3] M. Stefik, J.S. Aikins, R. Balzer, J. Benoit, L. Birnbaum, F. Hayes-Roth and E.D. Sacerdoti, The organization of expert systems, a tutorial, *Artif. Intell.* **18** (2) (1982) 135–173.

Systems

Artificial Intelligence 59 (1993) 227–232
Elsevier

ARTINT 980

STRIPS, a retrospective

Richard E. Fikes and Nils J. Nilsson

Computer Science Department, Stanford University, Stanford, CA 94305, USA

Introduction

During the late 1960s and early 1970s, an enthusiastic group of researchers at the SRI AI Laboratory focused their energies on a single experimental project in which a mobile robot was being developed that could navigate and push objects around in a multi-room environment (Nilsson [11]) . The project team consisted of many people over the years, including Steve Coles, Richard Duda, Richard Fikes, Tom Garvey, Cordell Green, Peter Hart, John Munson, Nils Nilsson, Bert Raphael, Charlie Rosen, and Earl Sacerdoti. The hardware consisted of a mobile cart, about the size of a small refrigerator, with touch-sensitive "feelers", a television camera, and an optical range-finder. The cart was capable of rolling around an environment consisting of large boxes in rooms separated by walls and doorways; it could push the boxes from one place to another in its world. Its suite of programs consisted of those needed for visual scene analysis (it could recognize boxes, doorways, and room corners), for planning (it could plan sequences of actions to achieve goals), and for converting its plans into intermediate-level and low-level actions in its world. When the robot moved, its television camera shook so much that it became affectionately known as "Shakey the Robot".

The robot, the environment, and the tasks performed by the system were quite simple by today's standards, but they were sufficiently paradigmatic to enable initial explorations of many core issues in the development of intelligent autonomous systems. In particular, they provided the context and motivation for development of the A* search algorithm (Hart et al. [7]), the STRIPS (Fikes and Nilsson [4]) and ABSTRIPS (Sacerdoti [14]) planning systems, programs for generalizing and learning macro-operators

Correspondence to: R.E. Fikes, Knowledge System Laboratory, 701 Welch Road, Bldg. C, Palo Alto, CA 94304, USA. E-mail: fikes@ksl.stanford.edu.

(MACROPS) (Fikes et al. [5]), "triangle tables"for plan execution (Fikes [3]), and region-finding scene analysis programs (Duda and Hart [1]). In this note, we focus on the development of the STRIPS (STanford Research Institute Problem Solver) automatic plan generator and its accompanying plan execution monitor.

The STRIPS automatic plan generator

STRIPS is often cited as providing a seminal framework for attacking the "classical planning problem" in which the world is regarded as being in a static state and is transformable to another static state only by a single agent performing any of a given set of actions. The planning problem is then to find a sequence of agent actions that will transform a given initial world state into any of a set of given goal states. For many years, automatic planning research was focused on that simple state-space problem formulation, and was frequently based on the representation framework and reasoning methods developed in the STRIPS system.

The integration of state-space heuristic search and resolution theorem proving which is the centerpiece of the STRIPS design was consistent with and motivated by the bringing together of our respective backgrounds and interests at the time. Fikes had come to SRI from CMU in 1969 steeped in a GPS-based heuristic problem solving tradition. In addition, he had just completed work on the REF-ARF problem solver (Fikes [2]) which had a multi-level design analogous to that of STRIPS in that it used a symbolic interpreter (of nondeterministic procedures) to build up (constraint-based) state descriptions that were then analyzed by a separate reasoner. Nilsson and his colleagues at SRI had been focused on logic-based representations and use of theorem proving techniques for problem solving. Notably, Cordell Green had just completed development of the QA3 [6] system for his Ph.D. thesis in which the situation calculus representation developed by McCarthy and Hayes [10] and a resolution theorem prover was used to do (among other things) automatic planning for the SRI robot domain.

Green's QA3 work focused our attention on the difficulties of describing in a formal logic the effects of an action, and particularly the difficulty of specifying those aspects of a situation that are not affected by an action (i.e., the "frame problem"). There were no default logic or circumscription theories to appeal to, and we did not invent them. Frustrated by these "technical" difficulties and driven by the pragmatic objective of developing an effective plan generator, we began considering "ad hoc" representations for robot actions and algorithms for modeling their effects, while still maintaining our logic-based representation of individual states. Those considerations produced what is arguably the key technical contribution of the STRIPS work, namely the STRIPS operator representation and the algorithm for modeling the effects of an operator based on the "STRIPS assumption" that a plan operator affects only those aspects of the world explicitly mentioned in the operator's deletions and additions lists.

Given that we had an effective means of representing robot actions and their effects, we were then faced with the task of designing a plan generator. Using GPS as our paradigmatic problem solving architecture, we needed to define meaningful "differences" between a situation described by a set of predicate calculus sentences and a goal situation in which a given predicate calculus sentence is true. Once differences were defined, we needed to specify what it meant for an operator to be "relevant" to "reducing" the difference.

Since we were using our resolution theorem prover to determine whether a goal was true in a given state, we were faced with the problem of extracting from the theorem prover's failed proof attempts "differences" between the given state and one in which the goal is true. We noted that what was needed to complete the proof were operators which would assert clauses that resolve with the clauses at the leaf nodes of the proof tree. Thus, we could use pattern matching techniques to find operators whose additions lists were relevant to reducing the difference between incomplete and complete proofs without the need for an explicit difference table.[1] This technique, which was another key technical idea in the design, was essentially the same as that used by backward chaining production rule interpreters developed many years later. In our case, each operator corresponded to a rule of the form

> if ⟨ preconditions ⟩
> then (retract ⟨ deletions ⟩) (assert ⟨ additions ⟩).

In retrospect, STRIPS was extremely limited in both the scope of planning issues it addressed and the complexity of problems it could solve. Whereas current planning research is concerned with multiple agents operating in dynamic environments, STRIPS assumed that only one action could occur at any time, that nothing changed except as a result of the planned actions, and that actions were effectively instantaneous. Also, the STRIPS "solution" to the frame problem was vague and flawed. It was many years before the ideas were made precise and a satisfactory formal semantics developed (see Lifschitz [9]). Even with those limitations, the STRIPS representation and reasoning framework was used as the basis for most automatic planning research for many years. Perhaps the severe simplifying assumptions of

---

[1]Note that the technique for finding relevant operators of matching goals to add lists is only a heuristic since the delete lists of operators are ignored. If an operator is selected to complete an incomplete proof and it deletes a clause used in the incomplete proof, then the proof attempt may fail after application of the operator because of the missing clause.

the STRIPS framework were needed in order to enable early progress to be made on the extreme difficulties of the general automatic planning problem. The STRIPS framework had sufficient intuitive appeal to most researchers for them to believe that it was a viable foundation on which to develop techniques that would be effective in more realistic models. For example, techniques for abstract planning were developed as direct extensions to STRIPS (Sacerdoti [14]), and even some frameworks for planning in dynamic worlds were formulated as extensions to the static STRIPS world (e.g., Hendrix [8] and Pednault [13]).

The STRIPS execution monitor

Given that STRIPS had produced a plan to achieve a goal state, the system was then confronted with the problem that when Shakey executed the plan in a real environment, the resulting state often differed from the state expected by the planner. The differences might result from inadequacies in the robot's world model, effectors, or both. Thus, some kind of "execution monitor" was needed to determine after execution of each plan step whether the plan was "on track" or whether replanning was needed. The problem becomes interesting when one realizes that an exact match between actual and planned states will rarely be achieved and is not needed, since most aspects of a given situation will be irrelevant to the success of a plan. Thus, the challenge is to determine the requirements that must be satisfied by the state produced after each plan step in order for the remainder of the plan to succeed.

Execution monitoring was a relatively unexplored problem at the time this work was done because most AI problem solving research until then had been focused on domains where actions are assumed to produce the results described in their models (e.g., chess, puzzles, theorem proving). Because we were working with an actual rather than a simulated robot, we were led to consider this important additional aspect of problem solving in the physical world.

There were basically two notable technical ideas in the STRIPS execution monitor. The first was a simple algorithm for computing a "kernel" set of sentences which must be true after each plan step in order for the remainder of the plan to succeed. The algorithm regressed plan goals and operator preconditions back through the plan to the states where they were expected to become true and then included them in the kernel of that state and all states through which they had been regressed.

The second notable technical idea in the execution monitor was the monitoring algorithm based on the "triangle table" plan representation. Given that a plan's kernels have been computed, a simple execution monitor might check whether the appropriate kernel is true after each plan step, execute the next plan step if it is, and initiate replanning if it is not. However, that simple algorithm is deficient in two important ways: it does not recognize situations in which the next plan step is unnecessary because the kernel sentences it is intended to achieve are already serendipitously true, nor does it recognize situations in which redoing some portion of the existing plan is a viable response to the expected kernel not being true. We designed a monitoring algorithm which overcame those deficiencies by asking after executing each plan step whether the goal (i.e., the final kernel) is true, then whether the kernel preceding the last plan step is true, then whether the kernel preceding the next to last plan step is true, etc. When a true kernel was found, the testing stopped and the appropriate action was taken; if no kernels were true, then replanning was initiated. The algorithm did not execute unnecessary steps, retried steps that had failed, and was non-redundant in that it checked each kernel sentence only once as it searched for true kernels.

The STRIPS execution monitor is a simple form of a goal-directed program interpreter in which the goal to be achieved by each program step is explicitly represented and monitored by the interpreter. Some current planning systems embed the monitoring algorithm in the plans they produce in the form of conditional actions that test the kernel sentences (e.g. Nilsson's "teleo-reactive" programs [12]). Given such embedding, execution monitoring occurs as a side-effect of simply executing the plan as a conventional program.

The STRIPS monitor's preference at each step for reusing portions of the existing plan or even to continue executing the existing plan rather than replanning is a heuristic choice except in the rare case where the states being produced during execution are identical to those anticipated by the planner. The choice is heuristic because if an actual state differs from the anticipated one, the planner may be able to produce a plan to achieve the goal from that state which is more efficient than the original plan. The preference for using the existing plan is based on an assumption that replanning is expensive.

Finally, note that the execution monitor takes as given the sensor feedback from the robot after each action is executed. It does not consider, for example, the possibility of sensor error when a kernel sentence is false nor does it consider obtaining additional sensor data when the truth value of a kernel sentence cannot be determined.

References

[1] R.O. Duda and P.E. Hart, Experiments in scene analysis, Tech. Note 20, Artificial Intelligence Center, SRI International, Menlo Park, CA (1970).

[2] R.E. Fikes, REF-ARF: a system for solving problems stated as procedures, *Artif. Intell.* **1** (1) (1970) 27–120.

[3] R.E. Fikes, Monitored execution of robot plans produced by STRIPS, in: *Proceedings IFIP Congress 71*, Ljubljana, Yugoslavia (1971).

[4] R.E. Fikes and N.J. Nilsson, STRIPS: a new approach to the application of theorem proving to problem solving, *Artif. Intell.* **2** (1981) 189–208.

[5] R.E. Fikes, P.E. Hart and N.J. Nilsson, Learning and executing generalized robot plans, *Artif. Intell.* **3** (4) (1972) 251–288.

[6] C.C. Green, Application of theorem proving to problem solving, in: *Proceedings IJCAI-69*, Washington, DC (1969) 219–239.

[7] P.E. Hart, N.J. Nilsson and B. Raphael, A formal basis for the heuristic determination of minimum cost paths, *IEEE Trans. Syst. Sci. Cybern.* **4** (2) (1968) 100–107.

[8] G. Hendrix, Modelling simultaneous actions and continuous processes, *Artif. Intell.* **4** (1973) 145–180.

[9] V. Lifschitz, On the semantics of STRIPS, in: M.P. Georgeff and A. Lansky, eds., *Reasoning about Actions and Plans* (Morgan Kaufmann, San Mateo, CA, 1987).

[10] J. McCarthy and P.J. Hayes, Some philosophical problems from the standpoint of artificial intelligence, in: B. Meltzer and D. Michie, eds., *Machine Intelligence* **4** (Edinburgh University Press, Edinburgh, 1969) 463–502.

[11] N.J. Nilsson, Shakey the Robot, SRI Tech. Note 323, Menlo Park, CA (1984).

[12] N.J. Nilsson, Toward agent programs with circuit semantics, Robotics Laboratory Tech. Note, Computer Science Department, Stanford University, Stanford, CA (1992).

[13] E. Pednault, Formulating multi agent dynamic world problems in the classical planning framework, in: M.P. Georgeff and A. Lansky, eds. *Reasoning about Actions and Plans* (Morgan Kaufmann, Los Altos, CA, 1987) 42–82.

[14] E. Sacerdoti, Planning in a hierarchy of abstraction spaces, *Artif. Intell.* **5** (2) (1975) 115–135.

Artificial Intelligence 59 (1993) 233–240
Elsevier

ARTINT 983

DENDRAL and Meta-DENDRAL: roots of knowledge systems and expert system applications

Edward A. Feigenbaum

Knowledge Systems Laboratory, Department of Computer Science, Stanford University, Stanford, CA 94305, USA

Bruce G. Buchanan

Computer Science Department, University of Pittsburgh, Pittsburgh, PA 15260, USA

During AI's first decade (1956–1966), the task environments in which AI scientists investigated their basic science issues were generally idealized "clean" task environments, such as propositional calculus theorem proving and puzzle solving. After the mid-1960s, a bolder and more applied inclination to choose complex real-world problems as task environments became evident. These efforts were both successful and exciting, in two ways. First, the AI programs were achieving high levels of competence at solving certain problems that human specialists found challenging (the excitement was that our AI techniques were indeed powerful and that we were taking the first steps toward the dream of the very smart machine). Second, these complex real-world task environments were proving to be excellent at stimulating basic science questions for the AI science, in knowledge representation, problem solving, and machine learning. To recognize and illuminate this trend, the *Artificial Intelligence Journal* in 1978 sponsored a special issue on applications of artificial intelligence.

Correspondence to: E.A. Feigenbaum, Knowledge Systems Laboratory, Department of Computer Science, Stanford University, Stanford, CA 94305, USA. E-mail: eaf@sumex-aim.stanford.edu.

Salient among the early applications of AI was the work of the DENDRAL group, applying AI to problems of the analysis of the mass spectra of organic molecules and the induction of new rules of mass spectral fragmentation. The paper "Dendral and Meta-Dendral: their applications dimension" [3] was solicited by the editor of the special issue. The article appeared in 1978, thirteen years after the start of the DENDRAL Project. In those thirteen years, many DENDRAL papers had been published in the literature of both AI and chemistry. Some of the results of DENDRAL and Meta-DENDRAL as applications to chemistry had been reported to chemists. The time was ripe for reporting these results not merely as chemistry but as applied AI, and the special issue provided us with the appropriate vehicle.

In this note, we will look both backward and forward from the 1978 publication date of the special issue. Though this note is necessarily short, two other and longer works have done this job thoroughly [8,9], the more recent paper having the advantages of perspective of time and experience with the technology transfer of DENDRAL to an industrial setting.

DENDRAL in the context of its time: more history

The DENDRAL Project began in 1965. Feigenbaum had been searching for a task environment in which to investigate processes of empirical induction (of models and theories from data) and had oriented his thinking toward finding such a task environment among the activities that scientists do. Lederberg, a geneticist whose work in 1965 on exobiology involved the mass spectra of amino acids, suggested the task of analyzing mass spectra—the formation of hypotheses of organic molecular structure from mass spectral data. Buchanan joined the effort shortly thereafter; his orientation was philosophy of science blended with AI, a concern for the nature of scientific discovery and the information processes underlying it.

DENDRAL work was largely experimental work. One of the earliest of the experimental results was also perhaps the most important. That was the *knowledge-is-power hypothesis*, which has become the slogan by which many in AI remember the DENDRAL Project. As we extended the limits of DENDRAL's abilities, what we found was that we needed, more than anything else, *more domain-specific knowledge* of chemistry and mass spectrometry (having more powerful AI problem solving methods was useful but not crucial to our success; more knowledge was crucial). Toward this end, we recruited the collaboration of Djerassi, a world-class specialist in mass spectrometry, and with Djerassi his team of researchers, visitors, and post-docs.

One of our important early motivations, investigating the processes of theory formation (in scientific work, and elsewhere) was postponed for several years. We made a decision (in retrospect correct) to achieve experimental results and gain system-building experience on a more concrete problem first: the hypothesis formation problem of inferring from one set of spectral data one (or a few) candidate molecular structure(s). Success with DENDRAL led us back to the original problem of theory formation, which now appeared in a quite specific and concrete form that was "meta" to DENDRAL (hence the project's name, Meta-DENDRAL). If the knowledge of mass spectrometry was crucial to the progress of DENDRAL, then we must codify it, and we knew of only two ways. Either work in the painstaking one-on-one fashion of our interaction with Djerassi's chemists (which has since become known as the knowledge acquisition part of knowledge engineering). Or, infer the knowledge directly from electronic libraries of mass spectral data and the known structures that gave rise to the data. The latter was the task of the Meta-DENDRAL learning program.

Did DENDRAL make a difference?

How did DENDRAL affect AI? The AI science of 1965 was largely dominated by the theme of the "*generality* dimension" of problem solving. At center stage was the program GPS, but the GPS model was being challenged by problem solvers based on theorem proving using the newly discovered and programmed resolution method. Hardly mentioned in the discussion was the role of knowledge in problem solving. For example, in a very important early paper by Newell, Simon, and Shaw [11] describing their chess playing program, the word "knowledge" is used only once, and that use is incidental to the paper's main line.

Because generality dominated the field's concerns, the issue of *levels of competence in performance* did not motivate the field very much in the early 1960s. That was odd, because the dream of human-level and beyond-human-level performance was strongly present at the birth of AI (e.g. predictions of world-class chess play; predictions of new theorems to be proved by AI programs; performance of an AI program on the New York State Regents geometry exam).

The DENDRAL group was strongly focused on the performance dimension of AI and played a key role in reinstating the view (the goal, the dream) that AI programs can perform at the level of the most competent humans performing the task (and perhaps beyond). It did this with enough specificity that its results could be extended by the group itself, and by others. For the DENDRAL group, the extension was to MYCIN, then to EMYCIN (the software generalization), then to applications in medicine, engineering, molecular biology, x-ray crystallography, submarine detection, etc. This system-building experimental AI effort, sustained over a period of fifteen years, engendered concepts, methods, techniques, software, and (not least) credibility for the approach. A new sector of AI was born, as well as a sector of the software industry.

How important was this to AI? In 1985, when the Editors of the *Artificial Intelligence Journal* asked key AI scientists for their views of the most important happenings in AI over the previous decade, Allen Newell responded:

> There is no doubt, as far as I am concerned, that the development of expert systems is the major advance in the field during the past decade.... The emergence of expert systems has transformed the enterprise of AI, not only because it has been the main driver of the current wave of commercialization of AI, but because it has set the major scientific problems for AI for the next few years.... [1, p. 385]

We think of DENDRAL as the "grandfather of expert systems". (Though, in the modern style, perhaps we should think of it as "the mother of all expert systems".) In 1968, we wrote a paper summarizing the first three years of the DENDRAL experiments, in which we used the DENDRAL results to challenge the "generality" paradigm. We stated and defended our knowledge-is-power hypothesis of problem solving. That paper, in several places, links the system's behavior with that of "the expert", and the felicitous phrase "expert system" came into use in our project thereafter. Much more important than the coining of a term was the fact that we helped to set in motion a shift in paradigm in AI from one based on generality to one that was *knowledge-based*. The knowledge-based paradigm is today the main operating paradigm of AI. For example, one of the major textbooks of AI (Rich and Knight [12] concludes the book with this:

> If there is one single message that this book has tried to convey, it is the crucial part that knowledge plays in AI programs. [12, p. 579]

DENDRAL was not the only agent that brought about the shift of paradigm (at MIT, Moses and the Mathlab/Macsyma group were influential supporters of and early contributors to the expert systems viewpoint), but it was one of the most significant agents.

By 1967, the DENDRAL project faced a crisis of knowledge representation. The amount of new knowledge (represented as LISP code) that was pouring in via the knowledge acquisition interactions with the chemists produced a complexity of the knowledge base that we could neither manage nor sustain. Inspired initially by the Newell–Simon use of productions as an architecture for problem solving, we conceptualized productions as modular situation–action "rules" in terms of which we could represent the knowledge of mass spectrometry. By early 1968, we had re-represented the entire knowledge base of DENDRAL, had provided a clean representation for the remainder of the DENDRAL Project, and had given ourselves the right representational leverage for the soon-to-happen MYCIN work. This contribution of DENDRAL to AI has been one of the most robust. As expert systems moved into industrial and commercial use, most of the implementations were rule-based systems.

Well, DENDRAL, what have you done for us lately?

Riding on the maturation of time-sharing technology and the birth of the ARPAnet, Lederberg and Feigenbaum established the SUMEX facility, a national computational resource for applications of AI to Medicine and Biology. DENDRAL was ported to SUMEX's PDP-10 and made available throughout the 1970s and early 1980s to a wide national community of academic and industrial chemists. They used DENDRAL primarily to gain the advantage of its superb structure elucidation methods (not, however, for its mass spectral analysis expertise).

In the original article that is the subject of this note, we pointed to a problem of technology transfer at that time: the absence of "satellite engineering firms" for AI that could "map research programs into marketable products" that would benefit the chemical industry. In this simplistic wish of our younger selves was a stunning naiveté: that such firms, if they existed would want to "harden" our software; and that buyers for our software existed in the industry. Also in the original article, as a way to improve the chances for technology transfer, and with some prescience, we called for a small computer to come into being, hopefully inexpensive, that would run advanced symbolic manipulation languages (we asked for INTERLISP)!

Several factors, not least among which was the impending end of federal funding for the DENDRAL Project, led Stanford to license the DENDRAL programs to a company specializing in software for chemical structure manipulation, synthesis planning, and literature searching. The key players of the DENDRAL Project in the 1980s were all of a breed that might be called "computational chemists". They were hired by the company to do the technology transfer, and more importantly for the company to guide and develop other projects within the firm. (Our former chemist collaborators regard the DENDRAL Project's training of many of the first generation of computational chemists as one of the most significant contributions of the Project).

DENDRAL as a software entity with a unique identity was "de-constructed". Its structure manipulation algorithms have been used in the various products of the firm, including three chemical database management systems.

These systems, using DENDRAL ideas, algorithms, and chemical structure representations, are used (according to the company) by the "overwhelming majority of the world's chemical and pharmaceutical industries to manage their chemical information".

The focus on mass spectrometry was apparently not a marketable focus. Nor apparently was DENDRAL's unmatched capability to do systematic structure elucidation—even when coupled with excellent modern interactivity that would allow a chemist to shape and control the search for structures.

As AI researchers, we seriously underestimated the problems of technology transfer and the nature of the barriers to technology diffusion. "Underestimate" is charitable: we really didn't have the foggiest idea. This same lack of understanding was to plague the embryonic AI software and applications industry throughout the 1980s. While the small, cheap symbol-manipulating computers we asked for did indeed help to lower acceptance barriers, we largely ignored the social, psychological, and business aspects of reluctance to try new tools. We comment on all of these, and give the subject extensive discussion in our recent case study paper [9]. We also failed to appreciate until 1988 [5] the crucial role played by champions of the technology in industry. A technology does not transfer itself; it is transferred on the strong shoulders of champions of the technology. None of the early industrial users of DENDRAL became an industrial champion for DENDRAL.

What about Meta-DENDRAL? What did it do for AI? For industry?

Around the time of Meta-DENDRAL's birth (circa 1970), work in the machine learning area was at a low ebb (exceptions were Waterman's work at our lab on learning of production rules, an ancestor of Meta-DENDRAL; Michalski's work on variable-valued logic and its application to learning; and Winston's thesis work on concept acquisition). Meta-DENDRAL was the stimulus that led to the resurgence of the machine learning area. This was due to three factors:

First, Meta-DENDRAL focused on knowledge: the learning of knowledge, not process. In addition, it took a knowledge-based approach to the learning task. Meta-DENDRAL demonstrated in a concrete way that "knowledge acquisition is itself a knowledge-based task". In the early 1970s, these were powerful ideas.

Second, it turned out that an important part of Meta-DENDRAL's learning algorithms were generalizable. The generalization—to Version Spaces—was done by Mitchell [10] in his thesis, spawned much research, and was very influential.

Third, Meta-DENDRAL had demonstrably significant results. A paper we published in 1976 [4] reported new mass spectral fragmentation rules for certain subfamilies of the chemical family called androstanes. As far as we know, it was the first paper in the literature of science that reports the discovery of new scientific knowledge (albeit of a routine kind) by a computer program (there is now another). Perhaps in the future that will be viewed as a landmark event.

We characterized Meta-DENDRAL's task as an induction problem with not many examples to start with and no teacher to pre-classify them. Some of the design considerations implied by this goal are still being addressed by the machine learning community. Here are several examples:

- *Noisy data*: We could not assume that the empirical data given to the program were complete and correct. The data were known to contain spurious (noisy) data points and to omit data points that the theory predicted should be present.
- *Multiple concepts*: Meta-DENDRAL had to learn the preconditions (LHSs) for more than one concept (mass spectral process), but did not know how many concepts needed to be learned.
- *Unclassified data*: Meta-DENDRAL was given sets of x–y points without having those points labeled as positive or negative instances of a concept. Thus we first had to generate possible explanations of each x–y point before we could consider positive and negative evidence associated with each explanation.

This is the stuff of excellent AI science. But did Meta-DENDRAL find any application in any industrial setting? No. Nor have any of the other complex machine learning procedures (however, machine induction based on algorithms of Quinlan have had a marginal success). The industry of AI applications is still awaiting the dawn of an era of knowledge engineering significantly aided by machine learning.

References

[1] D.G. Bobrow and P.J. Hayes, Artificial Intelligence—where are we? *Artif. Intell.* **25** (3) (1985) 375–415.

[2] J. Brinkley, R. Altman, B. Duncan, B.G. Buchanan and O. Jardetzky, The heuristic refinement method for the derivation of protein solution structures: validation of Cytochrome-b562, *J. Chem. Inf. Comput. Sci.* **28** (4) (1988) 194–210.

[3] B.G. Buchanan and E.A. Feigenbaum, Dendral and Meta-Dendral: their applications dimension, *Artif. Intell.* **11** (1978) 5–24.

[4] B.G. Buchanan, D.H. Smith, W.C. White, R. Gritter, E.A. Feigenbaum, J. Lederberg and C. Djerassi, Applications of artificial intelligence for chemical inference, XXII: automatic rule formation in mass spectrometry by means of the Meta-DENDRAL program, *J. Am. Chem. Soc.* **98** (1976) 6168.

[5] E.A. Feigenbaum, P. McCorduck and H.P. Nii, *The Rise of the Expert Company* (Times Books, 1988).

[6] P.D. Karp, Hypothesis formation and qualitative reasoning in molecular biology, Knowledge Systems Laboratory Tech. Report 89-52, Stanford University, Stanford, CA (1989).

[7] D.B. Lenat and E.A. Feigenbaum, On the thresholds of knowledge, in: *Proceedings IJCAI-87*, Milan, Italy (1987) 1173–1182; also: *Artif. Intell.* **47** (1991) 185–250.

[8] R.K. Lindsay, B.G. Buchanan, E.A. Feigenbaum and J. Lederberg, *Applications of Artificial Intelligence for Organic Chemistry: The DENDRAL Project* McGraw-Hill, New York, 1980).

[9] R.K. Lindsay, B.G. Buchanan, E.A. Feigenbaum and J. Lederberg, DENDRAL: a case study of the first expert system for scientific hypothesis formation, *Artif. Intell.* **60** (1993) (to appear).

[10] T.M. Mitchell, Version spaces: an approach to concept learning, Doctoral dissertation, Department of Electrical Engineering, Stanford University (1978).

[11] A. Newell, H.A. Simon and C. Shaw, Chess playing programs and the problem of complexity, E.A. Feigenbaum and J. Feldman, eds., *Computers and Thought* (McGraw-Hill, New York, 1963).

[12] E. Rich and K. Knight, *Artificial Intelligence* (McGraw-Hill, New York, 2nd ed., 1991).

Artificial Intelligence 59 (1993) 241–247
Elsevier

ARTINT 981

R1 ("XCON") at age 12: lessons from an elementary school achiever

John McDermott

Digital Equipment Corporation, 111 Locke Drive, Marlboro, MA 01752, USA

The R1 paper [7] claimed that the following two lessons emerged from our effort to develop a computer system configurer:

- "An expert system can perform a task simply by recognizing what to do, provided that it is possible to determine locally (i.e., at each step) whether taking some particular action is consistent with acceptable performance on the task."
- "When an expert system is implemented as a production system, the job of refining and extending the system's knowledge is quite easy."

If I had the paper to write over again, I would claim that three lessons emerged from this research.

One of the three lessons is the first lesson mentioned above; the paper almost got that lesson right, but as far as I can tell, failed to convince anyone that it is important. The second lesson mentioned above is a wildly simplistic formulation of another lesson that continues to emerge as R1 grows in size and shape; a better formulation of the second lesson is that today's most commonly touted programming heuristics (also known as "good software engineering principles") must be made substantially less parochial before they can be followed to develop and maintain a system like R1. The third lesson is that if usefulness is the primary criterion of success for an application program, then R1 didn't become much of a success until several years after the R1 paper was written.

Correspondence to: J. McDermott, Digital Equipment Corporation, 111 Locke Drive, Marlboro, MA 01752, USA. E-mail: mcdermott@airg.enet.dec.com.

The first lesson repeated

- For some tasks, a very significant fraction of the knowledge required to perform the tasks competently is domain-specific knowledge of how to decide what to do next (i.e., is domain-specific control knowledge).

The R1 paper suggested that the most interesting thing about R1 is that it manages to successfully search a large space without backtracking. It claimed that this is because R1 contains a large amount of domain-specific control knowledge. The paper described how R1 uses the Match method (Newell [8]) to perform its task. The Match method can be used for a task if there exists an implicit partial ordering on the decisions comprising the task such that the consequences of making the next decision bear only on aspects of the solution that have not yet been determined. For reasons that I don't understand, the description in the R1 paper of how R1 uses Match has given rise to a serious misconception. The misconception is that R1 knows, before it configures a system, the order in which it should perform its various subtasks. This exactly misses the point of R1 (and of Match).

R1's task has the feature (shared by almost all tasks that involve putting physical or mental things together) that the order in which various configuration decisions are made determines whether or not the agent doing the configuration will have to perform a combinatorial search. In other words, the order in which the configurer extends the configuration has strong implications for whether an acceptable configuration can be found. If the configurer makes a bad choice about what to do next, then it will at some later point run up against the consequences of that choice and have to backtrack. If the configurer makes many such bad choices, then the effort required to produce an acceptable configuration will be huge. What the development of R1 showed and continues to show is:

- The precise sequence in which R1's lowest level actions (rule firings) occur is usually not important.
- Getting the sequencing of R1's behaviors right at a slightly higher grain size (the subtask level—a few tens of rule firings) is critical if R1 is to avoid spending most of its time backtracking.
- A very significant fraction of R1's knowledge (i.e., of its 10,000 rules) is knowledge of how to decide what to do next.
- Given all of its domain-specific control knowledge, R1 makes the task look easy since it makes few missteps and appears to be pushed along by the consequences of its ever-growing set of past decisions.

Much the same point—that domain-specific control knowledge can change an intractable problem into a tractable one—has been made by the people who talk about problem solving in terms of Least Commitment (Stefik

[10]) instead of in terms of Match. They point out that search will be minimized if the problem solver acts at each step in a way that leaves the most options open. But what doesn't emerge for me from their writings and what apparently emerged for almost no one from the R1 paper is that the whole trick to preparing an agent to use Match or Least Commitment effectively is providing that agent with the know-how it will need in order to be smart about what to do next. Many considerations (i.e., many diverse pieces of knowledge) may need to be identified by the agent and brought to bear to make any one such decision. And hundreds of such decisions may need to be made to accomplish a task. R1, because it has by now an immense amount of knowledge about how to figure out what to do next, lives Least Commitment.

The second lesson reconstructed

- When a task has the characteristics that
  (1) only a small subset of the actions required to cover all task instances are relevant to any particular task instance, and
  (2) it makes a difference in what order some of the actions are performed,
  a production system implementation, because it is data driven, will make the job of extending and changing a system's knowledge easier than it would otherwise be—provided the Match method's requirements can be exploited to give visibility into and protection against potentially negative rule interactions.

What I think of, when I think of a "production system implementation", is a software artifact that has the character it has because it is trying to describe how to perform a task where what to do is very much dependent on a large collection of rapidly changing situational cues. Put another way, whenever there is a lot of conditionality in a task, some way needs to be found to describe and dynamically evaluate the conditions under which each action should be performed. If mostly all of the same actions are performed for each instance of a task, then a production system implementation doesn't add any value. The point here is that whether or not an official production system language (like OPS) is used as the implementation language, for such tasks the implementation has to find a way to address the issue of a lot of conditionality, and when you get right down to it, the options available are fairly limited.

The big problem that anyone who tries to automate tasks with lots of conditionality ends up being confronted by is the risk of incoherence. The problem is that the more we have to independently characterize the situation in which each action should be performed, the more risk there is that two apparently orthogonal descriptions will end up in unintended conflict. R1 is one of the few studies of how this risk can be reduced.

Before focusing on the one data point I know about, I want to discuss the general problem of abstraction misuse. Probably we all agree that abstracting is what allows us to get a handle on our experiences. Reality has too many facets for us to face them all at once, so we select. We abstract from all but a few facets, and this allows us to focus our attention on whatever it is in our current experience that happens to be relevant to our current goals (or maybe vice versa).

Now one of the things I've found myself doing in the course of writing application programs is trying to get clear, right from the start, what facets of reality each application program will need to attend to. Then I write descriptions (create concepts) that abstract from everything else. So far, so good. But what I mostly haven't done until lately is distinguish between facets that identify the properties of objects that someone sometime cares about ("sometimes interesting" facets) and facets that identify when those "sometimes interesting" facets are interesting ("when interesting" facets).

In my case, this failure has led to descriptions of the world that don't generalize at all well. Because I everywhere comingle the two types of facets, not much in the way of patterns emerge. Others have responded to their failure to distinguish in a quite different way. Their response has been to ignore the "when interesting" facets (or to relegate them to the nether world). Because this response denies that the "orthogonal collision" problem exists, it results in over-simplified characterizations of the real world (the fantasy of "always interesting" facets) and thus is a poor strategy for anyone even modestly desirous of writing application programs that are adapted to real world situations.

During 1986 and 1987, R1 was reimplemented (see Bachant [1,3]). The reports of this reimplementation make two important contributions to our understanding of how to automate tasks that are replete with conditionality:

- They document how the continued development of R1 became increasingly difficult precisely because the "sometimes interesting" facets and the "when interesting" facets were not distinguished (see Soloway et al. [9]).
- They describe a methodology that has proven itself to be of significant value in managing the development of programs that tackle tasks containing substantial amounts of conditionality.

RIME, the methodology developed during the reimplementation of R1, encourages developers to decompose tasks into problem spaces (relatively independent subtasks (see Laird [5]) and then for each of those pieces to create three things:

- a control structure (an algorithm) that defines the skeleton of the problem solving that will go on in that problem space,
- a body of knowledge describing how to determine what problem space should be active right now,
- a body of knowledge describing the various ways in which objects are operated on within this problem space.

To assist the developer in creating the second and third of these, RIME encourages the use, within each problem space, of multiple small facet hierarchies (abstraction graphs) that identify, for a body of knowledge within a problem space, the facets that are relevant. These facet hierarchies turn out to be a powerful aid to the developer because since they have no global aspirations, but are merely local accounts of what concepts (in this semantically rich and constantly changing world of ours) need to be attended to within each problem space, they avoid being pretentious and unwieldly. But even more important, by giving the same attention to "when interesting" and to "sometimes interesting" facets, the facet hierarchies promote paying serious attention to the multiplicity of ways in which relevance can manifest itself; in other words, they provide a way of thinking about serious conditionality.

RIME is an evolving methodology, but even in its current initial state, it provides substantial insight into how to effectively develop and maintain programs for real world tasks.

The third lesson

- To be useful, a system has to be able to do more than just correctly perform some task.

The R1 paper presented R1 as successful in virtue of the fact that it could correctly configure VAX-11/780 computer systems. The paper seems to suggest that if a program can perform some task correctly, then the program will be used. Later papers on R1 (McDermott [6] and Bachant [2]) suggested that it is also important that management buy in and be supportive. But none of the papers talked about how hard it is to place application programs in real workplaces (workplaces with organizations, processes, and individuals in place, each with their own attitudes, values, competencies, and incompetencies).

In retrospect, R1 owes its early feelings of self worth to its few initial target users. R1 was developed to assist with a very specific and a very new process—the configuration in the Salem, NH, plant of Digital's just-introduced VAX-11/780 computer systems. As Digital extended its VAX line and introduced other families (e.g., the 11/750, the 11/730), R1 was extended to deal with them. But even though R1's competence was significantly greater as each new family was introduced, R1's usage didn't correlate with its competence. Even though the configuration task was similar at each of Digital's manufacturing plants, some plants counted heavily on R1 and other plants used it only cosmetically. After several years of this very uneven dependency on R1, Digital introduced a low-end system that it expected to sell in high volume. The manufacturing engineer for that product designed R1 into his production process and so for that system family and for subsequent ones, Digital's reliance on R1 has been more uniform.

What strikes me most about this story is that its outcome relies so much on the particular attitudes of the individuals that R1 was developed to assist—their attitudes toward work, toward computers, toward assistance, toward process explicitness, etc. R1 was lucky. Its developers and some of its users managed to get enough into contact for it to amount to something. But the way the developers and users got into contact was not then, and is still not now, well understood.

Thus another area of research that the experience with R1 points to as critically important is research in workplace analysis—but more specifically, research in the identification of workplace analysis methodologies that provide, for any particular workplace, significant insight into the kinds of computer activity that would fit into that workplace in a helpful way (see Dallemagne et al. [4]).

Acknowledgement

Judy Bachant helped me recognize the lessons from R1. She, Bahar Ceceli, and Tom Mitchell also provided many valuable suggestions for how to make this retrospective more interesting and less misleading.

References

[1] J. Bachant, RIME: preliminary work toward a knowledge acquisition tool, in: S. Marcus, ed., *Automating Knowledge Acquisition for Expert Systems* (Kluwer, Dordrecht, Netherlands, 1988).

[2] J. Bachant and J. McDermott, R1 revisited: four years in the trenches, *AI Mag.* **5** (3) (1984) 21–32.

[3] J. Bachant and E. Soloway, The engineering of XCON, *Commun. ACM* **32** (3) (1989).

[4] G. Dallemagne, G. Klinker, D. Marques, J. McDermott and D. Tung, Making application programming more worthwhile, in: F. Schmalhofer, G. Strube and T. Wetter, eds., *Knowledge Engineering and Cognition* (Springer, New York, 1991).

[5] J. Laird and A. Newell, A universal weak method: summary of results, in: *Proceedings IJCAI-83*, Karlsruhe, Germany (1983).

[6] J. McDermott, R1: the formative years, *AI Mag.* **2** (2) (1981) 21–29.

[7] J. McDermott, R1: a rule-based configurer of computer systems, *Artif. Intell.* **19** (1) (1982) 39–88.

[8] A. Newell, Heuristic programming: ill-structured problems, in: J.S. Aaronofsky, ed., *Progress in Operations Research* (Wiley, New York, 1969).

[9] E. Soloway, J. Bachant and K. Jensen, Assessing the maintainability of XCON-in-RIME: coping with the problems of a very large rule-base, in: *Proceedings AAAI-87*, Seattle, WA (1987).

[10] M. Stefik, Planning and meta-planning (MOLGEN: Part 2), *Artif. Intell.* **16** (2) (1981) 141–169.

Allen Newell

Artificial Intelligence 59 (1993) 251–259
Elsevier

ARTINT 1023

Allen Newell: the entry into complex information processing

Herbert A. Simon

*Departments of Computer Science and Psychology, Carnegie Mellon University,
Pittsburgh, PA 15213, USA*

With the death on July 19, 1992 of Allen Newell, the field of artificial intelligence has lost one of its premier scientists, who was at the forefront of the field from its first stirrings to the present and whose research momentum had not shown the slightest diminution up to the premature end of his career. In this brief note I want to recount the events that led Allen into this field which he helped to create, and to which he devoted substantially his whole effort for 37 years. The history is partly my history also, and the history of Cliff Shaw [1], but the three of us followed quite different paths in the years that just preceded our intense collaboration, and the years that followed it, and I will focus on Allen's own path that brought him into the joint partnership. As the critical years ran from 1950 to 1956, my interpretations will derive mainly from a half dozen technical reports and papers that Allen authored or co-authored during that period. We will observe the scientist as a young man, and the knowledge and motives that set him on his career.

1. The career

A few preliminary comments. It is not strictly accurate to say that Allen devoted his entire research career to a single problem. In a remarkable talk about his research strategies and history given at Carnegie Mellon University in December 1991, he described his career as aimed at understanding the human mind, but admitted to having suffered four or five substantial

Correspondence to: H.A. Simon, Department of Computer Science and Psychology, Carnegie Mellon University, Pittsburgh, PA 15213, USA. E-mail: has@cs.cmu.edu.

[1] Although, for reasons that no longer are obvious, Cliff Shaw was not a co-author of this paper, he was a full partner in the entire research effort.

diversions from that goal—almost all of which produced major scientific products of their own. These "diversions" included the work with Gordon Bell that is recorded in *Computer Structures* [2] and its successor volumes, the work with Stu Card and Tom Moran that issued in *The Psychology of Human–Computer Interaction*, [5] a major role in the ARPA program of research on speech recognition, and several others.

For the rest, Allen's work aimed steadily, from the autumn of 1955 up to the present, at understanding and modeling the human mind, using computer simulation as the key research tool. After the first burst of activity, which produced the Logic Theorist [15], the General Problem Solver [14], and the NSS chess program [13], he focused increasingly on identifying and overcoming the limitations of these models that restricted their generality and flexibility and thereby impeded their extension directly into a wholly general theory of the mind. His final book, *Unified Theories of Cognition* [11], records the vast progress that he and others had made towards such generality over thirty years, progress that in the final decade of his life focused on the emerging Soar system that he and his colleagues have built.

The 1982 paper, "The knowledge level" [10], on which Allen comments in this special volume, represents that particular moment in his progress when he addressed the specific issue of top-level organization of rational mental activity, just above the symbolic level. One would be hard-pressed to identify many other research careers that combined, in as fruitful a way as Allen's did, single-mindedness about the goal with imagination and flexibility about the routes to it.

2. How it began

Let me now go back to the beginnings. I will not pause to examine Allen's decision to become a scientist, a decision not especially surprising for a bright young man raised in an academic environment, having for father a distinguished radiologist on the faculty of the Stanford Medical School. That decision, he once reported, was reached, shortly before he entered Stanford, while he was serving on a U.S. Navy ship that carried scientific observers to the Bikini nuclear tests.

Stanford, in addition to generally stimulating Allen's scientific interests (he majored in physics), exposed him in the classroom to George Polya, who was not only a distinguished mathematician but also a thoughtful student of mathematical discovery. Polya's widely read book, *How to Solve It* [16], published in 1945 (shortly before Allen first studied with him), introduced many people to *heuristic*, the art of discovery, a term and practice that Polya traced back to Greek mathematics. (In 1954, Polya expanded his discussion of heuristic into the two-volume *Mathematics and Plausible*

Reasoning [17], containing the ideas and many of the illustrative examples that Allen encountered in Polya's classes). Allen came away from that experience aware that the processes of discovery could be investigated and analyzed, and that heuristic—the art of guided search—played a key role in creative thinking. (I also encountered and was influenced by *How To Solve It* during these years, which may partly account for the rapidity with which Allen and I established common ground on first meeting early in 1952).

A year in mathematics (1949–1950) as a graduate student at Princeton, and exposure to game theory, invented shortly before by von Neumann and Morgenstern, convinced Allen that he preferred a combination of experimental and theoretical research to pure mathematics. He found a position at the RAND Corporation in a group that was studying the logistic problems of the Air Force. Two technical reports [6,12] he co-authored with Joseph B. Kruskal demonstrate his interest at that time in applying formal methods to complex empirical phenomena.

Of the first paper [6], the authors say, "This paper is an attempt to set down explicitly a model of 'physical reality' which will provide a suitable context for studying organizations and their properties." Of the second [12], they say, "The idea is simply to construct a language for discussing organizations which has the following properties ...", the properties including ability to express complex concepts unambiguously, and allowing "fairly automatic" transition from descriptive statements to models that would allow "rigorous deduction of testable conclusions". Both papers adopt a style of formal axiomatization that was fashionable at that time in game theory and economics.

A six-week field visit to the Munitions Board in Washington impressed Allen with the distance that separated the formal models from reality, and his trip report, "Observations on the science of supply" [8], exhibits his sensitivity to and sophistication about the organizational realities that he observed (probably reinforcing his brief naval experience and a summer's work in a wartime shipyard before he completed high school). Somewhat disillusioned with axiomatization as the route to reality, Allen then turned to the design and conduct of some laboratory experiments on decision making in small groups, a topic of considerable active interest at RAND at that time.

Dissatisfied also with small-group experiments as a way of studying organizations, the RAND team of John Kennedy, Bob Chapman, Bill Biel and Allen then conceived of constructing and operating a full-scale simulation of an Air Force Early Warning Station, in order to study the decision making and other organizational processes of the station crews. This effort was duly funded by the Air Force in 1952, leading to the creation of the Systems Research Laboratory at RAND. A major theme in the research was to record and analyze the crew's information processes—their interactions with their radar screens, with interception aircraft, and with each other—which provided the basis for their decisions and resulting actions. It was as a consultant to this laboratory that I first met Allen and his colleagues.

The work of the Systems Research Lab, while not diverting Allen from his goal of understanding human organizations, focused his attention on the information handling and decision making processes of individual participants, and the communication among them. It also continued to frustrate him (and all of us) in the attempt to define an appropriate language in which to carry out the analysis and model the process.

One of Allen's special responsibilities in the project was to find a way of simulating a radar display of the continually changing picture of air traffic. Short of sending up an armada of actual airplanes, no technology was available to the lab for making appropriate patterns of blips move over the radar screens. In searching for computational alternatives, Allen met Cliff Shaw, a RAND systems programmer, then working with a Card-Programmed Calculator, a prehistoric device that just preceded the first stored-program computers. Allen and Cliff conceived the idea of having the Calculator calculate the successive air pictures and print out (on 80-column IBM paper!) simulated radar maps—one for every sweep of each radar antenna. This not only proved to be a satisfactory solution for the laboratory simulation but also demonstrated to Al and Cliff (and to me, when I learned of it) that computers, even prehistoric computers, could do more than arithmetic: they could produce maps, spatial arrangements of symbols representing airplanes.

Now two of the preconditions were in place for Allen's shift from the research goal of understanding organizations to the goal of understanding human information processing, that is, thinking. He clearly saw information processing and the decision making it supported as central activities in organizations, and he had had a first experience in symbolic computing. A third precondition derived from other things going on in the RAND environment, reflecting an even broader stirring outside. The stored-program computer had recently been freed from its wartime wraps, and John von Neumann was committed to designing one for RAND, to come into operation about 1954.

At the same time, the ideas of cybernetics, as well as the associated ideas of artificial life, were attracting considerable public attention. W. Ross Ashby had published, in 1952, his *Design for a Brain* [1], and the appropriateness of the "giant brain" metaphor for computers had been widely discussed since E.B. Berkeley's book of that title was published in 1949 [3]. Grey Walter in England had constructed some mechanical "turtles", capable of wandering about a room and of searching for a wall outlet if their batteries ran low, and similar creatures were built by Merrill Flood's group at RAND.

By 1950, both Turing [4] and Shannon [18] had described (but not actually programmed) strategies for computer chess. Shannon's strategies even including provision for selective search. In the summer of 1952, von Neumann gave a talk at RAND, rather pessimistic, about the prospects of building a good chess-playing program. That inspired me to describe (but not to implement on a computer) a program extending Shannon's ideas and adding to the heuristics he had proposed. (The program was appended to a technical report on human decision making in the face of complexity issued in 1953, but the appendix was never published.) On a day-long auto trip en route to observing some Air Force exercises in the summer of 1954, Allen and I discussed at length the possibilities of using a computer to simulate human problem solving. But neither of us was then diverted from our current research agenda of studying organizations.

3. The commitment

In October of 1954, Allen attended a seminar at RAND given by Oliver Selfridge of Lincoln Laboratories, in which Selfridge described a running computer program, developed with G.P. Dinneen, that learned to recognize letters and other patterns. While listening to Selfridge characterizing his rather primitive, but operative, system, Allen experienced what he always referred to as his "conversion experience".

"It was instantly clear to Newell", he has said in a third-person autobiographical account of the experience, "that intelligent adaptive systems could be built that were far more complex than anything yet done and that they would be programmed on digital computers". And in an interview with Pamela McCorduck some twenty years later, he added, "And that just fell on completely fertile ground. I hate to use the phrase, but it really was a case of the prepared mind". To the knowledge Allen already had about computers (including their symbolic capabilities), about heuristic, about human information processing to solve problems in organizations, about cybernetics and early proposals for chess programs was now added a concrete demonstration of the feasibility of computer simulation of complex processes. His knowledge of and strong interest in these matters was converted right then into a determination to devote his life to understand human learning and thinking by simulating it. The student of organizations became almost instantly a student of mind.

In the months immediately following Selfridge's visit, Allen wrote the paper, "The chess machine: an example of dealing with a complex task by adaptation" [9], which outlined a highly imaginative design for the program of a computer to play chess in humanoid fashion. By "humanoid", I mean that the scheme introduced notions of goals, aspiration levels for terminating search, satisficing with "good enough" moves, multi-dimensional evaluation functions, the generation of subgoals to implement goals, and something like best-first search. Information about the board was to be expressed symbolically in a language resembling the predicate calculus on which the program could reason. The design was never implemented, but ideas were later borrowed from it that went into the NSS program in 1958. It is interesting that chess, not pattern recognition, was the task Al selected for his investigation, thereby drawing on his contacts with this task during the immediately preceding years, and staying closer to the kinds of problem solving processes that were implicated in the SRL simulation.

But the best indication of the long-term vision that inspired this effort is to be found in the opening paragraphs of the chess paper [9]. In the application of general-purpose computers, Allen says, "There has been a growing concern over problems ... [that] ... satisfy the condition that (1) The relevant information is inexhaustible; (2) The set of potential solutions is neither enumerable nor simple representable; (3) The processing to be accomplished is unknown until other processing is done; and (4) An acceptable solution is required within a limited time."

"Most design problems, including programming a computer, are of this nature;" he continues, "so are the very complex information processing tasks like translating languages or abstracting scientific articles". The current arguments about thinking machines and general-purpose robots also revolve about whether computers can deal with problems of this general nature.

"The problem of playing good chess certainly falls into this class of ultracomplicated problems .... The aim of this effort, then, is to program a current computer to learn to play good chess. This is the means to understanding more about the kinds of computers, mechanisms, and programs that are necessary to handle ultracomplicated problems."

What is striking here, and what distinguishes this proposal and the research that followed it in the next two years from previous work on computer chess (or Samuel's contemporaneous work on checkers) is the broad context in which it is placed: the aim is not simply to build a chess program, however powerful it might be, but to reach an understanding of complex information processing and all the cognitive tasks that require it. When the paper was presented in March at the 1955 Western Joint Computer Conference (and subsequently published in its Proceedings) Walter Pitts, the commentator for this session, said, "But, whereas Messrs. Farley, Clark, Selfridge, and Dinneen [the authors of the other papers] are imitating the nervous system, Mr. Newell prefers to imitate the hierarchy of final causes traditionally called the mind. It will come to the same thing in the end, no doubt ...". From the very beginning, something like the physical symbol system hypothesis was embedded in the research.

4. The Logic Theorist

Even before the "conversion", Allen had been making plans to move to Pittsburgh early in 1955 to work with me in organizational research and earn his "union card", a doctoral degree. This plan was duly executed, but with the crucial alteration that the research was to be on programming a chess machine. It was arranged that Cliff Shaw would collaborate with us, and the actual program would run on RAND's Johnniac. As the events that followed have been recounted before (by Pamela McCorduck [7] and in my autobiography [19]), they do not need to be repeated here. For various technical and accidental reasons, chess changed to geometry and geometry to logic, and the Logic Theory Machine emerged as a hand simulation by the end of 1955 and a running program in the summer of 1956. Work was pursued simultaneously on an appropriate programming language, leading to the invention of the Information Processing Languages, the first list-processing languages. I think it is fair to say that LT and its successor, the General Problem Solver, laid the foundation on which most of the artificial intelligence programs of the following decade were built.

The question may well be raised as to why this particular work was as influential as it has been, for as we have already seen (and as could be documented a great deal more fully) it was part of a *Zeitgeist* that was already well under way and that had attracted the attention of many able scientists. The answer to this question probably has at least two parts. First, a running program performing a task of some sophistication (discovering proofs for theorems in the propositional calculus) has a great deal more persuasive and educational power than do general discussions of ideas. (Allen's reaction to Selfridge and Dinneen's program had earlier demonstrated that.) A running program is the moment of truth.

Second, and perhaps most important, LT and its successors were not directed simply at programming a single task; they were addressed broadly at the basic problems of constructing complex information processing systems. The specific programs were to be constructed in such a way as to contribute to the solution of the general problem—they were steps along the way to our long-run objective of understanding the human mind.

The strategy is stated boldly and at once in the title and the abstract of our first publication on LT: "The logic theory machine: a complex information processing system" [15]:

> "In this paper we describe a complex information processing system, which we call the logic theory machine, that is capable of discovering proofs for theorems in symbolic logic. This system, in contrast to the systematic algorithms that are ordinarily employed in computation, relies heavily on heuristic methods

similar to those that have been observed in human problem solving activity. The specification is written in a formal language, of the nature of a pseudo-code, that is suitable for coding for digital computers .... The logic theory machine is part of a program of research to understand complex information processing systems by specifying and synthesizing a substantial variety of such systems for empirical study.

It is all there: complex information processing, symbolic computation, heuristic methods, human problem solving, a programming language, empirical exploration.

These are the components of the fundamental strategy underlying our research in 1955 and 1956, and the strategy that continued to guide Allen Newell's scientific work throughout all the rest of his career. It was what led him continually to identify and diagnose the limitations of the programs he built and to ponder about architectures that would remove these limitations. It was what led him, in the last decade, to Soar—not as the final answer, for he knew that there are no final answers in science, only better approximations. It led him to Soar as the next step of progress along a path that he intended to follow, and did follow, as long as he was able to work. And it is the legacy he leaves for those of us who are aiming at the same goal he aimed at: to advance continually our understanding of the human mind.

References

[1] W.R. Ashby, *Design for a Brain* (Wiley, New York, 1952).
[2] C.G. Bell and A. Newell, *Computer Structures: Readings and Examples* (McGraw-Hill, New York, 1971).
[3] E.C. Berkeley, *Giant Brains, or Machines That Think* (Wiley, New York, 1949).
[4] B.V. Bowden, ed., *Faster Than Thought* (Pitman, New York, 1953). (Contains Turing's description of a chess-playing program.)
[5] S. Card, T.P. Moran and A. Newell, *The Psychology of Human–Computer Interaction* (Erlbaum, Hillsdale, NJ, 1983).
[6] J.B. Kruskal Jr and A. Newell, A model for organization theory, Tech. Rept. LOGS-103, The RAND Corporation, Santa Monica, CA (1950).
[7] P. McCorduck, *Machines Who Think* (Freeman, San Fransisco, CA, 1979).
[8] A. Newell, Observations on the science of supply, Tech. Rept. D-926, The RAND Corporation, Santa Monica, CA (1951).
[9] A. Newell, The chess machine: an example of dealing with a complex task by adaptation, in: *Proceedings 1955 Western Joint Computer Conference* (1955) 101–108; also Tech. Rept. P-620, The RAND Corporation, Santa Monica, CA.
[10] A. Newell, The knowledge level, *Artif. Intell.* **18** (1982) 87–127.
[11] A. Newell, *Unified Theories of Cognition* (Harvard University Press, Cambridge, MA, 1990).
[12] A. Newell and J.B. Kruskal Jr, Formulating precise concepts in organization theory, Tech. Rept. RM-619-PR, The RAND Corporation, Santa Monica, CA (1951).

[13] A. Newell, J.C. Shaw and H.A. Simon, Chess-playing programs and the problem of complexity, *IBM J. Res. Develop.* **2** (1958) 320–335.

[14] A. Newell, J.C. Shaw and H.A. Simon, Report on a general problem solving program for a computer, *Information Processing: Proceedings of the International Conference on Information Processing*, Paris (1960) 256–264.

[15] A. Newell and H.A. Simon, The logic theory machine: a complex information processing system, *IRE Trans. Inf. Theory* **2** (3) (1956) 61–79.

[16] G. Polya, *How To Solve It* (Princeton University Press, Princeton, NJ, 1945).

[17] G. Polya, *Mathematics and Plausible Reasoning* (Princeton University Press, Princeton, NJ, 1954),

[18] C.E. Shannon, Programming a digital computer for playing chess, *Philos. Mag.* **41** (1950) 256–275.

[19] H.A. Simon, *Models of My Life* (Basic Books, New York, 1991).

Artificial Intelligence 59 (1993) 261–263
Elsevier

ARTINT 1008

Editorial

Eight reviews of *Unified Theories of Cognition* and a response

Mark J. Stefik and Stephen W. Smoliar (Review Editors)

Theories of mind seem to be inherently interdisciplinary. Few would disagree that research has only scratched the surface of what there is to be known about minds and brains. Nonetheless, researchers approach the study of mind from the perspectives and methodologies of many different fields. Facing this diversity, Allen Newell proclaimed in 1990 that the time was ripe to consider unified theories. His book, *Unified Theories of Cognition*, serves up a challenge and an invitation. It invites us to look at a specific model (realized in part by the Soar system) and to consider the questions it tries to answer and the data on which those answers are based. It also invites the development and comparison of other theories.

In this issue, nine reviewers consider and answer the challenge. As is customary in this column, the reviewers begin by considering the book itself but carry the discussion to perspectives beyond those in the book. As is appropriate for a work so wide-ranging, we have chosen reviewers from a range of scientific and philosophical backgrounds.

The first review is by Michael A. Arbib, Professor of Computer Science, Neurobiology and Physiology, as well as of Biomedical Engineering, Electrical Engineering, and Psychology at the University of Southern California. Arbib's current research focuses on mechanisms underlying the coordination of perception and action. An overview of this work is given in *The Metaphorical Brain* 2: *Neural Networks and Beyond*.

The second review is by Daniel Dennett, Distinguished Professor of Arts and Sciences and Director of the Center for Cognitive Studies at Tufts University in Medford, Massachusetts. Dennett is the author of several books dealing in part with AI, as well as of articles on specific issues and problems in the field. His most recent book, *Consciousness Explained*, 1991, includes a discussion of Newell's influence on cognitive science.

The third review is by Michael Fehling, Director of the Laboratory for Intelligent Systems in the Department of Engineering–Economic Systems at Stanford University. Fehling is best known in AI for his work on knowledge-based system architectures for use in real-time, distributed problem-solving applications. His current research focuses on the nature of organizational problem solving and development of mathematical and computer-based technology to support it. Fehling is also working extensively on theories of limited rationality as a foundation for unified theories of cognition.

The fourth review is by Barbara Hayes-Roth of the department of Computer Science at Stanford University. Hayes-Roth is best known for her work on intelligent control and its embodiment in the BB1 system. Her current research interests are in the area of adaptive intelligent systems, which integrate multiple reasoning tasks and interact with other dynamic entities in real time.

The fifth review is by Marvin Minsky, Toshiba Professor at MIT in the EECS Department, the MIT AI Laboratory, and the MIT Media Laboratory. Minsky is well known for research on knowledge representation, machine vision, robotics, computational complexity, and confocal microscopy. He is currently working on the use of multiple representations, and his most recent books are *The Society of Mind* and *The Turing Option*, a novel about the future of AI (with Harry Harrison, 1992).

Our sixth review is by Dale Purves, George Barth Geller Professor and Chairman of the Department of Neurobiology at Duke University Medical Center. Purves is best known for his work in developmental neurobiology. In 1988 he published *Body & Brain: A Trophic Theory of Neural Connections.*

Our seventh review is by Jordan B. Pollack of the Laboratory for AI Research at the Ohio State University. Pollack is known for his work at the border between the connectionist and symbolic approaches to language and representation. His current research interests are in the area of machine learning, neural networks, and dynamical systems.

Our eighth review is co-authored by Roger C. Schank and Menachem Jona of the Institute for the Learning Sciences at Northwestern University. Schank is best known for his work on natural language processing, story understanding, models of learning and memory, and case-based reasoning. His current research interests are in the area of developing innovative computer-based learning environments based on cognitive theories of learning, memory, and reasoning. Menachem Jona is a graduate student working on representing knowledge about teaching for use in building educational software.

Planning for this set of reviews began in December 1990 when we heard that the book was in preparation and when drafts of it became available. In August 1991 we began seriously recruiting reviewers. Throughout this process Newell was anticipating reading the reviews and responding to them. Part of the motivation for many of the reviewers was knowing that Newell would respond to counterexamples and challenges raised by the reviews. Final versions of most of the reviews were ready by July 1992, ironically days before Newell died. Part of Newell's living legacy to the community is the Soar project which involves colleagues at several universities. As Newell's health worsened, he arranged for Paul Rosenbloom to help him draft a response to the reviews. After Newell died, Rosenbloom agreed to complete the response and collaborated on this with his colleague John Laird.

Paul Rosenbloom and John Laird received their Ph.D. degrees in Computer Science from Carnegie-Mellon University in 1983, with Allen Newell as their thesis advisors. Since 1983, Rosenbloom, Laird, and Newell have formed the core of the team that has been developing Soar as both an integrated intelligent system and a unified theory of human cognition. Rosenbloom is currently an Associate Professor of Computer Science, and a Project Leader in the Information Sciences Institute, at the University of Southern California. Laird is currently an Associate Professor of Electrical Engineering and Computer Science at the University of Michigan. Their primary research focus is the development and application of architectures capable of supporting general intelligence; and, in particular, on the Soar architecture. Related to this overall focus are interests in machine learning, problem solving and planning, models of memory (and their implementation), robotics, autonomous agents in simulation environments, expert systems, neural networks, and cognitive modeling.

Artificial Intelligence 59 (1993) 265–283
Elsevier

ARTINT 1009

Book Review

Allen Newell, *Unified Theories of Cognition**

Michael A. Arbib

*Center for Neural Engineering, University of Southern California, Los Angeles,
CA 90089-2520, USA*

Received September 1991
Revised September 1992

1. Soar: a general cognitive architecture

Among the classics of AI is GPS, the General Problem Solver (Newell, Shaw and Simon [17] in 1959). Its key notion was that solving a problem consisted in finding a sequence of operators for transforming the present state into some goal state. A given problem area would be characterized by a finite set of *differences* and an *operator-difference table*. Given two states, one would compute the differences to be reduced between them, and then, for each difference, consult the table to find an operator that had proven fairly reliable for reducing that difference in a variety of situations. However, the given operator was not guaranteed to reduce the difference in all circumstances. GPS then proceeds with search by a process called *means–end analysis*: pick a difference, apply an operator, look at the new goal and the new state, look at the new difference and so on until the goal is attained. The challenge is to keep track of these states, operators, and differences to extract a "good" path, i.e., a relatively economical sequence of operators which will carry out the desired transformation.

More than a decade after developing GPS, Newell and Simon (1972) published a huge book called *Human Problem Solving* [18] in which they

Correspondence to: M.A. Arbib, Center for Neural Engineering, University of Southern California, Los Angeles, CA 90089-2520, USA. E-mail: arbib@pollux.usc.edu.
* (Harvard University Press, Cambridge, MA, 1990); xvi + 549 pages.

looked at protocols showing how people solve numerical puzzles or word problems. They used such studies to develop means–end analysis into a psychological model of how people solve problems. In this way, GPS contributed to work in both classic AI and cognitive psychology, with each state represented as a small structure of symbols, and with operators providing explicit ways of manipulating symbols in some serial fashion to search a space to find an answer.

Another two decades have passed and, in *Unified Theories of Cognition*, Allen Newell offers us a specific symbolic processing architecture called Soar which may be seen as the culmination of the GPS paradigm. Instead of just measuring a difference and reducing it, Soar can consult a *long-term memory* that has many productions of the form: "if X is the problem, then try Y". It also has a *working memory* containing the current set of goals, the relationships between them, and information about what means have already been tried. Rather than relying on a single operator-difference table as in GPS, Soar can invoke a variety of *problem spaces*, each providing a set of tools appropriate for some subclass of problems (Fig. 1). Rather than always applying an operator to reduce a difference, Soar may recognize that attaining a particular goal suggests a specific problem space which then invokes a particular set of methods to be used. *Subgoal generation* remains a key issue. After applying an operator or using the methods in a particular space, Soar has either solved the problem or it has not—in which case further subgoals must be generated in the attempt to move towards the overall goal. Soar also offers a simple learning mechanism called *chunking*. In trying to achieve a goal, Soar may generate many subgoals and subsubgoals to yield a large tree of different subgoals. Eventually, Soar will grow the tree to the point where it can find a path leading from the present state to the goal state by applying a sequence of operators—at which stage the rest of the search tree can be discarded. Soar can then store this successful "chunk" of the search tree in memory so that when it next encounters a similar problem it can immediately use that sequence of subgoals without getting into extensive search. Soar can have multiple goals and these need not agree, and the system can be set either to pick any one goal and try to achieve it or to take some numerical measure and come up with the best possible result even if it must ignore some of the goals in the process.

I plan to address Newell's bold claim (see especially his Chapter 2, "Foundations of Cognitive Science") that the specific choices which he and his colleagues made in developing Soar are central to the study of cognitive science in general and of human cognitive architecture in particular. I will argue that those choices are so heavily rooted in the classic serial symbol-processing approach to computation that they lead to an architecture which, whatever its merits within AI, is ill-suited to serve as a model for human cognitive architecture. This critique will be grounded in the view that cognitive science is to be conducted in terms of a vocabulary of interacting functional units called

LONG-TERM KNOWLEDGE

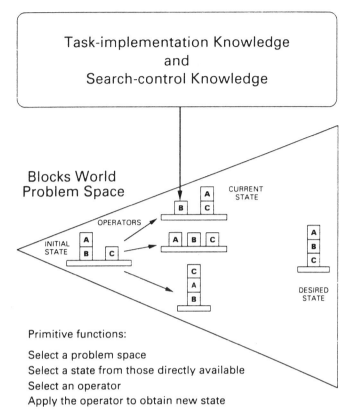

Fig. 1. In Soar, the basic unit of processing is a problem space, as shown here. For different problem domains, different problem spaces may be invoked, each with its own representations and appropriate set of operators to carry out *problem search*. Part of Soar's knowledge is used to determine which is the appropriate knowledge to apply to attack a specific problem—this is *knowledge search*. Acting on a problem in one problem space may create subgoals which require the instantiation of new spaces for their attainment. (Figure 2-16 of Newell's *Unified Theories of Cognition*.)

schemas whose functional definition can in many (but not all) cases be constrained by neurological data. The review will then question the utility of Newell's use of a notion of knowledge akin to Chomsky's notion of competence by asserting that cognitive science must address data on human performance. However, the review closes on a more positive note, suggesting a research plan which links the schema-based approach to intelligence with some of Newell's key insights into the nature of problem solving. In particular, we will pay specific attention to Newell's notion of the "Great Move" from using specialized materials to support different schemas to using a medium in which it is possible to compose copies of whatever schemas are needed to form novel representations.

2. Differing criteria for a human cognitive architecture

What is an appropriate general framework for human cognitive architecture? Newell's approach to cognitive science is close to the following "extreme AI" position:

Position (a). Cognitive tasks rest on a set of basic processes, such as pattern recognition, search, memory, and inference, whose properties and interactions can be characterized in an abstract way independent of implementation. In particular, properties and interactions that we understand by implementing them on serial symbol processors are equally valid for the human mind.

Newell feels that problem spaces and the mechanisms that Soar provides to control them (Fig. 1) underlie any cognitive architecture. However, data may be employed to help constrain the specific problem spaces employed in any specific cognitive system. For a variety of human problem-solving tasks, Newell offers models which not only simulate *what* a human can do, but also have their structure constrained by data on the timing and errors of human performance. As such, these models certainly contribute to cognitive psychology, but in no way meet the demands of *cognitive neuroscience* which seeks to link cognitive capability to the brain mechanisms which subserve it. Timing data is not enough. In particular, Newell fails to make appropriate use of a wealth of data (experimental and clinical) about the effects of brain lesions on human and animal behavior. His approach also fails to connect gracefully with data and theories about instinctual behavior and the basis these provide for cognitive functions. Obviously, much useful work, including Newell's, can be done at a level of aggregation above that requiring the distribution of function over brain regions. I am not making the false claim that no good cognitive science can be done within the Soar framework. Rather, I am claiming that it is an approach that seems ill-suited to unify cognitive science if it is conceded that cognitive science must address, amongst other things, the data of clinical neurology.

Unfortunately, Newell's discussion of the "Foundations of Cognitive Science" (Chapter 2) offers neither an adequate concept of mind nor a well thought out characterization of cognitive science. He offers no "place to stand" from which to evaluate Soar, and takes no account of observations which suggest the importance of neurological data in dissecting cognitive processes. Newell takes "*mind* to be the control system that guides the behaving organism in its interactions with the dynamic real world" (p. 43). However, such a definition does not distinguish mind from brain, for it seems more correct to state that the *brain* is the control system that guides the behaving organism in its interactions with the dynamic real world. Again, he fails to address the notion that much of the control of such interactions is not mental, and that much of what is mental is subsymbolic and/or unconscious. Without offering a precise definition of "mental", let me just say that many people can agree on examples of mental activity (reading, thinking, etc.) even if they take the diametrically opposite philosophical positions of dualism (mind and brain are separate) or monism (mind is a function of brain). They would then agree that some mental activity (e.g., contemplation) need not result in overt "interactions with the dynamic real world", and that much of the brain's activity (e.g., controlling automatic breathing) is not mental. Face recognition seems to be a mental activity which we do not carry out through conscious symbol manipulation. And since Freud, even psychologists who reject his particular psychosexual theories accept his notion that much of our mental behavior is shaped by unconscious forces. (For an assessment of Freud and a schema-theoretic account of consciousness, see [5].)

Newell sees mind as providing "*response functions*. That is, the organism takes actions as a function of the environment. . . . However, many different response functions occur as the organism goes through time . . . such as one when you get yourself out of bed, one when you reach for your clothes, one when you face yourself in the mirror . . ." (p. 43). He then claims that "cognitive science needs a concept of knowledge that is used simply to describe and predict the response functions of a system" (p. 46). This ignores the issue of which response functions are cognitive and which are not. It also ignores the crucial distinction between being able to do something and having knowledge about it, a distinction related to "knowing how" versus "knowing that" which some (e.g., Squire [19]) take to underlie two kinds of human memory ("procedural" and "declarative") dissociable by brain lesions.

Despite his all too inclusive definition of "mind", when Newell (p. 61) charts the *Great Move* in evolution that distinguishes rational behavior from instinctive behavior, he gives the impression that he views rational behavior as the proper province of cognitive science, to the exclusion of instinctive behavior. By contrast, I believe it more fruitful to place human cognition in an evolutionary context rooted in mechanisms for instinctive behavior [1]. A famous example of this is provided by Humphrey's study [14] of "What the Frog's Eye Tells the Monkey's Brain". It had long been known that the role of tectum (the largest visual area in the midbrain) in directing whole body moments in frog is analogous to the role of superior colliculus (the mammalian homolog of tectum) in directing orienting movements in cat and monkey. It had also been believed by neurologists that a monkey (or human) without a visual cortex was blind. However, Humphrey argued that a monkey without visual cortex should have at least as much visual ability as a frog, but that such monkeys had not been taught to pay attention to available visual cues. After two years of attention training, the monkey without visual cortex that he worked with was able to use visual cues to grab at moving objects, and to use changes in luminance—such as an open door—for navigation, even though delicate processes of pattern recognition were never regained. Moreover, it was discovered that humans without visual cortex could also "see" in this sense—but, remarkably, they were not conscious that they could see. This phenomenon is referred to as *blindsight* (see Weiskrantz [21]). Clearly, blindsight is not in itself a rational behavior, being closely linked to the instinctive visually guided behavior of the frog. Yet, it seems to me that the above data are a crucial part of any theory of vision, and that anything that claims to be a "human cognitive architecture" must be able to address such data. This a Soar-based architecture does not do.

Many AI workers have used the slogan "aeroplanes don't flap their wings" to justify the claim that AI may be developed without reference to the study of biological systems. The same slogan equally justifies our skepticism that AI *per se* is adequate to address the needs of cognitive neuroscience. But if we reject Position (a) above (even for an AI informed by data on human performance but not on human neurology) must we go to the other extreme of what might be called "neurochemical reductionism"?:

Position (b). Any human cognitive architecture must take account of the way in which mood, emotion, and motivation affect human performance. We know that drugs can alter mood, and we know that the action of many of these drugs involves the way in which they bind to receptors in the cell membranes of neurons. Thus, no human cognitive architecture can be complete unless it incorporates the relevant specificities of neurochemistry.

Rather than discuss Position (b) explicitly, I will develop an intermediate position which encourages an interchange between *distributed* AI and cognitive neuroscience. To continue with the aeroplanes versus birds analogy, the bridging science of aerodynamics develops key concepts like lift, and then explains the different strategies of planes and birds in terms of the surface properties of the two kinds of wings and the way air is moved across them. Another discipline, materials science, has the task of understanding the surface properties. In the same way, we may hope (it is a research strategy which is yielding results but is by no means universally established) that the following approach may provide the right intermediate between Positions (a) and (b) above:

Position (c). Cognitive science is to be conducted in terms of a vocabulary of interacting functional units called *schemas*. Neuroscience then has the task of explaining the properties of these schemas in terms of neural circuitry or even the underlying neurochemistry and molecular biology. However, the functional definition of the schemas will in many cases be constrained by the data of clinical neurology and observations on modulation of behavior by variations in mood, emotion, and motivation.

To develop this argument, we must first turn to a brief exposition of schema theory, based on Arbib's [4].

3. Schema theory

Schema theory is an approach to knowledge representation that has been explicitly shaped by the need to understand how cognitive and instinctive functions can be implemented in a distributed fashion such as that involving the interaction of a multitude of brain regions. However, many of the concepts have been abstracted from biology to serve as "bringing" concepts which can be used in both distributed (DAI) and brain theory and thus can serve cognitive science whether or not the particular study addresses neurological or neurophysiological data:

(i) Schemas are ultimately defined by the execution of tasks within a physical environment. A set of *basic motor schemas* is hypothesized to provide simple, prototypical patterns of movement. These combine with *perceptual schemas* to form *assemblages* or *coordinated control programs* which interweave their activations in accordance with the current task and sensory environment to mediate more complex behaviors. Many schemas, however, may be abstracted from the perceptual-motor interface. Schema activations are largely task-driven, reflecting the goals of the organism and the physical and functional requirements of the task.

(ii) A schema is both a store of knowledge and the description of a process for applying that knowledge. As such, a schema may be instantiated to form multiple schema *instances* as active copies of the process to apply that knowledge. E.g., given a schema that represents generic knowledge about some object, we may need several active instances of the schema, each suitably tuned, to subserve our perception of a different instance of the object. Schemas can become *instantiated* in response to certain patterns of input from sensory stimuli or other schema instances that are already active.

(iii) Each instance of a schema has an associated *activity level*. That of a perceptual schema represents a "confidence level" that the object represented by the schema is indeed present; while that of a motor schema may signal its "degree of readiness" to control some course of action. The activity level of a schema instance may be but one of many parameters that characterize it. Thus the perceptual schema for "ball" might include parameters to represent size, color, and velocity.

(iv) The use, representation, and recall of knowledge is mediated through the activity of a network of interacting computing agents, the schema instances, which between them provide processes for going from a particular situation and a particular structure of goals and tasks to a suitable course of action (which may be overt or covert, as when learning occurs without action or the animal changes its state of readiness). This activity may involve passing of messages, changes of state (including activity level), instantiation to add new schema instances to the network, and deinstantiation to remove instances. Moreover, such activity may involve self-modification and self-organization.

(v) The key question is to understand how local schema interactions can integrate themselves to yield some overall result without explicit executive control, but rather through *cooperative computation*, a shorthand for "computation based on the competition and cooperation of concurrently active agents". For example, in VISIONS, a schema-based system for interpretation of visual scenes (Draper et al. [13]), schema instances represent hypotheses that particular objects occur at particular positions in a scene, so that instances may either represent conflicting hypotheses or offer mutual support. Cooperation yields a pattern of "strengthened alliances" between mutually consistent schema instances that allows them to achieve high activity levels to constitute the overall solution of a problem; competition ensures that instances which do not meet the evolving consensus lose activity, and thus are not part of this solution (though their continuing subthreshold activity may well affect later behavior). In this way, a schema network does not, in general, need a top-level executor, since schema instances can combine their effects by distributed processes of competition and cooperation, rather than the operation of an inference engine on a passive store of knowledge. This may lead to apparently emergent behavior, due to the absence of global control.

(vi) Learning is necessary because schemas are fallible. Schemas, and their connections within the schema network, must change so that over time they may well be able to handle a certain range of situations in a more adaptive way. In a general setting, there is no fixed repertoire of basic schemas. New schemas may be formed as assemblages of old schemas; but once formed a schema may be tuned by some adaptive mechanism. This tunability of schema assemblages allows them to become "primitive", much as a skill is honed into a unified whole from constituent pieces. Such tuning may be expressed at the level of schema theory itself, or may be driven by the dynamics of modification of unit interactions in some specific implementation of the schemas.

The words "brain" and "neural" do not appear in criteria (i)–(vi). We next spell out just what makes a schema-theoretical model part of brain theory:

(BTi) In brain theory, a given schema, defined functionally, may be distributed across more than one brain region; conversely, a given brain region may be involved in many schemas. A top-down analysis may advance specific hypotheses about the localization of (sub)-schemas in the brain and these may be tested by lesion experiments, with possible modification of the model (e.g., replacing one schema by several interacting schemas with different localizations) and further testing.

(BTii) Once a schema-theoretic model of some animal behavior has been refined to the point of hypotheses about the localization of schemas, we may then model a brain region by seeing if its known neural circuitry can indeed be shown to implement the posited schema. In some cases the model will involve properties of the circuitry that have not yet been tested, thus laying the ground for new experiments. In DAI, individual schemas may be implemented by artificial neural networks, or in some programming language on a "standard" (possibly distributed) computer.

Schema theory is far removed from serial symbol-based computation. Increasingly, work in AI now contributes to schema theory, even when it does not use this term. For example, Minsky [16] espouses a *Society of Mind* analogy in which "members of society", the agents, are analogous to schemas. Brooks [9] controls robots with layers of asynchronous modules that can be considered as a version of schemas (more of this later). Their work shares with schema theory, with its mediation of action through a network of schemas, the point that no single, central, logical representation of the world need link perception and action—the representation of the world is *the pattern of relationships between all its partial representations*. Another common theme, shared with Walter [20], Braitenberg [8], and Arbib [2], is the study of the "evolution" of simple "creatures" with increasingly sophisticated sensorimotor capacities.

We may now return to the claim of Position (c) that cognitive science is to be conducted in terms of a vocabulary of interacting schemas (or schema instances), and that neuroscience then has the task of explaining the properties of these schemas in terms of neural networks. Even though cognitive science itself is thus relieved of responsibility for explaining how schemas are implemented, it must still (a feathered flexible wing is different from a rigid metallic wing) be based, at least in part, on schemas which represent the functioning of hundreds of simultaneously active regions of the human brain. But there is nothing in the GPS tradition, or in Newell's book, that looks at distributed processing in any detail, let alone neurological data which constrains how the different parts of the computation might be located in the different parts of the brain. The point is *not* that all good cognitive science *must be* cognitive neuroscience. It is rather that a general framework for cognitive science must *include* cognitive neuroscience. In fact, given the current state of scientific knowledge, any current schema-level model of a cognitive system must be heterogeneous in that some schemas can be modeled in terms of detailed neural circuitry, some can be related to brain regions for which few details of circuitry are known, while others represent hypotheses about functional components for which little or no constraining neural data are available.

4. A cognitive architecture rooted in computer architecture

To understand why Newell's approach to cognitive science is so little adapted to the needs of cognitive neuroscience, we must see how his view of *cognitive architecture* is rooted in his 1971 work in *computer architecture* (Bell and Newell [6]), and in particular shaped by the hierarchy of computer systems in which the levels are (p. 47):

> *Bell–Newell computer hierarchy*
>   program-level systems
>   register-transfer systems
>   logic circuits
>   electrical circuits
>   electronic devices

Newell states (p. 87) that such architectures emerged in the 1960s as the complexity of computer systems increased and that the enabling key was the development of the register-transfer level as an abstract description of the processing of bit vectors as a bridge between programs and the circuits that implement them. In developing his views of cognitive architecture, Newell makes three changes: he adds the knowledge level as an AI-motivated addition above the Bell–Newell hierarchy, he equates the symbol system level with the program level, and he does not specify the downward elaboration from the register-transfer level:

> *Newell cognitive hierarchy*
>   knowledge-level systems
>   symbol-level systems ($\approx$ programs)
>   register-transfer systems

The knowledge level "abstracts completely from the internal processing and the internal representation. Thus, all that is left is the *content* of the representations and the *goals* toward which that content will be used" (p. 48). The program level in the Bell–Newell hierarchy is based on sequential operation of programs, and this feature of 1971-style computers (namely, seriality) has colored Newell's view of cognition:

> A knowledge system is embedded in an external environment, with which it interacts by a set of possible actions. The behavior of the system is the *sequence* of actions taken in the environment over time. . . . Its body of knowledge is about its environment, its goals, its actions, and the relations between them. It has a single law of behavior: the system takes actions to attain its goals, using *all* the knowledge that it has. . . . The system can obtain new knowledge from external knowledge sources via some of its actions. . . . Once knowledge is acquired, it is available *forever* after. The system is a single *homogeneous* body of knowledge, *all* of which is brought to bear on the determination of its actions. (p. 50, my italics)

The italicized *forever* and *all* stress the point that the knowledge level is an unattainable ideal, unconstrained by implementation limits of computing space or time (as in Chomsky's preference for theories of "competence" rather than "performance"). Newell's claim that "all the person's knowledge is always used to attain the goals of that person" (p. 50) is not even approximately true of normal human behavior—or even of highly aberrant behavior such as seeking to complete this review. The words *sequence* and *homogeneous* already predispose the theory against a distributed view of AI (coordinated problem solving by a network of heterogeneous schemas) let alone providing a conception of knowledge that can be related to the functioning of human brains. Moreover, Newell carries over from computer science the view that function at each level can be studied without attention to its implementation at lower levels:

> [Behavior at each level is] determined by the behavior laws, as formulated for that level, applying to its state as described at that level. The claim is that abstraction to the particular level involved still preserves all that is relevant for future behavior described at that level of abstraction. . . . Thus, to claim that humans can be described at the knowledge level is to claim there is a way of formulating them as agents that have knowledge and goals, such that their behavior is successfully predicted by the law that says: all the person's knowledge is always used to attain the goals of the person . . . no details of the actual internal processing are required. This behavior of an existing system can be calculated if you know the system's goals and what the system knows about its environment. (pp. 49–50)

My point is not to throw away the idea of a level of abstract specifications (call it the knowledge level, if you will). Rather, it is my point that for cognitive science we need specifications which take timing and real-world interaction into account. Thus "hit the ball" is far removed from the level of retinal activity and muscle contractions, but the task imposes a concreteness of interaction that is far removed from the mere abstract knowledge that, e.g., a bat would serve the task better than a hand. The latter "knowledge" provides a useful annotation, but cannot provide a complete specification that can be refined level by level with logical exactness and without revision of the initial specification.

In Newell's cognitive science, symbol systems play the role of the program level. Newell (pp. 80–81) then defines an *architecture* as the fixed structure that realizes a symbol system. In the computer systems hierarchy it is the description of the system at the register-transfer level, below the symbol level, that provides the architecture. The architecture is the description of the system in whatever system description scheme exists next below the symbol level. This raises the question of what system description scheme exists next below the symbol level (i.e., what is the "register-transfer systems" level of the mind?). The "pure AI" approach of Position (a) would accept any system convenient for mapping symbol systems onto serial computers. However, the move towards brain function takes us away from seriality. We focus on competition and cooperation of concurrently active schema instances. More boldly, I claim that the schema level in the Position (c) approach to cognitive science replaces the symbol-system level in Newell's Position (a) approach, but I add that the Position (c) approach also dispenses with a knowledge level that is distinct from the schema level. The schema theorist may still want a "level" in which to talk about generic properties of schemas without reference to their particular specifications, but I view this as talk *about* cognitive systems, rather than a level of representation *of* those systems. On this account, symbols are replaced by schemas which, by combining representation and execution, are far richer than symbols are often taken to be.

Research in the neurophysiology of vision, memory, and action gives information a non-symbolic representation distributed in patterns that do not lend themselves immediately to a crisp description with a few symbols. It is thus a daunting, but exciting, challenge to show how the insights of Newell's approach can make contact with the study of neural networks and issues in cognitive neuroscience. Some members of the Soar community have begun to look at implementations on parallel computers, or at the use of artificial neural networks to implement Soar's memory functions (Cho, Rosenbloom, and Dolan [10]), but I know of no attempt to make extended contact between Soar and neuroscience.

5. Connectionism ≠ brain theory

In developing Soar and the various cognitive models in his book, Newell ignores the biological substrate save for some timing constraints in Chapter 3, and he emphasizes a serial symbol-computation perspective throughout. However, he does offer a few hints of possible changes. He states that "One of the major challenges in the development of massively parallel connectionist systems is whether they will find a different hierarchical organization. In any event, the computer-systems hierarchy is an important invariant structural characteristic, although its [*sic*] seems to be the only one" (p. 88); and he devotes Section 8.3 to some comparisons of Soar with connectionism. However, Section 8.3, "The Biological Band", is misnamed since the comparisons are with the artificial networks of connectionism, not with biological data on the (human) brain. The "neural networks" of connectionism are nets of abstract computing elements, rather than models of the actual circuitry of the brain.

Since our present focus is to determine the extent to which Soar can provide a framework for cognitive science broad enough to encompass cognitive neuroscience, it is thus important to know how relevant Newell's views are to this extension, and in particular to assess the extent to which the organization of "massively parallel connectionist systems" is the same as that of the brain. The connectionist comparison is, in fact, so undernourished and underconstrained by comparison with what is needed for a cognitive neuroscience that I need to emphasize the claim of the section title: *connectionism ≠ brain theory*.

For some "connectionists", all connectionist systems have the same structure, namely large randomly connected neural-like networks which become increasingly adapted to solve some problem through training and/or self-organization. In such an approach, there seem to be only two levels, the specification of what a network is to do (akin to the knowledge level?) and the tuned neural network itself (akin to the logic-circuit level), with nothing in between. However, brain theory is not connectionism, even though progress in connectionism may enrich our vocabulary of the computations that neural networks, viewed abstractly, can perform. Analysis of animal behavior or human cognition should yield a model of how that behavior is achieved through the *cooperative computation* of concurrently active regions or schemas of the brain (the two analyses are not equivalent: regions are structural units; schemas are functional units), rather than in terms of any simple one-way flow of information in a hierarchically organized system.

Items (BTi) and (BTii) of Section 3 embody the eventual goal of cognitive *neuro*science—that functional and structural analyses be rendered congruent. However, experience with brain modeling shows that a distribution of function across schemas that may seem psychologically plausible may not survive the test of neurological data which demand that the schemas be structured in such a way that their subschemas are allocatable across brain regions to yield a model that predicts the effects of various brain lesions.

For example, a model of our ability to make saccadic eye movements to one or more targets even after they are no longer visible requires a schema to inhibit reflex responses, as well as schemas for working memory (holding a "plan of action") and dynamic remapping (updating the "plan" as action proceeds). But this does not imply that a distinct *region* of the brain has evolved for each functionally distinct *schema*. More specifically, a neural refinement of the model (Dominey and Arbib [12]) distributes these three schemas across a variety of brain regions (parietal cortex, frontal eye fields, basal ganglia, and superior colliculus) in a way that responds to and explains a variety of neurophysiological data. (The reader may recall the data on blind-sight, showing how the superior colliculus of monkeys can support a range of subconscious visual functions, but that these nonetheless seem to provide a basis for the totality, dependent on cerebral cortex, of our visual repertoire.)

To summarize, functions that appear well separated in an initial top-down analysis of some behavior or cognitive function may exhibit intriguing inter-dependencies as a result of shared circuitry in the neural model whose construction was guided by, but which also modifies, that initial analysis. I am thus sceptical of Newell's view (pp. 49–50, cited earlier) that each of the levels in his cognitive hierarchy can be operationally complete with no details of the actual internal processing being required. In particular, schema change may be driven by the dynamics of modification of unit interactions in some specific implementation of the schemas. The learning curve of two different neural networks may be dramatically different even though they come under the same symbolic description of their initial behavior.

As noted earlier, Newell's idea of architecture is rooted in the conceptually serial register-transfer level, and does not really come to terms with the possibility of a framework (cooperative computation) that *drastically* expands the concept of computation to embrace the style of the brain. Although Newell notes that massive parallelism can result in *qualitatively* different computations since real-time constraints reveal the effective amount of computation available within specified time limits, I do not find this issue returned to in the attempt to understand the nature of information processing in the human cognitive system, or in the brain that underlies it. By contrast, schema theory emphasizes the distributed, cooperative computation of multiple schema instances distrib-uted across distinctive brain regions; it is delegation of schema functionality to neural networks that brings in massive parallelism. The hierarchy then be-comes:

> *Schema-based cognitive hierarchy*
>   descriptions of behaviors
>   schemas ($\approx$ programs)
>   interacting brain regions
>   neural circuitry
>   neurons
>   sub-neural components (synapses, etc.)

We map schemas onto brain regions where possible, though accepting computer programs as a "default" when constraining neuroscience data are unavailable or inappropriate. In the brain, we might view successive refinements of the overall architecture as involving (i) the segregation into anatomically distinct regions, (ii) the classifications of different circuits and cell types in each region, and (iii) the overall specification of which cell type synapses on what other cell types and with what transmitter. Changes in the detailed pattern of, e.g., cell-by-cell synaptic weighting could then give the architecture its adaptability. The bulk of these changes will be seen as the dynamics of the "software", with changes in "architecture" corresponding only to overall shifts in "computing style" resulting from cooperative effects of myriad small changes.

6. The Great Move: searching for a conclusion

The tone of this review has been negative, in that it has emphasized the problems posed to those of us interested in the role of the brain in cognition by the use of a serial symbol-processing approach, or the use of the knowledge level as providing a performance-independent characterization of cognitive competence. I have not reviewed the many substantial contributions that Newell has made to AI and cognitive psychology, and which are well documented in his book. To somewhat redress the balance, this final section suggests a viable research plan which links the schema-based approach to intelligence with some of Newell's key insights into the nature of problem solving. We may start with Newell's discussion of ethology which sets the stage for his discussion of what he properly calls *the Great Move*:

> Finding feasible representations gets increasingly difficult with a richer and richer variety of things to be represented and richer and richer kinds of operational transformations that they undergo. More and more interlocking representation laws need to be satisfied. . . . [E]thologists have [studied] the adaptive character of lower organisms. . . . Unfortunately, not all adaptations require representations, and the examples, from the digger wasp to the stickleback, are not sorted out to make it easy to see exactly what is representation and what is not. . . . Instead of moving toward more and more specialized materials with specialized dynamics to support an increasingly great variety and intricacy of representational demands, an entirely different turn is possible. This is the move [the Great Move] to using a neutral, stable medium that is capable of registering variety and then *composing* whatever transformations are needed to satisfy the requisite representation law. Far from representational constriction, this path opens up the whole world of indefinitely rich representations. (p. 61)

The line between representation and non-representation is a sticky one. Does the stickleback lack a representation of males with which it is to compete, or is the representation too inclusive to discriminate the experimentalist's simulacrum from the actual opponent? Perhaps the key point is that the stickleback lacks the ability to recognize when it is mistaken and change its ways accordingly (and this is only the beginning of the necessary refinements—cf. Bennett [7] for all the ingredients that a bee would have to exhibit for its "language" to be a true index of rationality).

We may note here a controversy about the nature of AI fomented, e.g., by Brooks [9] which sets an ethologically inspired hierarchy of levels of control (mentioned earlier as being in the spirit of schema theory), each biasing rather than replacing the one below it, in opposition to the "classical" view of abstract operators applied to uniform representations. Newell offers a somewhat broader version of classical AI, since he allows a variety of problem spaces— but nonetheless sees these each as being implemented in some uniform medium, like that offered by the register-transfer level in the Bell–Newell hierarchy. However, it seems mistaken to see this as a sharp dichotomy in which one school or the other must prove triumphant. The schema theorist (as in our discussion of blindsight) explains a complex cognitive function through the interaction of "instinctive" schemas, implemented in specifically evolved circuitry, and "abstract" schemas that are developed through learning and experience in "general-purpose" (highly adaptive, post-Great-Move) circuitry. An intelligent system needs to combine the ability to react rapidly (jumping out of the way of an unexpected vehicle when crossing the street) with the ability to abstractly weigh alternatives (deciding on the best route to get to the next appointment).

In summary, a satisfactory account of Newell's "Great Move" should not seek a complete break from using specialized materials to support different schemas to using a medium in which it is possible to compose copies of whatever schemas are needed to form novel representations. Rather, we should provide—in the manner of schema theory—insight into how instinctive behavior provides a basis for, and is intertwined with, rational behavior. When I study frogs [2], I see the animal's behavior mediated by the dynamic interaction of multiple special-purpose schemas implemented in dedicated neural circuitry. But when I seek to understand human vision, I combine a model of low-level vision implemented across a set of dedicated brain regions (DeYoe and Van Essen [11]) with a general-purpose medium in which copies of schemas (schema instances) can be assembled, parameterized, and bound to regions of the image as they compete and cooperate in a process of distributed planning which creates an interpretation of a visual scene (recall item (v) of Section 3; cf. Arbib [3, esp. Sections 5.1, 5.2, 7.3, and 7.4]). The contrast between frog visuomotor coordination and the flexibility of human visual perception makes explicit the contrast between those schema assemblages that are "evolutionarily hardwired" into patterns of competition and cooperation between specific brain regions, and those which can, through multiple instantiations (both data- and hypothesis-driven), yield totally novel forms to develop new skills and represent novel situations. It is this latter form of "creative" representation that Newell espouses:

> The great move has forged a link between representations and composable response functions. If a system can compose functions and if it can do it internally in an arena under its own control, then that system can represent. How well it can represent depends on how flexible is its ability to compose functions that obey the needed representation laws—there can be limits to composability. However, representation and composability are not inherently linked together. If the representations are realized in a special medium with appropriate . . . transformations, there need be no composability at all. (p. 63)

Such flexibility of composition, of being able to link in new problem spaces (recall Fig. 1) as the need arises to provide a complex problem-solving structure, is one of the great strengths of Soar. Even though I remain sceptical of Newell's sharp division between knowledge and its application, I feel that he advances our understanding when he makes the key distinction between *problem search* and *knowledge search*:

> There are two separate searches going on in intelligence. One is *problem search* which is the search of [a] problem space. . . . The other is *knowledge search*, which is the search in the memory of the system for the knowledge to guide the problem search. . . . [For] a special purpose intelligent system [only problem search need occur]. [For] agents that work on a wide range of tasks. . . [w]hen a new task arises, [their] body of knowledge must be searched for knowledge that is relevant to the task. . . . [K]nowledge search goes on continually—and the more problematical the situation, the more continuous is the need for it. (pp. 98–99)

All this suggests a rapprochement in which future work explores the integration of key insights from Soar with the distributed approach in which action is mediated through a network of schema instances in which no single, central, logical representation of the world need link perception and action. This would add to Newell's scheme the distinction between *off-line planning* which finds a sequence of operators to go all the way to the goal and *then* applies them in the world, and *dynamic planning* which chooses the next few (possibly concurrent) actions which may help achieve the goal, applies them, and then factors new sensory input into continued activity (cf. the "reactive planning" of Lyons and Hendriks [15]).

Perhaps a starting point is to regard a problem space as the analog of a schema, and the creation of a new problem space to meet a subgoal as the analog of schema instantiation. The key question then becomes: How do we restructure Soar when many problem spaces/schema instances can be simultaneously active, continually passing messages, both modulatory and symbolic, to one another? When this question is answered, the seriality that dominates Newell's book will be sundered, and the full-throated dialog between the Soar community and workers in cognitive neuroscience and distributed AI can truly begin.

References

[1] M.A. Arbib, Perceptual motor processes and the neural basis of language, in: M.A. Arbib, D. Caplan and J.C. Marshall, eds., *Neural Models of Language Processes* (Academic Press, New York, 1982) 531–551.

[2] M.A. Arbib, Levels of modeling of mechanisms of visually guided behavior (with commentaries and author's response), *Behav. Brain Sci.* **10** (1987) 407–465.

[3] M.A. Arbib, *The Metaphorical Brain 2: Neural Networks and Beyond* (Wiley Interscience, New York, 1989).

[4] M.A. Arbib, Schema theory, in: S.C. Shapiro, ed., *The Encyclopedia of Artificial Intelligence* (Wiley Interscience, New York, 2nd ed., 1992).

[5] M.A. Arbib and M.B. Hesse, *The Construction of Reality* (Cambridge University Press, Cambridge, England, 1986).

[6] C.G. Bell and A. Newell, *Computer Structures: Readings and Examples* (McGraw-Hill, New York, 1971).

[7] J. Bennett, *Rationality: An Essay towards an Analysis* (Routledge & Kegan Paul, London, 1964).

[8] V. Braitenberg, *Vehicles: Experiments in Synthetic Psychology* (Bradford Books/MIT Press, Cambridge, MA, 1984).

[9] R.A. Brooks, A robust layered control system for a mobile robot, *IEEE J. Rob. Autom.* **2** (1986) 14–23.

[10] B. Cho, P.S. Rosenbloom and C.P. Dolan, Neuro-Soar: a neural-network architecture for goal-oriented behavior, in: *Proceedings 13th Annual Conference of the Cognitive Science Society*, Chicago, IL (1991).

[11] E.A. DeYoe and D.C. Van Essen, Concurrent processing streams in monkey visual cortex, *Trends Neurosci.* **11** (5) (1988) 219–226.

[12] P.F. Dominey and M.A. Arbib, A cortico-subcortical model for generation of spatially accurate sequential saccades, *Cerebral Cortex* **2** (1992) 153–175.

[13] B.A. Draper, R.T. Collins, J. Brolio, A.R. Hanson and E.M. Riseman, The schema system, *Int. J. Comput. Vision* **2** (1989) 209–250.

[14] N.K. Humphrey, What the frog's eye tells the monkey's brain, *Brain Behav. Evol.* **3** (1970) 324–337.

[15] D.M. Lyons and A.J. Hendriks, Planning, reactive, in: S.C. Shapiro, ed., *The Encyclopedia of Artificial Intelligence* (Wiley Interscience, New York, 2nd ed., 1992) 1171–1181.

[16] M.L. Minsky, *The Society of Mind* (Simon and Schuster, New York, 1985).

[17] A. Newell, J.C. Shaw and H.A. Simon, Report on a general problem-solving program, in *Proceedings International Conference on Information Processing*, UNESCO House (1959) 256–264.

[18] A. Newell and H.A. Simon, *Human Problem Solving* (Prentice-Hall, Englewood Cliffs, NJ, 1972).

[19] L.R. Squire, *Memory and Brain* (Oxford University Press, Oxford, 1987).

[20] W.G. Walter, *The Living Brain* (Penguin Books, Harmondsworth, England, 1953).

[21] L. Weiskrantz, The interaction between occipital and temporal cortex in vision: an overview, in: F.O. Schmitt and F.G. Worden, eds., *The Neurosciences Third Study Program* (MIT Press, Cambridge, MA, 1974) 189–204.

Artificial Intelligence 59 (1993) 285–294
Elsevier

ARTINT 1010

Book Review

Allen Newell, *Unified Theories of Cognition* *

Daniel C. Dennett

Center for Cognitive Studies, Tufts University, Medford, MA 02155-7068, USA

Received August 1991
Revised September 1992

The time for unification in cognitive science has arrived, but who should lead the charge? The immunologist-turned–neuroscientist Gerald Edelman [6] thinks that neuroscientists should lead—or more precisely that he should (he seems to have a low opinion of everyone else in cognitive science). Someone might think that I had made a symmetrically opposite claim in *Consciousness Explained* [4]: philosophers (or more precisely, those that agree with me!) are in the best position to see how to tie all the loose ends together. But in fact I acknowledged that unifying efforts such as mine are proto- theories, explorations that are too metaphorical and impressionistic to serve as the model for a unified theory. Perhaps Newell had me in mind when he wrote in his introduction (p.16) that a unified theory "can't be just a pastiche, in which disparate formulations are strung together with some sort of conceptual bailing wire", but in any case the shoe more or less fits, with some pinching. Such a "pastiche" theory can be a good staging ground, however, and a place to stand while considering the strengths and weaknesses of better built theories. So I agree with him.

> It is not just philosophers' theories that need to be made honest
> by modeling at this level; neuroscientists' theories are in the same
> boat. For instance, Gerald Edelman's (1989) elaborate theory of

Correspondence to: D.C. Dennett, Center for Cognitive Studies, Tufts University, Medford, MA 02155-7068, USA. E-mail: ddennett@pearl.tufts.edu.

*(Harvard University Press, Cambridge, MA, 1990); xvi + 549 pages.

"re-entrant" circuits in the brain makes many claims about how
such re-entrants can accomplish the discriminations, build the
memory structures, coordinate the sequential steps of problem
solving, and in general execute the activities of a human mind, but
in spite of a wealth of neuroanatomical detail, and enthusiastic
and often plausible assertions from Edelman, we won't know what
his re-entrants can do—we won't know that re-entrants are the
right way to conceive of the functional neuroanatomy—until they
are fashioned into a whole cognitive architecture at the grain-level
of Act* or Soar and put through their paces. [4, p. 268]

So I begin with a ringing affirmation of the central claim of Newell's
book. Let's hear it for models like Soar. Exploring whole cognitive systems
at roughly that grain-level is the main highway to unification. I agree,
moreover, with the reasons he offers for his proposal. But in my book
I also alluded to two reservations I have with Newell's program without
spelling out or defending either of them. This is obviously the time to make
good on those promissory notes or recant them. "My own hunch", I said,
"is that, for various reasons that need not concern us here, the underlying
medium of production systems is *still* too idealized and oversimplified in its
constraints" [4, p. 267]. And a little further along I expressed my discomfort
with Newell's support for the traditional division between working memory
and long-term memory, and the accompanying notion of *distal access* via
symbols, since it encourages a vision of "movable symbols" being transported
here and there in the nervous system—an image that slides almost irresistibly
into the incoherent image of the Cartesian Theater, the place in the brain
where "it all comes together" for consciousness.

Preparing for this review, I re-read *Unified Theories of Cognition*, and
read several old and recent Newell papers, and I'm no longer confident
that my reservations weren't based on misunderstandings. The examples
that Newell gives of *apparently* alternative visions that can readily enough
be accommodated within Soar—semantic and episodic memory within the
single, unified LTM, Koler's proceduralism, Johnson-Laird's mental models,
for instance—make me wonder. It's not that Soar can be all things to all
people (that would make it vacuous), but that it is easy to lose sight of
the fact that Soar's level is a *low* or foundational architectural level, upon
which quasi- architectural or firmware levels can be established, at which
to render the features and distinctions that at first Soar seems to deny. But
let's put my reservations on the table and see what we make of them.

On the first charge, that Soar (and production systems in general) are still
too idealized and oversimplified, Newell might simply agree, noting that we
must begin with oversimplifications and use our experience with them to
uncover the complications that matter. Is Soar *the* way to organize cognitive

science, or is it "just" a valiant attempt to impose order (via a decomposition) on an incredibly heterogeneous and hard-to-analyze tangle? There's a whole messy world of individualized and unrepeatable mental phenomena out there, and the right question to ask is not: "Does Soar idealize away from these?"—because the answer is obvious: "Yes, so what?" The right question is: "Can the *important* complications be reintroduced gracefully as elaborations of Soar?" And the answer to that question depends on figuring out which complications are really important and why. Experience has taught me that nothing short of considerable mucking about with an actual implementation of Soar, something I still have not done, would really tell me what I should think about it, so I won't issue any verdicts here at all, just questions.

First, to put it crudely, what about pleasure and pain? I'm not just thinking of high-urgency interrupts (which are easy enough to add, presumably), but a more subtle and encompassing focusing role. Newell recognizes the problem of focusing, and even points out—correctly, in my view—that the fact that this can be a problem for Soar is a positive mark of verisimilitude. "Thus the issue for the standard computer is how to be interrupted, whereas the issue for Soar and Act* (and presumably for human cognition) is how to keep focused" (Newell, Rosenbloom and Laird [10]). But the Soar we are shown in the book is presented as hyperfunctional.

> Soar's mechanisms are dictated by the functions required of a general cognitive agent. We have not posited detailed technological limitations to Soar mechanisms. There is nothing inappropriate or wrong with such constraints. They may well exist, and if they do, they must show up in any valid theory. (p. 354)

Doesn't this extreme functionalism lead to a seriously distorted foundational architecture? Newell provides an alphabetized list (Fig. 8.1, p. 434) of some mental phenomena Soar has not yet tackled, and among these are daydreaming, emotion and affect, imagery, and play. Soar is all business. Soar is either working or sound asleep, always learning-by-chunking, always solving problems, never idling. There are no profligate expenditures on dubious digressions, no along-for-the-ride productions cluttering up the problem spaces, and Soar is never too tired and cranky to take on yet another impasse. Or so it seems. Perhaps if we put just the right new menagerie of operators on stage, or the right items of supplementary knowledge in memory, a sprinkling of sub-optimal goals, etc., a lazy, mathophobic, lust-obsessed Soar could stand forth for all to see. That is what I mean about how easy it is to misplace the level of Soar; perhaps all this brisk, efficient problem solving should be viewed as the biological (rather than psychological) activities of elements too small to be visible to the naked eye of the folk-psychological observer.

But if so, then there is a large element of misdirection in Newell's advertising about his functionalism. "How very functional your teeth are, Grandma!" said Red Riding Hood. "The better to model dysfunctionality when the time comes, my dear!" replied the wolf. Moreover, even when Soar deals with "intendedly rational behavior" of the sort we engage in when we are good experimental subjects—comfortable, well-paid, and highly motivated—I am skeptical about the realism of the model. Newell acknowledges that it leaves out the "feelings and considerations" that "float around the periphery" (p. 369), but isn't there also lots of *non*-peripheral waste motion in human cognition? (There certainly seems to me to be a lot of it when I think hard—but maybe Newell's own mental life is as brisk and no-nonsense as his book!)

Besides, the hyperfunctionality is *biologically* implausible (as I argue in my book). Newell grants that Soar *did* not arise through evolution (Fig. 8.1), but I am suggesting that perhaps it *could* not. The Spock-like rationality of Soar is a very fundamental feature of the architecture; there is no room *at the architectural level* for some thoughts to be harder to think *because they hurt*, to put it crudely. But isn't that a fact just as secure as any discovered in the psychological laboratory? Shouldn't it be a primary constraint? Ever since Hume got associationism under way with his quasi-mechanical metaphors of combination and attraction between ideas, we have had the task of describing the dynamics of thought: what makes the next thought follow in the heels of the current thought? Newell has provided us, in Soar, with a wonderfully deep and articulated answer—the best ever—but it is an answer that leaves out what I would have thought was a massive factor in the dynamics of thought: pain and pleasure. Solving some problems is a joy; solving others is a bore and a headache, and there are still others that you would go mad trying to solve, so painful would it be to contemplate the problem space. Now it *may just be* that these facts are emergent properties at a higher level, to be discerned in special instances of Soar chugging along imperturbably, but that seems rather unlikely to me. Alternatively, it may be that the *Sturm und Drang* of affect can be piped in as a later low-level embellishment without substantially modifying the basic architecture, but that seems just as unlikely.

David Joslin has pointed out to me that the business-like efficiency we see in the book is largely due to the fact that the various implementations of Soar that we are shown are all special-purpose, truncated versions, with tailor-made sets of operators and productions. In a fully general-purpose Soar, with a vastly enlarged set of productions, we would probably see more hapless wandering than we would want, and have to cast about for ways to focus Soar's energies. And it is here, plausibly, that an affective dimension might be just what is needed, and it has been suggested by various people (Sloman and Croucher [13], de Sousa [5]) that it cannot be packaged within the contents of further knowledge, but must make a contribution orthogonal to the contribution of knowledge.

That was what I had in mind in my first reservation, and as one can see, I'm not sure how sharply it cuts. As I said in my book, we've come a long way from the original von Neumann architecture, and the path taken so far can be extrapolated to still brainier and more biological architectures. The way to find out how much idealization we can afford is not to engage in philosophical debates.

My second reservation, about symbols and distal access, opens some different cans of worms. First, there is a communication problem I want to warn other philosophers about, because it has bedeviled me up to the time of revising the draft of this review. I think I now understand Newell's line on symbols and semantics, and will try to explain it. (If I still don't get it, no harm done—other readers will set me straight.) When he introduces symbols he seems almost to go out of his way to commit what we philosophers call use–mention errors. He gives examples of symbol tokens in Fig. 2-9 (p. 73). He begins with words in sentences (and that's fine), but goes on to *numbers* in equations. We philosophers would say that the symbols were *numerals*—names for numbers. Numbers aren't symbols. He goes on: atoms in formulas. No. Atom-symbols in formulas; formulas are composed of symbols, not atoms; molecules are composed of atoms. Then objects in pictures. No. Object-depictions in pictures. I am sure Newell knows exactly what philosophers mean by a use–mention error, so what is his message supposed to be? "For the purposes of AI it doesn't matter"? Or "We AI-types never get confused about such an obvious distinction, so we can go on speaking loosely"? I don't believe it. There is a sort of willful *semantic descent* (the opposite of Quine's semantic ascent, in which we decide to talk about talk about things) that flavors many AI discussions. It arises, I think, largely because in computer science the expressions up for semantic evaluation do in fact refer very often to things inside the computer—to subroutines that can be called, to memory addresses, to data structures, etc. Moreover, because of the centrality of the domain of arithmetic in computers, the topic of "discussion" is often numbers, and arithmetical expressions for them. So it is easy to lose sight of the fact that when you ask the computer to "evaluate" an expression, and it outputs "3", it isn't *giving* you a number; it's *telling* you a number. But that's all right, since all we ever want from numbers is to have them identified—you can't eat 'em or ride 'em. (Compare "Gimme all your money!" "OK. $42.60, including the change in my pocket.") Can it be that this confusion of symbols and numbers is also abetted by a misappreciation of the fact that, for instance, the binary ASCII code for the *numeral* "9" is not the binary expression of the number 9?

Whatever its causes—or even its justifications—this way of speaking creates the impression that, for people in AI, semantics is something entirely internal to the system. This impression is presumably what led Jerry Fodor into such paroxysms in "Tom Swift and his Procedural Grandmother" [7]. It is too bad he didn't know how to put his misgivings constructively. I tried once:

> We get the idea [from Newell [9]] that a symbol designates if it gives access to a certain object or if it can affect a certain object. And this almost looks all right as long as what we're talking about is internal states .... But of course the real problem is that that isn't what reference is all about. If that were what reference was all about, then what would we say about what you might call my Julie Christie problem? I have a very good physically instantiated symbol for Julie Christie. I know it refers to her, I know it really designates her, but it doesn't seem to have either of the conditions that Professor Newell describes, alas. [2, p. 53] (See also Smith [14].)

Newell's answer:

> The criticisms seemed to me to be a little odd because to say that one has access to something does not mean that one has access to *all* of that thing; having some information about Julie Christie certainly doesn't give one complete access to Julie Christie. That is what polite society is all about .... The first stage is that there are symbols *which lead to internal structures*. I don't think this is obscure, and it is important in understanding where the aboutness comes from ... the data structures *contain knowledge about things in the outside world*. So you then build up further symbols which access things that you can think of as knowledge about something—knowledge about Julie Christie for instance. If you want to ask why a certain symbol says something about Julie Christie, you have to ask why the symbolic expression that contains the symbol says something about Julie Christie. And the answer may be ... because of processes that put it together which themselves have knowledge about Julie Christie .... Ultimately it may turn out to depend upon history, it may depend on some point in the history of the system when it came in contact with something in the world which provided it with that knowledge. ([2, p. 171], emphasis mine)

What we have here, I finally realize, is simply a two-stage (or *n*-stage) functional role semantics: *in the end* the semantics of symbols is anchored to the world via the knowledge that can be attributed to the whole system *at the knowledge level* in virtue of its capacity, exercised or not, for perspicuous

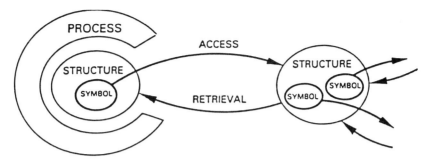

Fig. 1. Symbols provide distal access. (Originally, Fig. 2.10 (p. 75) in *Unified Theories of Cognition.*)

behavior vis-a-vis the items in the world its knowledge is about. And that's my view, too. What makes a data structure about Julie Christie is that it's the part of the system the presence of which explains my capacity to pick her out of a crowd, answer questions about her in quiz shows, etc., etc. That's all there is to it. But it is certainly misleading to say that the symbol gives one *any* "access" (partial access, in polite society!) to the object itself. (It turns out that Julie Christie and I have a mutual friend, who sent her an offprint of [2]. And what do you know, she ... sent me a Christmas card. "Getting closer", I thought. "Maybe Newell's right after all! You just have to be patient. Porsche, Porsche, Porsche.")

Newell's diagram in Fig. 1 makes it all clear (in retrospect) as long as you realize that it is not just that he concentrates (in his book and in his earlier writing) on the semantic link-arrows in the middle of the diagram—the access links tying symbols to their distal knowledge-stores—but that he simply *assumes* there is a solution to any problems that might arise about the interpretation of the arrows on the right-hand side of the diagram: those arrows, as I understand him now, lead one *either* to more data structures or eventually to something in the external world—but he is close to silent about this final, anchoring step. This is fine by me, but then I'm one of the few philosophers who thinks Twin-Earth and narrow content are artifactual philosophical conundrums of no importance to cognitive science [1,3]. Make no mistake, though: serious or not, Newell sweeps them under the rug right here. [1]

---

[1] In a more recent paper, he goes a bit further in defense of this interpretation: "The agent's knowledge is embodied in the knowledge of the four problem space components. However, this latter knowledge is about the problem space, states and operators; hence it cannot of itself be the knowledge of the agent, which is about the goal, actions and environment. It becomes the agent's knowledge by means of the relationships just described. That is, states are about the external world because of KL perception; operators are about the external world because of KL actions; the desired states are about the goal of the KL agent because of formulate-task; and the means-ends knowledge of select-operator is about performing tasks in the environment because it links environment-referring operators on environment-referring states to descriptions of environment-referring desired states." (Newell et al. [11, p. 23])

What concerns him is rather the interesting question of Plato's aviary: how does an intelligent agent with more knowledge than it can "contemplate" all at once get the right birds to come when it calls? (Dennett [4, p. 222–225]). And how do you do this without relying on a dubious *transportation* metaphor, which would require shipping symbol-tokens here and there in the system? I'm not sure I understand his answer entirely, but the crucial elements are given on p. 355:

> Functionally, working memory must be a short-term memory. It is used to hold the coded knowledge that is to be processed for the current task. It is necessary to replace that knowledge when the task changes. That replacement can be achieved in many ways, by moving the data [bad idea!—DCD], by moving the processes [better!—DCD], or by changing the access path [best!—DCD] .... Working memory for cognition has no continued functional existence outside these limits, however, since elements that are no longer linked to the goal stack become unavailable. Furthermore, problem spaces themselves have no existence independent of the impasses they are created to resolve.

I find these ideas some of the most difficult to understand in cognitive science, for they require setting aside, for once, what we might call the concrete crutch: the lazy picture of places (with boxes around them) and things moving to and fro. *That* vision, for all its utility at the symbol level, is a dangerous companion when we turn to the question of mapping computational processes onto brain processes. When Newell says "Search leads to the view that an intelligent agent is always operating within a *problem space.*" (p. 98) we should recognize that this is really being presented as an *a priori* constraint on how we shall interpret intelligent agents. Show me an intelligent agent, and whatever it does, I'll show you a way of interpreting it as setting up a problem space. Since the key term "distal" is defined relative to *that* space—that logical space—we should be cautious of interpreting it too concretely (cf. Fodor and Pylyshyn [8]).

So my second reservation is blunted as well. Two strikes, or maybe foul balls. There is one more issue I want to take a swing at as long as I'm up at bat. Newell's silence on the issue of natural language as a symbolic medium of cognition in human beings is uncanny. We know that Soar can (in principle) learn from taking *advice* (e.g., p. 312), and Newell sketches out the way Soar would or might handle language acquisition and comprehension (pp. 440–449; see especially his discussion of redundant encoding, p. 453), but I cannot figure out from these brief passages what Newell thinks happens to the overall shape of the competence of a cognitive system when it acquires a natural language, and I think his reticence on this score hides major issues. Early on he gives an eloquent survey of what he calls the "efflorescence of adaptation" by the human (and only the human) species (pp. 114–115), but does this paean to productive versatility proclaim that the symbols of an *internalized natural language* are necessary, or is it rather that one needs a pre-linguistic language of thought—in which case we may wonder why the human language of thought gives us such an edge over the other species, if it does not get most of its power from the external language we learn to speak. For instance, Newell's discussion of annotated models (pp. 393ff) is a fine perspective on the mental models debates, but I am left wondering: can a non-human intelligent agent—a dog or dolphin or ape, for instance—avail itself of an annotated model, or is that level of cognitive sophistication reserved for language-users? This is just one instance of a sort of empirical question that is left curiously burked by Newell's reticence.

This gap is all the more frustrating since in other regards I find Newell's treatment in Chapters 1 and 2 of the standard debating topics in the philosophy of cognitive science a refreshing challenge. These chapters are simply required reading henceforth for any philosophers of cognitive science. [2] Newell doesn't waste time surveying the wreckage; he gets down to business. He says, in effect: "Sit down and listen; I'll show you how to think about these topics." He simply *makes moves* in all the games we play, and largely leaves it to us to object or play along. This should be a model for all non-philosopher scientists who aspire (correctly!) to philosophical probity. Don't try to play the philosophers' games. Just make your moves, clearly and explicitly, and see if you can get away with them.

I very largely agree with his moves, and it will be a pity if philosophers who disagree with him don't rise to the bait. They may not, alas. At times Newell underestimates how ingrown his jargon is. I have pushed portions of his text on some very smart philosophers and neuroscientists, and they are often completely at sea. (These issues are awfully hard to communicate about, and I am well aware that the alternative expository tactics I have tried in my own writing run their own risks of massive misconstrual.)

It might seem odd, finally, for me not to comment at all on Newell's deliberate postponement of consideration of consciousness, which gets just a brief apology on p. 434. Is this not unconscionable? Not at all. Newell's

---

[2] Philosophers will find important material throughout the book, not just in the foundational chapters at the beginning. For instance, the discussion of the discovery of the data-chunking problem in Soar and its handling (pp. 326–345) can be interpreted as a sort of inverse version of Meno's paradox of inquiry. The problem is not how can I search for something if I don't already know what it is, but how can I set myself up so that when I confront a real Meno-problem, there will be a way I can solve it? (Alternatively, if Soar couldn't solve the data-chunking problem, Meno's claim would not be paradoxical when applied to Soar, but simply true.) I think the memory-management search control strategies that are adopted can be read as part of an explicit answer—much more explicit than any philosopher's answer—to Meno's challenge.

project is highly compatible with mine in *Consciousness Explained* [4]. For instance, I endorse without reservation his list of multiple constraints on mind in Fig. 1-7 (p. 19). How can he achieve this divorce of consciousness? Just look! The enabling insight, for Newell and for me, is that handsome is as handsome does; you don't need any *extra witnesses* in order to explain cognition. Newell modestly denies that he has yet touched on consciousness; I disagree. He's made a big dent.

References

[1] D.C. Dennett, Beyond belief, in: A. Woodfield, ed., *Thought and Object* (Clarendon Press, Oxford, 1982).

[2] D.C. Dennett, Is there an autonomous "Knowledge Level"? in: Z.W. Pylyshyn and W. Demopoulos, eds., *Meaning and Cognitive Structure* (Ablex, Norwood, NJ, 1986) 51–54.

[3] D.C. Dennett, *The Intentional Stance* (MIT Press/Bradford Books, Cambridge, MA, 1987).

[4] D.C. Dennett, *Consciousness Explained* (Little Brown, Boston, 1991).

[5] R. de Sousa, *The Rationality of Emotion* (MIT Press, Cambridge, MA, 1987).

[6] G.M. Edelman, *The Remembered Present: A Biological Theory of Consciousness* (Basic Books, New York, 1989).

[7] J.A. Fodor, Tom Swift and his Procedural Grandmother, *Cognition* **6** (1978) 229–247.

[8] J.A. Fodor and Z.W. Pylyshyn, Connectionism and cognitive architecture: a critical analysis, *Cognition* **28** (1988) 3–71; also in: S. Pinker and J. Mehler, eds., *Connectionism and Symbol Systems* (MIT Press, Cambridge, MA, 1988) 3–71.

[9] A. Newell, The symbol level and the knowledge level, in: Z.W. Pylyshyn and W. Demopoulos, eds., *Meaning and Cognitive Structure* (Ablex, Norwood, NJ, 1986) 169–193.

[10] A. Newell, P.S. Rosenbloom and J.E. Laird, Symbolic architectures for cognition, in: M. Posner, ed., *Foundations of Cognitive Science* (MIT Press, Cambridge, MA, 1989).

[11] A. Newell, G. Yost, J.E. Laird, P.S. Rosenbloom and E. Altmann, Formulating the problem-space computational model, in: R. Rashid, ed., *Carnegie Mellon Computer Science: A 25-Year Commemorative* (ACM Press/Addison-Wesley, Reading, MA, 1992).

[12] Z.W. Pylyshyn and W. Demopoulos, eds., *Meaning and Cognitive Structure* (Ablex, Norwood, NJ, 1986).

[13] A. Sloman and M. Croucher, Why robots will have emotions, in: *Proceedings IJCAI-81*, Vancouver, BC (1981).

[14] B.C. Smith, The link from symbol to knowledge, in: Z.W. Pylyshyn and W. Demopoulos, eds., *Meaning and Cognitive Structure* (Ablex, Norwood, NJ, 1986) 40–50.

Artificial Intelligence 59 (1993) 295–328
Elsevier

ARTINT 1011

Book Review

Unified theories of cognition: modeling cognitive competence *

Michael R. Fehling

Laboratory for Intelligent Systems, Stanford University, Stanford, CA, USA

Abstract

Fehling, M., Unified theories of cognition: modeling cognitive competence, Artificial Intelligence 59 (1993) 295–328.

In his recent text, *Unified Theories of Cognition,* Allen Newell offers an exciting mixture of theoretical and methodological advice to cognitive scientists on how to begin developing more comprehensive accounts of human problem solving. Newell's perspective is at once both exciting and frustrating. His concept of a unified theory of cognition (UTC), and his attempt to illustrate a UTC with his Soar problem solving architecture, is exciting because it suggests how scientists might use the computational methods of cognitive science and artificial intelligence to formulate and explore both broader and deeper aspects of intelligence in people and in machines. Newell's perspective is equally frustrating because it dictates a behaviorist methodology for evaluating cognitive models. Newell views a UTC as a simulation of behavior. I explore the surprising similarity of Newell's approach to theory to the approaches of classical behaviorists such as John Watson and Edward Chace Tolman. I suggest that Newell's behaviorist methodology is incompatible with his commitment to building theories in terms of complex computational systems. I offer a modification to Newell's approach in which a UTC provides an architecture in which to explore the nature of competence—the requisite body of knowledge—that underlies an intelligent agent's ability to perform tasks in a particular domain. I compare this normative perspective to Newell's commitment to performance modeling. I conclude that his key theoretical concepts, such as the problem space hypothesis, knowledge level systems, and intelligence as approximation to the knowledge level are fundamentally competence constructs. I raise specific concerns about the indeterminacy of evaluating a UTC like Soar against performance data. Finally, I suggest that competence modeling more thoroughly exploits the insights of cognitive scientists like Newell and reduces the gap between the aims of cognitive science and artificial intelligence.

Correspondence to: M. Fehling, Laboratory for Intelligent Systems, Stanford University, CA, USA. E-mail: fehling@bayes.stanford.edu.
* (Harvard University Press, Cambridge, MA, 1990); xvi + 549 pages.

1. Introduction

A great many psychologists, linguists, and other students of human behavior have expressed the hope that their studies might eventually be embedded within a comprehensive theory of human information processing. Over the last twenty years or so this hope has given rise to the research discipline known as cognitive science (Stillings et al. [46]). According to Herbert Simon (Simon and Kaplan [43]) "[c]ognitive science is the study of intelligence and intelligent systems, with particular reference to intelligent behavior as computation". The focus on computational models of cognition establishes a strong and direct relationship between cognitive science and the field of artificial intelligence (AI).

In *Unified Theories of Cognition*, Allen Newell presents cognitive scientists with a bold and exciting challenge, one that should also interest many AI scientists. Newell is very enthusiastic about progress made by cognitive scientists in measuring diverse types of human problem solving behavior. However, his enthusiasm is tempered by the observation that no overarching theory has yet been developed to explain the broad range of data describing human behavior.

Newell proclaims that the time has come to build such a comprehensive theory:

> Psychology has arrived at the possibility of unified theories of cognition—theories that gain their power by positing *a single system* of mechanisms that operate together to produce the *full range* of human cognition .... Such *[comprehensive theories] are within reach and we should strive to attain them.* (p. 1) [emphasis added]

1.1. Toward unified theories of cognition

Newell's primary objective is, therefore, to persuade cognitive scientists to build unified theories of cognition (UTCs). He perceives some urgency in this matter. He declares that "it is time to get going on producing unified theories of cognition" before the body of facts to be explained grows even larger (p. 25). This remark, despite its rather curious logic, illustrates Newell's commitment to developing UTCs. He explicitly distinguishes this goal from that of espousing one particular UTC:

> I am not asserting that there is a unique unified theory and we should all get together on it. ... [M]ultiple theories are the best we can do. The task at hand is to get *some* candidate theories ... to show ... that they are real. The task is somehow to cajole

> ourselves into putting it all together, even though we don't know many of the mechanisms that are operating. (p. 17)

One might reasonably expect Newell to pursue his ambitious objective by comprehensively surveying and comparing a broad range of candidate UTCs, or even partial UTCs. Instead, he focuses his attention exclusively on his own work. Newell's candidate UTC is *Soar*, a problem solving architecture he and his students have been developing over much of the last decade (cf., Laird et al. [28]). Although he worries that Soar's more contentious features "may detract a little from using Soar simply as an exemplar for a unified theory of cognition" (p. 39), Newell is satisfied that Soar will illustrate his proposal for building UTCs. For Newell, research on Soar typifies what a UTC is, how to build one, and how to assess its adequacy as a theory of human behavior.

At the least, Newell's monograph contributes significantly by integrating many of his most important theoretical concepts about human cognition. Over his long career, Newell has formulated a powerful set of fundamental concepts for describing human cognition as knowledge-based, heuristic search (Newell et al. [5,39,40]). His concepts have influenced the thinking of most cognitive scientists as well as many in AI. Newell brings these ideas together in this work and describes their role in building a solid foundation for theory in cognitive science.

However, I suggest in this commentary that, on balance, *Unified Theories of Cognition* will fall somewhat short of achieving its major objective. This is not because cognitive scientists will reject Newell's counsel to build UTCs. In fact, many of them have been at this task for quite some time (e.g. Anderson [1,2], Holland et al. [24], MacKay [29]). Nor is it due, as Newell fears, to Soar's "contentious" claims. I can think of no better stimulus to the development of competing UTCs than offering a contentious or unconvincing theory.

The fundamental problem that I see with Newell's book stems from his insistence that UTCs accurately describe and predict human behavior. This commitment is a cornerstone of his methodology for interpreting and evaluating UTCs. For Newell a good theory, whatever its scope, is one that "you can really make predictions with" ... (p. 5). And, a UTC simply extends this commitment more broadly. A UTC embodies "a single set of mechanisms for all of cognitive behavior" (p. 15). Of course, Newell shares this commitment to performance prediction with most cognitive scientists as well as many other theorists who choose not to formulate their psychological theories in computational terms.

Newell's discussion of theory as behavior simulation and the role of Soar as such a model illustrates this doctrine with revealing clarity. This provides an important reason for examining Newell's proposal so carefully.

A number of cognitive scientists (e.g., Anderson [1], Townsend and Ashby [48]) claim that it is impossible to distinguish competing predictive models using performance data alone. Cognitive theorists accepting this argument will be far less inclined to concern themselves with Newell's proposal and to expend enormous effort to develop and compare UTCs. In contrast, Newell seeks to convince us that competing UTCs can be distinguished on the basis of performance prediction. If he can do so then his approach will be interesting. I argue below that he fails in his attempts to overcome the limitations of predictive modeling.

I offer an alternative approach to evaluating and exploring cognitive theories such as Newell's UTCs. I argue that the distinct value of a computational model of cognition emanates from its ability to rigorously depict the knowledge that enables intelligent problem solvers to adequately perform specific tasks. I refer to such embodied knowledge as a *cognitive competence.* A UTC such as Newell's Soar serves as a framework within which to interpret and explore models of cognitive competence.

Although my alternative approach differs radically from Newell's on methodological grounds, it seems to me to be quite consistent with many of his more fundamental theoretical pronouncements about cognition. In this light, I also suggest that this alternative approach to cognitive theory is more consistent with Newell's fundamental theoretical distinctions than is his commitment to performance simulation.

1.2. Modeling cognitive competence

The notion of cognitive competence may be unfamiliar to some readers. I now briefly review some of the central features of competence theories before continuing my commentary on Newell.

Noam Chomsky [6] is perhaps the best known proponent of this approach to cognitive theory. Chomsky revolutionized the study of language by suggesting that a grammar be viewed as a description of the knowledge tacitly or implicitly held by an idealized speaker-listener. An idealized linguistic agent is not subject to errors while generating or comprehending well-formed linguistic utterances. So, a grammar does not make predictions about *actual* performance. Rather, it provides a set of *ideal* performances, here, the set of acceptable sentences of some language. Chomsky proposed that linguistic competence be represented as a collection of recursive production rules. An adequate set of rules must generate all and only the acceptable sentences of the idealized speaker-listener's language. He called such a collection of rules a *generative grammar.*

Moravcsik [33] discusses some important features of a competence account. First, a competence account postulates a *disposition toward a structured class of behaviors.* By "disposition" I mean here a capacity to act in certain restricted ways, and perhaps an inclination toward these actions under certain abstract conditions. For example, a complete theory of an English speaker's competence accounts for her ability to utter syntactically, semantically, and pragmatically acceptable sentences in that language and perhaps her propensity to utter them under hypothesized conditions of intent (e.g., to convey meaning or accomplish a speech act). A disposition embodies knowledge about the structure of these idealized action. For example, an English speaker's competence also manifests itself in the agent's capacity to acknowledge (Chomsky would say to have intuitions about) structural relations among sentences. In particular, a complete competence theory must also account for the English speaker's ability to recognize that one sentence in the passive voice paraphrases (i.e., conveys the same meaning as) another sentence in the active voice, or that one sentence is the negation of another.

Second, although the disposition embodies knowledge of a structured class of behaviors, the competent agent need not be able to directly articulate that knowledge. For example, while competent English speakers can be expected to follow the rules of subject–verb agreement, they may not be able to state those rules. Chomsky labeled this kind of knowledge as "tacit". For example, Chomsky's generative grammar embodies this kind of tacit knowledge by specifying "what the speaker actually knows, not what he may report about his knowledge" (Chomsky [7, p. 8]).

Third, theorists can distinguish a competent agent's disposition toward a set of behaviors from the concrete manifestations of that disposition. A competence theory focuses on *ideal* performance as distinguished from actual, possibly erroneous, performance. A theory of English-speaking competence does not predict when or whether an agent will utter a particular sentence. Nor does it predict that an utterance will or will not be grammatically correct. However, it does claim that, under ideal circumstances, competent English speakers can agree on whether any given construction is acceptable in English, is related to other constructions, etc. Competence is described in a form that is abstracted away from factors idiosyncratically influencing real performance.

Finally, and most importantly for this paper, theories can be developed and explored that characterize competences other than linguistic competence. Moravcsik [33] proposes that cognitive theorists "can characterize grammatical, logical, mathematical, etc. competences, and add ... later characterizations of several other competences or in some cases ... psychological or environmental factors that influence actual performance or occurrence" (p. 86).

In sum, a cognitive theory of competence focuses on describing dispositional knowledge, embodied as generative processes, underlying idealized performance. This outlook on cognitive theory contrasts sharply with Newell's commitment to cognitive theory as a basis for predicting or simulating behavior. Having reviewed this alternative approach to cognitive theory, I am now ready to consider Newell's proposal in more detail.

2. The elements of Newell's approach

This section outlines four central features of Newell's approach—his stance on the goals of cognitive theory, his biologically inspired view of the human cognitive architecture, his view of UTCs as knowledge systems, and his exemplar UTC, the Soar problem solving architecture.

2.1. Theories of cognition

Newell believes that a cognitive theory is concerned above all else with describing human behavior, especially in chronometric terms. He points to the impressive body of experimental data amassed by experimental psychologists and cognitive scientists and in need of explanation. Newell illustrates his view of commendable psychological theory by reviewing such "microtheories" as Fitts' Law [17] and the Power Law of Practice (Snoddy [44]). Fitts' Law predicts the time it will take a subject to move a finger or pointer to a target location. This time varies in proportion to the logarithm of the ratio of the distance moved to the size of the target region. According to the Power Law, the logarithm of some measure of performance, e.g, performance time, is linearly related to the logarithm of the number of practice trials (Fitts and Posner [18]). These chronometric laws illustrate Newell's concern with predicting the time-dependent course of behavior. He also offers information processing mechanisms as hypotheses of the cognitive processes that produce these behavioral regularities.

Newell offers yet another illustration of acceptable theorizing. This example, a model of search in problem solving, differs somewhat from the examples of chronometric laws in being a bit more abstract. The observations in this case take the form of a detailed record of a chess player's verbal report of the sequence of candidate moves (s)he considers at a point in a game. For Newell, these verbal reports, called a *protocol* (Ericsson and Simon [11]), provide observable manifestations of the subject's mental search among possible moves. Unlike the two previous cases, the regularities that Newell observes are qualitative. He finds that the subject engages in a specific pattern of search that he calls "progressive deepening". Here, as in the two previous examples, Newell seeks to illustrate how one can construct an information processing mechanism capable of simulating these behavioral regularities.

Newell also wants to diverge from the strictest approaches to behavior modeling in which a single predictive failure suffices to falsify an entire theory. Newell argues that "theories are ... like graduate students" (p. 14). That is, once a theory is adopted one aims to "nurture" it, to find ways to tune or adapt it in the face of contradictory evidence rather than simply reject it. This decidedly non-Popperian view of theorizing is an important aspect of Newell's approach. A UTC approximates a complete or exact account of all the evidence. Theorists strive to refine and modify the UTC to better account for the evidence and to gradually expand the theory's scope. Nevertheless, simulation or prediction of physically measurable performance data comprises the core of Newell's approach regardless of the diversity of types of data or the degree of approximation that he is willing to accept.

2.2. The human cognitive architecture

Newell carries his theme of simulating physical events to the biological level. He presents his picture of the neural system that produces intelligent behavior, the "human cognitive architecture". His architecture is a hierarchy that is built, as he puts it, out of "neural technology". He begins by composing basic neuronal units hierarchically out of even more elemental biophysical units. He then constructs a hierarchy of ever more complex combinations of neuronal units. Newell identifies "levels" in this hierarchy in terms of compositional complexity. He further aggregates adjacent levels in the hierarchy into what he calls "bands". Newell focuses particularly on postulating relationships between bounds on performance capabilities of structures at a particular level (of complexity) and bounds on the performance times required by those units to carry out their functions.

Individual neural elements form a low level of this hierarchy. The first level of composition, in which neural elements are connected, Newell calls the "lowest level of the cognitive band" (p. 132). These element-to-element connections allow information stored at one location to be accessed at another. Distal access is, for Newell, the defining capability for producing and using symbols. Newell postulates that simple distal access takes place within approximately 10 milliseconds. This fixes the functional or processing capability of this level of the hierarchy and associates with it a bound on performance time. Newell emphasizes the inherent inflexibility of this level of processing. Assuming fixed connections, an element's response is entirely determined by the contents of the fixed locations to which it is connected and which may be accessed.

At the next higher level, combinations of these basic connections are hypothesized to produce the simplest forms of what Newell calls "deliberation" (p. 133). Essentially, circuits at this level are composed of a selection element having distal access to some set of remote units. The selection element distally accesses information stored in the remote units, computes over it, and produces a response on the basis of that fixed computation. So, the response of a deliberative unit reflects a comparison of the content of multiple, distal sources of information during one or more cycles of access. Newell estimates the processing time at this level to be on the order of 1/10 of a second. This increase in processing time accompanies the increase in functionality. However, Newell emphasizes the inflexibility of circuits at this basic level of deliberation. The response produced by such a circuit depends upon the information from fixed connections and a fixed choice function.

The next level of circuits provides more flexibility in response. Newell posits that this level provides the minimum flexibility to produce "characteristic interactions with the environment which ... evoke cognitive considerations" (p. 129). Circuits at this level select among the alternatives at the next lower level. Thus, these circuits realize "operations" that give more cognitive flexibility by allowing choices or compositions among alternative basic deliberation mechanisms. Alternative deliberation methods can be distally accessed, selected among, or composed. Newell proposes that these operations take on the order of 1 second to occur. Newell suggests that behaviors resulting from operations at this level of the human cognitive architecture correspond to highly practiced responses such as pushing the appropriate button in a reaction time task.

Newell adds yet another level, the "unit task" level. Circuits at this level are composed from combinations of the "operations" at the immediately preceding level. Accordingly, he calls this the "first level of composed operations". Newell postulates another order-of-magnitude increase in performance times at this level, to approximately 10 seconds. This increase in performance time, of course, corresponds to a further increase in the flexibility and processing power that can be achieved at this level. Newell associates the responses produced by the unit task level with elementary, reportable problem solving steps such as the reportable elements of task performance by skilled computer users (Card et al. [5]) or moves selected in a chess game (Newell and Simon [40]).

Newell names these four levels the "cognitive band". The cognitive band is built hierarchically from the more basic constituents of the "neural technology" in the subordinate "biological band". Newell suggests that the cognitive band constitutes the lowest level of the human cognitive architecture that can manifest the essential functions of problem solving—*symbolic representation, composed representation, knowledge as response capacities, and search.*

Newell extends his hierarchy to higher composed levels. He describes the "intendedly rational band" as immediately superior to the cognitive band. Three levels comprise this band. The functions defined there are, of course, selected and composed from lower level circuits. Rational band functions search even more thoroughly and flexibly among distally accessed alternatives. The rational band's most distinctive feature is, according to

Newell, the ability to perform functions enabling the cognitive system to adapt its responses to attain goals. Newell says little about how goals arise or how they are encoded except to indicate that goals represent a cognitive system's limited "knowledge of [its] environment" (p. 150). He suggests that search in this band, implemented by compositions of composed functions from lower levels provides the flexibility to operate in a goal-driven manner. Of course, these flexible operations also consume more time, taking anywhere from a couple of minutes at the lowest level of this band to a couple of hours at the rational band's highest level.

Still higher level bands are hierarchically composed from the rational, cognitive, and biological bands. Newell calls these the "social, historical, and evolutionary bands". He has even less to say about these bands. Here again, Newell seems primarily concerned to show how structural complexity leads to greater functional capacity and adaptivity, on the one hand, and longer required operating times, on the other.

This brief summary should provide a general feel for Newell's "human cognitive architecture". It illustrates his predominant concern for identifying physical events whose chronometric and other properties provide cognition with a basis in physical reality. By including this architecture as part of his monograph's presentation, Newell seems to be telling us specifically that a UTC's mechanisms must be reducible to measurable biophysical phenomena. Moreover, he makes a concerted (and, in this case, heroic) effort to use performance timings to shed light on other aspects of cognition. He is quite willing, as he freely admits, to construct highly speculative hypotheses of neurophysiological architecture in order to "get some general guidelines for the cognitive architecture regardless of any specific proposal" (p. 157).

2.3. UTCs as knowledge systems

Other than this speculative foray into neurophysiological modeling, Newell focuses most of his discussion on computational rather than neurophysiological mechanisms from which to build UTCs. He develops a comprehensive theory depicting "the symbol processing required for intelligence" (p. 158). Newell presents his AI architecture, Soar, as both the embodiment of this cognitive theory and as a guiding example of UTCs in general. As an exemplar UTC, Soar embodies some constructs that Newell believes are fundamental to any UTC. This section reviews these foundational UTC constructs.

For Newell, a UTC is a theory taking "*mind* to be the control system that guides the behaving organism in its complex interactions with the dynamic real world" (p. 43). Although mind is a control system, Newell rejects the language of control science (Wiener [50]). He chooses instead to describe this control system as "having knowledge and behaving in light of it" (p. 45).

A UTC explains the performance produced by a *knowledge system*. Newell also rejects the analyses of knowledge produced by epistemologists and other philosophers. He presents a concept of knowledge "that is used simply to describe and predict the *response functions* of a system ... to predict (with varying degrees of success) the behavior of the system" (p. 46). The knowledge that a cognitive system embodies provides its capacity to behave—perform tasks, solve problems, and enact decisions—under various conditions.

Newell's presentation of knowledge systems recapitulates ideas he has published previously over more than thirty years. This includes his well-known discussions of physical symbol systems [36], the knowledge level [38] and the problem space hypothesis [37]. His contribution in his current monograph is to integrate these ideas in a common framework, an *architecture*. In fact, Newell believes that the knowledge system specified by a UTC must be embodied in an architecture. He proclaims that "to specify a unified theory of cognition is to specify an architecture" (p. 158). The architecture specified by a UTC constitutes basic mechanisms that realize and manage a knowledge system's most fundamental functions. Furthermore, he suggests that the functions carried out by this architecture itself contribute substantively to the behavioral predictions of the UTC. The architecture's properties show up in what Newell terms "the commonalties ... in behavior" (p. 159).

Newell's list of fundamental knowledge system functions include the use of *symbols, structured and composible representations, knowledge, and problem solving as search*. Because Newell has already written extensively about these things I can be very brief in reviewing them.

- *Symbols.* As already noted, Newell's basic idea of symbolic representation turns upon what he calls "distal access". A symbol is an object providing a cognitive system with the ability to gain access to some remote body of information. A UTC stipulates how symbols are constructed and used within an architecture to establish the laws of information availability and access.
- *Representation.* Symbol structures act as representations insofar as they obey Newell's basic representation law

  $$Decode[Encode[T](Encode[X])] = T(X).$$

  To explain this law, suppose that X is some actual situation in an agent's task environment. Let T be some transformation that can occur in that environment. T maps the situation, X, into another situation, $T(X)$. Newell's representation law says that application of a proper representation of T to a proper representation of X produces a proper representation of $T(X)$. This law specifies how composite representations are built up from simpler representations.

- *Knowledge.* A UTC specifies how knowledge engenders action. The dispositional quality of knowledge is its most fundamental characteristic to Newell. UTCs describe how a cognitive system's knowledge provides its capacity "to take actions to attain goals" (p. 50). Newell does not hold that knowledge must be encoded in some declarative form such as predicate calculus (cf., Genesereth and Nilsson [19]). For example, the knowledge in Newell's UTC, Soar, is encoded in procedural form, as productions, and in its architecture's functions such as the decision cycle that manages operations on Soar's goal stack. Newell does not arbitrarily rule out UTCs that hypothesize declarative encoding of knowledge such as Anderson's [2] ACT* architecture. He does, however, hold that one would need to understand how these declarations are interpreted and converted to action before one could confidently assert the knowledge specified by such a theory.

  Newell uses his dispositional definition of knowledge to show how UTCs can depict the overall capability, or *intelligence*, of a cognitive system. Newell defines a *knowledge level* system as one that uses all of its knowledge or beliefs in performing its tasks. This includes knowledge that is logically entailed by explicitly embodied knowledge. The *intelligence* of a knowledge system is the degree to which it makes complete use of its knowledge. That is, a cognitive system's intelligence is its degree of approximation to being a knowledge level system.

- *Search.* In Newell's view problem solving is fundamentally search. A UTC specifies problem solving amounts to search of a *problem space* for a solution state. The proposition that problem solving may be viewed as state space search is a predominant assumption in both AI and cognitive science. The most unique feature of Newell's version of this well-worn search hypothesis is his stipulation that problem spaces may be generated to solve problems arising from the incomplete or otherwise flawed character of a given problem space representation. For example, if an agent is searching a given problem space, she might find herself in a state for which no operators exist to enable further search. Newell calls this kind of problem solving event an *impasse*. Impasses define new problems which require search in their own associated problem spaces. In the present example, a problem space must be selected and searched to find new operators to add to the original problem space in order to resolve the "no operator" impasse. This hierarchical and generative view of search contrasts with most discussion of problem solving as search in AI and cognitive science that implicitly assume search in a single complete space.

Newell distinguishes between *knowledge search* and *problem search*. Problem search explores a given problem space. Knowledge search seeks information to guide or control problem search. For example, the result of knowledge search can initiate problem search as when the perceived occurrence—i.e., the encoding—of a problematic environmental condition triggers the selection of a particular state space to be searched to resolve that problematic condition. Knowledge search can constrain the steps taken in this problem search. The reaction to an impasse illustrates this case. In my previous example, impasse detection triggers a knowledge search that sets up the problem space to be searched for finding new operators.

2.4. Soar

Newell's problem solving architecture, Soar, embodies his vision of UTCs. I touch lightly those aspects of Soar that I refer to in subsequent discussion.

Soar is a production system architecture. It implements Newell's problem space hypothesis. Soar's key elements include a single *long-term* or *recognition memory*. Recognition memory is populated entirely by production rules. Thus, Soar's knowledge is procedurally encoded. This commitment distinguishes Soar from other UTCs, such as Anderson's ACT*, which encode some or all of the contents of long-term memory as declarative structures such as logic assertions, semantic network structures, or frames. As in any production system, Soar's *working memory* is another key component. The contents of Soar's working memory are object–attribute–value data structures. Working memory's specific contents cause appropriate production rules to execute. The left-hand side of each production rule in long-term memory describes a pattern of object–attribute–value combinations (with variables allowed) that can occur in Soar's working memory. Of course, working memory contents that trigger productions on a given cycle are the result of previous production rule firings (or possibly direct by sensor input, although Newell says little about this).

The *context stack* is a very important structure within working memory. It is an architectural feature of Soar. The context stack encodes a hierarchy of problem solving contexts. Each level in the stack represents a commitment to search a specific problem space, the goal (state) being sought in that space, the current state in the problem space which search has reached, and an operator to apply next to generate successors of the current state. These four items in each level of the context stack represent the current problem solving context. Since the context stack is in working memory, productions can respond to its contents. Among other things, productions may suggest how to complete or change the contents of the context stack. For example, a particular level of the stack may happen to specify only a problem space, goal, and current state. In this case, productions might fire that "propose" operators to fill out this context level. Once an operator has been proposed, accepted, and inserted into the proper level of context, long-term memory productions may then fire that propose the successor state to use to replace the current state entry.

Conflicts can occur in this process. For example, productions may propose multiple candidate operators to complete a level, or multiple candidate successor states in the problem space. So, certain productions insert *preferences* into working memory. These preferences order selection among competing proposals to change the context stack. These preferences will, hopefully, resolve to a single choice. If they do not, an impasse is created that triggers long-term memory productions to set up a new problem space with the goal of resolving the impasse. Thus, the principles that guide conflict resolution in Soar are largely driven by information in long-term memory rather than being defined strictly as part of the overall architecture.

Soar's *decision procedure* is the fixed component of the architecture that manages changes to working memory and resolves competition using the preferences just mentioned. Each cycle of Soar's operation begins with an elaboration phase. In this phase the current contents of working memory trigger concurrent firings of production rules. Rules that fire insert new items in working memory. This may cause more production rules to fire. This continues until no new working memory elements are created and, hence, no more rules fire. This ends the *elaboration phase*. Up to now the multiple, possibly competing proposals created by firing of production rules have not been incorporated in the context stack. This is done next, during the *decision phase.* Soar's *decision procedure* examines the proposals for changes to the context stack and the preferences that have been asserted to resolve conflicts. If the proposals and preferences combine to uniquely stipulate modifications to the context stack, then the indicated modifications are made and Soar moves to the elaboration phase of the next cycle of Soar's operation. An *impasse* may occur, however, if no changes are made or if the preferences in working memory do not specify a unique choice among competing proposals. If this occurs the decision procedure creates data elements encoding the specific type of impasse before a new cycle of rule firing begins. Production rules firing in response to impasse detection create a new level in the context stack. It is subordinate to the level in which the impasse occurs. This new level will identify a problem space to be searched with the goal of resolving the current impasse.

When an impasse is resolved, Soar invokes another important component of its architecture, the *chunking* mechanism. Chunking is Soar's single mechanism for learning. As I have just sketched, Soar resolves an impasse by creating and searching a problem space. Soar keeps a record of the elements of working memory that were involved in the creation of the impasse. When the impasse is resolved, a new rule is created that encodes the search result as the response to make in the future if the conditions leading to the impasse recur.

Soar is a very direct and elegant implementation of Newell's problem space hypothesis [37]. Soar encodes problem spaces implicitly. A problem space is generated by the sequence of production rule firings and the changes that they produce in working memory's context stack. Problem spaces can be created and searched by productions that respond to various working memory contents such as goals, impasses, and other data. So, one may conceptually group subsets of productions in Soar's long-term memory according to the problem space descriptors (problem space identity, goal, state, operator, or other assertions in the context stack) that are a prerequisite to their firing.

3. Critical appraisal

The previous section reviewed four elements of Newell's approach to cognitive theory. His general remarks on theories of cognition show him to be committed to simulation or prediction of specific performance, frequently emphasizing the time-dependent properties of behavior. His description of the human cognitive architecture suggests that a UTC must be reducible to biophysical processes and structures as well as concrete behavior. In contrast, the foundational elements of Newell's theory of knowledge systems emphasize dispositional knowledge as a generative capacity for intelligent behavior. Finally, Soar embodies this theory and provides a direct and elegant implementation of Newell's ideas about problem solving as search in a hierarchy of problem spaces.

As I stated in the introduction, my critical remarks about Newell's proposal focus mostly on problems caused by his view of UTCs, and Soar in particular, in terms of their ability to simulate or predict behavior.

3.1. Cognitive theory as behavior simulation

My most fundamental concern with Newell's approach is prompted by the similarity of Newell's proposal to classical behaviorism. This is surprising because behaviorism is the paradigm that he and others deem to have been displaced in a "paradigm shift" to cognitive science. Newell asserts that the theories and methods of cognitive science have "established a new paradigm" (p. 24). Newell sees the dominance of cognitive science reflected in the critical attention being given to it by recent challenges from such competing paradigms as ecological realism (Gibson [20,21]) and connectionism (McClelland et al. [30,41]). Newell thinks that it is high time that cognitive science has a theoretical manifesto to replace those provided by leading behaviorists such as Watson [49], Tolman [47] or Hull [25].

However, as I carefully studied Newell's exposition of UTCs, I found it increasingly difficult to distinguish his view as a cognitive scientist from the fundamental principles of the behaviorist paradigm. Many aspects of Newell's approach invite comparison to the behaviorist doctrine prescribed by John Watson, typically considered the founding expositor of behaviorism. Other aspects of Newell's approach seem similar to Tolman's version of behaviorism.

John Watson advocated a very rigorous version of behaviorism [49]. He sought to reduce the science of psychology in its entirety to the objective measurement of repeatable, observable performance. He felt that, to be properly scientific, psychologists must provide a physical, mechanistic explanation of psychological phenomena. For Watson, the mechanism was clearly the organisms neurophysiological system. He felt that, to be psychological, laws must describe the observable behavior produced by this neurophysiological system. Such behavioral descriptions would be objective and they would be expressed in physical terms that would be consistent with the physical reductionist language of biology as Watson understood it.

So, Watson wanted to unequivocally ban explanations in terms of purely mental objects and events such as consciousness, concepts, memory, etc. Psychological explanations could not be scientific unless their terms were merely shorthand for, or abstractions of, observable behavior patterns. For example, reference to a subject's "memory" of a set of stimuli must describe the measurable properties of some set of observable responses such as the subject's *verbal reports* of these stimuli at some time following their presentation. Watson felt that constructs defined in terms of behavior could ultimately be reduced to descriptions of neurophysiological structure and function; descriptions containing mental constructs could not. In sum, unlike many inaccurate accounts, Watsonian behaviorism did *not* eschew talk about a mechanism responsible for producing behaviors. Watson merely insisted that such talk either describe this mechanism's biophysical properties directly or else describe other observable physical events, behaviors, that could be reduced to descriptions of biophysical processes. One must interpret theoretical constructs entirely in terms of their relation to observed performance. And, all such constructs must be directly reducible to physical properties of an underlying neurophysiological system.

Newell's approach seems quite compatible with the behaviorist doctrine in its absolute commitment to a UTC as a system for simulating human performance. Newell, like Watson before him, seems to feel that a psychological theory is meaningful only in terms of its ability to describe or predict human performance. To illustrate what a psychological theory ought to be, Newell described two examples of chronometric performance models—Fitts' Law and the Power Law of Practice. The methodological and theoretical commitments of scientists who investigated those laws were, and for the most part still are, very much to mainstream behaviorism.

But, one might say, Newell also espouses using protocol analysis to investigate problem solving. Is that not a paradigmatic departure from behaviorism? It turns out not to be a departure at all, even from John Watson's rigorous version of behaviorism. Watson did *not* eschew the study of so-called cognition—e.g., language, problem solving, memory—as long as such phenomena are reducible to behaviors or to physiological operations. As long as a UTC is interpreted in terms of its capacity for predicting performance, then Newell's program seems to be challenging none of behaviorism's methodological preconceptions.

My conclusion is reinforced by Newell's reductionist account of the human cognitive architecture. It is quite reminiscent of Watson's concern for biophysical reduction. Unhappily, Newell's exposition is also all too reminiscent of the problems that behaviorists encountered in pursuing their reductionist goals. They found the gap between behavior and physiological processes to be much broader than they initially suspected. Attempts to bridge that gap turned out to be oversimplified and highly speculative.

So too with Newell's reductionist account. Newell's human cognitive architecture espouses a number of highly speculative and overly simplified reductions of psychological functions to neurophysiological processes. He builds up his picture of neural cognition from some admittedly controversial assumptions about (a) the complexity of neural activity required for specific classes of cognitive operations, and (b) implied bounds on these performance times. He provides only the most casual evidence for these very strong assumptions. Of course, given the current state of understanding of the relationship between brain function and cognition, he can do little more. Unfortunately, he feels compelled to press ahead. Perhaps Newell believes that he must provide this sort of reduction to provide an "objective" basis for his functional model. In this sense, his perspective seems remarkably similar to that of Watson and other psychologists who argue that psychology can only be scientific if the contents of its theories reduce directly to those of biology and ultimately those of physics. At the least, Newell's proposed human cognitive architecture suggests just how strongly he is committed to the psycho-physical reductionism of the behaviorists that he otherwise decries.

Perhaps one should look past Newell's talk about "neural technology" and regard his account from a purely functional viewpoint. Unfortunately, the functional content of Newell's human cognitive architecture is an old story. Newell basically says that

(a) simple, fast neural circuits manifest simple, inflexible responses,
(b) compositions of these circuits manifest more complex responses, including "cognitive behaviors" (sic), and
(c) the operation times of neural structures are proportionate to the complexity of the cognitive operations that they manifest.

From a functional standpoint, this sort of proposal is hardly new. For example, Miller and his colleagues [31] proposed a similarly hierarchical architecture of cognitive functions. Their architecture is composed of elemental functional units called "TOTEs" (for Test–Operate–Test–Exit). These seem quite similar to Newell's basic deliberative units. Miller et al.'s TOTEs can be composed to produce higher level units capable of more complex goal-oriented activities such as planning. In a concluding chapter these authors even speculate on the reduction of their functional, computational constructs to more basic neurophysiological mechanisms and their interconnections.

I wish to make two more points about Newell's commitment to performance prediction. First, even if one stresses Newell's emphasis on information processing functions that produce intelligent behavior, its contrast with behaviorism again seems minimal at best. Second, and more importantly, the problem of choosing among competing theories seems hopeless, in spite of Newell's claims to the contrary.

The UTCs envisaged by Newell present information processing mechanisms that emit the same behaviors as humans. To put it as Newell does at other places in his book, these information processing mechanisms mediate a system's response to stimuli. Perhaps this focus on mediating processes distinguishes Newell's brand of cognitive science from previous paradigms and their defects. Interestingly, many behaviorists such as E.C. Tolman have been as willing as Newell to postulate mediating processes in their accounts of human behavior. Tolman, like Newell, aimed to describe phenomena such as cognition, goal-directed or "purposive" behavior, and learning as fundamental psychological constructs. Tolman [47] referred to a general learning capability as "docility". Tolman sought what he called "intervening variables" that would explain how an organism's responses to specific stimuli could differ across occasions. Tolman believed that combinations of intervening variables could account for the way that cognition mediates an organism's responses. This, of course, is strikingly similar to Newell's conception of cognition as the control system for intelligent behavior. Tolman proposed that mediating variables could be identified and their effects estimated by abstracting over behavior episodes. For example, a rat that found its way blocked to a food dispenser on one trial might find another path on subsequent trials. This sequence of behaviors, said Tolman, would define a "goal" to get to the dispenser as an intervening variable in the rat's cognitive system. Tolman hoped to extend behaviorism beyond Watson's rather strict boundaries by devising methods to study and predict these mediating effects. For example, the rat's goal to reach the food dispenser might be a function of its level of hunger—another intervening variable—that could be predicted in turn by an objective measurement such as hours of food deprivation. Tolman hoped that his introduction of intervening variables could enable the objective investigation of many cognitive phenomena.

The fundamental differences between Tolman's and Newell's accounts of cognition seem to reside mainly in Newell's use of a computational language to describe mediating cognitive processes and objects such as the memory contents. However, for both Tolman and Newell, the validity of a mediating construct, whether it be computational or a quantitative intervening variable, derives from objective measurement of observable behaviors. Tolman [47, pp. 235–245] even anticipated Newell's use of verbal protocols (Ericsson and Simon [11]). Finally, Tolman, like Newell, stressed the need for unified theories by emphasizing how psychological theorists should build unified *systems* of cognitive mechanisms mediating the transition from stimulus to response.

Recognizing that an information processing model of performance is just a fancier system of intervening variables leads one to a rather serious problem with Newell's proposal. A theory must be *identifiable.* That is, one must be able to compare the predictions of one UTC with another and, eventually, determine which UTC does a better job of predicting human behavior. Unfortunately, psychologists have now experienced many cases in which multiple, competing models or theories predict identical behaviors (e.g., Townsend and Ashby [48]). It turns out that the problem of nonidentifiability of competing theories haunts any paradigm that proposes to uniquely identify complex mediating processes as the causal basis of observable behaviors.

Surprisingly, Newell treats the problem of nonidentifiability rather lightly. According to Newell, nonidentifiability "... is a methodological artifact. It shows up when attention is focused on one specific task, one specific type of data, and one specific inference situation" (p. 244). He asserts that the problem simply vanishes as one uses a UTC to predict the performance regularities of a sufficiently broad range of tasks. He suggests that data already collected on human performance contains "... enough constraining regularities ... to identify the architecture to all extents and purposes" (p. 243).

Newell does not attempt to prove this point. He defends it by describing the success of his own UTC, Soar, in predicting behavioral regularities produced by human subjects across a broad range of tasks. Soar's ability to simulate human performance is indeed impressive, especially given the diverse collection of tasks that Soar must perform. In addition, Soar's chunking mechanism evidently provides it with an equally impressive ability to mimic performance improvements, again on a wide range of tasks.

However, a demonstration of Soar's plausibility does not prove that another, distinct theory could not do as well. In this light, I feel that it is particularly unfortunate that Newell has chosen to focus his exposition on Soar alone. It is highly unlikely that cognitive scientists will be persuaded to endorse *any* single theory, whether that theory is Soar or not. Consequently, Newell's pleas to develop UTCs risk being overshadowed by speculative arguments about Soar's shortcomings. Had Newell compared Soar to other UTCs such as ACT* (Anderson [1]) or the theory offered by John Holland and his colleagues [24], he would have been better able to illustrate how UTCs could be compared. For example, how would Newell compare the implications of Soar's uniform long-term (production) memory with ACT*'s division of long-term memory into procedural and declarative components? How does Soar's chunking mechanism compare to *knowledge compilation* in ACT* (Neves and Anderson [34]) in which declarative information is translated into production rules? In general, the plausibility of Newell's proposal to build UTCs would be greatly enhanced if he had shown how to make such comparisons and illustrate how they could lead to the selection of one UTC over another, competing theory.

Even without comparing one UTC to another, questions about theory validation remain unanswered in Newell's discussion. For example, how would one determine whether to provisionally accept Soar, or under what conditions would it be proper to reject Soar as a UTC? Newell specifically discards the idea that a UTC should be rejected because it fails to predict some specific aspect of human performance. He supplants the Popperian notion of theory falsification with the idea of accumulation or approximation. The scientific community should not reject Soar just because it falsely makes certain specific predictions. Instead, it should alter the theory to bring its predictions in closer correspondence to existing data. Of course, as it does so, it must strive to maintain Soar's ability to emulate performance on other tasks. In this way Soar will simulate an ever-increasing range of intelligent behavior. Problems also arise from the broad coverage of a UTC. For example, one predictive failure might lead the theorist to make a repair that degrades the UTC's ability to predict other types of performance. What should the theorist do in this case? Newell provides no overall guidance on the degree of correspondence needed before one can comfortably accept a UTC's predictions as adequate. Does a required level of predictive adequacy depend on whether Soar is being used to simulate individual behavior or as a simulation of aggregate performance of many subjects? How massive a degradation would be required before Soar were rejected altogether?

All these questions reflect the problem of nonidentifiability. Such questions must go unanswered for Newell because he is embracing an experimental methodology that corresponds to a very different and far simpler form of theorizing. Performance prediction was the forte of behaviorism. Watsonian behaviorism assumed minimal complexity of processes intervening between stimulus and response. Tolman's version admitted complex mediating variables but suffered from the very problems of nonidentifiability I have been discussing. Modern information processing models of cognition, especially

UTCs like Soar, postulate even more complex mediation between stimulus and response. Indeterminacy arises because of the enormous number of degrees of freedom in a UTC's process model. When faced with an error of prediction, the theorist just has too many ways to change the model. Newell claims, but does not demonstrate, that this problem goes away when the theory gets larger. I conclude that a UTC can be neither refuted unambiguously nor validated as a cognitive simulation/prediction model.

3.2. Architectures versus frameworks

UTCs as Newell envisions them describe how intelligent behavior arises from the operation of multiple, diverse cognitive mechanisms. An encapsulating *architecture* manages the execution of these mechanisms. I sketched the essential components of Soar's architecture at the end of Section 2. Basic Soar provides this general framework. The actual cognitive theory that Soar embodies depends on its substantive contents—namely, the production rules in long-term memory—that this framework encapsulates.

However, Newell makes it quite clear that the architecture's features also contribute substantively to the claims of a UTC. As Newell asserts, "There is no alternative for a [UTC] based on information processing but to be a theory of the architecture" (p. 431). The properties of the architecture influence the effects of the cognitive subsystems encapsulated within it: "[T]he total theory is an amalgam of information spread over ... the *general principles* and the *simulation details*" (p. 10) [emphasis added]. From a methodological perspective, an implemented architecture provides a framework for generating and exploring the complex and often subtle implications of the UTC it embodies. Or as Newell says, "An important aspect of each architecture-embodied unified theory of cognition is its capacity for generating ... possibilities" (p. 306). For example, Soar's architecture makes no structural or functional distinction between so-called semantic and episodic long-term memory. However, Newell asserts that the semantic–episodic distinction, and many others not yet foreseen, arise as distinctions in Soar's functions. These functional distinctions are due to the content of specific groups of productions that Soar creates together with the way these productions are created and managed by the architecture. Thus, Newell seems very clear in his conviction that an architecture like Soar comprises an information processing framework the design of which makes a substantive theoretical contribution over and above its specific contents.

Newell repeatedly stresses another important way in which a UTC serves as a theoretical or exploratory framework. At various times he emphasizes that a UTC like Soar must be capable of incorporating the full range of more specific models or "microtheories". These smaller scale theories represent theorists' best accounts of specific classes of intelligent behavior. A UTC must smoothly incorporate these microtheories. In this sense, a UTC is not a theory that proposes a new and distinct paradigm. Rather it provides a framework within which "to integrate and synthesize knowledge within the existing paradigm [of cognitive science], not to propose new questions and radically different answers .... The function of a unified theory is to precipitate and consolidate ... the saturated solutions of empirical results and successful microtheories that currently exist" (p. 395). In keeping with this principle, Newell presents numerous examples of Soar's ability to embody the predictive substance of many "microtheories", from chronometric performance models to the use of mental models in syllogistic reasoning.

In spite of his enthusiasm for Soar as an architectural framework in both the preceding senses, Newell seems curiously pessimistic about the work of others to develop general problem solving architectures. Although he briefly acknowledges AI's contribution to the "theoretical infrastructure for the study of human cognition" (p. 40), he summarily dismisses work in that field on what he calls "*frameworks* which are conceptual structures (frequently computational systems) *reputed to be relatively content free* that permit specific cognitive theories to be inserted in them in some fashion" (p. 16) [emphasis added]. Newell gives no examples of these "content free frameworks", nor does he say more beyond this cursory dismissal. However, I can suggest a number of problem solving architectures worthy of consideration, whose features have been substantively influenced by psychological theory. One very prominent example is, of course, the so-called blackboard architecture of the Hearsay-II speech understanding system (Erman et al. [12]). Hearsay-II, and blackboard systems in general, have provided a substantive architectural framework for many modeling efforts in cognitive science (e.g., Hayes-Roth and Hayes-Roth [23]). Does Newell really wish to dismiss such systems as "content free" frameworks? If Soar's properties *as an architecture* have substantive theoretical implications, then why do not these architectures?

I think that Newell misses an important opportunity to clarify and defend his thesis with this rather parochial dismissal of other work on problem solving frameworks. If cognitive scientists are to receive clear guidance on building and exploring UTCs, then clear comparisons are needed among competing hypotheses. And, if one accepts Newell's claims regarding the central theoretical significance of the information processing architecture that a UTC specifies, then sharp comparisons among competing architectures are imperative. Newell's exposition would have benefited significantly by comparing Soar directly with other information processing frameworks, even if they are, as Newell claims, lacking Soar's broad scope (cf., Hayes-Roth's BB1 architecture [22] or my own [13] real-time problem solving architecture, called Schemer). In sum, I find this aspect of Newell's expository strategy to be a major barrier to understanding and accepting his recommendations.

3.3. Cognition and intelligence

Newell believes that a successful UTC should tell us how humans exhibit *intelligence* (e.g., p. 429). Section 2 of this commentary presented his definition of intelligence—the degree of a cognitive system's approximation to the knowledge level. Unfortunately, I find this definition inadequate. More importantly, it seems to contradict other views that Newell expresses on the nature of intelligence and its relationship to cognition.

Newell's definition aims to decouple the knowledge embodied in a cognitive system from its intelligence. A system is intelligent to the extent that it makes full use of whatever knowledge it has. Recall that Newell defines knowledge as a disposition. A system's knowledge is whatever underlies its capacity to perform. A knowledge level system makes full use of its knowledge. It always produces the most appropriate performance up to the limitations of its knowledge. It is the gold standard in terms of which the intelligence of humans and UTCs must be measured.

These commitments force Newell to the rather curious conclusion that a very simple system, such as a thermostat, is more intelligent than a human. In contrast to human problem solvers, the thermostat has an extremely limited body of dispositional knowledge (e.g. a small, closed set of "rules" for starting and stopping the furnace). It uses this knowledge fully in performing its task. A thermostat is, thus, a knowledge level system. Humans possessing far more complex knowledge can only approximate this ideal level of performance, and probably not very closely at that. Newell tries to dismiss this *reductio ad absurdum* critique by asserting that "knowledge-level [systems] cannot be graded by intelligence ..." (p. 90). One is just not allowed to compare the capabilities of knowledge level systems to human performance. Unfortunately, with this move the scale for measuring intelligence seems to suffer a rather serious discontinuity.

More generally, Newell's definition rests upon a hopelessly subjective criterion. One must assess a system's intelligence strictly in terms of that system's knowledge. So, the intelligence of two cognitive systems cannot be compared. I doubt the utility of a concept of intelligence that does not admit comparisons. At the very least, such a subjective definition directly conflicts with Newell's manifest concern for objective theory validation that I discussed earlier in this section.

3.4. Conclusions

Many of these criticisms could have as easily been directed at positions taken by other cognitive scientists. Allen Newell's extensive contributions, on which his monograph is based, have had a powerful and positive impact on psychology and cognitive science. As a consequence, many elements of his bold proposal have already been enthusiastically embraced by the cognitive science community. In particular, Newell's commitment to behaviorist methods and modeling typify assumptions made by most cognitive scientists about the experimental validation of computational, information processing theories of human cognition. His materialist and reductionist perspective of the human cognitive architecture typifies a current trend among many cognitive scientists toward materialist and functionalist reductions of psychological phenomena to biological processes (e.g., Dennett [10], Churchland [8]). As a consequence, the criticisms that I have raised, and the alternative view that I offer below as a response, really address difficulties in the mainstream paradigm (it can be called such) of cognitive science as much as any limitations of Newell's presentation.

On the other hand, Newell's position on the Soar architecture versus other information processing frameworks, and his curiously subjective definition of intelligence seem to articulate less commonly held views. My critical interest in them is tied to the alternative view of cognitive theory that I present in the next section.

4. Theories of cognitive competence

Newell's interest in measuring, simulating, and predicting of concrete performance contrasts sharply with the focus of competence theories as described in the introduction. The criticisms I advanced in the previous section were meant to draw out the weaknesses of Newell's focus on predictive modeling. I now develop my proposal that UTCs be viewed as competence models, a view that better exploits the significant strengths of Newell's theories of knowledge systems and intelligent cognition.

4.1. Cognitive competence

UTC should identify and elucidate the *idealized competences of an intelligent agent*. This statement entails a number of commitments that are worth spelling out.

First, a competence theory is a theory of *knowledge-based agency* (Fehling and Shachter [16]). It explains intelligent agents' interaction with their environment the knowledge that these agents possess. A competence theory also accounts for agents' knowledge of structural relations among these potential actions. For language this includes intuitions about such structural relations as paraphrase, negation among potentially expressible linguistic acts (utterances), and the ability to embed one utterance as a component in another. The importance of structural relations holds for other types of cognitive competence as well. Consider, for example, a competence explanation of agents' ability to construct, execute, monitor, and revise plans. Plans, like linguistic constructions, may stand in "paraphrase" relations as when distinct plans achieve the same objectives with different courses of action. One plan may be "structurally embedded" in another if it may be used as a component to achieve a subgoal, say. A pair of plans may differ only in that one honors a particular constraint while the other relaxes or "negates" that constraint. In general, a psychological (or AI) theory of planning competence would explain how agents synthesize (i.e., learn) and exploit such structural knowledge as well as their ability to construct individual plans from first principles. Newell's concept of a knowledge system and knowledge as a capacity for effective action seem particularly congenial to this aspect of competence theories.

Second, a unified theory of cognitive competence would depict intelligent agents as possessing multiple, distinct competences. Each particular competence would represent the knowledge (tacit or otherwise) sufficient to accomplish a specific set of tasks. In addition, each competence would account for agents' abilities to meet certain criteria of acceptable task performance. For example, a theory of linguistic competence usually takes the task to be the production or comprehension of linguistic expressions in a particular dialect (or even idiolect) of a specific language. In general, competence theory depicts the knowledge required to produce only those expressions having acceptable grammatical form, semantic content, and pragmatic force as components of a conversation. Identification of the defining tasks and acceptance criteria circumscribe the theorist's search for a particular body of knowledge. Change the task definition or criteria and the competence being sought also changes. Here again, non-linguistic cognitive skills, such as planning, decision making, or playing a game like chess, seem equally amenable to this approach. Theorists building unified competence theories would strive to identify bodies of knowledge that are sufficient to generate acceptable completion of an ever-increasing range of tasks. Here again, Newell's knowledge systems would seem to provide a very congenial framework in which to explore candidate competence accounts.

Third, a competence account describes the logical form of generative processes that can produce the potential actions of competent agents. The competence is a disposition. It does not predict that the actions will be taken, it explains how they could be. Furthermore, the agent's knowledge of her competence may be tacit. Though she will act in accordance with the disposition, she may or may not be able to articulate its logical content. For example, a competent English speaker can recognize that an utterance violates a rule of subject–verb agreement whether or not she is capable of describing that rule. The tacit nature of the relevant knowledge may hold for many other types of competence, too. The potentially tacit nature of knowledge embodied in a competence implies that a competence theory is fundamentally neutral on whether agents encode explicit descriptions of the distinctions they are able to manifest. If one expresses that competence theory in computational terms, then this means that a competence theory is essentially neutral regarding the controversy in AI over whether knowledge in a computational agent should be entirely procedural or entirely declarative (Winograd [51]). The far more important commitment is to describe the logical form of knowledge entailed by the disposition (Chomsky [6,7]). This aspect of a competence seems to me to be similar to Rosenschein's concept of "grand strategy" in an AI theory of agency (cited in Genesereth and Nilsson [19]. With the grand strategy a declarative formalism like predicate calculus may be used "to describe the knowledge of an agent, but may or may not be used in the implementation" [19, p. 327].

My fourth point generalizes the previous one. A competence theory may remain essentially neutral to reductionist versus non-reductionist explanations of the generated behavior. A competence theory is an epistemic theory, a theory about knowledge. It focuses on the structural and functional properties of knowledge giving rise to particular cognitive skills. One may explore the epistemological commitments of a particular competence theory without ever being concerned with the ontological status of the embodiment of that knowledge.

Fifth, and perhaps most significantly, while a competence theory is still a theory of behavior, it offers an idealized account. As Moravcsik puts it

> It is reasonable for the study of cognition to borrow a page from the books of the other successful sciences, and conceive of the study of cognition as the study of [cognition and action] abstracted from the real everyday context, and described under idealizations. [33, p. 85]

In sum, a cognitive theory of competence focuses on describing knowledge embodied as generative processes or dispositions that give rise to idealized performance. It does not attempt to predict situation-specific behaviors. Specific deviations in performance are abstracted away from the descriptive content of the theory. If the theory does focus on errors, it does so by showing how they arise systematically and again as idealized performance from a body of knowledge whose content is inadequate (cf., Brown and VanLehn [4]). In this way, the problems of identifiability in predictive modeling are bypassed. On the other hand, this type of theory still provides substantive explanations. It can tell why an agent is or is not capable of acting intelligently in some task context. This alone establishes the value of competence accounts. What I now hope to establish is that this type of theory is quite compatible with Newell's most fundamental theoretical concepts.

4.2. Knowledge systems as competence models

While I remain sharply critical of Newell's commitment to performance prediction and his reductionist account of the human cognitive architecture, I find his theoretical foundations for knowledge systems to be quite compatible with my proposal to use UTCs for exploring cognitive competences. The elements of his theory seem to provide a valuable and powerful vocabulary for articulating the content of a competence.

Newell proposes that one view the goal of UTCs as showing how intelligent systems build and manage structured symbolic representations encoding knowledge that is used to achieve similarly represented goals by a process of knowledge-based search. I am particularly taken by his focus on knowledge as the *abstract capacity to act* to achieve goals, and his lack of emphasis on parametric features of such knowledge or how such features would arise. Knowledge for Newell is abstract in that it is "abstracted from representations and processing" (p. 108). It seems clear that, using Newell's suggested theoretical terms, one is no longer talking about performance, but rather about tacit knowledge embodying performance dispositions. In Newell's own UTC such tacit knowledge is embodied as procedural rules and, he claims, in the architecture's ability to create them and manage their operation. In all these ways, Newell's fundamental terms for cognitive science correspond remarkably well to fundamental commitments of a competence theory.

In addition, Newell offers a dispositional and agent-oriented definition of knowledge that closely matches these aspects of competence theory. For Newell, knowledge is the logical form of the capacity to "select actions to attain goals" (p. 108). Agents employ this knowledge to react to, and interact with, their perceived environment. Or, in Newell's words, agents must use this knowledge to "operate in a rich, complex, detailed environment" (p. 233). Newell's notion of a symbol system is equally dispositional—a symbol embodies the *function* of distal access. One may readily interpret his description of human memory (Chapter 6) as specific competence for the tasks of recognition, recall, or savings in relearning based on the function of distal access.

The problem space hypothesis is a very important element of Newell's view of human cognition that seems to be quite central to competence accounts. Search is a very powerful model of deliberation—successively generating or selecting alternatives and evaluating them until one or some combination provides a solution to the problem being deliberated. Newell's profound contribution has been to extend this abstract model to account for the circumscribed nature of any search space, on the one hand, and the necessary capacity of an agent to cope with incompleteness and other limitations of a given search process by defining a new search to resolve the impasse. The formalism of a problem space hierarchy is likely to provide a basis for describing the collection of competences that an intelligent agent possesses and important relationships among these competences. In particular, each problem space (more properly, the dispositions for selecting and searching it) represent one particular deliberative competence of the agent.

Recasting Newell's UTCs as competence theories also helps to sort out some of my concerns regarding his concept of intelligence. Recall that Newell defines intelligence as the degree to which a cognitive system can approximate a knowledge level system, one that uses all of its knowledge. Of course, if there were no constraints on a cognitive system's use of its knowledge, then all such systems could be knowledge level systems. Unfortunately, constraints introduced by the task environment, such as limitations of time or task-critical information, limit a knowledge system's ability to use its full knowledge. In addition, the system's own capacities determine how constraining these limitations become. So, is the ability to approximate the knowledge level a fixed capacity, independent of knowledge as Newell proposes? Or, is intelligence itself reflective of some form of knowledge? I agree with Newell's description of central cognition as a knowledge-based control system that mediates between perception and motor actions. To intelligently adapt to conditions in its environment, such a control system must augment its basic knowledge for completing tasks with knowledge that allow it to use the most appropriate quality and quantity of that knowledge in the face of contextual constraints. In other words, cognitive scientists must also account for a cognitive system's competence in adapting its deliberations and actions in the face of encountered constraints.

Recently, a great deal of attention has come to be focused on these issues of constrained rationality (Russell [42], Fehling and Shachter [16]). This recent literature suggests significant value in using UTCs based on Newell's concept of a knowledge system to explore the competence required for constrained rationality. In particular, the notion of competence as dispositional knowledge can be used to elucidate a system's idealized ability to adapt its problem solving performance. A number of specific techniques have been proposed that could be incorporated in such a theory and examined for adaptive adequacy. For example, since search takes time, a system may benefit from learning and using decision procedures that trade solution quality for speed of solution construction (Fehling and Breese [15]). Alternatively, a system could exploit knowledge of special methods such as "anytime algorithms" that provide solutions of steadily increasing quality until time runs out (Dean and Boddy [9]). In Newell's terms, these two approaches could enhance a system's manifest intelligence by improving either knowledge search or problem search, respectively.[1] Such knowledge enables the cognitive system to cope with the constraints that specified conditions impose on its ability to approximate its knowledge level competence.

The concept of constrained rationality suggests that intelligence as the degree of approximation to the knowledge level is a knowledge-relative measure. This contrasts sharply with Newell's aim to decouple knowledge and intelligence. However, it has the virtue that one is now free to explore hypotheses that intelligence can be affected by environment or experience. This is not a possibility if the degree of intelligence is independent of the knowledge content of a cognitive system. (Embracing Newell's idea strictly, one must conclude that intelligence reflects fixed properties of the cognitive architecture.) This modification of Newell's definition of intelligence also addresses my concerns about the subjective nature of his definition. A useful measure of intelligence must now include some objective specification of the effectiveness of the agent's actions that are engendered by the portion of its knowledge that it can effectively use.

Finally, I note that, under this view of a UTC as a competence account, a system's intelligence would not be depicted as a monolithic or uniform capacity. Rather, the extent of a system's knowledge can differ widely with respect to different task domains. So too can its ability to approximate the full use of its knowledge for distinct task domains. A UTC specifies a system's intelligence as a collection of competences and the capacity to integrate and situationally adapt them. This non-monolithic view of intelligence corresponds reasonably well to recently developed theories in psychology (Sternberg [45]).

4.3. Methodology—constructing and evaluating competence theories of cognition

UTCs as competence models help cognitive scientists to undertake an important form of theory development that, for the most part, has been restricted to investigations of linguistic behavior. Newell's conception of a knowledge system is happily compatible with this perspective on theory and allows theorists to sidestep the drawbacks of UTCs as behavioral simulations discussed earlier. A few words are in order about the overall methodology that competence theorists would follow.

Moravcsik [32,33] has articulated the general methodology for exploring competence. The following questions paraphrase his exposition of this methodology:

---

[1] The use of a decision procedure differs from assumptions that Newell makes about knowledge search being simply the retrieval of fixed rules for problem search. However, we see no reason to preclude a more constructive process, such as decision modeling, as another, more flexible form of knowledge search. This generalization does no damage to Newell's distinction of these two forms of search.

(1) What does the possessor of a competence need to accomplish to have successfully completed a task?
(2) What are the varying conditions under which the problem solver must possess and exercise the competence?
(3) What are the essential cognitive processes that are required?
(4) How are these processes organized to cope with
   (i) variations in the task requirements or
   (ii) task conditions?

A UTC like Newell's Soar could be used as a framework for answering these questions. Answers to the first two questions would be represented in the goals that Soar encodes and the conditions that trigger assertion of those goals into working memory (in the context stack). Answers to the last two questions come from an analysis of the content of Soar's recognition memory when it has been shown to be adequate for meeting the requirements defined by (1) and (2). There are three salient facts in this regard. First, this methodology aims to populate Soar with a collection of rules that enable it to succeed in completing some specified tasks of interest under a plausibly complete range of expected conditions. Competence theorists have no direct concern for predicting the idiosyncratic details of actual human performance. In particular, they have no concern for modeling error, *per se*. Second, once such a version of Soar has been formulated, investigators will focus primarily on elucidating the basic elements of this competence and the *structural relations* among these elements. Third, in contrast to Newell's assertion, the properties of the framework itself will probably turn out to be theory-neutral. Such a framework is, after all, equivalent to a universal Turing machine. What counts is the substantive content of the knowledge encapsulated in the system. Theorists will focus their attention on the encapsulated knowledge and its sufficiency for producing task performance that meets specified criteria. They can defer concern with most architectural distinctions. Competence explanations focus on the logical content of the architecture and the adequacy of this content for completing specific tasks. Or, as Newell would say, one focuses on characterizing claims about the required knowledge content of the system that may be abstracted from its encoded productions and other processes.

The existence of criteria for defining successful task completion gives a competence theory a normative flavor. The normative aspects of UTCs as competence theories mark a radical shift in focus from the predictive/descriptive focus of Newell's methodology for performance prediction. Because a competence account seeks to elucidate knowledge that enables a system to meet task performance criteria, this type of theory may be of interest to AI investigators who do not share the cognitive scientists concern for explaining human cognition.

5. Conclusions

My commentary has stressed a contrast between Newell's view of UTCs as predictive performance models and the notion of UTCs as providing competence characterizations. Predictive models fall prey to the problems of identifiability, regardless of their scope. If one examines proofs of nonidentifiability in formal logic and automata theory, one sees that the problem really has to do with insufficient density of observation states compared to the functional state sequences in the hypothesized system. This problem can arise regardless of the absolute size of the system. Newell could only make a convincing case by showing formally that the set of distinct observable behaviors grows much more rapidly than the complexity of the internal structure of the formal systems generating such behaviors. Although I have not completed a formal proof, this seems to me to be unlikely in general.

In contrast, a competence account focuses theorists primarily on the job of articulating knowledge embodied by an agent in order to adequately perform some range of tasks. Performance considerations are raised only in the idealized context provided by the competence account. This form of theory has dramatically improved our understanding of important phenomena in cognitive science such as language comprehension and production. Newell's proposal to build UTCs would be dramatically improved by adopting this competence perspective. As Newell himself pointed out many years ago (1973), performance modeling leads to a game of "twenty questions with nature" [35]. It is a game that theorists cannot win. I am persuaded by Newell's profound insight into the problems of validating performance models. I disagree with him in believing that the limitations of performance modeling are resolved simply by building much larger models.

Although I have focused specifically on Allen Newell's proposals, the concerns raised here apply more broadly to the theoretical and methodological presumptions of most cognitive scientists (e.g., Anderson [2]). Newell's proposal illustrates a tension that has existed in cognitive science and, in fact in psychology and other related disciplines, for at least two centuries—a tense self-consciousness over the scientific status of investigations of mental phenomena.

The recent emergence of cognitive science as a discipline has been both exciting and frustrating. It has been exciting because it has turned scientific attention toward things truly psychological, viz., mental or cognitive phenomena. Cognitive science has broadened our perspective on the range of phenomena that may be studied, methodologies for collecting them, and—most importantly here—the use of computational methods to describe and explain these phenomena. Cognitive scientists have reestablished the legitimacy of subjective phenomena such as thinking (Johnson-Laird [26]), imagery (Kosslyn [27]), and the nature of conscious awareness (e.g., Dennett [10], Baars [3], Fehling et al. [14]).

But, the emergence of this cognitive science as a discipline has also been frustrating. Many cognitive scientists seem as engaged as psychologists ever were in a perpetual struggle to reduce cognitive phenomena to either behavioral or biophysical measurement (e.g., Churchland [8]). Accordingly, controversies over dualist, functionalist, or materialist interpretations of cognitive phenomena arise frequently. Sometimes these controversies shed new light on cognition. More often, they simply distract attention from the substantive issues of the nature of thought and, as Newell would have it, thought's role as the control system for a behaving agent. Progress in cognitive science has sometimes been frustrated because cognitive scientists have struggled to adapt their studies to satisfy the methodological and conceptual biases of behaviorism and biophysical reductionism.

The perspective offered by Newell in *Unified Theories of Cognition* is similarly frustrating. It is exciting because Newell offers a carefully worked out conceptual framework that provides a rich and powerful set of distinctions for describing cognition. However, his methodological commitments fail to be equally satisfying. So, is the glass half empty or half full? If one fixates on Newell's idea of cognitive simulation, one will probably conclude that it is half empty. If, on the other hand, one adopts the perspective of a UTC as a theory of cognitive competence, a theory of knowledge in service of effective action, then Newell's contribution is profound. From this perspective, his work has for a long time contributed significantly to our understanding of human cognition. I hope that cognitive scientists will carefully explore his proposal that one view intelligence as the degree of approximation to the knowledge level. They should be able to largely ignore his preoccupation with performance prediction. It is far more interesting and important to focus on Newell's suggested framework—yes, that is what it is—for modeling cognitive competences. From this perspective, Newell gives us the beginnings of a methodology for discovering the knowledge required by humans and machines to manifest important problem solving skills.

I would like to add a final word about the relevance of all this to AI scientists who are not compelled by the excitement of theories of human cognition. As long as cognitive scientists continue to engage in purely *descriptive* modeling, their results will be of only passing interest to many AI practitioners. However, cognitive modeling is a *normative* exercise. This type of model, with its emphasis on task analysis and analysis of knowledge requirements, increases the overlap in the objectives of AI researchers and cognitive scientists. A cognitive scientist's explanation of required competence for a given task domain may well be useful to the designer of an AI system intended for use in that domain. Whether or not the AI designer is willing to model the performance of humans performing her target task,

she will benefit from a description of the task and its knowledge requirements. Conversely, a cognitive scientist can extract useful guidance from
the analysis and design of AI systems that reflect rigorous consideration
of their intended task domain. I hope that this commentary encourages
those interested in other forms of human or machine problem solving to
take advantage of this communality. If they do, they are likely to find that
many of the theoretical constructs discussed by Newell in *Unified Theories
of Cognition* will help them in their efforts.

References

[1] J.R. Anderson, *Language, Memory, and Thought* (Lawrence Erlbaum, Hillsdale, NJ, 1976).

[2] J.R. Anderson, *The Architecture of Cognition* (Harvard University Press, Cambridge, MA, 1983).

[3] B.J. Baars, *A Cognitive Theory of Consciousness* (Cambridge University Press, Cambridge, England, 1988).

[4] J.S. Brown and K. VanLehn, Repair theory: a generative theory of bugs in procedural skills, *Cogn. Sci.* **4** (1980) 397–426.

[5] S.T. Card, P. Moran and A. Newell, *The Psychology of Human-Computer Interaction* (Lawrence Erlbaum, Hillsdale, NJ, 1983).

[6] N. Chomsky, *Syntactic Structures* (Mouton, The Hague, Netherlands, 1957).

[7] N. Chomsky, *Aspects of a Theory of Syntax* (MIT Press, Cambridge, MA, 1965).

[8] P.S. Churchland, *Neurophilosophy: Toward a Unified Science of the Mind/Brain* (MIT Press/Bradford Books, Cambridge, MA, 1986).

[9] T. Dean and M. Boddy, An analysis of time-dependent planning, in: *Proceedings AAAI-88*, St. Paul, MN (1988).

[10] D.C. Dennett, *Consciousness Explained* (Little, Brown, and Co., Boston, MA, 1991).

[11] K.A. Ericsson and H.A. Simon, *Protocol Analysis: Verbal Reports as Data* (MIT Press, Cambridge, MA, 1984).

[12] L.D. Erman, F. Hayes-Roth, V.R. Lesser and D.R. Reddy, The Hearsay-II speech understanding system: integrating knowledge to resolve uncertainty, *ACM Comput. Surv.* **12** (2) (1980) 213–253.

[13] M.R. Fehling, A. Altman and B.M. Wilber, The heuristic control virtual machine: an implementation of the Schemer computational model of reflective, real-time problem solving, in: V. Jagannathan, R. Dodhiawala and L. Baum, eds., *Blackboard Architectures and Applications* (Academic Press, Boston, MA, 1989).

[14] M.R. Fehling, B.J. Baars and C. Fisher, A functional role for repression, in: *Proceedings 12th Annual Conference of the Cognitive Science Society*, Cambridge, MA (1990).

[15] M.R. Fehling and J.S. Breese, Decision theoretic control of problem solving under uncertainty, Tech. Rept. 329-88-5, Rockwell International Science Center, Palo Alto Laboratory, Palo Alto, CA (1988).

[16] M.R. Fehling and R. Shachter, Constrained rational agency: foundations for an interactionist theory of intelligent systems, Tech. Rept. No. 92-7, Laboratory for Intelligent Systems, Stanford University, Stanford, CA (1992) (Manuscript currently being revised).

[17] P.M. Fitts, The information capacity of the human motor system in controlling the amplitude of movement, *J. Experimental Psychol.* **47** (1954) 381–391.

[18] P.M. Fitts and M.I. Posner, *Human Performance* (Books/Cole, Belmont, CA, 1969).

[19] M.R. Genesereth and N.J. Nilsson, *Logical Foundations of Artificial Intelligence* (Morgan Kaufmann, Los Altos, CA, 1987).

[20] J.J. Gibson, *The Senses Considered as Perceptual Systems* (Houghton Mifflin, Boston, MA, 1966).

[21] J.J. Gibson, *The Ecological Approach to Visual Perception* (Houghton Mifflin, Boston, MA, 1979)

[22] B. Hayes-Roth, A blackboard architecture for control, *Artif. Intell.* **26** (2) (1985) 251–321.

[23] B. Hayes-Roth and F. Hayes-Roth, A cognitive model of planning, *Cogn. Sci.* **3** (1979) 275–310.

[24] J.H. Holland, K.J. Holyoak, R.E. Nisbett and P.R. Thagard, *Induction: Processes of Inference, Learning, and Discovery* (MIT Press, Cambridge, MA, 1986).

[25] C.L. Hull, *Principles of Behavior: An Introduction to Behavior Theory* (Appleton-Century-Crofts, New York, 1943).

[26] P. Johnson-Laird, *Mental Models: Towards a Cognitive Science of Language, Inference, and Consciousness* (Cambridge University Press, Cambridge, England, 1983).

[27] S. Kosslyn, *Imagery and Mind* (Harvard University Press, Cambridge, MA, 1980).

[28] J.E. Laird, A. Newell and P.S. Rosenbloom, Soar: an architecture for general intelligence, *Artif. Intell.* **33** (1987) 1–64.

[29] D.G. Mackay, *The Organization of Perception and Action* (Springer, New York, 1987).

[30] J.L. McClelland, D.E. Rummelhart and the PDP Research Group, eds., *Parallel Distributed Processing: Explorations in the Micro-Structure of Cognition*, Vol. 2: *Psychological and Biological Models* (MIT Press, Cambridge, MA, 1986).

[31] G.A. Miller, E. Galanter and K.H. Pribram, *Plans and the Structure of Behavior* (Holt, Rinehart and Winston, New York, 1960).

[32] J.M. Moravcsik, Competence, creativity, and innateness, *Philos. Forum* **1** (1969) 407–437.

[33] J.M. Moravcsik, *Thought and Language* (Routledge, London, 1990).

[34] D.M. Neves and J.R. Anderson, Knowledge compilation: mechanisms for the automatization of cognitive skills, in: J.R. Anderson, ed., *Cognitive Skills and Their Acquisition* (Lawrence Erlbaum, Hillsdale, NJ, 1981) 57–84.

[35] A. Newell, You can't play twenty questions with nature and win: projective comments on the papers of this symposium, in: W.G. Chase, ed., *Visual Information Processing* (Academic Press, New York, 1973).

[36] A. Newell, Physical symbol systems, *Cogn. Sci.* **4** (1980) 135–183.

[37] A. Newell, Reasoning, problem solving, and decision processes: the problem space as a fundamental category, in: R. Nickerson, ed., *Attention and Performance* VIII (Lawrence Erlbaum, Hillsdale, NJ, 1980).

[38] A. Newell, The knowledge level, *Artif. Intell.* **18** (1982) 87–127.

[39] A. Newell, J.C. Shaw and H.A. Simon, Elements of a theory of human problem solving, *Psychol. Rev.* **65** (1958) 151–166.

[40] A. Newell and H.A. Simon, *Human Problem Solving* (Prentice-Hall, Englewood Cliffs, NJ, 1972).

[41] D.E. Rumelhart, J.L. McClelland and the PDP Research Group, eds., *Parallel Distributed Processing: Explorations in the Micro-Structure of Cognition*, Vol. 1: *Foundations* (MIT Press, Cambridge, MA, 1986).

[42] S. Russell and E. Wefald, *Do the Right Thing: Studies in Limited Rationality* (MIT Press, Cambridge, MA, 1991).

[43] H.A. Simon and C.A. Kaplan, Foundations of cognitive science, in: M.I. Posner, ed., *Foundations of Cognitive Science* (MIT Press/Bradford Books, Cambridge, MA, 1989) 1–47.

[44] G.S. Snoddy, Learning and stability, *J. Appl. Psychol.* **10** (1926) 1–36.

[45] R.J. Sternberg, *Handbook of Human Intelligence* (Cambridge University Press, Cambridge, England, 1982).

[46] N.A. Stillings, M.H. Feinstein, J.L. Garfield, E.L. Rissland, D.A. Rosenbaum, S.E. Weisler and L. Baker-Ward, *Cognitive Science: An Introduction* (MIT Press/Bradford Books, Cambridge, MA, 1987).

[47] E.C. Tolman, *Purposive Behavior in Animals and Men* (Appleton-Century-Crofts, New York, 1932).

[48] J.T. Townsend and F.G. Ashby, *Stochastic Modeling of Elementary Psychological Processes* (Cambridge University Press, Cambridge, England, 1983).

[49] J.B. Watson, *Behaviorism* (Norton, New York, 1930).

[50] N. Wiener, *Cybernetics: Or Control and Communication in the Animal and the Machine* (MIT Press, Cambridge, MA, 1948).

[51] T. Winograd, Frame representations and the declarative/procedural controversy, in: D.G. Bobrow and A. Collins, eds., *Representation and Understanding: Studies in Cognitive Science* (Academic Press, New York, 1975) 185–210.

Artificial Intelligence 59 (1993) 329–341
Elsevier

ARTINT 1012

Book Review

On building integrated cognitive agents: a review of Allen Newell's *Unified Theories of Cognition* *

Barbara Hayes-Roth

Department of Computer Science, Stanford University, 701 Welch Road, Bldg. C., Palo Alto, CA 94304, USA

1. Introduction

Twenty years ago, Allen Newell and Herbert Simon gave us a landmark book, *Human Problem Solving*, in which they introduced the method of protocol analysis, reported the parameters of human cognition, and set the stage for the emerging field of cognitive science. It is only fitting that, with his new book, *Unified Theories of Cognition*, Newell should set our course for the next twenty years. Once again he challenges us to shift paradigms, in this case to leave behind our focus on isolated cognitive tasks and to aim instead for the development of unified theories that account for the full range of cognitive function.

The book retains the easy conversational style of Newell's 1987 William James Lectures at Harvard University, on which it is based. It reflects his characteristic comprehension of the issues, attention to detail, and intellectual honesty. It is spiced with casual metaphors, witty asides, and wry ripostes to colleagues who hold different opinions. Reading it,

Correspondence to: B. Hayes-Roth, Department of Computer Science, Stanford University, 701 Welch Road, Bldg. C., Palo Alto, CA 94304, USA. E-mail: bhr@camis.stanford.edu.
 * (Harvard University Press, Cambridge, MA, 1990); xiv + 549 pages.

one can easily imagine Newell's intent gaze and, behind it, his passion for the quest. In short, except for being entirely one-sided, reading *Unified Theories of Cognition* is very much like having a conversation with Allen Newell—stimulating, enlightening, and very pleasurable, indeed.

Newell reminds us repeatedly that his "book argues for unified theories of cognition—the plural, not the singular ... I am much more concerned with figuring out how a theory could put it all together, and what could be the plausible yield from doing so, than I am for arguing that Soar is the best or even the favored choice" (p. 234). Nonetheless, he has chosen to deliver his message by example with Soar, the particular theory of human cognition on which he, Paul Rosenbloom, John Laird, and their students have been working for the last ten years. Indeed, after three introductory chapters that explain the objective and give brief tutorials in cognitive science and human cognition, the remainder of the book tells us in great detail what requirements Soar is designed to meet, how it works in general, how it performs a number of specific tasks, and how it might perform others. This progress report is extremely important. A great deal of research has been done on Soar, perhaps more than on any other cognitive theory, and the whole is truly greater than the sum of its parts. We need to have all of the parts in this one place so that we can appreciate the very large picture Newell has begun to paint for us.

To preview the discussion below, my response to *Unified Theories of Cognition* is generally positive. I endorse Newell's goal of developing comprehensive cognitive theories, his research paradigm of empirical evaluation of mechanistic theories, his efforts to identify functional requirements of intelligence as a basis for theory formation, and his demand for generality of candidate theories over many tasks. However, within each of these areas of agreement, I disagree with some of Newell's specific claims. While sharing his long-term goal of developing unified cognitive theories, I would establish more measured intermediate-term research objectives. While advocating empirical evaluation of mechanistic theories, I would develop a more rigorous empirical methodology. While advocating the identification of functional requirements of intelligence, I would emphasize a different set of requirements to drive early theory development. While recognizing the need for generality, I would propose integration as the ultimate evaluation criterion for candidate theories and, with that in mind, I would impose a particular programmatic structure on the research effort. These issues are discussed in Sections 2–5 below. Finally, I disagree with Newell about candidate architectures—but I will save the comparison of Soar and BB1 (my candidate) for another paper.

2. The goal: unified theories of cognition

Newell begins by making his case for the new research goal, unified theories of cognition. "Divide-and-conquer" is a good strategy for coping with complexity; cognition is such a complex system of phenomena that both psychologists and AI researchers have divided and conquered with abandon. As Newell observes, we now have an extensive literature on diverse phenomena, such as how people remember lists of words, how they do syllogistic reasoning, how a computer could learn to recognize a conjunctive concept, how it could diagnose infectious diseases. For each phenomenon, we have competing micro-theories and earnest efforts to support or demolish them. But identifying and discriminating among competing micro-theories is not an end in itself. The ultimate goal is a comprehensive theory that explains all of the phenomena. Ironically, as Newell points out, we face a growing complexity of our own making in the unbounded accumulation of observations to be explained in a comprehensive theory. If we wish to incorporate our observations and micro-theories as elements of a comprehensive theory, we have enough of them to begin the work of theory construction now.

I would add to Newell's arguments that, by studying phenomena in isolation, we virtually guarantee that our most successful micro-theories will be incorrect—they will not survive as elements of a comprehensive theory and may divert us from the path to one. Why? Individual phenomena offer so little constraint that it is easy to generate micro-theories and easy for them to perform well against local optimality criteria. Moreover, it is easy to carry this strategy too far, oversimplifying phenomena so that they will be amenable to careful analysis, but perhaps of limited relevance to the original question. A comprehensive theory is unlikely to comprise a complete set of locally optimal micro-theories. It is one of the commonest and costliest lessons of computer science (and engineering in general) that independently developed software components resist subsequent integration in a smoothly functioning whole. Components need to be designed for integration right from the start. We can expect this lesson to hold as well when the components represent micro-theories of cognitive function. Indeed, in the case of human intelligence, full integration has been the prevailing "design constraint". Nature has had no alternative but to mold diverse cognitive functions around one another within the architectural confines of a single, extremely versatile individual. Newell's quote from Voltaire (p. 16), "The best is the enemy of the good", is apt here. If the goal is a unified theory, we had better strive for integration right from the start even if that means sacrificing optimal micro-theories to achieve a graceful integration of merely good ones.

On the other hand, should we really aim for complete unified theories of all cognition? At this point in time, we can't even agree on what that would mean. Newell will be criticized for the grandiosity and patent unrealizability of his goal. Critics will claim that unified theories are impossible or at least premature. They will riddle his candidate, Soar, with its own faults and limitations. Although these criticisms are probably correct in a literal sense, I believe they are misguided in spirit. We probably never will have a unified theory of cognition. But that is an empirical question, which the Soar team is trying to answer. It almost certainly is premature to think of having one now. But it is not premature to begin working toward one, as the Soar team is doing. In fact, Newell acknowledges that his objective is ambitious, controversial, even presumptuous. He acknowledges that Soar is only a partial theory of selected phenomena. Newell might have avoided criticism by calling for more measured intermediate objectives. For example, I would advocate two such objectives: "multi-faceted systems" that integrate several (not all) individually challenging cognitive capabilities in a graceful, synergistic manner; and "adaptive intelligent systems" that integrate cognition with perception and action in dynamic real-time environments. Pursuit of these kinds of objectives requires a paradigm shift, but not a leap of faith.

Perhaps Newell's call for unified theories of cognition is, in part, a public relations strategy; he certainly has got our attention! But more than that, Newell is sending a fundamental message to the AI and cognitive science communities. He is reminding us what the long-term goal is, where we should be going as a scientific enterprise, and how to insure that short-term and intermediate-term research leads to long-term progress. He is tutoring us in the new paradigm by showing us what he and his colleagues have accomplished with Soar. And, far from being guilty of his "sin of presumption" (p. 37), Newell is urging us to give Soar some serious competition.

3. The paradigm: mechanistic theories and empirical evaluation

Newell's commitment to theory as mechanism is another important message. In the AI community, the term "theory" has been specialized to refer to formal descriptions of computational techniques, accompanied by mathematical or logical analysis of their soundness, completeness, and complexity. By default, mechanistic theories, especially if they are implemented in computer programs, are disparaged as "engineering" or "applications", with the implication of lesser scientific significance. In psychology, the concept of theory is less idiosyncratic and less exalted. With few exceptions, psychological theories abstract only the gross features of observed cognitive phenomena; they typically have neither the rigor of formal AI theories nor the explanatory power of mechanistic AI theories. Newell claims to hold an "unexceptional—even old-fashioned" view: a theory is any "body of explicit knowledge, from which answers can be obtained to questions by inquiries" (p. 13). Whether a theory is cast as a set of facts, axioms, or mechanisms is less important than that it explicitly represent a body of knowledge from which predictions, explanations, prescriptions, etc. can be derived objectively. A good theory is not necessarily formal or elegant or parsimonious—although these might be pleasing attributes, other things being equal. Quite simply, a good theory is one that gives good answers to the questions of interest. In the present context, a good theory is one that correctly accounts for the cognitive behavior of human beings or intelligent computer programs.

Despite this ostensibly catholic view, Newell's own theoretical work is almost exclusively mechanistic. For him, a theory of cognition is an architecture—a fixed computational structure that can process variable content to produce the desired cognitive behavior. In the tension between necessity and sufficiency, Newell is unambiguous: "*Necessary* characteristics are well and good, but they are substantially less than half the story. *Sufficiency* is all-important" (p. 158). Only by actually producing the behaviors in question can a theory claim to explain them. As with other complex systems, a sufficient theory of cognition will not comprise a small number of elegant laws, but rather a carefully designed and coordinated system of mechanisms working in concert. Thus, although Newell accords formal theories a place in the enterprise, for him "God is in the details".

To evaluate whether a theory explains cognitive behavior, Newell advises us to implement the theory in a computer program and evaluate its performance. The objective of a given evaluation is not to confirm or disconfirm the theory—any plausible cognitive theory would be too complex for binary decisions. Rather, the objective is to accumulate evidence that supports the theory and to identify aspects of the theory that need amendment. Thus, we approach the ultimate goal, a unified theory of cognition, by a Lakatosian process of successive approximation; in the meantime, we have a partial theory to use. Most AI researchers will feel comfortable with Newell's frank rejection of Popperian refutation (p. 14); there may be several theories that explain the phenomena of interest and any one will do. Most psychologists will object; their goal is to identify the one psychologically correct theory. Because Newell shares this goal, Soar eventually must undergo the test of necessity. However, he is right to insist on first constructing a more comprehensive and, therefore, more interesting and promising theory that meets the sufficiency test for a diverse set of observations.

Even accepting Newell's empirical approach, however, we are left with tough methodological issues.

First, the concept of "sufficiency" needs definition. Is an implemented theory sufficient if it produces a particular response? If it follows a particular line of reasoning? If its reasoning or behavior follows a particular time course? If it makes particular kinds of errors? Is sufficiency all-or-none or are there degrees of sufficiency? Which is more sufficient: a theory that perfectly models the designated line of reasoning or a theory that imperfectly models both the line of reasoning and its time course? We need measures that allow us to reliably evaluate different aspects of the sufficiency of an implemented theory. Given the goal to unify an array of behaviors within a single theory, we need measures that compare the sufficiency of competing theories that account for overlapping subsets of the full array. Finally, we need measures that evaluate the sufficiency of a theory with respect to unification *per se*, as well as for component behaviors.

Second, what is the relationship between a theory and its implementation? Newell acknowledges that, in his own case, "Soar, like any computer system, is a system always in a state of becoming something else. Many aspects are not yet operational, or only operational in some limited way" (p. 231). For purely practical reasons, a computer implementation must lag behind the theory it represents and it must contain many extra-theoretical hacks. It inevitably reflects the skill and style of its programmers. When instantiated for a particular task, it also reflects the skill and style of the application developers. As a result, given the performance of an implemented theory on a particular task, it is not a pure theory, but this hybrid that we are evaluating. We must distinguish the theory and non-theory in a computer implementation and correctly assign credit between them for important aspects of performance. One approach would be to experimentally manipulate an implementation in order to test predictions about the effects of excising or replacing (non-)theoretical code segments. Another approach would be to lift the theory out of its implementation and replicate its performance in a completely different implementation.

Third, given the complexity of our theories, we must look inside them and understand why they take the shape they do. Which aspects of the theory influence which aspects of behavior? Perhaps, as Newell says, all of the theory influences even apparently simple behaviors. We need to have some evidence that this is so and we need to understand how and why it is so. As our theories evolve, we must determine whether old elements still play their original roles or have become vestigial in the presence of new elements. We need measures of how theoretical complexity increases with the scope of the phenomena being explained. We must assess whether a repeatedly improved theory should be overhauled and streamlined or reconceived anew.

Finally, I would suggest that the proper companion to empirical development of sufficient theories is analysis. Many of the ambiguities inherent in particular implementations of complex theories can be resolved by abstracting theoretical constructs out of the implementation and analyzing the formal relationships among them.

At this time we do not have a rigorous methodology for describing, analyzing, and empirically evaluating complex cognitive theories. Developing that methodology should be a first-order goal of the research community. Implementing and evaluating experimental applications of a complex theory is hard, resource-intensive, and time-consuming. But it is the only way we really come to understand and believe in an architecture.

4. Requirements for intelligence

Newell evaluates the sufficiency of his own theory, Soar, against two categories of requirements for intelligence. First, it must replicate the behavior of two ostensibly intelligent creatures: human beings and AI programs. Second, it must exhibit the characteristics of behavior entailed in a definition of intelligence formulated by Newell himself.

4.1. Replicating the behavior of intelligent creatures

Psychological data are the objective facts that Soar, as a theory of human cognition, is bound to replicate. Newell devotes three of his eight chapters to showing how Soar models three kinds of psychological data. "Immediate behavior" (Chapter 5) refers to simple perceptual-motor reactions, for example pressing a button when a light comes on or pressing one of two buttons depending on which of two lights comes on. "Memory, learning, and skill" (Chapter 6) refers to verbal learning tasks, for example studying and then recalling a list of items or studying a list of cue–item pairs and then recalling the items, given the cues. "Intendedly rational behavior" (Chapter 7) refers to simple verbal puzzles, for example solving cryptarithmetic problems, syllogisms. I am impressed by Newell's discipline and perseverance in working through the details of Soar's treatment of these tasks.

On the other hand, I have reservations about Newell's choice of tasks. Most of them represent low-level cognitive functions, perhaps artifacts of biological hardware that we may never model successfully in a computer program. Put in a positive light, I think we can take this as a measure of Newell's seriousness about Soar as a true psychological theory. What is more problematic, the tasks seem artificial. Who but a cognitive psychologist would find the performance of choice reaction tasks (at which pigeons excel) or cryptarithmetic tasks (which leave most people cold) to be hallmark manifestations of human intelligence? Psychological experiments are notorious for oversimplifying the phenomena of interest—and for good reason: that is the only way to control enough variables to get reliable and interpretable results. I can accept Newell's determination that Soar, as a psychological theory, must explain these carefully documented data. However, I do not think the data offer much in the way of constraint on a comprehensive theory or that they give us insight into other cognitive functions—especially for those who are concerned primarily with producing intelligent computer programs, rather than with modeling psychological truths *per se.*

Newell also reports Soar's replication of the performance of AI programs on four classes of tasks: toy problems and weak methods (e.g., Eight Puzzle, Towers of Hanoi, hill climbing), expert systems applications (e.g., R1, Neomycin), learning programs (e.g., explanation-based generalization), and programs that interact with the external world (e.g., control of a Puma arm with a vision system). Again, I applaud Newell for his determination to "put [Soar] through its paces" (p. 159).

But again, I also have reservations about Newell's choice of these tasks and his implicit rationale. Newell seems to be inferring that these tasks require intelligence simply because researchers have decided to build AI programs to perform them. Somehow, it is incumbent upon Soar to follow in the footsteps of AI programs: "Thus, the demonstration that Soar can exhibit intelligence is only as good as the current state of the art. Indeed, this question must be re-asked continually as AI advances—Soar must keep up with the art, if we are to be able to assert that it predicts that humans are intelligent, according to an increasingly improving view of the nature of intelligence" (p. 220). I disagree. Given the rudimentary state of AI as a discipline, our current view of the nature of intelligence can hardly be bound by its limits. We learn at least as much from the other cognitive sciences. Conversely, it is obviously possible that special-purpose AI systems might perform in a "super-intelligent" manner that cannot be replicated by a unified cognitive theory because of the other constraints a unified theory must meet. This leaves open the question of how we know which AI programs' performances a unified theory must replicate and which we can simply admire.

In addition to the abstract tasks Newell and his colleagues have studied, I would like to see candidate cognitive theories perform important real tasks that intelligent human beings perform in their real lives. These could include everyday tasks familiar to all, such as maneuvering a car through traffic while looking for a parking place close to a destination. They could include esoteric instances of familiar classes of tasks, such as planning and executing a sequence of therapeutic interventions under uncertain conditions in a medical context. Real tasks have several attractive properties. They have "ecological validity"; we do not risk modeling phenomena that occur only in the laboratory. They present important cognitive demands in the context of messy incidental details; we do not risk modeling phenomena that occur only under extraordinarily austere conditions. And they carry extra-theoretical requirements that stimulate theory expansion. In my opinion, as discussed below, one of the most important such requirements is the integration of knowledge and reasoning for several "tasks" within a larger mission. Certainly, the Soar research team has investigated some "real" tasks, notably in R1-Soar. I would like to see more in this category.

4.2. Meeting a definition of intelligence

If we are in the business of building theoretical architectures to support "intelligence", the logical first step would be to define intelligence. How better to know when we have succeeded or failed? However, while many psychologists and AI researchers play fast and loose with the term "intelligence", few have been forthcoming with a definition. Some have declared the very idea misguided—which may be true if we aim immediately for a single universal definition.

Indeed, even informal reflection reveals our fundamental ambivalence about the nature of intelligence. Are all (any?) non-human animals intelligent? What about human neonates? Which is more intelligent: a dog that has a repertoire of 20 command-driven tricks and can fend for itself in the world or a human neonate? Is computer vision a core element of AI? If so, are congenitally blind humans less intelligent than the normally sighted? Do humans who lose their sight lose some of their intelligence? Are eagles more intelligent, in visual matters, than humans? Who was more intelligent: Albert Einstein or Virginia Woolf? Pablo Picasso or Virginia Woolf? Albert Einstein or Marilyn Vos Savant (who reputedly has the highest IQ ever recorded and currently writes the "Ask Marilyn" column for *Parade* magazine)? It quickly becomes obvious that there is no single property that we intuitively call intelligence and no simple rule by which we intuitively determine how intelligent particular individuals are. Rather, there exists a multitude of factors whose differential contributions make an individual appear to be more or less intelligent in particular ways.

Nonetheless, I agree with Newell that we should start by identifying some of the important components of intelligence. If we turn out to be mistaken in the end, at least in the meantime, our colleagues will understand what it is we are trying to achieve with our theories and they will be able to argue with us about that as well as about the theories themselves. Newell distinguishes himself by giving us both a universal definition and an array of component requirements for intelligence.

First, consider Newell's universal definition: "A system is *intelligent* to the degree that it approximates a knowledge-level system." More specifically: "1. If a system uses all of the knowledge that it has [to achieve its goals], it must be perfectly intelligent .... 2. If a system does not have some knowledge, failure to use it cannot be a failure of intelligence .... 3. If a system has some knowledge and fails to use it, then there is certainly a failure of some internal ability ..." (p. 90). This definition is impressive in its simplicity, but it doesn't tell us enough about how to distinguish between "knowledge" and "intelligence", which I take to be the use of knowledge. Can't the ability to use knowledge be viewed as a kind of knowledge? To avoid tautology, the definition must operationalize this distinction. To illustrate, a meta-level exercise of Newell's definition leads to paradox. Assume a system has failed to solve a problem requiring knowledge k1. Is this is a failure of knowledge or intelligence? If the system knows k1, it's a failure of intelligence. But, if the system lacks k2, the knowledge that it ought to use k1 for this problem, it's only a failure of knowledge. Moving up a level, if the system knows k2, but fails to use it, it's a failure of intelligence. But if it lacks k3, the knowledge that it ought to use k2, it's only a failure of knowledge. The continuing regression of meta-levels is obvious—can't we recast every apparent failure of intelligence as a failure of the next meta-level of knowledge? For us to use Newell's definition well—that is, to determine whether a system is or is not behaving intelligently, we need an operational definition of what counts as knowledge, a way to assess the system's current knowledge and goals, and a way to determine what part of the system's knowledge it ought to apply in a given situation.

The universal definition also leads to some conclusions I find unintuitive. A simple computer program that knows the rules of addition and has a single goal to solve addition problems is perfectly intelligent, while a human being who can do a lot of things imperfectly, including arithmetic, is imperfectly (less) intelligent. A system that uses all available reasoning methods to insure a reliably correct answer is more intelligent than one that chooses to use only one of them—even though both get the same answer. A system that solves 100 of 100 problems by retrieving solutions from a table is more intelligent than a system that solves only 10 of them by reasoning imperfectly from a sufficient set of first principles. A system that always uses all of a fixed knowledge base is as intelligent as one that always uses all of a growing knowledge base. I think Newell should extend his universal definition to account for the amount of knowledge a system has, its tendency to use the most effective knowledge, and its ability to acquire knowledge.

Finally, the universal definition ignores several cognitive phenomena I consider fundamental: a system's allocation of limited cognitive resources, its ability to focus attention, its efforts to meet real-time constraints, its balancing of competing demands and opportunities for action, its considered decisions not to apply knowledge that is available, its inclination to satisfice. How can these phenomena be accounted for in a knowledge-level definition?

To complement his universal definition, Newell gives us several lists of component requirements for a unified theory of cognition: "areas to be covered by a unified theory of cognition" (p. 15), "multiple constraints that shape mind" (p. 19), "characteristics of Soar that agree with the basic shape of human cognition" (p. 227), and "potpourri of things Soar has not done" (p. 434). Together, these lists comprise a long, heterogeneous collection of requirements, such as: "Behave flexibly as a function of the environment".

"Be self-aware and have a sense of self." "Be realizable as a neural system." "Operate in real time." "Use language." "Use an indefinitely large body of knowledge."

I find all of Newell's proposed requirements interesting and worth examining in more detail. For example, the constraint that a system operate in real time is fundamental. Because it potentially affects every element of a cognitive architecture and all of their interactions, it can be used to prune severely the space of possible architectures. Given his commitment to model the biological details of human cognition, Newell operationalizes the real-time requirement in terms of constraints imposed by the underlying biological hardware: "There are available only ~ 100 operation times (two minimum system levels) to attain cognitive behavior out of neural-circuit technology" (p. 130). Because Soar's component computations meet these constraints, Newell reports that it has been shown to operate in real time. By contrast, I would operationalize the real-time requirement in terms of constraints imposed by the environment: The utility of the agent's behavior depends on its timing with respect to exogenous events. To show that Soar meets this definition of real time, we need a different kind of evidence. Soar must produce goal-effective behavior within externally imposed time constraints and degrade the quality of its behavior gracefully when necessary. Newell's and my operationalizations of the real-time requirement are not incompatible. In fact, there is a potential bridge between them if we can show how the biological constraints adapt human beings to their particular environmental constraints and, similarly, how the corresponding constraints restrict the environments in which AI programs can function effectively. But the two definitions are separable and individually important.

Critics will object that Newell's combined list of requirements is arbitrary, incomplete, and vulnerable to exceptions. But I think that is a natural consequence of trying to characterize this multi-dimensional thing we call intelligence. The problem is not specific to Newell's effort to build unified theories; anyone who is trying to model intelligence must communicate and establish the significance of whatever requirement(s) they have chosen to address. Mapping out the space of requirements, uncovering their relationships to one another, identifying the constraints they impose on our theories—these are necessary precursors to understanding the nature of the complete problem and the significance of individual research results within that larger context.

5. Generality, integration, and the structure of the research program

Newell's overall argument on behalf of Soar is one of generality: "We are interested in coverage—in whether a single theory, as an integrated conceptual structure, can address many different cognitive phenomena, ranging in time scale and task" (p. 303). So he and his collaborators have given us a proliferation of different versions of Soar—R1-Soar, Designer-Soar, Robo-Soar, etc.—each of which performs a different task. It's an impressive accomplishment, but ambiguous. How much of what we see reflects the theoretical principles embodied in Soar and how much reflects the skill of accomplished AI system builders? Newell recognizes and guards against the weakness in his argument: "It is important that Soar be seen to be a theory and not a framework of some kind. For example, it is not a loose verbal framework, which guides the form of invented explanations but does not itself provide them. ...Soar is a specific theory by means of which one calculates, simulates, and reasons from its fixed structure" (p. 433).

I think that a stronger argument could be made for Soar's (or any theory's) generality if we combined the sufficiency criterion with a "constraint" criterion. A would-be theory has theoretical content to the degree that it constrains the appropriate form in which to model each new demonstration task. Of course, this poses a new construct to be operationalized and measured, but there is a straightforward (if labor-intensive) empirical method for measuring degree of constraint. Ask 10–20 people (Soar experts presumably), working independently, to apply Soar to each of several tasks. Ask another group of people to apply architecture X (a standard of comparison) to the same tasks. If Soar offers a lot of theoretical constraint, there should be substantial agreement among the designs produced by the Soar experts, more than among the designs produced by the architecture X experts. Other things being equal, we prefer a more constraining theory over a less constraining one.

Even with the additional requirement for constraint, generality over many individual tasks in a series of localized demonstrations is a weak test for a unified cognitive theory. The hard test is integration. Acknowledging this, Newell claims: "One should think of [R1-Soar and Designer-Soar] being added together to make a single Soar system with the knowledge of the two tasks. They are kept separate simply because they are worked on by separate investigators at different times" (p. 216). But the assertion that R1-Soar and Designer-Soar are separate for purely logistical reasons is glib and the phrase "added together" is mysterious. What would it mean to integrate these two applications in a substantive way and what difference would it make? Would the integrated knowledge base be smaller (non-redundant) and more interconnected than a simple composite of the original two? What about the problem spaces? Would performance quality or speed on the original tasks be improved or hindered in any way? Would any new capabilities be potentiated? Would Soar be able to combine elements of independently acquired knowledge bases to perform new tasks? Newell does report integration of two algorithm domains (sorting and sets) within

Designer-Soar, with some sharing of problem spaces but no transfer of learning. He also reports integration of an instruction-taking capability with performance of a sentence-verification task. These are promising steps, but I would like to see more of a concerted effort to integrate knowledge and reasoning capabilities that interact in multiple ways—not all of them fully anticipated—and to extend those capabilities in an incremental fashion. In other words, I propose a more programmatic structure to the research effort, in which we incrementally develop an increasingly sophisticated, integrated "cognitive agent".

Let me presume to offer a friendly challenge to the Soar team. Give us "Agent-Soar", integrating all of the "content" of the existing Soar applications in a graceful, principled fashion within a single instance of the Soar architecture. Show us the resulting economies of storage and Agent-Soar's global perspective on its knowledge. Show us how Agent-Soar can exploit all of its content to meet several of the component requirements for intelligence simultaneously. For example, show us Agent-Soar operating continuously, selectively perceiving a complex unpredictable environment, noticing situations of interest, setting and modifying its own goals, and going about achieving them. Show us how it integrates concurrent tasks and coordinates their interacting needs for knowledge, inferences, perceptual information, computational resources, and real time. Show us synergy—unplanned desirable capabilities arising from interactions among independently acquired contents. Show us Agent-Soar learning in the natural course of these activities to produce incremental growth in unanticipated areas of its knowledge. Show us that Agent-Soar is self-aware, possessing and applying knowledge of itself as an agent that possesses and applies knowledge. Show us how it modifies its knowledge based on experience and makes the best use of dynamic, but limited resources under real-time constraints. Finally, show us how Agent-Soar grows and develops and successively approximates the ideal knowledge-level agent.

Acknowledgement

Preparation of this paper was supported by NASA contract NAG 2-581 under DARPA Order 6822.

Artificial Intelligence 59 (1993) 343–354
Elsevier

ARTINT 1013

Book Review

Allen Newell, *Unified Theories of Cognition* *

Marvin Minsky

*Media Lab, Room E-15-489, Massachusetts Institute of Technology, Cambridge,
MA 02139, USA*

1. Introduction

This book can be seen as at least four different books—about Soar, about
the prospects of psychology, about AI, and about philosophy of mind. Its
range and depth make it a landmark in our understanding of how minds
must work. I found it hard to write this review because whenever I found
something to argue about I would soon discover another page in which
Newell either answered it or explained why Soar was not ready to attack
that issue. Soar itself appears to be a wonderfully economical yet powerful
way both for using knowledge to solve problems, and for learning from
that experience. But as for the thesis of this book—the search for a Unified
Theory of Mind, I'm not sure that this is a good idea.

The Introduction tries to justify that search:

> ... a single system (mind) produces all aspects of behavior. It
> is one mind that minds them all. Even if the mind has parts,
> modules, components, or whatever, they all mesh together to
> produce behavior. (p. 17)

This might be true in some simple sense, but it can lead to bad philosophy.
Whatever one may think of Freud, we owe to him the insight that the parts

---

Correspondence to: M. Minsky, Media Lab, Room E15-489, Massachusetts Institute of
Technology, Cambridge, MA 02139, USA. E-mail: minsky@ai.mit.edu.
  * (Harvard University Press, Cambridge, MA, 1990); xvi + 549 pages.

of the mind don't always mesh, and that there need be *nothing* to mind them all. When Newell adds, "Unification is always an aim of science" (p. 18), one might reply that new ideas were often made by first disunifying older ones. Chemistry's hundred-odd elements came from the ashes of an older theory based on only four. To be sure, the properties of the new elements were subsequently derived from many fewer principles—but in this review I'll try to show why we can't expect this to happen in regard to the brain. Chapters 5-8 of *Unified Theories of Cognition* (*UTC*) show that Soar can be made to simulate the outcomes of a variety of psychological experiments. A critic might fear that that's not enough, because the mind can do so many things that *any* theory could be made to look good by selecting which tasks to simulate. The list of domains (Fig. 8-1) unexplored by Soar includes some very important ones, such as understanding stories, and reasoning by analogy. But mainly I'll be less concerned with what Soar can do than with how much it could do concurrently.

2. The organic brain

In earlier times, physical science was split into separate "branches" that focused on different phenomena, such as mechanics, optics, electricity, heat, and chemistry. Then heat became part of mechanics, light turned out to be electrical, and then these (and virtually everything else) were "reduced" to a few quantum principles. The term "unified theory" celebrates this discovery that the laws of the universe are few. But we know that this can't happen in biology—because we know too much about the nature of an animal. The trouble is that the structures and functions of an animal's organs are not much constrained by those basic physical laws. This is because the functional details of each organ are determined by the activities of great numbers of specialized genes. Recent research (Sutcliffe [7]) appears to show that in this respect, the brain is unique, because as much as half of the entire mammalian genome is involved in coding for the nervous system.

What is an animal, anyway? Essentially, its body consists of a bizarre collection of organs, each specialized to do only certain jobs. In order for "higher" such forms to survive, those complex assemblies had to evolve along with networks of systems to regulate them; some of these are chemically distributed, while others take the form of additional organs—most notably the brain. The brain itself resulted from several hundreds of megayears of adapting to different environments, and now consists of hundreds of specialized sub-organs called brain centers, each one linked by more-or-less specific connections to several others, to form a huge system of what clearly must be a myriad of mechanisms for synchronizing, managing, and arbitrating among different functions. Newell recognizes this complexity in

Section 4.1 and proposes, at least for the time being, to seek a unified theory only for what he calls central cognition.

> ... the total system is too complex to handle all at once, and the sorts of considerations that go into perception and motor action seem too disparate to integrate. So the strategy is divide and conquer. (p. 160)

My question is, has Newell divided enough? In Section 3.5 he explains with great clarity how each theory in psychology must be applied only at the right level, lest its claims become too strong to be true or too weak to be useful. At the lowest level,

> ... the neural-circuit level remains a realm governed by natural science. The types of laws are those of physics and chemistry. (p. 129)

But because those individual cells could be assembled into unlimited varieties of computational circuitry, the properties of the neurons themselves do not constrain cognition much. Theories based on high-level models of computation provide no guidance for psychology, because it is so easy to design such machines to do whatever we can describe. If we ignore the issue of speed, this applies almost as well to people, too: disciplined humans can instruct themselves to do virtually anything, by combining symbolic thinking and long-term memory. In this regard we differ from all other animals.

Accordingly, in Section 3.3 Newell argues that we'll need different kinds of psychological theories for dealing with the scales of time that he calls biological, cognitive, rational, and social. For Soar he reserves the "cognitive band" of activities that take place over intervals between 0.1 and 10 seconds. The slow and deliberate "rational band", which works on time scales of minutes and hours, will be built over that—whereas Soar itself will be built upon the biological band of events shorter than 0.01 seconds in duration. One could hardly object to any of this—except to note that some low-level events may have longer durations. For example, such attachment events as bonding, infatuation, and mourning take place on scales of weeks and months. Is this because our social relationships are involved with certain synapses that are peculiarly slow to forget? Or is it merely because it takes a long time to rearrange certain large and complex mental structures?

3. The speed of thought

All the things that Soar can do are accomplished by selecting and executing productions—that is, IF–THEN rules—one at a time. The body of Chapter 5 shows that if cognitive activities are indeed production-based, then those productions cannot execute in less than the order of 20-odd milliseconds. Newell's accumulation of evidence for this is as strong as anything of that sort I've ever seen in psychology. He then applies these time-constraints quite forcefully. Whatever we do in that "cognitive band"—that is, any psychological function that can be accomplished in one second or so—Soar must accomplish by executing no more than a few dozen productions. No theory would be acceptable that demands thousands of such steps per second.

This neatly prevents Soar from exploiting its computation potentiality to simulate other theories. Newell's ferocious time-constraint precludes any such trick: Soar cannot appear to succeed because of any "Turing leak". It cannot admit even a single level of "interpreting" of one language in terms of another because, in practice, such simulations expand time scales by factors of hundreds. Then, despite this constraint, almost half of the volume of *UTC* describes ways in which Soar is able to do (and learn to do) significant tasks. This is truly a remarkable claim, for in many of those one-second instances, the human subjects routinely make not merely a recognition, but also a knowledge-based inference and an action decision. It is surely a significant accomplishment to have shown that so many significant things can be done in so few steps.

On second thought, we must ask *which* things. Yes, Soar can indeed do surprising things with just one production at a time. But do there remain important things that Soar can*not* so do? I faced the same question twenty years ago when I first read *Human Problem Solving* [6]. Some simulations worked very well for minutes at a time—until the system would suddenly fail as the human problem solver switched to a different strategy or "changed the subject". Some of those "episodes" could be explained in terms of switching to another pre-established problem space. But other times it seemed to me that the subject must have switched over to a new representation of the problem that was *already adapted* to the situation. To do this so quickly, it seemed to me that the system would need to have been updating that other representation all along—and that would require more productions. Thus, Soar's simulation (Fig. 7-5) of cryptarithmetic gave me a sense of *déjà vu*. Although the system was able to simulate the interiors of each episode, again there was the question of whether Soar could be made to handle more of those impasse-escaping jumps, still using only one production at a time? Surely so, when it is merely a matter of switching to another pre-constructed problem space. But if the new scheme needs extensive updating, then that would need too many productions—and Soar would require more concurrent processes. Humans often change their viewpoints in less than a single second of time—for example, at the punch-line of a joke in which a complex description that first seemed strange (or commonplace) suddenly becomes more meaningful (or the opposite), when one trait of a person is replaced by another, or when a physical interpretation is abruptly replaced by a sexual one. Were both of them running in parallel?

For another perspective, contrast the sorts of problems discussed in *UTC* with the more prosaic kinds of contexts considered in *The Society of Mind* [2, 1.3]. Imagine yourself sipping a drink at a party while moving about and talking with friends. How many streams of processing are involved in shaping your hand to keep the cup level, while choosing where to place your feet? How many processes help choose the words that say what you mean while arranging those words into suitable strings? What keeps track of what you've said to whom; what takes into account what you know of your friends so as not to hurt their feelings? What about those other thoughts that clearly go on in parallel, as one part of your mind keeps humming a tune while another sub-mind plans a path that escapes from this person and approaches that one. Perhaps Soar could be trained to do any of those, but to do them all concurrently would seem to require an order of magnitude more productions per second. If this is correct, then either (1) we could raise the level of Soar up into that rational band, or (2) we might consider using several Soars at once, or (3) we could try to maintain the basic idea while replacing the single-production idea by some more active type of memory. It seems to me that the very rigor of Newell's analysis comes close to showing that a single Soar cannot by itself account for enough of what goes on in each second of human thinking-time.

If a mind consisted of several Soars, what could bind them together? A programmer might instantly say, "Let's put yet one more Soar in charge". A Freudian might counter with, "you must install some set of long-range values into an almost-read-only memory, to serve as a superego to keep the system from drifting away. You must also supply some Censors, too, for the child to learn what *not* to do." A Piagetian might insist that you'll need some more machinery to sequence certain stages of development, to ensure that certain things be learned. A disciple of Warren McCulloch might say that no single processor could suffice: you'll need "redundancy of potential command" to keep the thing from going mad.

4. A framework for representing knowledge?

AI researchers have found many problems that seemed intractable when described in one way but became easy in another representation. Some domains seem well suited to logical expressions, others work well with production systems, yet others prosper when frames are employed—or scripts, semantic nets, fuzzy logic, or neural nets. Perhaps the most radical aspect of Soar is that it employs only a single, universally accessible workspace that supports nothing but the pairs of sets of symbol strings that constitute productions. An obvious alternative would be to use a variety of different, more specialized representations. Newell opposes this idea because, as he says in Section 2.3, using several representations in concert, each along with its own operational procedures, might lead to a combinatorial explosion. In my view, that concern is misplaced. It would indeed apply to an *arbitrary* collection of representation schemes—but might not if we searched for centuries to find some much more compatible set! Now consider that for millions of years our ancestors were doing precisely that! Among the known results of this are those hardware schemes found in the sensory and motor areas that constitute much of our brains. Newell explicitly places these beyond the scope of present-day Soar, because he considers them more likely to be less uniform. But why would evolution have changed its ways, only within the cognitive realm? Ironically, Newell's ideas about processing speed led me in the other direction. For example, human thought seems so proficient at making "chains of reasoning" that one would expect to find that our brains contain special structures for doing this—perhaps in the form of script-like representation schemes. Then because we're very quick at hierarchical reasoning, perhaps we should look for hardware trees. Language-like kinds of reasoning might best be supported by hardware designed to deal with case-frames or semantic nets.

Shortly I'll discuss the processes that I suspect are most vital of all— the ones that deal with *differences*. To manipulate these as fast as we do, we might need hardware for pairs of frames. Much of Newell's previous work emphasized the importance of finding good representations. The position of *UTC* seems to be that we need not provide for these in advance. This faces us with two alternatives. One way would be to simulate such structures at least one level above the productions—thus challenging real-time Soar's potential speed. The other way is to remain at the base level, and "non-simulate" the required functions by building huge look-up tables. But while this could be done at a constant speed, it exposes us to another risk—of exponential growth of memory size and of learning time. Such systems might appear to work on small-sample problems, but then rapidly fail when we try to export them to reality. I myself am more inclined to look for good representations at some lower level of neurology. But going that way would not escape the question of how the mind could so quickly switch between different representation schemes. My conjecture is that this must be the end result of *forcing the different representations to learn to work together from the stages of development.* We must cross-link them by making them "grow up" together.

5. Society of Mind theories

Perhaps the most novel aspect of Soar is the idea of dealing with impasses—and this is why I've dwelt so much on multiple representations. This is based on my belief that *metaphors may constitute our most powerful ways to escape from cognitive impasses—and a multiplicity of representations could systematically support our most pervasive metaphors.* With metaphor, when one type of representation fails, you can quickly switch to another one without the need to start over. It seems to me that, in this regard, *UTC* has tried to avoid a crucial aspect of psychology: how peculiarly good we humans are at exploiting the uses of metaphor in the temporal, spatial, and social realms. Theory: to move among these so fluently, our systems must have learned to assign the same symbols to analogous links of representations in different realms. I see no basic reason why we could not make Soar do such things—but could it do this at lifelike speeds, in ways that infants are likely to learn?

A major goal in designing what Seymour Papert and I called the "Society of Mind" (SOM) theory was to facilitate thinking by analogy. Evidently Newell never read *The Society of Mind* [2] in detail; its only citation in *UTC* is this single remark: "The society-of-mind metaphor is built around relatively small communication channels, but inside each mind it is not that way at all." This seems intended to contrast *SOM*'s assumption that the interiors of agencies are generally opaque to one another against Soar's assumption that all memories share the same uniform space. But that distinction might end up with little effect because Soar productions of different sorts will tend to become insulated from one another. In another respect the two theories might seem strongly opposed in regard to the idea of "unified"; Soar has very few basic mechanisms and a single representation, whereas SOM assumes quite a few different kinds of representations and machinery for employing them. Still, the two theories also have so many common aspects that I think they could serve as alternative ways to interpret the same psychological data. In Soar, everything is learned by forming new "chunks" (which are simply new productions) whereas in SOM almost everything that is learned is ultimately composed of K-lines [1;2, 8.2]. (K-lines are agents that, when activated, arouse sets of other agents, including other K-lines.) The two schemes are rather similar in that both chunks and K-lines serve as ways to reify the "net" effects of recent input-output activity; as such, they are also learned in much the same way. Newell emphasizes (p. 140) that chunk-memories have the property that, once activated, they can then interact to form "reconstructed memories". The same is true of K-lines as well; indeed, they reconstruct (albeit by interacting in parallel) not only declarative, but also procedural and dispositional memories. Both Soar's "objects" and my "polynemes" are little more than attribute–value sets, and most of the "frames" described in [2, 24.8] could be represented in Soar as sets of objects appearing as elements of productions. However, the more complex structures called "frame-arrays" incorporate more innate structure. Some of their terminals (i.e., attributes) are indexed by special activation lines called "pronomes" (which resemble the role-markers of case grammars) that enable the system to quickly switch between frames without recomputing their value-assignments. If the same kinds of role-symbols are applied more globally, they can be used to bridge between corresponding slots in the other representations used in grossly different realms of knowledge—and that would automatically yield some capabilities to reason by analogy. (This is different from the more general, higher-level idea of being able to construct correspondences between different things. Here it is a matter of evolving innate hardware preparations for a small and pre-selected group of "pervasive" metaphors, e.g., between events in time and space, or between spatial and social proximity.)

The discussion of impasse resolution in *UTC* seems somewhat vague:

> Soar responds to an impasse by creating a subgoal to resolve it.
> What resolves an impasse is knowledge that would lead Soar not
> to make that impasse at that decision point. There are many ways
> in which this might happen. (Section 4.1.5)

We're told that one way Soar can accomplish this is by inserting a new entry on a subgoal stack. In *SOM* as well, impasses are recognized and then engaged in various ways. One scheme that pervades the whole system is the idea I called Papert's Principle: throughout child development, knowledge becomes organized through the construction of new agents that serve as "middle level managers". (Some of these manager agents may correspond roughly to Newell's "problem spaces," but I'm not really sure about that.) The managers themselves are installed as consequences of impasse-resolving episodes. One typical function of a manager agent is to resolve conflicts by making other agents "resign". That is, whenever related agents disagree, if they have a common manager, its activation is weakened so that its competitors can "take over". Of course, this will be helpful only if some more competent agent is lying in wait. Another assumption I made in *SOM* is that a typical agency is equipped with provisions for dealing with the most common kinds of impasses. For example, each agent at a certain level could operate under the supervision of some impasse-detecting specialists at another level. (The text of *SOM* calls these the A-Brain and the B-Brain.) These "B-brain" specialists are particularly suited for detecting looping, meandering, and other forms of lack of progress. Of course, the extent to which such functions could be made innate depends on the extent to which they can be done in content-free ways. I presume that such "quasi-reflective" functions could be programmed into Soar, presumably in the form of recursive activations of the same system. But the critical question is, I think, *would enough such structures evolve by themselves if a Soar were raised as a human child?* Eventually, at higher knowledge levels, all normal humans eventually acquire some serial-conscious reflective-memory systems. We could ask of both SOM and Soar how likely such things are to come about without any pre-arranged help. In [2, 10.9 and 31.4] I assume that infants start out with a substantial endowment of pre-constructed machinery or the staging of infant development. This appears to be another domain unexplored by Soar.

6. Reformulation and natural language understanding

"Something seems to have gone wrong here. Just what was I trying to do?" In this typical rational mental scene, you notice that you've got stuck and try to re-describe the situation to yourself. Almost instantly, then, you hear yourself think things like this: *"Gosh that was stupid! The '5' in the third column has nothing at all to do with the 'M' in the first column. What could I have been thinking of?"* This sort of "reformulation" process could be our most powerful impasse-resolving technique—at least in Newell's rational band. But how might reformulation work? I'll argue that from the Society of Mind viewpoint, reformulation needs machinery that must be a lot like GPS. But my reasons may seem wrong from the viewpoint of Soar. This is because in Soar all knowledge is assumed to be uniformly accessible, so there is nothing to bar the central processor from accessing anything—including the current situation-description. However, in a SOM-type theory, higher-level processes will often have to build their own representations of other agencies' plans and goals, because they have such poor access to what happens inside other parts of the brain.

How could one closed agency examine a structure inside another? In [2, 22.10], I proposed a way of doing this, and called it the "re-duplication" method. This scheme is actually nothing more than a variant of Newell and Simon's GPS. Suppose you were given an opaque box that contains an unknown symbol-tree, and you want to find out what's inside? Assume that (1) you're allowed to use list-processing operations to build new things inside the box and (2) that you have a way to detect the "highest-level differences" between two things in the box. Then you can solve the problem in the following way: the goal is to make a *copy* (inside that box) of the unknown tree inside that box. Simply begin with an empty copy—that is, a blank representation. Then continue top-down recursively, to build up the copy by detecting and removing the differences between it and the original; at every step performing whichever operation promises to remove or reduce the last-noticed difference. You need never see the trees themselves because—if everything works—the stream of operations that you have performed is a serial description of that hidden tree.

If this mechanism is invoked when you're stuck in an impasse, the result may be to produce a different and perhaps more suitable representation of the situation or goal because the copying process will be affected by your current choice of GPS-type difference priorities—which in turn you'll adjust to represent your current goals and concerns. Elements that your current copier considers to be irrelevant to the current goal will be considered unworthy of notice and will automatically be stripped out of the copy. This editing could make that impasse disappear—or at least make the problem seem simpler, more abstract, or more easy to match to available knowledge.

How is this related to that "What was I trying to do?" Simply, I think, because language itself may use something like this. Suppose that Mary has a certain idea and wants to explain it to Jack. What might ensue, mechanically? Well, let's assume that somewhere in the Broca region of Mary's brain is a pointer to a certain knowledge representation. The latter might be a complex semantic network that includes pointers to other sorts of trans-frames and scripts, but let's assume for simplicity that Mary's "idea" is merely a tree. Then as that copy-duplication activity proceeds, the resulting stream of operations could be used by Mary's Broca region to produce a serial stream of verbal sounds. If Jack "understands" that language stream (and this is as good a way as any to explain what "understand" means), then the Wernicke region of Jack's brain will interpret that phonemic stream to construct a copy of Mary's tree somewhere in Jack's brain. To do such things, each typical agency should be equipped with at least a pair of high-speed, temporary K-line memories. Let's assume that typical agents (like typical neurons) can serve as temporal change-detecting agents. Then any agency could easily compare two descriptions simply by first activating one description, then the other, and responding to the differences. Cognition constantly involves comparisons. Accordingly I would expect to find pervasive systems in the brain for efficiently comparing things (including ideas) and then reacting to detected differences. The concept of "difference" itself seems notably absent in *UTC*. It does not even occur in the index. In contrast, I predict that the most useful of all the representations proposed in *SOM* will be the trans-frames introduced in [2, 21.3]. A trans-frame is a type of frame that includes a pair of "before–after" frames, along with additional slots to describe their differences and pointers to the operations or "trajectories" that one might use to change one into the other. Trans-frames (which are modeled on older ideas of Roger Schank) are almost perfectly suited, not only to represent knowledge in forms well suited for scripting, chaining, and reasoning, but also for generating verb-centered sentences. If I hadn't rejected that thought from the start, I could have presented SOM as a "unified theory of cognition" based on representing all knowledge in trans-frame form.

Speaking of language, should not a unified theory try to explain why every language has nouns and verbs? I don't know quite how to obtain these from Soar, but it's easy as pie to derive them from SOM, because among our most basic representations are "polynemes" for describing "things" and trans-frames for describing changes and actions. Our ancestors must have evolved those object-nouns at some very early stage, and the action-verbs then later evolved so that they could think one more step ahead. So in spite of some language theorists' view that language is a separate thing, I claim that our brains must first have evolved representations to serve as nouns and verbs. Without having something resembling these, Soar might find it hard to speak.

This leads us into another area. Any unified theory in biology must eventually address the question of how it could have evolved. For example, how could my re-duplication scheme evolve? Perhaps the original function of that machinery was less for social communication and more for communication between different domains of the brain! This, in turn, most likely evolved for an even more critical function: to enable good communication from a mental agency to itself! How could an animal use such a thing? So far as I can see, neuro-cognitive theorists seemed to have overlooked this important problem: *how to produce new copies of the functions embodied in neural nets.* This appears to be a deficiency, for example, in what I understand of Edelman's "Neural Darwinism", which proposes an Ashby-like way to learn by selection—but lacks any way to produce new versions for further development. To be sure, Soar would have no problem *doing* this, either directly or by simulating a recursive re-duplicator—but how long would it take for Soar to *learn* such a thing?

7. Conclusions

We certainly need better "large-scale" theories for psychology, and Soar is a powerful stimulus. But we must also take care not to overshoot. It is always important to discover that a system can do more than we thought it would do—but that should not be our only goal. In this regard, it seems to me, the AI community has turned away from an equally important opportunity. Today, if you wanted to build a machine that used several different representations, you'd find that we have virtually no good ideas about how to do this. I would hope that now, future work will be aimed toward finding ways to synthesize and manage systems that can exploit that diversity. From the moment I met him in 1956, Allen Newell was one of my heroes. At least five times his ideas transformed mine; I was never the same person after understanding LT, GPS, HPS, or MERLIN, and now Soar in the context of *UTC*. This latest work will surely stand as a basic advance in AI's theories of knowledge machines. Reading this monumental book recalled to me my sense of awe in seeing the power of GPS, first in its original form [4] and then in the version with learning [5]. I hope others who read it carefully will have the same experience.

References

[1] M. Minsky, K-lines: a theory of memory, *Cogn. Sci.* **4** (1980) 117–133.

[2] M. Minsky, *The Society of Mind* (Simon and Schuster, New York, 1986).

[3] A. Newell, J.C. Shaw and H.A. Simon, Empirical explorations of the logic theory machine, in: *Proceedings Western Joint Computer Conference* (1955) 218–230.

[4] A. Newell, J.C. Shaw and H.A. Simon, Report on a general problem-solving program, in: *Proceedings International Conference on Information Processing*, Paris, France (1959).

[5] A. Newell, J.C. Shaw and H.A. Simon, A variety of intelligent learning in a general problem solver, in: M.T. Yovitts and S. Cameron, eds., *Self-Organizing Systems* (Pergamon Press, New York, 1960).

[6] A. Newell and H.A. Simon, *Human Problem Solving* (Prentice-Hall, Englewood Cliffs, NJ, 1972).

[7] J.G. Sutcliffe, mRNA in the mammalian central nervous system, *Am. Rev. Neurosci.* **2** (1988) 157–198.

Artificial Intelligence 59 (1993) 355–369
Elsevier

ARTINT 1014

Book Review

On wings of knowledge: a review of Allen Newell's *Unified Theories of Cognition* *

Jordan B. Pollack

Laboratory for AI Research, The Ohio State University, 2036 Neil Avenue, Columbus, OH 43210, USA

Received January 1992
Revised July 1992

1. Introduction

Besides being a status report on the Soar project, *Unified Theories of Cognition* is Allen Newell's attempt at directing the field of cognitive science by example. Newell argues that his approach to "unification", which involves the programmed extension of a single piece of software-architecture-as-theory to as many psychological domains as possible, is the proper research methodology for cognitive science today:

> In this book I'm not proposing Soar as *the* unified theory of cognition. Soar is, of course, an interesting candidate. With a number of colleagues I am intent on pushing Soar as hard as I can to make it into a viable unified theory. But my concern here is that cognitive scientists consider working with *some* unified theory of cognition. Work with ACT*, with CAPS, with Soar, with CUTC, a connectionist unified theory of cognition. Just work with some UTC. (p. 430)

Correspondence to: J.B. Pollack, Laboratory for AI Research, The Ohio State University, 2036 Neil Avenue, Columbus, OH 43210, USA. E-mail: pollack@cis.ohio-state.edu
* (Harvard University Press, Cambridge, MA, 1990); 549 pages

Over the past decade, Newell and his colleagues at numerous universities (including my own) have applied Soar to a number of different domains, and have adopted a goal of making it toe the line on psychological results. This is a very ambitious goal, and Newell knows it:

> The next risk is to be found guilty of the sin of presumption. Who am I, Allen Newell, to propose a unified theory of cognition ... Psychology must wait for its Newton. (p. 37)

Newell is clearly entitled by a life of good scientific works to write a book at such a level and, in my opinion, it is the most substantial and impressive, by far, of recent offerings on the grand unified mind. My entitlement to review his book is less self-evident, however—who am I to stand in judgement over one of the founding fathers of the field? And so I fear I am about to commit the sin of presumption as well, and to compound it, moreover, with the sin of obliqueness: Because my argument is not with the quality of Newell's book, but with the direction he is advocating for cognitive science, I will not review his theory in detail. Rather, I will adopt a bird's eye view and engage only the methodological proposal. I will, however, belabor one small detail of Newell's theory, its name, and only to use as my symbolic launching pad.

2. Artificial intelligence and mechanical flight

The origin of the name Soar, according to high-level sources within the project, was originally an acronym for three primitive components of the problem-space method. But shortly, these components were forgotten, leaving the proper noun in their stead, a name which evokes "grand and glorious things", and also puts us in mind of the achievement of mechanical flight, AI's historical *doppelgänger.*

> Among those who had worked on the problem [of mechanical flight] I may mention [da Vinci, Cayley, Maxim, Parsons, Bell, Phillips, Lilienthal, Edison, Langley] and a great number of other men of ability. But the subject had been brought into disrepute by a number of men of lesser ability who had hoped to solve the problem through devices of their own invention, which had all of themselves failed, until finally the public was lead to believe that flying was as impossible as perpetual motion. In fact, scientists of the standing of Guy Lussac ... and Simon Newcomb ... had attempted to prove it would be impossible to build a flying machine that would carry a man. (Wright [25, p. 12][1]

---

[1] This book is a reissued collection of essays and photographs about the Wright's research and development process. It includes three essays by Orville Wright, and two interpretive essays by Fred C. Kelly. Subsequent citations are to this edition.

I will leave the substitution of contemporary scientists to the reader. Simply put, the analogy "Airplanes are to birds as smart machines will be to brains", is a widely repeated AI mantra with several uses. One is to entice consumers by reminding them of the revolution in warfare, transportation, commerce, etc. brought about by mechanical flight. Another is to encourage patience in those same consumers by pointing to the hundreds of years of experimental work conducted before the success of mechanical flight! A third is to chant it, eyes closed, ignoring the complex reality of biological mechanism.

Although it is quite likely that the analogy between AI and mechanical flight arose spontaneously in the community of AI pioneers, its earliest written appearance seems to be in a "cold war for AI" essay by Paul Armer, then of the Rand Corporation, in the classic collection *Computers and Thought*:

> While it is true that Man wasted a good deal of time and effort trying to build a flying machine that flapped its wings like a bird, the important point is that it was the understanding of the law of aerodynamic lift (even though the understanding was quite imperfect at first) over an airfoil which enabled Man to build flying machines. A bird isn't sustained in the air by the hand of God—natural laws govern its flight. Similarly, natural laws govern what [goes on inside the head]. Thus I see no reason why we won't be able to duplicate in hardware the very powerful processes of association which the human brain has, once we understand them. (Armer [1, p.398])

We all agree that once we understand how natural law governs what goes on in the head, we will be able to mechanize thought, and will then have the best scientific theory of cognition, which could be refined into the technology for "general intelligence". But our field has basically ignored natural law, and settled comfortably upon methodologies and models which involve only the perfect simulation of arbitrary "software" laws. I believe that we are failing to integrate several key principles which govern cognition and action in biological and physical systems, and that the incorporation of these should be the priority of cognitive science rather than of the writing of large programs.

3. Deconstructing the myths of mechanical flight

There are two myths in Armer's analogy which are important to correct. The first is that flight is based mainly upon the principle of the airfoil. The second is that the mechanical means by which nature solved the problem are irrelevant. Translating through the analogy, these two myths are equivalent to believing that cognition is based mainly upon the principle of universal computation, and that the mechanical means by which nature solved the problem are irrelevant.

Although my favorite sections of Newell's book are those in which he emphasizes the importance of constraints from biology and physics, he conducts his research in a way which is consistent with the myths. Indeed the myths are principally supported by his arguments, both the Physical Symbol System Hypothesis [17], which is the assertion that Universal Computation is enough, and the Knowledge Level Hypothesis [16], which legitimizes theories involving only software laws, even though their very existence is based only upon introspection.

In order to see why these myths are a stumbling block to the achievement of mechanical cognition, I will examine several aspects of the solution to mechanical flight, using the reports by Orville Wright.

3.1. The airfoil principle

The principle of aerodynamic lift over an airfoil was around for hundreds of years before the advent of mechanical flight. The Wright brothers just tuned the shape to optimize lift:

> The pressures on squares are different from those on rectangles, circles, triangles or ellipses; arched surfaces differ from planes, and vary among themselves according to the depth of curvature; true arcs differ from parabolas, and the latter differ among themselves; thick surfaces from thin ... the shape of an edge also makes a difference, so thousands of combinations are possible in so simple a thing as a wing .... Two testing machines were built [and] we began systematic measurements of standard surfaces, so varied in design as to bring out the underlying causes of differences noted in their pressures (Wright [25, p. 84])

Assume that the principle of Universal Computation is to AI what the principle of aerodynamic lift is to mechanical flight. In Chapter 2 of this book, Newell reiterates, in some detail, the standard argument for the status quo view of cognition as symbolic computation:

- Mind is flexible, gaining power from the formation of "indefinitely rich representations" and an ability to compose transformations of these representations. (pp. 59–63).
- Therefore mind must be a universal symbol processing machine (pp. 70–71).
- It is believed that most universal machines are equivalent (p. 72).

If one holds that the flexibility of the mind places it in the same class as the other universal machines (subject to physical limits, of course), then the mathematics tells us we can use any universal computational model for describing mind or its subparts (and the biological path is irrelevant). So, for example, any of the four major theories of computation developed (and unified) this century—Church's lambda calculus, Post's production system, Von Neumann's stored program machine, and universal automata (e.g. Turing's Machine)—could be used as a basis for a theory of mind. Of course, these theories were too raw and difficult to program, but have evolved through human ingenuity into their modern equivalents, each of which is a "Universal Programming Language" (UPL): LISP, OPS5, C, and ATN's, respectively.

If we plan to express our UTCs in UPLs, however, we must have a way to distinguish between these UPLs in order to put some constraints on our UTCs, so that they aren't so general as to be vacuous. There are at least five general strategies to add constraints to a universal system: architecture, tradition, extra-disciplinary goals, parsimony, and ergonomics.

The first way to constrain a UPL is to build something, anything, on top of it, which constrains either what it can compute, how well it can compute it, or how it behaves while computing it. This is called architecture, and Newell spends pages 82–88 discussing architecture in some detail. In a universal system, one can build architecture on top of architecture and shift attention away from the basic components of the system to arbitrary levels of abstraction.

The second method of constraining a universal theory is by sticking to "tradition", the practices whose success elevates them to beliefs handed down orally though the generations of researchers. Even though any other programming language would serve, the tradition in American AI is to build systems from scratch, using LISP, or to build knowledge into production systems. Newell is happy to represent the "symbolic cognitive psychology" tradition (p. 24) against the paradigmatic revolutions like Gibsonianism [10] or PDPism [21].

A third way we can distinguish between competing universals is to appeal to scientific goals outside of building a working program. We can stipulate, for example, that the "most natural" way to model a phenomenon in the UPL must support extra-disciplinary goals. Algorithmic efficiency, a goal of mainstream computer science, can be used to discriminate between competing models for particular tasks. Robust data from psychological experiments can be used to discriminate among universal theories on the basis of matching an implemented system's natural behavior with the observed data from humans performing the task. Finally, as a subset of neural network researchers often argue, the model supporting the theory must be "biologically correct". Newell, of course, relies very heavily on the psychological goals to justify his particular UPL.

Fourth, parsimony can be called into play. Two theories can be compared as to the number of elements, parameters, and assumptions needed to explain certain phenomena, and the shorter one wins. Newell makes a good point that the more phenomena one wishes to explain, the more benefit is gained from a unified theory, which ends up being shorter than the sum of many independent theories. This is called "amortization of theoretical constructs" (p. 22) and is one of Newell's main arguments for why psychologists ought to adopt his unified theory paradigm for research. However, such a unification can be politically difficult to pull off when different subdisciplines of a field are already organized by the parsimony of their own subtheories.

Fifth, we might be able to choose between alternatives on the basis of ergonomics. We can ask the question of programmability. How easy is it to extend a theory by programming? How much work is it for humans to understand what a system is doing? The Turing Machine model "lost" to the stored program machine due to the difficulty of programming in quintuples. Systems which use explicit rules rather than implicit knowledge-as-code are certainly easier to understand and debug, but may yield no more explanatory power.

However, unless the constraints specifically strip away the universality, such that the cognitive theory becomes *an application of* rather than *an extension to* the programming language, the problem of theoretical under-constraint remains. Following Newell's basic argument, one could embark on a project of extensively crafting a set of cognitive models in any programming language, say C++, matching psychological regularities, and reusing subroutines as much as possible, and the resultant theory would be as predictive as Soar:

> Soar does not automatically provide an explanation for anything just because it is a universal computational engine. There are two aspects to this assertion. First from the perspective of cognitive theory, Soar has to be universal, because humans themselves are universal. To put this the right way around—Soar is a universal computational architecture; therefore it predicts that the human cognitive architecture is likewise universal. (p. 248)

Thus, just as the Wright brothers discovered different lift behaviors in differently shaped airfoils, cognitive modelers will find different behavioral effects from different universal language architectures. The principle of the airfoil was around for hundreds of years, and yet the key to mechanical flight did not lie in optimizing lift. Using a UPL which optimizes "cognitive lift" is not enough either, as practical issues of scale and control will still assert themselves.

3.2. Scaling laws

> Our first interest [in the problem of flight] began when we were children. Father brought home to us a small toy actuated by a rubber [band] which would lift itself into the air. We built a number of copies of this toy, which flew successfully, but when we undertook to build a toy on a much larger scale it failed to work so well. (Wright [25, p. 11])

The youthful engineers did not know that doubling the size of a model would require eight times as much power. This is the common feeling of every novice computer programmer hitting a polynomial or exponential scaling problem with an algorithm. But there were many other scaling problems which were uncovered during the Wrights' mature R&D effort, beyond mere engine size:

> We discovered in 1901 that tables of air pressures prepared by our predecessors were not accurate or dependable. (Wright [25, p. 55])

> We saw that the calculations upon which all flying-machines had been based were unreliable, and that all were simply groping in the dark. Having set out with absolute faith in the existing scientific data, we were driven to doubt one thing after another .... Truth and error were everywhere so intimately mixed as to be indistinguishable. (Wright [25, p. 84])

Thus it is not unheard of for estimates of scaling before the fact to be way off, especially the first time through based upon incomplete scientific understanding of the important variables. Estimates of memory size [12,13] for example, or the performance capacity of a brain [15,24] may be way off, depending on whether memory is "stored" in neurons, synapses, or in modes of behaviors of those units. So the number of psychological regularities we need to account for in a UTC may be off:

> Thus we arrive at about a third of a hundred regularities about [typing] alone. Any candidate architecture must deal with most of these if it's going to explain typing .... Of course there is no reason to focus on typing. It is just one of a hundred specialized areas of cognitive behavior. It takes only a hundred areas at thirty regularities per area to reach the ~~3000 total regularities cited at the beginning of this chapter .... Any architecture, especially a candidate for a unified theory of cognition, must deal with them all—hence with thousands of regularities. (p. 243)

There is a serious question about whether thousands of regularities are enough, and Newell recognizes this:

> In my view its it time to get going on producing unified theories of cognition—before the data base doubles again and the number of visible clashes increases by the square or cube. (p. 25)

While Newell estimates 3000 regularities, my estimate is that the number of regularities is unbounded. The "psychological data" industry is a generative system, linked to the fecundity of human culture, which Newell also writes about lucidly:

> What would impress [The Martian Biologist] most is the efflorescence of adaptation. Humans appear to go around simply creating opportunities of all kinds to build different response functions. Look at the variety of jobs in the world. Each one has humans using different kinds of response functions. Humans invent games. They no sooner invent one game than they invent new ones. They not only invent card games, but they collect them in a book and publish them .... Humans do not only eat, as do all other animals, they prepare their food ... inventing [hundreds and thousands of] recipes. (p. 114)

Every time human industry pops forth with a new tool or artifact, like written language, the bicycle, the typewriter, Rubik's cube, or rollerblades, another 30 regularities will pop out, especially if there is a cost justification to do the psychological studies, as clearly was the case for typing and for reading. This is not a good situation, especially if programmers have to be involved for each new domain. There will be a never-ending software battle just to keep up:

> Mostly, then, the theorist will load into Soar a program (a collection of productions organized into problem spaces) of his or her own devising...The obligation is on the theorist to cope with the flexibility of human behavior in responsible ways. (Newell, p. 249)

If the road to unified cognition is through very large software efforts, such as Soar, then we need to focus on scalable control laws for software.

3.3. Control in high winds

Although we might initially focus on the scaling of static elements like wing span and engine power, *to duplicate the success of mechanical flight, we should focus more on the scaling of control.* For the principal contribution of the Wright brothers was not the propulsive engine, which had its own economic logic (like the computer), nor the airfoil, a universal device they merely tuned through experiments, but their insight about how to control a glider when scaled up enough to carry an operator:

> Lilienthal had been killed through his inability to properly balance his machine in the air. Pilcher, an English experimenter had met with a like fate. We found that both experimenters had attempted to maintain balance merely by the shifting of the weight of their bodies. Chanute and all the experimenters before 1900, used this same method of maintaining the equilibrium in gliding flight. We at once set to work to devise a more efficient means of maintaining the equilibrium .... It was apparent that the [left and right] wings of a machine of the Chanute double-deck type, with the fore-and-aft trussing removed, could be warped ... in flying ... so as to present their surfaces to the air at different angles of incidences and thus secure unequal lifts .... (Wright [25, p. 12])

What they devised, and were granted a monopoly on, was the *Aileron principle*, the general method of maintaining dynamical equilibrium in a glider by modifying the shapes of the individual wings, using cables, to provide different amounts of lift to each side. (It is not surprising that the Wright brothers were bicycle engineers, as this control principle is the same one used to control two wheeled vehicles—iterated over-correction towards the center.)

Translating back through our analogy, extending a generally intelligent system for a new application by human intervention in the form of programming is "seat of the pants" control, the same method that Lilienthal applied to maintaining equilibrium by shifting the weight of his body.

Just as the source of difficulty for mechanical flight was that scaling the airfoil large enough to carry a human overwhelmed that human's ability to maintain stability, the source of difficulty in the software engineering approach to unified cognition is that scaling software large enough to explain cognition overwhelms the programming teams' ability to maintain stability.

It is well known that there are limiting factors to software engineering [5], and these limits could be orders of magnitude below the number of "lines of code" necessary to account for thousands of psychological regularities or to achieve a "general intelligence". Since software engineers haven't figured out how to build and maintain programs bigger than 10–100 million lines of code, why should people in AI presume that it can be done as a matter of course? [7].

What is missing is some control principle for maintaining dynamical coherence of an ever-growing piece of software in the face of powerful winds of change. While I don't pretend to have the key to resolving the software engineering crisis, I believe its solution may rest with building systems from the bottom up using robust and stable cooperatives of goal-driven modules locked into long-term prisoner's dilemmas [2], instead of through the centralized planning of top-down design. The order of acquisition of stable behaviors can be very important to the solution of hard problems.

3.4. On the irrelevancy of flapping

> Learning the secret of flight from a bird was a good deal like learning the secret of magic from a magician. After you know the trick and know what to look for, you see things that you did not notice when you did not know exactly what to look for. (Wright (attributed) [25, p. 5])

When you look at a bird flying, the first thing you see is all the flapping. Does the flapping explain how the bird flies? Is it reasonable to theorize that flapping came first, as some sort of cooling system which was recruited when flying became a necessity for survival? Not really, for a simpler explanation is that most of the problem of flying is in finding a place within the weight/size dimension where gliding is possible, and getting the control system for dynamical equilibrium right. Flapping is the last piece, the propulsive engine, but in all its furiousness, it blocks our perception that the bird first evolved the aileron principle. When the Wrights figured it out, they saw it quite clearly in a hovering bird.

Similarly, when you look at cognition, the first thing you see is the culture and the institutions of society, human language, problem solving, and political skills. Just like flapping, symbolic thought is the last piece, the engine of social selection, but in all its furiousness it obscures our perception of cognition as an exquisite control system competing for survival while governing a very complicated real-time physical system.

Once you get a flapping object, it becomes nearly impossible to hold it still enough to retrofit the control system for equilibrium. Studying problem solving and decision making first because they happen to be the first thing on the list (p. 16) is dangerous, because perception and motor control may be nearly impossible to retrofit into the design.

This retrofit question permits a dissection of the "biological correctness" issue which has confounded the relationship between AI and connectionism. The naive form, which applied to work in computational neuroscience but not to AI, is "ontogenetic correctness", the goal of constructing one's model with as much neural realism as possible. The much deeper form, which could be a principle someday, is "phylogenetic correctness", building a model which could have evolved bottom up, without large amounts of arbitrary top-down design. Phylogenetically correct systems acquire their behaviors in a bottom-up order that could, theoretically, recapitulate evolution or be "reconverged" upon by artificial evolution. Thus, while the airplane does not flap or have feathers, the Wrights' success certainly involved "recapitulation" of the phylogenetic order of the biological invention of flight: the airfoil, dynamical balance, and then propulsion.

4. Physical law versus software law

By restricting ourselves to software theories only, cognitive scientists might be expending energy on mental ornithopters. We spin software and logic webs endlessly, forgetting every day that there is no essential difference between Fortran programs and LISP programs, between sequential programs and production systems, or ultimately, between logics and grammars. All such theories rely on "software law" rather than the natural law of how mechanisms behave in the universe.

Software laws, such as rules of predicate logic, may or may not have existed before humans dreamed them up. And they may or may not have been "implemented" by minds or by evolution. What is clear is that such laws can be created *ad infinitum*, and then simulated and tested on our physical symbol systems: The computer simulation is the sole guaranteed realm of their existence.

An alternative form of unification research would be to *unify cognition with nature*. In other words, to be able to use the same kind of natural laws to explain the complexity of form and behavior in cognition, the complexity of form and behavior in biology, and the complexity of form and behavior in inanimate mechanisms.

I realize this is not currently a widely shared goal, but by applying Occam's razor to "behaving systems" on all time scales (p. 152) why not use the ordinary equations of physical systems to describe and explain the complexity and control of all behavior? In an illuminating passage, Newell discusses control theory:

> To speak of the mind as a controller suggests immediately the language of control systems—of feedback, gain, oscillation, damping, and so on. It is a language that allows us to describe systems as purposive. But we are interested in the full range of human behavior, not only walking down a road or tracking a flying bird, but reading bird books, planning the walk, taking instruction to get to the place, identifying distinct species, counting the new

additions to the life list of birds seen, and holding conversations about it all afterward. When the scope of behavior extends this broadly, it becomes evident that the language of control systems is really locked to a specific environment and class of tasks—to continuous motor movement with the aim of pointing or following. For the rest it becomes metaphorical. (p. 45)

I think Newell has it backwards. It is the language of symbol manipulation which is locked to a specific environment of human language and deliberative problem solving. Knowledge level explanations only metaphorically apply to complex control systems such as insect and animal behavior [4,6], systems of the body such as the immune or circulatory systems, the genetic control of fetal development, the evolutionary control of populations of species, cooperative control in social systems, or even the autopoetic control system for maintaining the planet. Certainly these systems are large and complex and have some means of self-control while allowing extreme creativity of behavior, but the other sciences do not consider them as instances of universal computing systems running software laws, divorced from the physical reality of their existence!

We have been led up the garden path of theories expressed in rules and representations because simple mathematical models, using ordinary differential equations, neural networks, feedback control systems, stochastic processes, etc. have for the most part been unable to describe or explain the generativity of structured behavior with unbounded dependencies, especially with respect to language [8]. This gulf between what is needed for the explanation of animal and human cognitive behavior and what is offered by ordinary scientific theories is really quite an anomaly and indicates that our understanding of the principles governing what goes on in the head have been very incomplete.

But where might governing principles for cognition come from besides computation? The alternative approach I have been following over the past several years has emerged from a simple goal to develop neural network computational theories which gracefully admit the generative and representational competance of symbolic models. This approach has resulted in two models [18,19] with novel and interesting behaviors. In each of these cases, when pressed to the point of providing the same theoretical capacity as a formal symbol system, I was forced to interpret these connectionist networks from a new point of view, involving fractals and chaos—a dynamical view of cognition, more extreme than that proposed by Smolensky [23]. I have thus been lead to a very different theoretical basis for understanding cognition, which I will call the "Dynamical Cognition Hypothesis", that:

> The recursive representational and generative capacities required for cognition arise directly out of the complex behavior of non-linear dynamical systems.

In other words, neural networks are merely the biological implementation level for a computation theory not based upon symbol manipulation, but upon complex and fluid patterns of physical state. A survey of cognitive models based upon nonlinear dynamics is beyond this review [20], however, I can briefly point to certain results which will play an important role in this alternative unification effort.

Research in nonlinear systems theory over the past few decades has developed an alternative explanation for the growth and control of complexity [11]. Hidden within the concept of deterministic "chaotic" systems which are extremely sensitive to small changes in parameters is the surprise that precise tuning of these parameters can lead to the generation of structures of enormous apparent complexity, such as the famous Mandelbrot set [14].

There is a clear link between simple fractals, like Cantor dust, and rewriting systems ("remove the middle third of each line segment"), and Barnsley has shown how such recursive structures can be found in the limit behavior of very simple dynamical systems [3]. The very notion of a system having a "fractional dimension" is in fact the recognition that its apparent complexity is governed by a "power law" [22].

The equations of motion of nonlinear systems are not different in kind from those of simpler physical systems, but the evoked behavior can be very complicated, to the point of appearing completely random. Even so, there are "universal" laws which govern these systems at all scales, involving where and when phase transitions occur and how systems change from simple to complex modes, passing through "critical" states, which admit long-distance dependencies between components.

The logistic map $x_{t+1} = kx_t(1 - x_t)$ is a well-studied example of a simple function iterated over the unit line where changes in k (between 0 and 4) lead to wildly different behaviors, including convergence, oscillation, and chaos. In a fundamental result, Crutchfield and Young have exhaustively analyzed sequences of most significant bits generated by this map[2] and have shown that at critical values of k, such as 3.5699, these bit sequences have unbounded dependencies, and are not describable by a regular grammar, but by an indexed context-free grammar [9].

Without knowing where complex behavior comes from, in the logistic map, in critically tuned collections of neural oscillators, or in the Mandelbrot set, one could certainly postulate a very large rule-based software system,

---

[2]They analyzed the bit string $y_t = floor(0.5 + x_t)$.

operating omnipotently behind the scenes, like a deity whose hand governs the fate of every particle in the universe.

5. Conclusion

I want to conclude this review with a reminder to the reader to keep in mind the "altitude" of my criticism, which is about the research methodology Newell is proposing based upon the status quo of myths in AI, and not about the detailed contents of the book. These are mature and illuminated writings, and Newell does an excellent job of setting his work and goals into perspective and recognizing the limitations of his theory, especially with respect to the puzzles of development and language.

Despite my disagreement with Newell's direction, I was educated and challenged by the book, and endorse it as an elevator for the mind of all students of cognition. But still, I would warn the aspiring cognitive scientist not to climb aboard any massive software engineering efforts, expecting to fly:

> You take your seat at the center of the machine beside the operator. He slips the cable, and you shoot forward .... The operator moves the front rudder and the machine lifts from the rail like a kite supported by the pressure of the air underneath it. The ground is first a blur, but as you rise the objects become clearer. At a height of 100 feet you feel hardly any motion at all, except for the wind which strikes your face. If you did not take the precaution to fasten your hat before starting, you have probably lost it by this time .... (Wright, [25, p. 86])

References

[1] P. Armer, Attitudes towards artificial intelligence, in: E.A. Feigenbaum and J.A. Feldman, eds., *Computers and Thought* (McGraw Hill, New York, 1963) 389–405.

[2] R. Axelrod, *The Evolution of Cooperation* (Basic Books, New York, 1984).

[3] M.F. Barnsley, *Fractals Everywhere* (Academic Press, San Diego, CA, 1988).

[4] R. Beer, *Intelligence as Adaptive Behavior: An Experiment in Computational Neuroethology* (Academic Press, New York, 1990).

[5] F.P. Brooks, *The Mythical Man-Month* (Addison-Wesley, Reading, MA, 1975).

[6] R. Brooks, Intelligence without representation, *Artif. Intell.* **47** (1–3) (1991) 139–160.

[7] C. Cherniak, Undebuggability and cognitive science, *Commun. ACM* **31** (4) (1988) 402–412.

[8] N. Chomsky, *Syntactic Structures* (Mouton, The Hague, Netherlands, 1957).

[9] J.P. Crutchfield and K. Young, Computation at the onset of chaos, in: W. Zurek, ed., *Complexity, Entropy and the Physics of Information* (Addison-Wesley, Reading, MA, 1989).

[10] J.J. Gibson, *The Ecological Approach to Visual Perception* (Houghton-Mifflin, Boston, MA).

[11] J. Gleick, *Chaos: Making a New Science* (Viking, New York, 1987).

[12] W.D. Hillis, Intelligence as emergent behavior; or, the songs of eden, *Daedelus* **117** (1988) 175–190.

[13] T.K. Landauer, How much do people remember? Some estimates on the quantity of learned information in long-term memory, *Cogn. Sci.* **10** (1986) 477–494.

[14] B. Mandelbrot, *The Fractal Geometry of Nature* (Freeman, San Francisco, CA, 1982).

[15] H. Moravec, *Mind Children* (Harvard University Press, Cambridge, MA, 1988).

[16] A. Newell, The knowledge level, *Artif. Intell.* **18** (1982) 87–127.

[17] A. Newell and H.A. Simon, Computer science as empirical inquiry: symbols and search, *Comm. ACM* **19** (3) (1976) 113–126.

[18] J.B. Pollack, Recursive distributed representation, *Artif. Intell.* **46** (1990) 77–105.

[19] J.B. Pollack, The induction of dynamical recognizers, *Mach. Learn.* **7** (1991) 227–252.

[20] R. Port and T. Van Gelder, Mind as motion (in preparation).

[21] D.E. Rumelhart, J.L. McClelland and the PDP Research Group, eds., *Parallel Distributed Processing: Experiments in the Microstructure of Cognition* (MIT Press, Cambridge, MA, 1986).

[22] M. Schroeder, *Fractals, Chaos, Power Laws* (Freeman, New York, 1991).

[23] P. Smolensky, Information processing in dynamical systems: foundations of harmony theory, in: D.E. Rumelhart, J.L. McClelland and the PDP Research Group, eds., *Parallel Distributed Processing: Experiments in the Microstructure of Cognition*, Vol. 1 (MIT Press, Cambridge, MA, 1986) 194–281.

[24] J. Von Neumann, *The Computer and the Brain* (Yale University Press, New Haven, CT, 1958).

[25] O. Wright, *How we Invented the Airplane* (Dover, New York, 1988).

Artificial Intelligence 59 (1993) 371–373
Elsevier

ARTINT 1015

Book Review

Brain or mind?
A review of Allen Newell's
Unified Theories of Cognition *

Dale Purves

*Department of Neurobiology, Duke University Medical Center, Box 3209, Durham,
NC 27710, USA*

Received August 1991
Revised September 1992

Cognitive sciences, as defined by its practitioners, seeks to understand a variety of "higher" brain functions, examples of which are thinking, memory, perception, and language. The purpose of Newell's book, based on the William James Lectures he delivered at Harvard in 1987, is to bring together the various aspects of this complex field under the intellectual scepter of a single theory. Not surprisingly, Newell finds the unifying catalyst to be his own Soar program developed over the last three decades. Soar is a computer architecture for artificial intelligence that has been the object of considerable interest (and some controversy) among those interested in AI (see Waldrop [2,3]). Newell argues that the entire spectrum of cognitive functions is subsumed in—and can be explained by—this architecture.

Whatever the value of Newell's program to those interested in artificial intelligence, neurobiologists—that is, reductionists who take it as axiomatic that cognition must be understood in terms of the brain and its component parts—will find this book wanting. The tenor of the discourse is foreshadowed on page 17 of the Introduction where Newell states that his aim is to understand cognition in the context of *mind*, rather than *brain*. Indeed,

---

Correspondence to: D. Purves, Department of Neurobiology, Duke University Medical Center, Box 3209, Durham, NC 27710, USA. Telephone: (919) 684-6122.
   * (Harvard University Press, Cambridge, MA, 1990); xiv + 549 pages.

there is no entry in the index of this nearly-five-hundred page book of the word "brain", a surprising omission in a decade dedicated to this singular organ. Newell does pay some attention to the neurobiology of cognition, but this is scant; only a few pages in the middle of the book are devoted to nerve cells, neural circuits, and their role in cognition. The biological part of Newell's argument rests on two facts: that the generation of an action potential takes about a millisecond, and that the conduction of impulses along nerve fibers is quite slow (p. 124). According to Newell, the time consumed by the generation of an action potential, plus the conduction time within local circuits (more milliseconds), allow only about a hundred steps in a minimal cognitive event (which empirically requires about a second). This temporal restriction is considered of basic importance in Soar's design and its relevance to human cognition. "There is no way to put a collection of neurons together", says Newell, "and get them to operate in the $\sim\sim 1$ msec range" (p. 127). For Newell, the "neuron is a statistical engine in which nothing occurs with precise timing" (p. 128).

Although Newell's reasoning is logical enough, the brain has developed strategies that allow it to calculate faster and more precisely than he imagines. A good example is found in the auditory system. Many animals, including man, accurately localize sound in space. This feat is based on the ability of the brain to detect differences in the time of arrival and intensity of a sound at the two ears. Given the velocity of sound (340 m/sec) and the width of the head (about 25 cm), the differences that can be resolved are on the order of tens of microseconds. How the brain can make such precise temporal analyses was suggested in principle, ironically enough, by a cognitive psychologist about forty years ago (Jeffress [1]). Recent studies in cats, owls, and chickens have provided good evidence that Jeffress' hypothesis of how neurons compute tiny differences in binaural sounds with high precision is correct. Evidently, the brain can encode cognitive information with a temporal efficiency that transcends the limitations of its elements. To his credit, Newell does deduce that human cognition must involve a computational system that is "massively parallel", but this conclusion was reached by neurobiologists years ago based on brain structure and function.

From the perspective of a neuroscientist, the basic problem in this book is its consistent failure to deal with the essence of cognition, that is, the brain and what is presently known about it. Achieving (and maintaining) literacy in neuroscience is, to be sure, a daunting prospect for the cognitive scientist (or anyone else). This dilemma has been made more profound by the explosion of information about the brain in the last 25 years. Nonetheless, there is a corpus of principles and important facts about brain structure, function and development that can be assimilated by anyone determined to make the effort.

This criticism of Newell's book should not be taken to mean that neuroscience has no place for those disposed to consider cognition in terms of strategies, goals, and algorithms. Quite the contrary. But ignoring the machinery in which these abstractions must be embedded is no longer an option. Reading Newell's book brings an analogy to mind—a distant race of intelligent beings limited to observing automobiles on the surface of the earth by some primitive telemetry. Having no means to appreciate cars and their purposes other than observation from afar, their speculation would be wide-ranging (and legitimate). If, however, such aliens developed a spacecraft and retrieved a 1973 Dodge, they would no doubt hasten to get inside it, take it apart, and see what, in fact, a car is all about. The opinions of Newell and others who continue to speculate about cognition without considering the wealth of relevant information about the brain now available will not generate much interest outside of their own circle. After reading this book, one can only exhort Newell and any like-minded colleagues to put on their overalls, open the hood, and take a look.

References

[1] L.A. Jeffress, A place theory of sound localization, *J. Comput. Physiol. Psychol.* **41** (1948) 35–39.
[2] M.M. Waldrop, Toward a unified theory of cognition, *Science* **241** (1988) 27–30.
[3] M.M. Waldrop, Soar: a unified theory of cognition?, *Science* **241** (1988) 296–298.

Artificial Intelligence 59 (1993) 375–388
Elsevier

ARTINT 1016

Book Review

Issues for psychology, AI, and education: a review of Newell's *Unified Theories of Cognition* *

Roger C. Schank and Menachem Y. Jona

The Institute for the Learning Sciences, Northwestern University, Evanston, IL 60201, USA

Received August 1991
Revised September 1992

1. Introduction

With *Unified Theories of Cognition*, Newell has presented us with ideas developed over a twenty-year period. The book touches on so much of both psychology and AI that it provides an opportunity to discuss some important problems currently facing both fields. In fact, it is specifically because it covers so much ground that many real problems that are ignored, overlooked, or simply never discovered in less ambitious bodies of work come to the fore and demand to be addressed.

Newell has had a strong influence on our views of both psychology and AI. As AI researchers, we share many of the same opinions about the field of psychology. Our views on AI, however, while initially quite similar, have diverged. Despite this divergence, we still concur on many points and, as one would expect, people with similar viewpoints tend to find themselves disagreeing on small matters. It is important that this type of disagreement not be mistaken for acrimony, however.

Correspondence to: R.C. Schank, The Institute for the Learning Sciences, Northwestern University, Evanston, IL 60201, USA. E-mail: schank@ils.nwu.edu.

* (Harvard University Press, Cambridge, MA, 1990); xvi + 549 pages.

Unified Theories of Cognition raises interesting issues about three fields, psychology, AI, and education, the first two being fields close to Newell's heart and the third being a field close to ours. The structure of this review is organized around the issues raised for each of these fields.

In preview, we find ourselves in agreement with his criticisms of psychology's methodology, particularly his opposition to the obsession with falsifiability. We also agree with him on the importance of studying natural tasks, but feel that he has sometimes violated his own principle and used an unnatural task as a basis for constructing his theory.

In terms of AI, we also find ourselves in agreement with Newell on fundamental issues such as the importance and nature of learning. Yet there are a number of areas of disagreement as well. The work on Soar fails to provide what, in our opinion, is a realistic model of memory organization and access, and nearly completely ignores the importance of knowledge. Finally, while providing lip-service to the necessity of building non-brittle systems, Soar does not address the issue of scale-up in a satisfactory way.

While the book has little to say explicitly about education, there are some elements of it that are implicitly relevant and that raise important issues pertaining to education. In particular, the applicability of a unified theory of cognition, such as the one proposed in the book, should not end at the borders of the research labs of psychology and AI. Rather, it should also be put to practical use by informing the educational system. Researchers in cognitive science need to realize that, by virtue of their work, they have a role to play in educational reform.

2. On psychology

If one could take away only one thing from reading the book, it should be Newell's criticisms of the field of psychology. It is on this point that we are in strongest agreement. Psychology, perhaps in a quest for legitimacy, adopted the "physics model" of science, an obsession with theory falsifiability and an attraction to studying phenomena describable in mathematically rigorous ways. AI too, in spasms of angst over its scientific legitimacy compared to the "hard sciences", is now becoming threatened by this trend. But psychology, the older of the two fields, has been the more affected.

2.1. Psychology's malediction: a crippling methodology

Sadly enough, as Newell himself notes, many of the points he makes about the state of psychology in this book, he made nearly twenty years ago in his "twenty questions" paper [13]. We can only hope that this time someone will listen. In that paper, reflecting on the state of psychological theories at the time, he argued for three methodological changes that are as needed today in the field of psychology as they were then. We repeat them here because of their importance. They are:

- Psychology should construct complete processing models.
- Psychology should take particular tasks and analyze all the psychological phenomena involved in them.
- Psychology should apply a model of a single phenomenon to diverse situations where that phenomenon arises.

Newell has taken these three principles to heart and they have evolved into the main theses of the book, specifically that psychology is ready for unified theories of cognition and that it is scientifically worthwhile to attempt to formulate such unified theories. Following from the above principles, a unified theory of cognition is defined as one that, with a single system of mechanisms, can account for significantly more phenomena than previous theories have.

The research goal here is straightforward. The theory needs to have sufficient scope so that it will be possible to bring to bear a large number of constraints on the shape of the overall theory. This is a very important lesson that AI can provide psychology. By focusing on small, well-defined, and easily testable tasks, psychology has painted itself into a methodological corner. It has expended so much effort in pursuit of clean results, whittling away cognitive tasks until they bear little or no resemblance to anything real, that the important constraints imposed on any plausible theory of cognitive architecture have been lost. AI, having not yet succumbed to the restrictive methodology of the "physics model" of science, has used the power of bringing many diverse constraints to bear to be, in our opinion, much more successful in generating interesting theories of cognition and cognitive architectures.

That psychology is too limited by its own methods is one of the important points of the book. Newell points this out quite explicitly. He argues, and we agree, that psychological theorizing is too discriminating and should be more approximating instead. He also rejects the traditional approach that, as he puts it, "falsifiability is next to godliness" (p. 23). If psychology is to begin to contribute seriously to theories of cognition, it must throw off the methodological shackles that it has placed on itself. To do this, along with Newell's suggestions, it must begin to look at larger, more realistic tasks so that it can bring to bear the constraints that this approach provides.

2.2. The importance of studying realistic cognitive tasks: a case study

Despite Newell's criticisms of psychology's methodologies, he nevertheless goes on to use Soar to explain the results of several experiments that studied unrealistic cognitive tasks. This is a bad idea for at least two reasons. First, AI programs should worry more about examining phenomena that can't be studied in psychology, that is, until psychology's methodology can be changed so that interesting things can be studied. Second, the danger of studying artificial tasks as a basis for cognitive theories is as real in AI as it is in psychology.

What do we mean when we say that AI programs should worry more about examining phenomena that can't be studied in psychology? Newell's position to the contrary, we believe that it is a mistake to attempt to fit an AI program to data gathered from unrealistic and unnatural tasks.[1] It is very debatable whether fitting an AI program to data gathered from an unrealistic, unnatural task helps to build a system that will perform well in a realistic, natural task. Furthermore, advising this as a methodology not only serves to distract research attention from more profitable areas, but also invites the danger of reducing AI models to curve-fitting. AI researchers should not limit the topics they choose to study because of the overly restrictive methodology that another field has chosen to constrain itself with, nor should they try to make their programs conform to data that has been compromised by those same methodological constraints.

A good example of the danger of studying artificial tasks as a basis for cognitive theories and its unfortunate results is the use of the cryptarithmetic task described in Chapter 7. The cryptarithmetic task is used as evidence that people search problem spaces when solving problems. Of course, given the task, what else is there to do but search and backtrack through a space of possible solutions? One can easily imagine how the choice of this unnatural task shaped the early formulations of Soar in such a way that the notions of search and problem spaces became the cornerstones of the Soar architecture. What would have the theory looked like if the task chosen had been more naturalistic, for example, summarizing a newspaper article or explaining why the U.S. should or shouldn't have got involved in the Persian Gulf war? Here is a clear case of Newell falling into the same trap that has plagued psychological theorizing for so long: a bad choice of task leading to a bad choice of theory.

Lest we come across as being too critical of psychology, let us look at an example of the value of psychological studies when they are grounded in an overarching theory and when the task chosen to study is a reasonably natural one. Schank and Abelson [21] developed a theory of memory structures and processing based on the notion of a script. This theory proved not only quite popular, but also quite fruitful as it led to the development of many

---

[1] This is not to say that it is unprofitable to study human performance on a particular task when building an AI program to do that task. Rather, we are focusing on data at the level of, for example, reaction time.

interesting computer models of natural language parsing and understanding (DeJong [4,5], Schank and Riesbeck [23]).

As development continued on these models, problems with script theory began to emerge (see Schank [18], for a discussion). What really put the nail in the coffin, so to speak, and forced a radical rethinking of the theory was a study by Bower, Black and Turner [3]. In that study, subjects confused events from stories about visits to doctor and dentist offices in a way that could not be accounted for by script theory. This forced a reformulation of script theory that eventually became the theory of dynamic memory detailed by Schank [18]. The two points of this case study are first, the importance of grounding empirical studies in sound theory and second, that studying natural tasks like story understanding and recall, as opposed to artificial ones like cryptarithmetic, is the best way to insure having a sound theory to start with.

3. On AI

While Newell's arguments about the state of psychology in general, and psychological theorizing in particular, explicitly point out the problems with the field of psychology and the need for a (more) unified theory of cognition, his exemplar of one such unified theory, Soar, implicitly illustrates several important issues about AI. In fact, the scope of the work forces us to examine what AI is really about and whether and how Soar deals with the important issues.

3.1. What is AI?

To understand the value of *Unified Theories of Cognition's* contribution from the perspective of AI, we need to think about what AI is about. For the purpose of the present discussion, we can categorize AI as being primarily concerned with four things:[2]

- AI is learning.
- AI is memory organization and access.
- AI is functional constraints + knowledge analysis.
- AI is scale-up.

We have always believed that to build an intelligent system, one must build a system that learns. Intelligence means adapting to the environment and improving performance over time. Thus, if the goal of AI is to build intelligent systems, one of the things that AI has to be about is the study

---

[2]There are obviously other ways one might carve up the field as well.

of learning. The second thing that AI is about is memory organization and access. How a system gains access to its knowledge, and how it organizes its memory to facilitate that access, provide fundamental functional constraints on the nature of cognitive architectures. This brings us to the third thing that AI is about and the thing that sets it apart from other fields. The discovery and application of functional constraints imposed on cognitive processing and the analysis of the knowledge used in that processing form the bread-and-butter of AI research. Psychology's tools are experiments and t-tests and AI's are functional constraints and knowledge analysis.

The final thing that AI is about is scale-up. What does scale-up mean? An intelligent system that can only behave intelligently in two or three carefully selected situations is not really intelligent. AI is about building systems that can handle hundreds or even thousands of examples, not just two or three. The process of scaling up a system from handling two or three examples to handling hundreds provides so many functional constraints on the nature of the system that without it one has to be skeptical of the system's architecture and its ability to really perform the task it was designed to do.

How does Soar address these four aspects of AI? What lessons does the Soar project have for us as AI researchers?

3.2. The fundamental nature of learning

One of the points on which we find ourselves in strong agreement with Newell and his work on Soar is on the importance of learning and memory in cognition. As he puts it, "The ubiquity of learning is clearly a phenomenon that characterizes human behavior, and one that a unified theory of cognition should explain" (p. 313). This echoes the arguments about the fundamental importance of learning that we have been making for years, starting with the work on dynamic memory [18]. Real AI entails building systems that learn [20]. We would not consider a human who failed to learn from experience very intelligent and any AI system that has any hope of being "intelligent" that doesn't learn from its experiences and interactions is doomed to failure as an intelligent system. The integration of learning with every phase of cognitive processing is one of the most important lessons AI researchers can take from Soar.

There are two other points about learning made by Soar that we feel strongly about as well. The first is that chunking, the mechanism of learning in Soar, is impasse-driven. That is, chunking, or learning, occurs when there is a failure of some sort. Another way of putting this is that learning is failure-driven [18]. While we may disagree with some of the particulars of how learning takes place in Soar, we share the belief that nearly all learning is prompted by failures in processing. People have all sorts of expectations about what will happen next, and these expectations are continuously being violated. When an expectation fails, we are curious about why it failed, and we try to construct an explanation for why it did [18,22]. If we encounter a situation where none of our expectations are violated, we are often bored and tend not to learn much. It is primarily when our expectations fail, and trigger the construction of an explanation, that learning takes place. The importance of learning being driven by processing failures is that the system can be more efficient by allowing it to focus its cognitive effort on only those areas that caused the failure and hence are in need of modification (see, e.g., Birnbaum, Collins, Freed and Krulwich [1], Hammond [7], Simmons [24] and Sussman [26]).

The second point of value that Soar points out about learning is that it is always goal-oriented. While it is possible for a system to "learn" without being oriented towards a particular goal (e.g., inductive category learning), that is not the way people learn in natural situations (see, e.g., Schank, Collins and Hunter [22]). This is an important point. Not only is learning goal-oriented, meaning that learning occurs in pursuit of a goal, but *what* is learned in a given situation can change dramatically depending on what goal or goals the learner has. Many cognitive theories fail to include goals in their descriptions of learning, and many psychology experiments are designed without regard for the goals the subject may have and how they influence cognitive processing. This is a big mistake and Soar's position on goal-oriented learning should be taken seriously.

3.3. Memory organization and access

Inseparable from the importance of learning, however, is the importance of memory organization and access [18]. Both of these form the cornerstone of any theory of cognition. Newell seems to concur, saying "learning and memory can not be separated from the rest of Soar" (p. 310). Yet while this statement may be true in a limited sense, Newell seems to ignore the important functional constraints that can be obtained from examining memory access and organization. How do we become reminded of X when we see Y? How do we organize the millions of items we have stored in memory and gain access to them at just the moment when we need them?

A good example of the constraints that arise from considering the issues surrounding memory organization and access and their effect on the development of cognitive processing theories is recent work by our colleagues on natural language understanding. Our work in this area has changed from being focused primarily on word-based expectation-driven parsing (see, e.g., Birnbaum and Selfridge [2], Riesbeck and Schank [15])—the technique implemented in Soar (Section 7.3)—to a new style of natural language understanding called Direct Memory Access Parsing (DMAP) (Martin [12], Riesbeck and Martin [16]). Why have we changed our tune? Because of the constraints that come from looking at how people understand natural language and how they use and organize their memory when doing so.

We were forced to move beyond straight word-based expectation-driven parsing because when we compared how our systems read stories and how people read them in real life we saw that there was a significant difference. For all practical purposes, the systems we built had no memory of having read a particular story. They could have read it repeatedly, doing the same work over and over and never get bored. This stands in strong contrast to how people operate. For example, if you read something in a newspaper that you have already seen, you quickly recognize this fact and skip to the next article. What this means is that, like all other experience, reading text alters the state of the understander's memory. DMAP operates in just this way, altering its memory structures each time it reads a new text, and recognizing when it is reading something it has seen before. On the other hand, despite the fact that Soar uses its memory to improve its reading performance by storing new chunks, it is not clear how or whether Soar would have any recollection of having read a story it had already seen.

How memory is altered, and how it is used to understand natural language has provided important constraints on the development of our theory of natural language understanding. Newell seems to concur in principle, asserting that Soar is a system in which "... the language mechanisms can be related to the mechanisms used for all other cognition and in which all these mechanisms mutually constrain each other" (p. 418). Yet, on closer analysis, the theory of language understanding described in the book suffers some serious shortcomings as an even moderately realistic model of how humans perform this task.[3] An important reason for this is the lack of attention to the constraints that arise when language understanding is integrated with a real model of memory. One of Soar's major weaknesses as an AI program, and as a candidate unified theory of cognition, is its lack of attention to memory organization and access. The functional constraints that can be derived from the careful consideration of how memory is used and organized are too important to ignore when building a theory of any type of cognitive process.

The dynamic nature of memory is a fundamental characteristic of an intelligent system [18]. Memory is constantly changing as a result of experience. This seems almost a truism, and if you believe in the ubiquity of learning as Newell does (and we do), it has to be. But having a dynamic memory means more than simply having a bigger list of productions after processing an experience than before, as is the case in Soar. It means, among other

---

[3] For example, the chunking mechanism used by Soar in the natural language processing task essentially caches inferences at the lexical level. This is really a zeroth-order theory of how memory is used when understanding language.

things, organizing and reorganizing the elements of memory so that they can be easily retrieved when they are needed to understand new experiences (see, e.g., Kolodner [11]).

Knowledge in Soar is atomized in productions, and learning means simply aggregating more of these atomic units. There is no notion that the elements of memory cohere in any real sense. To build larger concepts in memory, one must specify how the component concepts relate to each other, that is, how they are structured. The essence of the problem with Soar's model of memory, and a possible explanation for why knowledge in Soar is just aggregates of atomic productions, is that one can't talk about memory organization without also talking about memory contents. This leads us directly to our next point.

3.4. Architecture versus content

Earlier, we said that one of the things that AI is about is the analysis of knowledge. This is one of the most basic tools of AI research, and one that sets it apart from related disciplines. The reason we bring it up here is its glaring absence from the work on Soar. This is unfortunate in our view, because Soar could be used to make valuable contributions in this area. The analysis and careful description of the knowledge needed to get Soar to perform various tasks, if done in a systematic way, would be immensely valuable. It is puzzling, then, that most of the work described in the book seems to be dancing around the need to tackle the hard problem of knowledge analysis. This is especially surprising given that Newell's important "knowledge level" paper [14] was a central voice in arguing for the importance of knowledge.

Newell carves Soar up into two pieces, architecture and content, and asks the obvious question: "... What is embodied in the architecture and what is moved out into the content?" (p. 82). Unfortunately, he focuses on the former to the exclusion of the latter, despite asserting later that "... the architecture itself does not exhibit intelligence. It must be augmented with knowledge ..." (p. 216). This statement seems to reflect the view that, while the architecture is interesting, the factor that provides the bulk of intelligent behavior is the knowledge the system has and how it is used. What follows from this is that the important thing to study, if one wants to understand the nature of intelligence and build intelligent systems, is content not architecture. [4] Or, as Guha and Lenat [6] put it, "[a]lthough issues such as architecture are important, no powerful formalism can obviate the need for a lot of knowledge" (p. 33).

---

[4] See Hayes [8] for a more detailed argument about the importance of tackling the problem of knowledge analysis and representation.

Why does the Soar project seem to shy away from knowledge analysis and stick to the architecture instead? There are at least two answers. One possible answer is that the difficulty of doing a careful analysis of knowledge tends to lead away from unified theories and towards separate micro-theories. Doing knowledge analysis right is hard. Developing a deep content theory for even a single domain requires a great deal of effort. Doing a more superficial analysis is easier, but tends to yield content theories that appear too disparate to unify. Getting such a theory of one domain to interface with one in another domain usually requires radical revision of both theories. Thus, it is usually safer (for the longevity of the theories) to avoid attempts to unify content theories and they tend to get left as separate micro-theories.

One attempt to bite the bullet and face this problem head-on is, of course, the Cyc project (see, e.g., [6]). That project can be seen as both similar to and opposite of Soar. The two projects are similar in that they both are attempting to elucidate functional constraints by trying to do very large tasks. They are opposite in that Soar, as just mentioned, concerns itself primarily with architecture issues, while Cyc is addressing content issues. Both Soar and Cyc are ambitious, interesting projects; yet, because of our perspective on what is important in AI, given a choice of one or the other we would pick Cyc.

A second, and more likely, answer is that Soar has fallen prey to the same misconception that plagues expert system shells, what we call the "I'll build the architecture so all you have to do is put in the knowledge" fallacy. This view is just plain wrong. Knowledge is what determines the architecture. What power expert systems have comes not from their architecture, which is really fairly simple, but from the analysis, organization, and encoding of the important knowledge about a certain domain. The recent hype over connectionism is similar in that there exists a belief among many people both in and outside the field that it is possible to discover a general connectionist architecture, and all that will be required to get intelligent behavior from it will be to "put in the knowledge".

3.5. Why think? Preparation, deliberation, and case-based reasoning

Another facet of the architecture versus content dichotomy is reflected in what Newell calls the preparation and deliberation components of cognition. When facing a given problem, a system can either have a solution already prepared by retrieving and adapting one that worked before, or it can deliberate to find one. In Soar preparation means knowledge search and deliberation means problem search.

The relative contributions of preparation and deliberation to human cognition is another area that we disagree with Newell's work on Soar. Soar's emphasis is obviously on deliberation, or search, while our work (and others) on case-based reasoning (CBR) emphasizes the importance of preparation, that is, of retrieving and adapting old solutions (see, e.g., Hammond [7], Kass [10], Riesbeck and Schank [17], Slade [25], or Jona and Kolodner [9]) for an overview). Most people prefer not to have to think hard if they can help it. They will try to get by with whatever worked before, even if it is less than optimal. We believe that, roughly speaking, people's everyday cognition consists of about 90% retrieving of past solutions and only about 10% or less of actual novel problem solving. Because of our belief about the relative importance of retrieval, it follows that if one wants to understand what it takes to model human intelligence one should focus on the type of processing that contributes the most to people's everyday behavior, namely retrieval and adaptation of old solutions. Even Newell seems to admit that the locus of intelligence resides more with retrieval than it does with constructing a solution from scratch, saying that "... for a given system, with its fixed architecture, improvement comes from adding knowledge, not adding search volume" (p. 106).

This is not so much a right versus wrong issue but rather a focus of research attention issue. Studying processes that account for only a small proportion of human cognition is not wrong, but it makes more sense to focus one's effort where most of the action is, so to speak. In addition, thinking seriously about what it means to retrieve the most relevant past solutions from a very large memory when they are most needed to solve a new problem raises numerous interesting and difficult issues for how all those past solutions are organized and retrieved. For example, one of the most difficult issues that must be faced is how past solutions are labeled, or indexed. This problem is known to CBR researchers as the *indexing* problem (see, e.g., Jona and Kolodner [9] for an overview). It is not clear how Soar could be extended to handle the kinds of memory-intensive tasks typically studied in the CBR community, and especially, as we discuss next, how it could handle very large memories consisting of thousands or tens of thousands of items.

3.6. The scale-up problem

The touchstone of real AI systems is whether they can scale up to handle a large number (i.e., hundreds or thousands) of examples. Even Newell seems to concur on this point, at least in principle, saying that one goal of AI is to build "nonbrittle systems" (p. 231). He believes that Soar architecture will permit it to be scaled up, but unfortunately has not given us much evidence that this has even been attempted. He even admits this explicitly:

> Soar is structured to have a very large knowledge base. That is what the production system provides and the design is for Soar to have a large number of productions ($\sim\sim 106$ or more). However,

none of the tasks explored with Soar has dealt with such large memory, so we can only project that Soar would behave plausibly under such conditions (p. 230).

This is a serious flaw, especially for a system aiming to be a large, general architecture for intelligence. The process of scaling up a system may fundamentally alter its architecture, in fact it seems almost certain that it will [8]. This is a lesson we have learned mostly from personal experience, however [20].

Even if we were to suspend disbelief at Soar's ability to scale up to a large memory size, the evidence presented in the book points directly against the likelihood of this happening. When Designer-Soar, a system that designs algorithms, was given two different algorithm design tasks, the transfer of learning from one task to the other was only 1% (p. 216). And this is for two tasks in exactly the same domain! What should we project from this in terms of scaling up to more general cross-contextual learning?

This points to another problem that is related to the issue of memory organization and access described above. The implicit claim made by Soar is that all the productions (knowledge) used in all the different tasks for which Soar has been programmed could all be eventually loaded into the system at one time producing a system that was somehow more than the sum of its parts (that is, it would produce some type of general intelligent behavior by transferring learning from one domain to another). The problem is that loading separate sets of productions into Soar at the same time does not produce a unified system any more than does loading many separate Lisp programs into core memory at once produce a unified program. In addition, what will happen to Soar's constraint of operating in real time when it has to search and match not 100 or 1000 productions, but 100,000 or 1 million? This is why facing the scale-up problem is essential. You can get away with too many insupportable assumptions if you don't.

4. On education

Newell devotes almost no attention at all to education in the book. This is at the same time both surprising and not surprising. It is not surprising because the focus of the book is on theories of cognition, not education. He certainly has enough to talk about trying to unify the field of psychology without trying to tie in education as well. Nonetheless, we strongly believe that a unified theory of cognition should bear some relation to education:

After all, both cognition and education are concerned with how people learn, and what we know about how people learn should inform how they are taught. Moreover, how people can be best taught will likely provide invaluable insights into the underlying cognitive processes of learning.

What Newell says explicitly about education, and what follows from it, is worth noting and thinking about. He says, "The notion of intelligence as a scientific construct defined entirely by a technology for creating tests is set in opposition to a notion of defining it by cognitive theories and experiment" (p. 89). If it is time for psychology to pursue unified theories of cognition, then it is also time for psychology, AI, and the rest of the cognitive sciences to realize that their work is really about the nature of intelligence. We may not have a full-blown, proven theory of all of cognition yet (although this book has started us down that road), but what we do know now about how people think, and how they learn, puts us in a much better position to define intelligence and what it takes to create it in both people and machines than those who are currently in the business of creating tests that measure, and therefore define, intelligence in our children.

Newell argues that it is time for psychologists to come out of their experimental laboratories and put their heads together to build more unified theories of cognition. That is a step in the right direction, but it does not go far enough. More importantly, it is time for all cognitive scientists to realize that, by virtue of their work on learning, memory, and cognition, they have a voice in the debate on education. Good theories of cognition have a practical and important role to play in restructuring the process of education.[5] The separation of the fields of education and cognitive science is both artificial and harmful. A unified theory of cognition must, now more than ever, be put into practical use as the cornerstone of the educational system.

Acknowledgement

The authors thank Jerry Faries, Gregg Collins, Chris Riesbeck, and especially Larry Birnbaum for their insights and comments during the preparation of this review. The Institute for the Learning Sciences was established in 1989 with the support of Andersen Consulting, part of The Arthur Andersen Worldwide Organization. The Institute receives additional support from Ameritech, an Institute Partner, and from IBM.

---

[5]Newell, in Section 8.5, discusses the need for a theory to have practical applications. What we are arguing for here could be restated in Newellæs terms by saying that restructuring the educational system is a useful and necessary practical application for good theories of cognition. In fact, we would argue that it is currently the most important possible application.

References

[1] L. Birnbaum, G. Collins, M. Freed and B. Krulwich, Model-based diagnosis of planning failures, in: *Proceedings AAAI-90*, Boston, MA (1990) 318–323.

[2] L. Birnbaum and M. Selfridge, Problems in conceptual analysis of natural language, Tech. Rept. No. 168, Computer Science Department, Yale University, New Haven, CT (1979).

[3] G.H. Bower, J.B. Black and T.J. Turner, Scripts in text comprehension and memory, *Cogn. Psychol.* **11** (1979) 177–220.

[4] G.F. DeJong, Skimming stories in real time: An experiment in integrated understanding, Ph.D. Dissertation, Yale University, New Haven, CT (1979).

[5] G.F. DeJong, An overview of the FRUMP system, in: W.G. Lehnert and M.H. Ringle, eds., *Strategies for Natural Language Processing* (Lawrence Erlbaum, Hillsdale, NJ, 1982) 149–176.

[6] R.V. Guha and D. Lenat, Cyc: a midterm report, *AI Mag.* **11** (3) (1990) 33–59.

[7] K.J. Hammond, *Case-Based Planning: Viewing Planning as a Memory Task* (Academic Press, Boston, MA, 1989).

[8] P.J. Hayes, The second naive physics manifesto, in: J.R. Hobbs and R. Moore, eds., *Formal Theories of the Commonsense World* (Ablex, Norwood, NJ, 1985) 1–36.

[9] M.Y. Jona and J.L. Kolodner, Case-based reasoning, in: S.C. Shapiro, ed., *Encyclopedia of Artificial Intelligence* (Wiley, New York, 2nd ed., 1992) 1265–1279.

[10] A.M. Kass, Developing creative hypothesis by adapting explanations, Ph.D. Disseration, Computer Science Department, Yale University, New Haven, CT (1990).

[11] J.L. Kolodner, *Retrieval and Organization Strategies in Conceptual Memory: A Computer Model* (Lawrence Erlbaum, Hillsdale, NJ, 1984).

[12] C.E. Martin, Direct memory access parsing, Ph.D. Dissertation, Yale University, New Haven, CT (1990).

[13] A. Newell, You can't play twenty questions with nature and win: projective comments on the papers at this symposium, in: W.G. Chase, ed., *Visual Information Processing* (Academic Press, New York, 1973) 283–308.

[14] A. Newell, The knowledge level, *Artif. Intell.* **18** (1) (1982) 87–127.

[15] C. Riesbeck and R.C. Schank, Comprehension by computer: expectation-based analysis of sentences in context, in: W.J.M. Levelt and G.B.F. d'Arcais, eds., *Studies in the Perception of Language* (Wiley, Chichester, England, 1976) 247–294.

[16] C.K. Riesbeck and C.E. Martin, Direct memory access parsing, in: J.L. Kolodner and C.K. Riesbeck, eds., *Experience, Memory and Reasoning* (Lawrence Erlbaum, Hillsdale, NJ, 1986) 209–226.

[17] C.K. Riesbeck and R.C. Schank, *Inside Case-Based Reasoning* (Lawrence Erlbaum, Hillsdale, NJ, 1989).

[18] R.C. Schank, *Dynamic Memory* (Cambridge University Press, Cambridge, England, 1982).

[19] R.C. Schank, *Explanation Patterns: Understanding Mechanically and Creatively* (Lawrence Erlbaum, Hillsdale, NJ, 1986).

[20] R.C. Schank, Where's the AI? *AI Mag.* **12** (4) (1991) 38–49.

[21] R.C. Schank and R. Abelson, *Scripts, Plans, Goals, and Understanding* (Lawrence Erlbaum, Hillsdale, NJ, 1977).

[22] R.C. Schank, G.C. Collins and L.E. Hunter, Transcending inductive category formation in learning, *Behav. Brain Sci.* **9** (1986) 639–686.

[23] R.C. Schank and C.K. Riesbeck, *Inside Computer Understanding* (Lawrence Erlbaum, Hillsdale, NJ, 1981).

[24] R.G. Simmons, A theory of debugging plans and interpretations, in: *Proceedings AAAI-88*, St. Paul, MN (1988) 94–99.

[25] S. Slade, Case-based reasoning: a research paradigm, *AI Mag.* **12** (1) (1991) 42–55.

[26] G.J. Sussman, *A Computer Model of Skill Acquisition* (American Elsevier, New York, NY, 1975).

Artificial Intelligence 59 (1993) 389–413
Elsevier

ARTINT 1017

Response

On *Unified Theories of Cognition*: a response to the reviews

Paul S. Rosenbloom

Information Sciences Institute & Department of Computer Science, University of Southern California, 4676 Admiralty Way, Marina del Rey, CA 90292, USA

John E. Laird

Artificial Intelligence Laboratory, 1101 Beal Street, The University of Michigan, Ann Arbor, MI 48109, USA

Received August 1991
Revised September 1992

1. Introduction

This is a tough one. Clearly, neither of us is Allen Newell, and there is no way that we can do the job he would have liked to have done in responding to these thought-provoking reviews of *Unified Theories of Cognition* (henceforth, *UTC*). However, it was very important to Allen— and is very important to us—that the work on Soar and unified theories of cognition carry on. So, here we will do what we can based on our combined understanding of Soar, cognitive science, Allen, and how he would have likely responded to the issues raised by these reviews. In this latter, we have been greatly aided by a prepublication print of [12] that was graciously provided to us by the editors of Behavioral and Brain Sciences, and by Newell's follow-on paper to *UTC* [13]. In general, we will try to be clear about when we are conveying how we think Allen would have responded, and when we are just giving our own views.

Correspondence to: P.S. Rosenbloom, Information Sciences Institute & Department of Computer Science, University of Southern California, 4676 Admiralty Way, Marina del Rey, CA 90292, USA. E-mail: rosenblo@isi.edu. Telephone: (310) 822-1511.

UTC has three principal themes:

(1) "Psychology has arrived at the possibility of unified theories of cognition—theories that gain their power by positing a single system of mechanisms that operate together to produce the full range of human cognition. I do not say they are here. But they are within reach and we should strive to attain them" (p. 1).

(2) There is a common foundation underlying cognitive science.

(3) Soar is a candidate unified theory of cognition that is useful as an exemplar of the concepts introduced in the book.

The first theme is most contentious among traditional experimental psychologists. As none of the present reviewers fit this mold, it is not too surprising that this issue is not a major source of concern for them. Most of the reviewers range from neutral (i.e., they don't mention it) to strong support. The one exception is Minsky, who is "not sure that this is a good idea". However, our impression is that Minsky is really disagreeing with a stronger form of this theme than Newell actually intended. By "unified theory" Newell was referring to any theory that integrates together a set of mechanisms that are intended to model a broad swath of human cognition. Newell's (and our) approach to building such a theory is biased towards having a small set of mechanisms that produce most of the action through their interactions (an issue that we will get back to later). However, the call for the development of unified theories is not limited to just this form of unification. In particular, an integrated architecture built out of a, possibly large, set of specialized modules—such as the Society of Mind theory might ultimately lead to—seems well within the scope of the call.

Though the first theme was clearly the central one in *UTC*, Minsky's comments were the only ones about it, so we won't say anything more about it in the remainder of this response.

The second theme covers basic material on behaving systems, knowledge systems, representation, machines and computation, symbols, architectures, intelligence, search and problem spaces, preparation and deliberation, system levels, and the time scale of human action. Much of this material is common knowledge by now in cognitive science, though still by no means universally accepted (in particular by those more closely tied to the structure of the brain). The new material that might be expected to raise the most controversy comprises:

(1) *The refinement of the notion of symbol and the resulting distinction between symbols and representation.* In Newell's usage, a symbol is a pattern that provides access to distal structures (so that local processing can make use of structures which are initially not localized).

Symbols are involved whenever such distal access occurs. A representation, on the other hand, is defined by encoding and decoding functions, such that if you decode the situation that results from applying an encoded transformation to an encoded situation, then you have exactly the situation that would have been generated if the original transformation had been applied to the original situation; that is:

$$\text{Decode}(\text{Encode}(\textit{Transformation})[\text{Encode}(\textit{Situation})])$$
$$= \textit{Transformation}[\textit{Situation}].$$

Using a representation need not involve distal access, nor must distal access involve representation. Thus our interpretation of this distinction is that it should be possible to have representation without symbols and symbols without representation.

(2) *The definition of intelligence in terms of approximation to a knowledge-level system.* This definition distinguishes the concept of intelligence from the concepts of knowledge, level of performance, and generality by defining intelligence *with respect to a goal* to be how well the *extant knowledge* is used in selecting actions for the goal. So, lack of knowledge implies ignorance, but not lack of intelligence. Failure to perform at a high level could result from a lack of intelligence, but could just as well arise from a lack of either the appropriate knowledge or goals. Generality, rather than being an inherent attribute of intelligence, becomes the scope of goals and knowledge possessed; and general intelligence becomes the ability to exhibit intelligence across a wide range of goals and knowledge. Note that though intelligence is defined in a universal manner, the intelligence exhibited by an agent need not be unitary, and can in fact be quite domain-specific because the ability to use knowledge effectively may not be the same across different ranges of goals and knowledge.

(3) *Describing human action in terms of a hierarchy of system levels which are characterized by time scales roughly an order of magnitude apart.* For example, at 1 ms is the neuron level, at 10 ms is the neural circuit level, and at 100 ms is the deliberate-act level. These levels then aggregate into bands that share a phenomenal world. The biological band consists of three levels concerned with the physical structure of the brain: the neuron and neural-circuit levels, plus one lower level. The cognitive band consists of three levels concerned with symbol processing: the deliberate-act level plus two higher ones. The rational band consists of three levels concerned with intendedly rational behavior; that is, humans at these levels approach knowledge-level systems.

Many of the reviewers comments are focused on foundational topics, though not limited to just these novel contributions.

The third theme, not surprisingly, engenders a large number of comments from the reviewers. Even those who share the same assumptions on unified theories and foundations generally have quite different notions about what the right architecture is for cognition, and about how one ought to go about developing and studying it (including, in particular, what data should drive its development). This is in fact one of the major messages of *UTC*—that Soar is not being proposed as *the* right answer, but as an exemplar (both Purves and Arbib appear to overinterpret the claim being made about Soar), and that others should take up the challenge from their own perspectives (and with their own driving data) and develop alternative unified theories of cognition. However, it is also clear that with all of Soar laid out in *UTC*, it becomes an irresistible target for comment (and that this isn't really inappropriate). So, given that the reviewers go beyond the book's use of Soar, to fundamental comments on its nature, we will feel free to also go beyond the book in responding; in particular, we will refer to results generated since the book's completion wherever they seem relevant to discussions of the architecture and of how it is being developed and studied. In general, we will only provide references for work not already cited in *UTC*.

In the body of this response we focus on the principal comments on both of these latter two themes—foundations and Soar. Related analyses of some of these same issues, along with analyses of some additional issues, can be found in [8,16].

2. Foundations

Two of the three foundational themes that were expected to be controversial—(2) defining intelligence and (3) the bands (and levels) of human cognition—did indeed provoke the lion's share of comments, along with one topic that surprised us, though perhaps it shouldn't have: theories. These three topics are discussed in this section, along with two other topics that had fewer, but still significant, comments: natural language and evolution.

2.1. Defining intelligence

Fehling and Hayes-Roth have several questions about Newell's proposed definition of intelligence. We've already commented on the question of whether intelligence is a unitary quantity or whether intelligence can vary by domain. A second question is the extent to which intelligence is really independent of knowledge. Newell clearly meant that adding a new piece of knowledge relating goals to actions doesn't increase intelligence. However, we don't think he also meant that there is no way to increase intelligence by adding meta-knowledge. It seems quite consistent with the basic definition to say that adding a body of meta-knowledge, M, that makes the system better able to use another body of knowledge, B, can make the system more intelligent *with respect to the uses of B.*

A third question about the definition of intelligence is whether a system that performs perfectly within a very narrow region (such as a thermostat) is more intelligent than a system that performs less perfectly over a wide region (such as a person); or, similarly, whether a system that performs perfectly via a trivial method (such as table look-up) is more intelligent than one that performs less perfectly via a more sophisticated method (such as reasoning from first principles). This is an interesting question that seems to reduce to three fundamental components: ignorance, generality, and complexity. First, if an agent doesn't know the first principles, then it may certainly be ignorant, but not necessarily unintelligent. Likewise, if it knows both a perfect table and an imperfect set of first principles, it is more intelligent with respect to those goals to use the perfect table in answering rather than the first principles. Second, what should make the first principles advantageous is not their substandard use for goals where the table is applicable, but their use for other goals where the table is inapplicable. Thus this is an issue of generality rather than intelligence. Third, there appears to be an implicit appeal to the notion that something that is more complex (or sophisticated) is more intelligent. It is often assumed that complexity is a sign of intelligence, but what must really be meant is the ability to cope with complexity when needed (we've all seen too many complex descriptions that could really have been expressed quite simply). Using the first principles where the table is applicable would be inappropriate complexity. However, if the system knew the principles, but could not use them when they might help with other goals, that would indeed be a failure of intelligence.

A fourth question about the definition of intelligence is whether it ignores important phenomena such as: "a system's allocation of limited cognitive resources, its ability to focus attention, its efforts to meet real-time constraints, its balancing competing demands and opportunities for action, ..." (Hayes-Roth). The answer to this question is that intelligence is about how closely a physical system can approximate the knowledge level; that is, the issue is how the lower levels can provide a rational band. The phenomena Hayes-Roth mentions are precisely about how a physical system can best reflect its knowledge and abilities in resource-limited situations. Thus, systems exhibiting these phenomena are likely to be judged more intelligent by the knowledge-level definition than systems that do not.

Rather than being directly concerned about the definition of intelligence, Schank and Jona are concerned about the definition of AI. They take an

eclectic approach that has more in common with Newell's list of constraints
that shape the mind (p. 19) than with his proposed definition of intelligence. In Schank and Jona's view AI consists of four topics: learning,
memory organization and access, functional constraints + knowledge analysis, and scale-up. All of these topics, except for knowledge analysis (which is
discussed in Section 2.2.2), do appear to be covered in Newell's list. Schank
and Jona also appear to leave important topics out, such as performance,
reasoning, problem solving, planning, and natural language, but without a
more detailed description of what they had in mind, it is hard to say much
concrete about this apparent lack.

2.2. Bands and levels

Arbib has a general concern that the bands and levels described by Newell
are too influenced by their roots in serial 1971-style computers, and thus
generally inappropriate for describing human cognition. However, we don't
see how a careful reading of the relevant figures in *UTC* could be taken
as supporting this concern. Instead, it appears that Arbib is confusing the
hierarchy of computer systems (Fig. 2-3, p. 47) with the time scales of
human action (Fig. 3-3, p. 122). For example, though a register-transfer
level appears in the former figure, there is no sign of it in the latter figure.
Likewise, the symbol level in the latter figure—which occurs at ~~10 msec
and is identified with the biological level of neural circuits—is in no way
inherently serial (see, for example, how this level is mapped onto Soar in
Fig. 4-23 on p. 224). We thus don't see how Arbib's concerns are relevant
to the levels Newell describes in Fig. 3-3.

2.2.1. The cognitive band

The remaining concerns tend to be about Newell's focus in *UTC* on the
cognitive band, with only limited attention being paid to the rational and
biological bands (and even less to the others). This focus comes in for some
sharp criticism from the reviewers who think it is either too restricted or
completely misplaced.

In terms of the focus being too restricted, Arbib is concerned that an
attempt is being made to restrict the scope of cognitive science to rational
behavior, to the exclusion of everything else; and, in particular, to the
exclusion of subjects such as instinctive behavior. However, this seems to us
to be a misreading of *UTC* in several ways. First, Newell clearly recognized
that models of all of the bands were necessary for a complete model of
human behavior. Second, the rational band is the home of rationality, not the
cognitive band. In the cognitive band there can easily be procedures which
can be executed, but not examined, thus providing "knowing how" without
"knowing that". For example, Soar is "aware" of the contents of its working

memory, but it has no way to directly examine its productions—indeed, it can only execute them. Instinctive behavior could thus be represented at the cognitive band as unexaminable proceduralized content (such as productions) that is innate and fixed, or indeed simply as part of the architecture.

In terms of the focus being misplaced, Schank and Jona, and Arbib, are concerned that too much attention is being paid to the cognitive band and too little to the rational or biological bands (respectively). Fehling and Purves appear to go beyond this concern to a claim that only one band matters, though they are in complete disagreement as to whether it is the rational (Fehling) or biological (Purves) band. These concerns and claims about the misplacement of the focus are considered in more detail next.

2.2.2. The rational band

Fehling believes that the utility in models of cognition comes from competence theories, and that one key aspect of this is the utility of modeling knowledge rather than mechanism. This aspect is clearly a variation on the expert-system slogan that "Knowledge is Power", as are Schank and Jona's comments that "... the important thing to study, if one wants to understand the nature of intelligence and build intelligent systems, is content not architecture." and "Knowledge is what determines the architecture." We can't disagree with the importance of explicitly studying knowledge, nor with the claim that this has not so far been a central scientific component of the Soar research enterprise. There has been some focus on knowledge, particularly in situations where the functionality being provided is both particularly important and provided in a non-obvious manner (such as when it provides a new form of learning behavior). There has also clearly been a significant amount of informal study of knowledge in the context of applying Soar in various domains. Nonetheless, these activities have not been a large part of the overall enterprise.

Though we do expect the explicit study of knowledge to be a continually growing component of the Soar research effort, this should not be thought of as taking away from the central importance of studying the architecture. The human cognitive architecture is the fixed structure that makes the human mind what it is. It distinguishes people from other animals, and enables people to acquire and effectively use the wide range of knowledge that then lets them perform effectively in such a diversity of domains. In natural systems, at least, the architecture (plus the world and the already extant knowledge) determines what knowledge the agent can and does have, not the other way around. In general, without an architecture, knowledge is nothing more than useless scribbles, and without an appropriate architecture, intelligence (and thus performance) can be severely degraded.

Fehling also believes that a clean separation should be maintained between mind and brain (rather than attempting to ground mental constructs in the physical structures of the brain). He is therefore concerned that Newell is requiring all cognitive theory to be grounded in the physical structure of the brain, and that this is unworkable, unnecessary, and inappropriate. However, here we can only assume that Fehling has radically misunderstood *UTC*. The notion of a system level implies that it is possible to build theories at various levels of the hierarchy without attending to the details of lower levels. Such theories can, in fact, be extremely useful in their own right; a fact that Newell was well aware of, and himself took advantage of throughout his career. Thus there is definitely no intent in *UTC* to claim that all cognitive theories must be so grounded. However, to the extent that the desire is to get an understanding of human cognition at all levels and/or the extent to which the level boundaries are not hard, a one-level (or one-band) model is insufficient. This is not particularly pernicious nor behaviorist—it freely allows the use of "mental" terms—it just hopes to eventually understand how they are grounded, no matter how indirectly or complexly, in the lower levels/bands. What Chapter 3 of *UTC* represents is an initial attempt by Newell to help lay some of the groundwork for bridging the gap between the cognitive and biological bands (see [1] for a small additional step in this direction). There is a very long way to go here still, but the problem has to rank as one of the most important and challenging problems in modern science.

2.2.3. The biological band

Purves' primary concern with *UTC* is "its consistent failure to deal with the essence of cognition, that is, the brain and what is presently known about it." The strong version of this claim is that neurobiological evidence is primary, and that nothing of true importance can be done without it. We find such a claim hard to take seriously, for two reasons. The first reason is that equivalent claims can be made by all bands with respect to those above them; for example, physicists could just as easily claim that chemists should stop speculating about how the world works, and "put on their overalls, open the hood, and take a look"; and chemists could make the same claim about biologists. The fallacy, of course, in all of this is that each band talks about different phenomena and captures different regularities, and thus has its own appropriate technical languages and models. Understanding the relationships between the bands is ultimately of central importance to science; however, it can't replace studying each of the bands in its own right. The second reason is that ultimately the proof is not in such argumentation, but in what research paths lead to understanding cognition. To take one example from *UTC*, is Purves ready to claim that neurobiology can, any time in the near (or even relatively distant) future, make zero-parameter predictions about the amount of time it will take a human to execute a computer command as a function of how the command is abbreviated? Or, to take an important example from elsewhere, can it tell us anything about how students learn, and fail to learn, subjects like mathematics? These two tasks stand in for a whole class of results from the cognitive (and, indeed, rational) band that have both increased our understanding of human cognition and have had significant practical impact. On practical impact, though the command-abbreviation result has not itself had significant economic impact, closely related results have— just one such result saved NYNEX $2.4M per year [4]. More broadly, the whole area of expert systems is a spin-off from the study of the cognitive and rational bands.

The weak version of Purves' comment is that *UTC* is weaker than it would have been had it taken neurobiological data into account (a view which appears to match Arbib's). We are quite willing to believe that this might be true, as it is also likely true with respect to linguistic data and a variety of other bodies of data about human behavior. However, a significant breakthrough in bridging the gap between Soar and neurobiology will probably need to wait for the development of individual researchers who are sufficiently proficient in both of these topics.

Beyond Purves' general concern, he also has a more specific concern about the timings assigned to particular levels. He discusses how the brain can actually make discriminations based on time differences much smaller than the ~~1 msec rate suggested for the neuron level; in fact, it seems to be able to discriminate intervals as short as ~~10 μsec. While we are impressed with the cleverness of how the brain appears to accomplish this, it is hard to see how it bears on the issue of the time scale(s) on which the brain functions. The leading model of auditory localization appears to be that the brain can respond differentially as a function of the correlation between the signals from the two ears [17]. The problem is that there need be no relationship between the time to compute this correlation and the size of the temporal interval that the correlation then implies. Thus, it is quite consistent for the brain to take milliseconds to compute these microsecond differences (though we have not actually seen any data on the exact time course).

2.3. Theories

Concerns about Newell's usage of theories includes the (lack of) methodology for studying and evaluating them, the question of their identifiability, the nature of theoretical form and content, and competence theories.

2.3.1. Methodology

Hayes-Roth is concerned with the development of a "rigorous methodology for describing, analyzing, and empirically evaluating complex cognitive theories". We agree with her general call to arms, though realize that developing such a methodology will be a difficult and extended process. One subpoint worth additional comment is the relationship between a theory and its implementation. Based on the notion of theory development that Newell expressed, this issue, along with the related issue of when a theory should be adopted or rejected (Fehling), loses some of its force. To Newell, the implemented architecture was the theory, implementation hacks and all. The hacks are just part of the approximate nature of the theory. Since incorrectness of one part of a theory is not to be grounds for rejecting the whole theory, this amount of approximation is quite consistent. However, this doesn't preclude having part of the theory stated outside of the context of the implementation. It merely says that all of the implementation is part of it. It also doesn't obviate the development of a meta-theory; that is, an understanding of what parts of the theory are accurate, trustworthy, and significant. Such a meta-theory can be quite important in generating acceptance for the theory.

However, in general, Newell felt that a theory is adopted by an individual or community if it is useful to them. If it is not useful—because it is wrong in some way that matters to them, or because they do not trust or understand it, or because there is some other theory that is more attractive—then they will abandon it (or never even pick it up). He did believe that there should be a minimal threshold a theory should meet before being taken seriously, and that the threshold should evolve over time as the standards set by existing theories climb. But among the contenders, the ultimate success of a particular theory was more to be determined by how far you could get with the theory than by careful comparisons between it and other theories (though, of course, he did pay careful attention to a broad range of other theories, and particularly to whether they offered leverage in expanding the scope of extant unified theories). In the process, unsuccessful theories would just naturally be left by the wayside. He was thus much more concerned with extending his theories to cover new data than in detailed comparisons with other theories. In contrast, comparing his theories to data was always of central concern.

2.3.2. Identifiability

Fehling (along with Pollack) is concerned with the issue of theory identifiability, whether it ever really goes away, and whether it makes the modeling of behavior (rather than competence) impossible. It may be that in some fundamental manner the identifiability problem can never go away. However, what Newell probably meant here is not that the problem isn't still there in at least a technical sense, but that as the body of data gets larger, the issue of identifiability fades in significance because of the increasing constraints under which all of the theories must exist. If the total set of constraints on mind is finite, then ultimately any theory which satisfies them all is as good as any other. Even if there is an unbounded set of constraints—as Pollack might suggest—as long as the significance of the newly discovered constraints eventually follows a predominantly decreasing trend, the significance of the identifiability problem will also decrease correspondingly.

Even if you accept that the identifiability problem will always matter, the conclusion Fehling draws from this—that it is therefore only possible to focus on competence theories—just seems plain wrong. All scientific endeavors have identifiability problems, including the endeavor of developing competence theories—at best a competence theory provides one body of knowledge that is sufficient for generating some class of behaviors, but it does not show that it is the only such body of knowledge. What scientists in general must do is first find at least one theory that works, and then as other theories arrive, understand in what ways they are equivalent, and what the differences (if any) mean. In the area of unified theories of cognition we are still very much in the phase of trying to find just one theory that meets all of the relevant constraints. With respect to Pollack's concerns about basing a theory on a "Universal Programming Language", he is correct in surmising that Newell relies heavily on constraints derived from robust psychological results to distinguish among possible theories; however, these constraints are in no sense extra-disciplinary, as *UTC* is all about modeling the human mind.

2.3.3. Form and content

Pollack is concerned about the use of "natural law" versus "software law". However, it appears to us that he is conflating two distinct issues here—one of form and one of content—neither of which makes his point about *UTC*. The first issue is whether a theory is expressed in terms of mathematical equations versus process descriptions (i.e., what most programming languages provide). Neither form has an a priori claim to appropriateness as a basis for theory expression. What matters is whether a theory of the domain can be represented appropriately in the form—for example, whether a system's knowledge, goals, and processes can adequately be expressed—and whether the theory as so expressed supports answering the key questions we have about the domain. The second issue is whether or not a "theoretical" structure is *about* anything. Both mathematics and computer languages can be used to create arbitrary abstract structures that, while possibly quite beautiful, may have nothing to do with how the world (or the mind works). When AI engages in such activities, it has much in common with pure mathematics (in both the positive and negative senses). However, when the structures are used to model natural activities—such as the phenomena people exhibit when behaving in the world (or in a lab)—what is being talked about is as much natural law as are theories expressed as equations. Even such rational-band theories as competence models are statements of natural law to the extent that they model, at some level of abstraction, classes of activities that do (or can) occur in the world.

Fehling is concerned that Newell is relegating all AI theories other than Soar to the ashbin of "content-free" frameworks. However, it looks to us like Fehling has misinterpreted two parts of Newell's original statement. First, "content-free" is intended to refer to the fact that the frameworks make no content commitments that would keep them from being a neutral (but convenient) language for implementing any theory. It is *not* intended to imply that these frameworks are themselves vacuous in any way. Second, by saying that a unified theory of cognition is not a framework, Newell meant that it should really be a theory—that is, it should make commitments about how things work—rather than being a theoretically neutral (but expressive) framework or programming language within which anything could be encoded. Neither of these points was intended to denigrate existing frameworks, nor to say that other AI architectures could not be considered as possible unified theories of cognition.

2.3.4. Competence theories

Fehling believes that theories of competence are more useful than theories of behavior. However, utility clearly depends on application. If you actually do want to predict human behavior—so that you can teach effectively, or counterplan, or design an aircraft cockpit that minimizes the number of pilot errors, or any number of other important applications—a competence theory is not enough. Likewise, if you actually want to build a working system that can exhibit a behavior (or competence), a competence theory is not close to being enough. Being concerned with performance is clearly shared with the behaviorists—as in fact, it is shared with nearly all other approaches in cognitive psychology, AI, and cognitive science—but this certainly does not make the approach behaviorist. The behaviorists did get some things right.

2.4. Natural language

Dennett is concerned about the role natural language plays in providing a representational medium, and the extent to which this distinguishes humans from other animals. We'll have to be quite speculative here, as we don't know what Newell thought about this, and we are not ourselves experts in this area.

So, what we will do is use Soar as a stand-in for Newell. The most natural prediction from Soar here is that the key difference between human and other animal cognition is in the architecture, and that natural language is based on the basic efflorescence of adaptation provided by the human architecture, rather than itself being the primary source (see, for example, [9] for thoughts on natural language in Soar). However, this prediction doesn't rule out there being specialized problem spaces (and representations within these spaces) for natural language, and their providing general capabilities that can be recruited for use in arbitrary tasks. For example, recent work on *Linguistic Task Operators* in Soar is examining how natural-language representations, along with the operations defined on these representations, can be used in solving parts (or all) of specific problems [10].

Minsky wonders about the origins of nouns and verbs in Soar. This issue can also be dealt with only in a rather speculative fashion. However, it should not be too much of a stretch to imagine them as arising as the linguistic correlates of states (or parts of states) and operators, respectively. These are Soar's primitive notions of objects and actions.

2.5. Evolution

Understanding the evolutionary path by which the human mind evolved is a fascinating scientific problem, and one in which Pollack, Arbib, and Minsky are all deeply interested. Newell clearly understood the importance of the evolutionary constraint on the architecture—as evidenced by its presence in Fig. 1-7 (p. 19) as one of the core constraints on the shape of the mind— but was also just as clearly not ready to deal with it. We are also not ready to deal with this constraint in any detail, other than to notice, with respect to Minsky's comments, that evolution is constrained by both the material it has to start with—that is, the initial organism—and the environment in which the organism must exist (that is, the task environment). Only by understanding the interactions among these two constraints will we be able to get a true sense of the extent to which evolution prefers bizarre over elegant solutions and complex over simple solutions.

Despite the admitted importance of the evolutionary constraint, no one should be misled into believing that the ordering evolution imposes on cognitive functioning need provide the best—or even a particularly good— ordering in which to go about studying and modeling the mind. To use a problem-space metaphor, this would be equivalent to claiming that the best way to understand a state in a space is to understand its parts in the order they were generated by the sequence of operators that led to the state. What this neglects is that states (and organisms) tend to be structures with stable interactions among their parts—if organisms were not, they probably could not survive—and which can often best be understood directly in terms of these interactions, rather than through the possibly convoluted means by which the stability was reached.

3. Soar

The following discussion of Soar is organized around whether the comments being responded to are about memory, scaling up (including integration), task domains, seriality, emotion, or comparisons with other architectures.

3.1. Memory

Schank and Jona are concerned about a lack of organization of Soar's productions into higher-level units, a lack of attention to how memory should be accessed, and a lack of emphasis on preparation (that is, use of memory) rather than deliberation (that is, search). Minsky is also concerned about memory access and about whether Soar can have specialized representations (and whether they can be learned, or must be innate).

3.1.1. Organization

We surmise that Schank and Jona are being misled by the surface syntax of the memory structures and are thus missing the deeper semantic organization that does exist. Soar's productions do not simply comprise a flat memory structure. Instead, they are semantically organized around the objects— i.e., the goals, problem spaces, states, operators, and other miscellaneous subobjects—to which they are relevant. For example, each problem space has a cluster of productions that define it. Likewise, each operator has a cluster of productions that define how it should be applied (as well as when it should be considered and when it should be selected). Such clusters of productions are only eligible for execution when their corresponding objects are active in working memory. When examining Soar's productions it is easy to miss this structure, as it is buried in the conditions of the productions. However, one of the main advantages of this approach is that a large variety of objects can be dynamically (and flexibly) constructed during execution—according to the cluster of productions whose conditions make them relevant—rather than being limited to only instantiations of those object classes predefined in something like a long-term frame hierarchy.

In addition to the organization provided simply by having these objects, we have recently come to realize that the objects themselves are organized into a full-blown new processing level, called the *problem space computational model* [14]. At this level, Soar is appropriately described as consisting of a set of interacting problem spaces, where each problem space effectively realizes a constrained micro-world. Languages defined at the problem-space level, such as TAQL [21], specify systems directly in terms of problem-space components (and can be compiled automatically into Soar productions).

3.1.2. Specialized representations and innateness

Minsky is concerned about whether Soar has specialized representations. Soar definitely can utilize specialized representations because individual problem spaces may have their own representations that are constructed in terms of the uniform low-level attribute–value structure. This has proven adequate for the tasks so far investigated, but we do not yet know whether it will remain so in the future, or whether we will need to add new representations—for example, for spatial information—to the architecture.

Minsky also wonders about the knowledge-genesis issue of whether Soar would be able to acquire specialized representations, along with the ability to convert rapidly among them, or whether it really needs to be born with them. Soar currently doesn't come born with specialized representations—except for the limited way in which they are provided by the "default" rules that are always loaded into Soar on start-up—and though we don't currently know whether or not they could be learned in general, a two-pronged approach to resolving this issue does seem clear. One prong is to investigate in some detail whether (or how) such knowledge could indeed be learned by Soar. The other prong is to continue accumulating evidence about the capabilities humans have at birth. If the conclusion is that the representation and conversion capabilities must all be there at birth, there would then still be the question as to whether it exists as innate content (that is, as productions or whole problem spaces), or as architecture. Either could appear physically in the brain as "specialized sub-organs".

3.1.3. Access

Schank and Jona are concerned that the issue of how memory should be accessed has received insufficient attention in Soar. However, the problem really appears to be not that it hasn't been dealt with in Soar, but that it has been dealt with in a different manner than in, for example, case-based reasoning. In case-based reasoning, the usual assumption is that memory consists of large-grained declarative structures that are processed little at storage time, except for some work on indexing. The understanding and adaptation of the case happen later, at retrieval time. In Soar, much more of the processing occurs at storage time. In fact, storage effectively occurs as a side-effect of the understanding process, resulting in the information usually being proceduralized with respect to the current context into a set of small-grain rules, each of which becomes indexed by those aspects of the situation that determined its consequences. The only form of automatic (that is, architecturally driven) adaptation that occurs at retrieval time is instantiation and combination (of object fragments from multiple rules). More intensive adaptation of retrieved structures is possible, but must be driven by knowledge (i.e., productions) or by more deliberative processing in further problem spaces. It would be quite easy to get into an extended debate about the relative merits of these two approaches to memory access—and of whether phenomena such as *encoding specificity* (p. 321) favor one approach over the other—however, the important message to be taken from here is that significant attention has been paid to the indexing of knowledge in Soar. In fact, indexing is most of what the learning mechanism spends its time doing (i.e., figuring out what conditions to place on a production).

Minsky expresses related concerns about Soar having too easy a time in accessing arbitrary pieces of knowledge: "... in Soar all knowledge is assumed to be uniformly accessible, so there is nothing to bar the central processor from accessing anything ...". However, two factors make such accessing more difficult than it appeared to Minsky. The first factor is that, though the working-memory contents of one problem space can be examined by other problem spaces, the productions cannot be. Productions can only be executed, and then only in the context in which they match. The second factor is that the specialized representations which get built up within individual problem spaces can make it impossible for one problem space to understand the working-memory contents of another space without solving the kinds of integration problems that are discussed in Section 3.2.

3.1.4. Preparation versus deliberation

Here we can only surmise that our propensity to talk about how flexible Soar is as a searcher has misled Schank and Jona into believing that Soar favors deliberation (search) over preparation (use of memory). It was hopefully clear from *UTC* that Soar uses memory (encoded as productions) whenever it has it—and we usually try to make sure it does have it, or can learn it. Search only arises as a response to uncertainty and as a court of last resort when the available knowledge is insufficient (pp. 96–97). One of the things we have learned over the years is that problem spaces are about much more than search—they also provide a deferred-commitment control strategy that allows decisions to be postponed until run time (and which also turns out to make room for the kind of "dynamic planning" that Arbib is concerned about), constrained microworlds for focused deliberation, a forum for error recovery, and a means of bootstrapping into task formulation [14]. We thus have no strong quarrel with the claim that cognition is 90% preparation and 10% deliberation, though the exact numbers must be confirmed with good data.

3.2. Scaling up

Schank and Jona, Hayes-Roth, and Pollack are all concerned about scaling up, which is, of course, a major issue for any proposed intelligent system. Three subissues are raised by Schank and Jona:

(1) *Size*: Whether the architecture can cope with large numbers of productions.
(2) *Integration*: Whether you can scale the knowledge just by adding in the productions from a bunch of independent tasks.
(3) *Transfer*: The amount of cross-contextual transfer of learning that will occur.

Pollack's concerns about the construction of large-scale systems and Hayes-Roth's programmatic suggestions both fit in well with Schank and Jona's concern about integration, and are therefore discussed in that context.

3.2.1. Size

Recent evidence shows that, for at least one significant task—message dispatching—Soar can scale up to over 10,000 productions without a significant loss of speed [3], and more recent results extend this to over 100,000 productions [2]. More clearly needs to be done here—and will be—however, these results should at least allay some of the scale-up fears.

3.2.2. Integration

None of us believe that you can build an integrated large-scale system by just adding together a bunch of productions created for different tasks. Because problem spaces provide Soar with an approximation to a modular structure, you often can just throw the problem spaces from multiple tasks together. However, what you get then is a system which can do the tasks individually, but not particularly a system that understands how to combine them in any effective way. There is integration that needs to go on with knowledge—i.e., among the problem spaces—just as there is for the architecture.

What we do know about knowledge integration in Soar is that problem spaces interact through impasses; that is, when a problem space gets stuck, additional problem spaces can be brought in to discover the information that will allow the original one to proceed. Chunking then provides a permanent transfer of the knowledge integrated together from the additional spaces to the original space. The integration of the chunked rules into their new space is relatively straightforward, as the nature of chunking automatically ensures that the new rules are already in the language of the space for which they are learned—the chunks' conditions and actions are all derived from existing working-memory elements in this space—and the decision cycle provides an openness of knowledge access that enables new rules to contribute their preferences to whichever decisions they are relevant.

Problem-space interactions are normally modulated by hand-coded productions that:

(1) determine which spaces are considered and selected for which impasses;

(2) create initial and desired states in the new problem spaces as a function of the structure and content of the existing context hierarchy (particularly including the immediately preceding impasse and problem space); and

(3) return results to the original problem space.

This approach has worked fine as long as it is possible to predefine the classes of interactions that will arise. However, it falls short of the ideal, which would be to provide the potential for any problem-space to be used for any impasse for which it might be relevant—and to thus enable knowledge from arbitrary spaces to migrate, via chunking, into other spaces as appropriate. Soar does provide a framework that may make this ultimate integration possible, in that it allows the activities of problem-space generation and selection, initial and desired state creation, and result returning to become first-class tasks for the system to work on. However, the super-analogical problem of how, in general, two previously-unrelated problem spaces can be brought into correspondence, so that one can aid the other, is a question that we are only now beginning to seriously address within Soar. It is a great problem though (and clearly not just for us).

Hayes-Roth recommends a program of research that is focused on the cumulation and integration of knowledge (probably from much the same intuition that underlies the CYC project). That seems like a fine idea to us, though clearly a very difficult enterprise, as Hayes-Roth acknowledges. In our own judgement we have so far been reasonably successful in following her recommendation with respect to the architecture, but much less so with respect to the content within the architecture. The reasons are several, including:

(1) the architecture is tightly controlled by a small group of people, whereas the content is developed diffusely over a large loosely-coupled distributed community; and

(2) the architecture contains a relatively small number of reasonably robust algorithms, whereas the content houses a large amount of fragmentary, ill-specified, heuristic knowledge (as it should).

The research effort mentioned above, as well as some of the new tasks we are going after (partly described in Section 3.3), are intended to help drive us further in the direction of knowledge integration. Even so, it can still frequently be useful to back off from the ideal Hayes-Roth presents, and to look at independent integrations of partial capabilities in specific tasks. When it is not possible to see a straight-line path to the integration of a complete new robust capability—which is, in fact, frequently the case—such partial integrations can be a great way to build the scientific base that should eventually support the full integration required (and can also be an easy way to incorporate many loosely coupled researchers).

Pollack proposes "building systems from the bottom up using robust and stable cooperatives of goal-driven modules locked into long-term prisoner's dilemmas" (presumably based on nonlinear dynamical systems). There is a lot of general common sense in this prescription—creating stable, robust modules and developing a stable organization of them—though the effectiveness of the particular approaches he advocates (such as long-term prisoner's dilemmas) is much less clear, as is the relationship of these approaches to existing large-scale system-construction methodologies that attempt to resolve the same basic issues. Specifically with respect to Soar, we see that problem spaces provide "goal-driven modules" that interact through the relationship of impasse resolution. Within problem spaces there are semi-independent objects (states, operators, etc.) each constructed out of productions (or more problem spaces). The productions themselves tend to be significantly more independent than those in most systems because of the lack of conflict resolution—productions fire in parallel, with behavioral arbitration occurring outside of the production system, via preferences and the decision procedure. All of this gives Soar a form of modularity that should help in the construction of large-scale systems. However, it is impossible to tell at this time whether this is enough—even when combined with the growth potential provided by chunking—or whether it is any better or worse than the approach Pollack describes.

3.2.3. Transfer

We do currently see a lot of transfer within and across problems from the same class of tasks; however, we do not yet see a great amount of cross-contextual transfer. Since such transfer is likely to be a direct function of the amount of commonality among the processing across different contexts, it is also probably related to the degree to which particular problem spaces can be used in different contexts, and thus a function of the amount of integration that can be achieved (as just discussed). Additional integration will thus probably help, but we would never expect to see a huge amount of cross-contextual transfer. The evidence on analogy and encoding specificity suggest that such transfer is actually quite limited in humans.

3.3. Task domains

Both Hayes-Roth and Schank and Jona are concerned about the set of tasks used in driving the development of Soar. Hayes-Roth is concerned that the psychological tasks are too low-level and artificial to be informative—and may just "reflect artifacts of biological hardware"—and that the AI tasks may have nothing to do with intelligent behavior (or might reflect super-intelligent behavior). Schank and Jona are concerned that paying attention to "unrealistic and unnatural" psychological tasks—as opposed to the more realistic tasks that AI can study but that psychology has more trouble studying—will both lead to a distortion in the resulting theory and distract effort away from the more important realistic tasks. Let's divide this issue up into two parts: (1) whether there is a right set of tasks to be working on; and (2) if so, what they are, and where Soar stands with respect to them.

On the first part, we are pretty sure we know what Newell would have said: There is no right set of tasks. People are not special-purpose devices that can only work on one type of task. Indeed, any single task can lead to a micro-theory that is overoptimized with respect to its own narrow domain, and that is thus severely distorted with respect to the full complexity and richness of human cognition. So, what really matters is not what task is covered, but what diversity of tasks are covered.

On the second part, we sympathize with the call for AI to study more realistic and naturalistic tasks. A key feature of such tasks is that they often contain within themselves enough essential diversity to keep the resulting micro-theory from being extremely narrow to begin with. The Soar community has put a fair amount of energy into understanding how Soar can perform in reasonably complex knowledge-intensive domains, both in terms of replicating existing systems and in terms of constructing novel ones. The domains range over such areas as computer configuration, medical diagnosis, algorithm design, blood banking [7], message dispatching [3], factory scheduling [5], browsing [15], and playing video games [6]. These are realistic tasks that people do perform, but they may seem to fall somewhat short on the scale of "naturalism". We have not yet looked much at performing everyday tasks, and that would be a useful addendum to the classes of tasks that we have examined. Perhaps the closest we have come is nascent work on how Soar can be used as the basis for developing human-like intelligent agents in large-scale, simulated, physical environments. This is a "real" task in the sense that the simulation environments are developed by groups outside of the Soar community, the environments have significant value for those groups, and they have a direct need for intelligent agents in these environments. This is also a reasonably naturalistic task, as it deals with multiple intelligent agents—some human-controlled and some computer-controlled—in realistic physical situations; however, they do not quite tend to be "everyday" situations.

Despite our general sympathy with the reviewers' calls to more realistic and naturalistic tasks, we also believe that controlled experimentation with more limited tasks can provide valuable information that can be difficult-to-impossible to derive from more complex tasks; for example, the rich bodies of data on controlled versus automatized performance, on memory, and on practice. Newell has already stated the rationale for this better than we could have, but the basic idea is that these short time-scale tasks—i.e., tasks requiring hundreds of milliseconds up to small numbers of seconds—are the ones that get close to the architecture, by eliminating much of the flexibility that humans have at longer time scales. To date, Hayes-Roth's concern about these phenomena being mostly artifacts of the biology (or in Newell's terms, phenomena of the biological band) have not been realized. We have been successful in modeling a number of tasks at this level—such as visual attention [20] and transcription typing—with functional models based on ~~50 msec operator-execution times. In general, as long as you don't restrict yourself to the micro-theory developed from a single such task, and in fact strive for coverage across a broad range of both realistic and controlled tasks, the danger of getting a fundamentally distorted view can be reduced greatly, while the amount of useful information available can be increased greatly.

3.4. Seriality

Minsky is concerned about Soar's "selecting and executing productions—that is, IF–THEN rules—one at a time". However, here Minsky seems to have fundamentally misunderstood the parallel nature of Soar. It is serial at the level of problem-space operations, but quite parallel below that: productions match and execute in parallel, and preferences are generated and decisions made in parallel. (Of course, when we implement Soar on a serial machine, this parallelism can only be simulated, but parallel implementations have also been investigated [19]. Because Soar does embody this parallelism, many of Minsky's arguments about what would be difficult to do quickly enough in Soar don't go through. To take just one specific example, recent work on garden-path sentences in Soar shows precisely the kind of rapid shift of interpretation about which Minsky is concerned. In this work, an ambiguous sentence is not a garden-path sentence precisely when it is possible to repair, in real time, from the incorrect interpretation of the sentence to the correct one [11].

Arbib is also concerned about the seriality of computers (and Soar) versus the parallel/distributed nature of brains. Part of the problem with this concern is that, as with Minsky, Arbib appears to have missed Soar's inherently parallel nature. However, a further problem with this claim is that there is strong evidence for something like serial processing in human cognition; for example, the large body of results on (parallel) automatized processes versus (serial) controlled/attentive processes [18]. In his final remarks, Shiffrin summarizes as follows: "Behavior in general is accomplished by limited, perhaps serial, attentive processes operating in parallel with numerous automatic processes, with the two systems passing information back and forth at all levels of analysis." (p. 805). Soar is, at least at a gross level, consistent with these results, as the productions produce (parallel) automatized behavior while the problem spaces produce (serial) controlled behavior.

3.5. Emotion

Dennett's primary concern about Soar is its being all business, with no pain, pleasure, playfulness, laziness, etc. There is no question that this is a rather large gap with respect to Soar's coverage of human cognition. Even if you abstract away from the purely biological aspects of emotion, there are large and well-documented effects of emotion on cognition—in many ways the issues are not unlike those concerning the interactions between cognition and perceptual-motor systems. So it is an important constraint, but not one that we yet know how to deal with. It will clearly need to be addressed some day and, when it is, it will almost certainly have an impact on the architecture.

3.6. Comparisons with other architectures

One of the things Minsky does in his review is to compare Soar directly with the Society of Mind. On the whole, we think he did an excellent job. The comparison helped us both to understand the Society of Mind better, and to understand some of the ways in which it does map quite nicely onto Soar (and vice versa). However, there are two aspects of the comparison to which we would like to add.

The first addition is that, rather than mapping the Society of Mind's management function onto Soar's problem spaces, we would map it onto Soar's decision procedure, along with the knowledge and processing that generates the preferences used by the decision procedure. This knowledge may consist simply of productions that directly generate preferences upon execution, or it may consist of problem spaces that require arbitrary amounts of processing before being able to generate the appropriate preferences. When management is by the former, it doesn't require impasses or deliberate processing, and can proceed in parallel for many activities. This would also be quite compatible with Minsky's notion that "The managers themselves are installed as consequences of impasse-resolving episodes", as these are exactly the circumstances under which chunking installs new productions in Soar.

The second addition concerns Soar's apparent lack of the concept of a "difference", which is so central to the Society of Mind. Soar does indeed not have a large-grained, architectural, difference-detection mechanism that compares arbitrary pairs of structures. However, it does have at its very core a fairly general match capability that provides a small-grained difference-detection mechanism; that is, it can detect situations where a value bound in one condition of a production is not the same as the value bound in another condition. This capability supports, but does not mandate, large-scale structure comparisons. An important part of the philosophy underlying this choice is that difference detection is not a purely syntactic operation that can be applied to two arbitrary structures and yield meaningful answers. Instead it must be a knowledge-guided process that can be based on which differences really matter in particular contexts. The selective use of difference detection in the matcher is one way of accomplishing this. This choice is also consistent with the overall philosophy underlying Soar's approach to problem solving. In contrast to systems such as GPS, Soar is not locked into a single problem solving method such as means–ends analysis (MEA). Instead it is to be free to use whatever methods are supported by the knowledge it has about the task. Thus, if it has difference information, something like MEA is possible; when it doesn't have such knowledge, other methods should be appropriate; and when it has such knowledge plus additional knowledge, more powerful, possibly hybrid, methods should be usable.

Arbib also compares schema theory with Soar, and generates similar conclusions. In particular, he proposes to map schemata onto problem spaces, but is then concerned about the resulting seriality. However, as with the Society of Mind's management function, it is not at all clear why the mapping shouldn't be extended to, at least, include Soar's productions as schemata.

4. Summary

If we pull up from all of the details, there are three major themes that we hope the reader takes away from this response. The first theme is that studying the architecture is important. No matter how much domain-specific power comes from the knowledge, there is no way to build a unified and effective theory of cognition without significant study of, and effort on, the architecture.

The second theme is that no band of phenomena is special. Each band has its own data, methods, regularities, and applications. A complete model of human behavior requires understanding all of them. Newell focused primarily on the cognitive band in his career, and *UTC* represents his attempt to build a comprehensive theory of the architecture—that is, the fixed structure—that gives this band its distinct shape. Unified theories of the other bands may take on quite different shapes, as might unified theories of cognition that are based on other phenomena within the cognitive band.

The third theme is that there is plenty of room—in fact, Newell tried to explicitly encourage it—for others to develop their own unified theories of the cognitive (or any other) band. As the theories grow, and the set of phenomena covered by them begins to converge, we expect that some of the theories will die (from an inability to grow further), while others will themselves start to converge, if not in their surface structure, then at least in their essence. Be warned though, that the development of such theories can be an immense undertaking, requiring the integration of a rather vast amount of both expertise and manpower. And even then, there will always be significant gaps and inconsistencies that can be criticized. Nonetheless, there are few research paths more exhilarating than trying to put it all together.

References

[1] B. Cho, P.S. Rosenbloom and C.P. Dolan, Neuro-Soar: a neural-network architecture for goal-oriented behavior, in: *Proceedings Thirteenth Annual Conference of the Cognitive Science Society*, Chicago, IL (1991).

[2] B. Doorenbos, *Personal communication* (1992).

[3] B. Doorenbos, M. Tambe and A. Newell, Learning 10,000 chunks: what's it like out there? in: *Proceedings AAAI-92*, San Jose, CA (1992).

[4] W.D. Gray, B.E. John and M.E. Atwood, Project Ernestine: validating GOMS for predicting and explaining real-world task performance, NYNEX Science and Technology Center and School of Computer Science, Carnegie Mellon University, Pittsburgh, PA (1991).

[5] W. Hsu, M. Prietula and D. Steier, Merl-Soar: scheduling within a general architecture for intelligence, in: *Proceedings Third International Conference on Expert Systems and the Leading Edge in Production and Operations Management* (1989).

[6] B.E. John, A.H. Vera and A. Newell, Towards real-time GOMS, Tech. Rept. CMU-CS-90-195, School of Computer Science, Carnegie Mellon University, Pittsburgh, PA (1990).

[7] T.R. Johnson, J.W. Smith, K. Johnson, N. Amra and M. DeJongh, Diagrammatic reasoning of tabular data, Tech. Rept. OSU-LKBMS-92-101, Laboratory for Knowledge-based Medical Systems, Ohio State University, Columbus, OH (1992).

[8] J.E. Laird, M. Hucka, S.B. Huffman and P.S. Rosenbloom, An analysis of Soar as an integrated architecture, *SIGART Bull.* **2** (1991) 98–103.

[9] J.F. Lehman, R.L. Lewis and A. Newell, Integrating knowledge sources in language comprehension, in: *Proceedings Thirteenth Annual Conference of the Cognitive Science Society*, Chicago, IL (1991).

[10] J.F. Lehman, A. Newell, T.A. Polk and R.L. Lewis, The role of language in cognition, in: G. Harman, ed., *Conceptions of the Human Mind* (Erlbaum, Hillsdale, NJ, to appear).

[11] R.L. Lewis, Recent developments in the NL-Soar garden path theory, Tech. Rept. CMU-CS-92-141, School of Computer Science, Carnegie Mellon University, Pittsburgh, PA (1992).

[12] A. Newell, SOAR as a unified theory of cognition: issues and explanations, *Behav. Brain Sci.* **15** (1992) 464–488.

[13] A. Newell, Unified theories of cognition and the role of Soar, in: J.A. Michon and A. Akyürek, eds., *Soar: A Cognitive Architecture in Perspective* (Kluwer Academic Publishers, Dordrecht, Netherlands, 1992).

[14] A. Newell, G.R. Yost, J.E. Laird, P.S. Rosenbloom and E. Altmann, Formulating the problem space computational model, in: R.F. Rashid, ed., *CMU Computer Science: A 25th Anniversary Commemorative* (ACM Press/Addison-Wesley, New York, 1991).

[15] V.A. Peck and B.E. John, Browser-Soar: A computational model of a highly interactive task, in: *Proceedings CHI'92* (ACM Press, New York, 1992).

[16] P.S. Rosenbloom, J.E. Laird, A. Newell and R. McCarl, A preliminary analysis of the Soar architecture as a basis for general intelligence, *Artif. Intell.* **47** 289–325 (1991).

[17] B. Scharf and A.J.M. Houtsma, Audition II: loudness, pitch, localization, aural distortion, pathology, in: K.R. Boff, L. Kaufman, and J.P. Thomas, eds., *Handbook of Perception and Human Performance*, Vol. I: *Sensory Processes and Perception* (Wiley, New York, 1986).

[18] R.M. Shiffrin, Attention, in: R.C. Atkinson, R.J. Herrnstein, G. Lindzey and R.D. Luce, eds., *Steven's Handbook of Experimental Psychology*, Vol. 2: *Learning and Cognition* (Wiley, New York, 2nd ed., 1988).

[19] M. Tambe, D. Kalp, A. Gupta, C.L. Forgy, B. Milnes and A. Newell, Soar/PSM-E: investigating match parallelism in a learning production system, in: *Proceedings ACM/SIGPLAN Symposium on Parallel Programming: Experience with Applications, Languages, and Systems* (1988).

[20] M. Wiesmeyer and J.E. Laird, A computer model of 2D visual attention, in: *Proceedings Twelfth Annual Conference of the Cognitive Science Society*, Cambridge, MA (1990).

[21] G.R. Yost and E. Altmann, TAQL 3.1.3: Soar Task Acquisition Language user manual, School of Computer Science, Carnegie Mellon University, Pittsburgh, PA (1991).

Artificial Intelligence 59 (1993) 415–449
Elsevier

ARTINT 1024

Interview with Allen Newell

Philip E. Agre

Department of Communication D-003, University of California, San Diego, La Jolla, CA 92093-0503, USA

Introduction

The body of this article consists of an interview that I recorded with Allen Newell in his office at Carnegie-Mellon University on July 3rd, 1991, a little over a year before his recent death. My purpose was to explore the development of some of his central theoretical ideas, particularly the concept of a problem space. I especially wanted to reconstruct some of the interactions between architectures, theories, and evidence through which this development took place. Although my questions were influenced by my own analysis and critique of Newell's research project, the focus was on Newell's ideas and not on my own.

The text below is not a direct transcription of the interview. The editing process began with a careful transcript prepared by Beatrice Velasco at the University of California, San Diego. I then heavily edited the transcript for clarity, revising obscure passages and omitting many redundant and peripheral comments. In doing so, I tried to stick with Newell's vocabulary and meaning. Nonetheless, as with any interview, the final text is necessarily a creative interpretation of the interview itself. Along the way I sought the advice of several people, including Bill Clancey, John Laird, Richard Lewis, Brian Milnes, Frank Ritter, Paul Rosenbloom, Steve Smoliar, and Mark Stefik, but they do not necessarily endorse my interpretations. In particular, Newell himself wrote comments on the interview after one round of editing, but the interview subsequently underwent much more editing which he did not have the opportunity to check over or endorse. The interview and transcription were supported by a grant from the American Association for Artificial Intelligence, for which I would like to thank Pat Hayes and Carol

Correspondence to: P.E. Agre, Department of Communication D-003, University of California, San Diego, La Jolla, CA 92093-0503, USA. E-mail: pagre@weber.ucsd.edu.

Hamilton. I would also like to thank Frank Ritter for his kind logistical
help.

I have kept annotations and commentary to a minimum. Omissions in
the text have not been notated in any way. Ellipses (that is, …'s) denote
a speaker being interrupted or trailing off in the middle of a thought. I
have inserted several references, each enclosed in parentheses as in (Newell
1980). Some of these references reflect my attempt (with help from Newell's
colleagues) to identify a paper that Newell discusses explicitly. Sometimes
Newell slightly misstated the title or date of a paper. When it was clear
what he was referring to, I repaired his misstatement without comment. In
other cases I have inserted an editorial comment; these and other comments
are italicized. The section headings are my work as well; they correspond to
clear changes of topic in the interview itself. I had sent Newell a short list of
questions a week ahead of time, roughly corresponding to my initial questions in each section here. Nonetheless, Newell's responses were improvised
and should be interpreted in that spirit.

1. Search and interaction

Phil: The problem space idea has been developing over thirty years or
more. Soar brings that idea together with production systems, chunking, and
universal subgoaling, but for the moment I want to consider the problem
space notion in isolation. You write about problem spaces in terms of a
definite set of metaphors. In a problem space you're searching for something,
namely an object. You have a location in the space, and you move to
someplace else in the space by applying an operator. So there's that whole
metaphor of being in space and travel and search. And it's understood that
this is not actual traversal of Pittsburgh or anything?

Allen: Right.

Phil: It's a mental process. Yet it's striking to me, especially in some of
the early papers, that the activities that you're modeling with search spaces,
like cryptarithmetic or solving a logic problem, are being done in interaction
with a world. *[Later on we'll be more careful to distinguish between a search
space and a problem space.]*

Allen: Okay. But by a world now do you mean a problem space or a
physical world?

Phil: I mean a physical world. In the experimental situation described in
the *Computers and Thought* paper (Newell and Simon 1963), for example,
the physical world contains a series of logic formulas. Or in cryptarithmetic
the world contains some scratch paper with the partially solved puzzle
written out. And that physical world changes from time to time.

Allen: Yes, very little in the logic. A little more in cryptarithmetic, which we didn't much take into account.

Phil: And even in the logic the successive derivations are written out.

Allen: But only in one sense, along a single path. You can't erase them if you want to back up and think of alternatives. It's a sort of projection from internal space.

Phil: I think that's very much the intent methodologically, to make something visible through the whole taking of protocols and so forth. And in the logic case the list of derivations is a list of the states that have been traversed.

Allen: Right.

Phil: The devil's advocate objection would be that the problem space theory makes the false prediction that people can do cryptarithmetic problems in their heads. The theory models the problem solving process as a very much mental process even though there is this interaction with the environment going on in the event.

Allen: No, it doesn't actually make that prediction. If you have this generative space in your head—that is, you don't have the actual space laid out but you have a set of generators which can produce the next state along—that doesn't say anything about how much of that space you can actually explore. This is how things were formulated in the early AI systems, where the memory problem is secondary. And it's not a problem at all if you're only keeping the current state or the current path so you can back up and do depth-first search. It turns out, in actually looking at human behavior, there is indeed an issue of how much of that one can keep in one's head. That question was not asked in a sharp way early on. One of the reasons for this is that, if you look at cryptarithmetic in *Human Problem Solving* (Newell and Simon 1972), where we plot out the whole problem behavior graph, it's quite clear that the search must be going on in the guy's head since it's not going on in the outer world. You thus have plenty of evidence that he is in fact searching this space internally and that memory problems are not a big deal. Now maybe if he had a different memory organization he'd actually do things quite differently. He might try to do a breadth-first search or something like this, whereas in fact the search strategies do not keep very much information around. And you may even search a whole space, but all that has to be kept is some local context.

Phil: So one can make the argument that, given that he's using such and such a search strategy, we could prove by doing a computer simulation in GPS—as it was at that time—that he wouldn't have needed much fresh access to the world.

Allen: Right. Now we know experimentally that these subjects, in almost all of these situations, have access to a fixed point that becomes a starting point of a search, from which they do a fair amount of internal search. You know it's internal because nothing is going on externally. And in those task situations—which are not all task situations—somehow the memory problem is not a big deal. If the memory problem had empirically shown up to be a big deal, so that this guy was always forgetting where he was, then memory considerations would clearly have entered in very early. "Early" here means early in trying to apply that theory to human cognition as opposed to the actual early history of it. There is a development of the problem space which is just driven by AI, in which one first comes to an awareness that humans are doing ... Well we're always mixed up between humans and ...

Phil: Yes. *[The point, I think, is that they were often mixed up between humans and computer models. In interjecting my agreement, I meant to draw polite attention to that mixing-up, which I think sometimes causes confusion.]*

Allen: As Herb would say, that's one of our secret weapons. Maybe you don't know that about Herb. Herb has this great lecture in which he says, "if you wish to do good science you must always have a secret weapon, one that other people don't have". And that's been one of them. I've never done this in a scholarly way—but two or three books were written about thinking just before the cognitive revolution started. And I've read them all of course. And by gosh, they hardly mention search at all. I mean they do mention search but it's just one topic among many. So there really was this change in which we all, operating within AI to begin with, became aware that search is not just any old process but really is central. And that happens through the ubiquitous fact that everything interesting in the early days turns out to be one of these combinatorial search spaces. And that was, as far as I was concerned, a genuine empirical discovery.

Phil: Let me focus in on, say, the logic case and others like it. You say that memory problems weren't evident. I don't understand how they could be, given that the subject had visual access to the blackboard with the formulas.

Allen: Because that only provides a point in the space. It will not provide the rest of the space ... You started us down this path by picking up on the question that said, "could that be going on in a person's head?"

Phil: Yeah, okay.

Allen: You're certainly right, we only looked opportunistically at a certain set of task domains. In those domains we do in fact find an anchor point, for example the initial chess position. But that's not the space. That's only a point in the space. So when you ask, can the human search this space given that they don't have environmental support for the search, the answer is that they have precisely an anchor point, but they're off some other place in the space.

Phil: In the case of cryptarithmetic—although I think it's similar in the logic case—the subject (or the experimenter on behalf of the subject) is writing things down, changing what's visible to the subjects.

Allen: Yes. But in the logic case not much was written down, though there is actually a certain amount of additional information. Nonetheless, the subject actually is working quite a ways in advance of this. That is, not every trial thing that the subject is doing is getting written down. It is, however, also the case—and you're certainly absolutely right—that ... I don't know if you ever saw the tech report on crypto-arithmetic.

Phil: No I haven't seen tech reports about it.

Allen: Well, there was a tech report in '67 *[probably Newell 1967]* which had a fair amount of interesting talk up front about the external space and the internal space and how you have two problem spaces, one of which you're actually searching in out there and the other you're searching in your head. It set the context for the actual protocol analysis. It is absolutely the case that in the actual analyses, that *[that is, the issue of memory capacity]* was not taken into account very much. And if you ask me, "why?", I think the right statement is, "I don't know!" It sort of dropped out and the analyses were going very successfully and so forth.

Phil: Okay. Do you feel that historically, that the memory problem has come back in?

Allen: Ah, nope. But let me say a big thing about that, which is that the humans do have a memory problem.

Phil: Oh yeah.

Allen: We all do. It gets worse as you get older—though I'm not sure it does for cryptarithmetic. And the problem gets solved because methods get used which avoid the memory problem. So you don't see a subject having terrible memory problems. What you see is that the memory shapes the method. And the big thing that comes out is that the search strategy that humans use is essentially progressive deepening. And it's funny that the whole development of AI doesn't recognize progressive deepening as a strategy, though it's a big deal in *Human Problem Solving*. As you probably know, that book didn't introduce the notion of progressive deepening. That goes back to de Groot in chess (1965), although he never liked our formulation of it. He always believed that much more exotic reformulations of the problem were going on, where we had it more mundanely relating to the search strategy, which tends to solve the memory problem because you really only keep two states, plus one external state. So you're absolutely right, one state is external. And if it's not, it's at least a state that you can get back to, in part because you may have been there before and you have some independent reconstructive access to it. In the early protocol studies of progressive deepening, we never defined very well these issues of what information is brought back and the internal representation and control structures for handling that. Now, in fact these issues have shown up in Soar in a striking way: there turn out to be two forms of progressive deepening. One form is, I put some information into a state, perhaps even while I'm in a subgoal, and then it's there in the state when I get back to it. The other one, which we are more enamored with, is, you venture out and maybe you learn something, so then you simply start over again. In that case you needn't update the state at all—no deliberate process of bringing information back at all. The information I've learned is available insofar as it's re-evocable, with the usual issues on chunking of whether the chunks are too specialized or not (Steier 1989). But the real transfer of knowledge happens because of the learning, not because of a deliberate transfer. And you know, if we had investigated the issue back in '72, those two alternatives simply would never have occurred to us.

Phil: It definitely seems to me that results about progressive deepening are not simply a description of what the subjects are doing but actually motivated by a computational mechanism, and that's a good thing. It is cheering to be able to have that kind of explanation. Your book presents several such explanations: you'll say not only is such and such empirically adequate, but it's comparatively the most efficient way of doing it. Is that a general mode of explanation that you have strong allegiance to?

Allen: I have to decide whether I like the way you have expressed it. I mean, you see it throughout the book in terms of the slogan "listen to the architecture", which is clearly related to doing what is simple in the architecture. And "simple" may be a better word than "efficient". But they are closely coupled of course. I would take that, however, purely as a heuristic. So take the matter of progressive deepening. Not only does it address this general memory problem, but it turns out to be implementable in a natural way within the Soar architecture, as opposed to an elaborate or even interpreted way. And, of course, that still does not explain how the subjects come to use progressive deepening. I express that as a "genesis problem". The fact that it satisfies all these principles doesn't explain why the subjects actually use it. We can neglect evolution here since we're assuming, roughly speaking, that evolution provides the architecture. But the organism has a whole history; somehow the subjects come to be organized that way through a lot of experience, a process to which we have basically zero access at the moment. Nonetheless, one can ask, how would a certain system that couldn't do progressive deepening then come, through dealing with problems, to organize itself that way? Within Soar that genesis problem is sort of well posed, in that it has to happen through chunking. Another relevant example from Soar is data chunking, which is a scheme for using chunking to acquire knowledge from the external world in order to do paired associates. Right there is the genesis question: How do subjects end up with that organization?

So these other kinds of principles are just substitutes to hold you until you get to these other questions—and of course you never get back to all of them. In computational systems, every hint of artificiality is a red flag that says, "we can't leave it that way". But of course one puts artificialities in these systems all the time; one has no choice. There is a whole piece of Soar that you may not be familiar with—by now I can't keep track of what comes through in the book—about trying to get the simulations to be what I call "fine grained", so that they are, so to speak, right all the way down. As you well know, usually in these simulations when you get down to the levels that are directly responsible to the data, you begin to introduce artificialities. And so in Soar we are, so to speak, getting the back of the house painted also. We're really trying to get it right everywhere.

Phil: And so you're trying to match protocol data as finely as you can record the protocol.

Allen: Right, though in fact we have pursued this most strongly not with protocol data but in the syllogism work (Polk and Newell 1988). This is actually a dangerous thing to do. I mean, I don't know how familiar you are with VanLehn's (1990) work on Buggy and repair theory.

Phil: Sure.

Allen: That's a great lesson in how a great mass of data can actually blind you to certain things. The theories seem successful, but if you now take protocols of subjects doing these subtraction tasks, they don't follow these control regimes at all. The first thing they do is to mark all the carries across the entire number, and then they go back and do the other. But repair theory is a local stack control regime. So there's actually a real danger in doing what we've done on syllogisms. Nevertheless that is the place where we have pushed pretty hard on getting the theory right all the way in the simulation right all the way down.

2. Models and reasoning

[This section will make more sense if the reader first refers to the discussion of thought as mental simulation in Chapter 5 of Kenneth Craik's 1945 book "The Nature of Explanation". It will also help to know that Craik, a neurophysiologist at Cambridge, died in an accident at an early age.]

Phil: In the book *[i.e., Newell's "Unified Theories of Cognition"]* the engineering style of explanation also comes up in the notion of annotated models. You argue very nicely that if you have completely general world models then they're hard to compute with because everything is connected to everything else. But models are nice because if you can simulate a model then that solves the frame problem, at least within the model.

Allen: Providing you don't confuse that with whether you've actually been able to model the world right.

Phil: Which is a very interesting question.

Allen: Of course! But that question shouldn't be confused with the frame problem, although it very often is. If you look through the Pylyshyn volume (1987), most of that collection of authors has got that issue totally conflated.

Phil: So your position on models is presented in the book, at least for expository purposes, as an efficiency consideration. Given that matching is the fundamental machinery, matching needs to be local operation, and so forth.

Allen: It says that if you try to use a general (that is, of course, quantificational) propositional representation, then you get into, not just efficiency problems, but intractability problems.

Phil: That's right.

Allen: And of course, that's not hypothetical.

Phil: It's quite real.

Allen: And it's real not only theoretically. But also, if you remember, STRIPS actually did that (Fikes and Nilsson 1971). They didn't understand that—not that they should have. But the very first version of STRIPS, that Rich Fikes wrote, used resolution as its functional match routine and took a long time on occasion. The fundamental efficiency consideration there is pretty obvious.

Phil: Yes indeed. So let me then press you on the question of adequately representing the world for your purposes. You develop that argument in the context of the syllogism case we were just discussing, and it had already come up in Johnson-Laird (1983) and the related literature.

Allen: Right. This was not at all a novel contribution.

Phil: As so often in the book, you're building on thousands of other projects and saying, this is the way we interpret what they did.

Allen: Right.

Phil: Now, many sorts of things in the world need models made of them, and some of them are terribly bigger and more complicated than the simple tokens in those mental models. Maybe you're walking down the street or you're in a large organization, in complex physical and social worlds, and it's an important question, what are the limits of modeling those things? Can one model them well enough to reason about them? Do annotated models account for what happens as you keep scaling? How do you think about this strategically as Soar develops?

Allen: Good. The big answer is, "I don't know". Roughly speaking, the annotated models for syllogisms were small enough not to really raise the issue of focus. Certainly a person's model of something—insofar as they've constructed it—might be a lot bigger and more complicated than we've worked with in the past. But at any given moment, they only deal with a piece of it. So clearly some sort of focusing is going on. Now the syllogism program actually does a kind of focus. It's not a focus that moves around with a fixed size. It's a kind of an expansion around one particular place that just keeps expanding as it needs to. So it does deal to some extent with why some things come into consideration before other things, but the models are small enough that it can expand its focus anywhere it wants without it having to contract elsewhere. So it doesn't really address the issue of scaling. Focusing is clearly a big mechanism that we have to deal with. Now, along with that goes another issue that's strongly related to problem spaces, namely, although Soar works this way, the state in the problem space shouldn't be sitting in working memory. Those are logically independent notions. I can make that more precise if you want.

Phil: I want to come back to that a little later, actually.

Allen: Okay. But if you think of large states, most of that large state is sitting up in the recognition memory. In problem space terms the system still is in such and such state; it's just that most of this state is in the recognition memory. Only a piece of it is in working memory. And that's already a focusing device, though even more focusing may be necessary. Even for the information that has been assembled momentarily in the working memory, any number of focusing mechanisms are necessary. But clearly if we say "let's apply the problem space notion to wandering around the city", then clearly the person only sees a small piece of it at a time, and that's clearly a really big focusing mechanism already. We only talk as if the person sees the whole thing.

Phil: Right. And so what you have to understand is how it is you swap things, as it were, into the working memory from the recognition memory. These are reconstructed memories no doubt, given that it's not a big dead store of facts up there but actually productions.

Allen: Right. Because in fact you don't swap things the way you do in a normal computer.

Phil: That's right, that's quite different.

Allen: And therefore the underlying technical problem is that you can only pull stuff out of that recognition memory in terms of what you've got in working memory. You can't swap it in by block. So the question is, how do you organize learning so that when the right clues are around you get the right stuff in? Of course the only way you could arrange to do that perfectly is by various compulsive devices which you probably can't stand to do anyway. But the issue of effective organization is primary. A funny note: back when John Laird and I were working before Soar shaped up, we spent a lot of time figuring out how to keep most of the state in long term memory and how you would arrange the productions so you could assemble just the parts you needed.

Phil: And all the work you all have done with data chunking and exploring mechanisms, that's the general form of an answer ...

Allen: Yes, although it's easy to infer the wrong sort of answer from that because data chunking is a particularly compulsive sort of scheme. One of the interesting things in the last few months is understanding the space of different data chunking things you can do, one of which Rick Lewis calls situated reconstruction (Lewis 1991), where you use the redundancies from the original situation to the current environment to guide the search to build up the correct learning. Like lots of things in Soar, things sit on the stack for long periods. You'll find one solution with some interesting properties, and even though you know other solutions exist, they just go in the background. But then all of a sudden they get fired up and actually on this issue of data chunking they've gotten fired up here on the last six months.

Phil: Okay, let me regroup the question of scaling up in relation to models. At several stages during the book you develop what I take to be a pretty fundamental commitment to a modern version of Craik's original notion of mental model (Craik 1945). You know, you encode a world, reasoning is in some way a simulation through a manipulation of a model of the world.

Allen: No. First part yes, second part no.

Phil: Okay, set me straight then.

Allen: Well because if I'm thinking about a model of a piece of the world, certainly one of the operations you can perform on it is to simulate it. But you can do lots of other things on it. So to fire a shot across somebody's bow, what's wrong with a lot of envisionment and qualitative simulation is the notion that the intellectual operations to be formed on this qualitative model are fundamentally those of simulation, whereas in practice you want to abstract it, you want to do things which are not physically possible with it, and so forth. You want to do all kinds of other intellectual operations besides simulation. But fundamentally the commitment is that the model is a form of representation that shows up in the states of your problem spaces. Now, of course, nobody knows how much more generally Craik thought about it. Maybe he thought about it much more generally, although it actually seems a little unlikely.

Phil: Well I've observed that in a lot of AI work, the word "reasoning" often means simulation in a model, in much the way Craik articulates it in his book.

Allen: I don't really believe that. Here's another shot across someone's bow—I have no idea whose. I think of reasoning as a kind of cover word so you don't have to say much about the kind of processing that's going on. By contrast, if I talk about it as search, that's a clear commitment. And so the reason I don't think of the term "reasoning" in the terms you described, is that what most theorem provers do is reasoning. And that's not describable in the way you did. In fact I think if you traced it sociologically you would find that the word "reasoning" comes in from the theorem proving types.

Phil: I expect the words have a number of different lines of descent that would be interesting to trace.

Allen: For a word like "reasoning" that sort of has to be the case.

Phil: So let me get where I was going and maybe we'll finish demolishing it now with your clarification. One of the straightforward objections to the simulation view of reasoning is that when the world gets to be complicated it becomes computationally difficult to simulate it. So not only is it difficult simply to model the world, it's much more difficult to conduct a simulation of it. And so to the extent that those results really bite, we need to press your point much harder that there are other things to do besides simulation.

Allen: So let me ask you a question. I would not have said that the book presents any notion of simulation, in the way we've been talking about it here, as an essentially important mental process. I just don't think of the book presenting that. It uses "reasoning" when it wants to talk about doing syllogisms because that's the natural name to talk about those things but, in fact, in syllogisms what's going on is not in fact a simulation.

Phil: So maybe I'm reading something in ...

Allen: But your impression was that did come out ...

Phil: What exactly came out is in the first discussion of models early in the book, where you say there was this "Great Move" where we understood that it wasn't just a neural hardware thing.

Allen: Do I talk about Craik in this book?

Phil: Let's look in the original discussion of composed transformations.

Allen: I think you're wrong. And the Great Move refers to going to computation to provide transformations for the external world.

Phil *[flipping through the MS of UTC]*: Here's the Great Move. Oh my; Craik is actually an annotation I wrote in the margin, having vividly recognized something you had written.

Allen: You've just provided a new item of data, right?

Phil: You bet. Top of page 59 in my copy which is in Section 2.3 on representation, says, "Let's describe abstractly what's going on in Figure 2.6. The original external situation is *encoded* into an internal situation. The external transformation is also *encoded* into internal transformation. Then the internal transformation is *applied* to the internal situation, to obtain a new internal situation. Finally the new internal situation is *decoded* to an external situation."

Allen: Right!

Phil: There's a paragraph in Craik's *The Nature of Explanation*, which says almost precisely the same thing.

Allen: But now that isn't the Great Move ...

Phil: I understand ...

Allen: That is just the (I hate to say it) totally obvious and right way to think about representation. Okay. And so that's what a representation is. And I believe that that's in Craik. I mean I can't pin it down ...

Phil: Chapter 5.

Allen: But if you simply go around this loop, now that doesn't say anything about simulation. The picture of representation I laid out in the book—the transformations and the internal transformation on the representation relative to the correspondence—simply seems obvious to me. Sure there are lots of controversies about it, but I think definitely it's going to hang in there. But that notion of representation does not seem to me to make any commitment at all to the notion of simulation. Certainly I did not intend any such commitment. And I think that our notion of representation covers all the uses that one actually makes of representations. Any statement whatever, any reasoning process you wish to go through and finally get something that says something about something out there, that's precisely one of these transformations because there is a correspondence between what you say and what's out there. Simulation is like that, but so are all other forms of reasoning as well. So anyway, that was my intent, but I think it's rather interesting that you were reminded of Craik.

3. History of problem spaces

Phil: So far we've been talking about fairly fundamental concepts that are more or less invariant over the whole of your development, without much reference to Soar and Soar ways of explaining things. But Soar is committed to the notion of search …

Allen: Well, let's see. In your notes *[my electronic mail outlining questions for the interview]* you spoke of these commitments we make to problem spaces and so forth. And you're right. But one of the interesting transformations of our view of problem spaces is that now they're precisely not search spaces.

Phil: Can you expand on that?

Allen: A key property—one of two or three—of the problem space is that it's a programming control construct which is least-commitment. The received view is that a programming language is a control structure over a bunch of base operators, a way of specifying which operators will occur when. A problem space is a least-commitment control structure that says, "we will wait until the very last minute to decide what operators will be applied and we will decide that in terms of the knowledge that is available at that time", as opposed to all kind of standard programming languages which force you, by the way you write things down, to make commitments about what happens when. We were led to this view by noticing that Soar does almost no search. It is actually delaying its choices until the moment of action. So it is really the essence of non-programming. In a certain quasi-philosophical way it rallied to some stuff that floats through computer science all the time. It dissolves once and for all the notion that in building an intelligent agent you lay down plans in advance for that agent to perform. Soar is not laying down such plans. Soar is, as it were, trying to assemble its knowledge right at the moment of activity. Anyway, that's the big thing that problem spaces do. So the problem space has turned out not to be a search. I mean, it does still allow the search. It also allows error recovery. So its three properties, or at least three sort of functions that it performs, are: search, this least-commitment control structure—which I think is the key one—and then error recovery. If something goes wrong you always have a way of considering alternatives. We haven't yet exploited that error recovery property very strongly. We've done some error recovery stuff but fundamentally I would say that our development of Soar is quite weak along that direction. We can explore why that is, too. I think of Soar as perfectly able to deal with generalized flexible error control with respect to unanticipated errors and all those other things, but we certainly haven't gone out there and dealt with them. Anyway I'm glad to see us spike the notion of always coming back to search.

Phil: There is a historical development where an idea that started out as search ended up as problem spaces. And do you see most of the change as occurring during the time of the Soar project?

Allen: No.

Phil: Can you give me your chronology of major changes and their causes?

Allen: I can try. Problem spaces start out as heuristic search spaces. And they start out as an empirical idea—I mean, LT (Newell, Shaw, and Simon 1963) is sort of a search system, but then you have Slagle's system (1963) and the *Computers and Thought* papers (Feigenbaum and Feldman 1963) and they all turn out to be search programs. They all have this similar character. Nobody at the time had any notion that that was the right organization in general. And so, a key point in the chronology for me is a paper that Ernst and I gave in '65 which is entitled "The search for generality" (Newell and Ernst 1965) which pulls this hypothesis together and says—I'm kind of an empiricist, okay? —"here are all these data points showing that all of the interesting action is in programs that do search", and we tried to taxonomize a little bit on the different kinds of heuristics and the different kinds of strategies and so forth. And it was at that point in my own development that I saw the problem space as a key way of organizing a problem solver, whereas before these were all very interesting kinds of organization. Of course, in retrospect you can spell out combinatorial reasons why they had to happen, but still there was that sense of lots of possible kinds of organization coming out of the woodwork. That wasn't true any more after '65.

Before I go on, though, let me make a statement about something. At some point much of the field started assimilating all of this to state spaces. But—and I've actually said this in the literature a couple of times—in some sense there's just nothing intellectually interesting to say about state spaces. I mean, of course, there was that original very powerful notion that they could be applied in so many different ways because you could make very generalized spaces. But after you've said that—and, hey, I didn't invent that and computer science didn't invent that—then that's all there is to it.

So anyway, the next thing that happens—I'm not sure I've got this right but we'll try it—is the realization that the problem space entails a commitment to solving a problem in some definite arena and not some larger arena. It's the problem solver's commitment that this problem shall be formulated in this way—a representational commitment—and that the problem solver in general has actually no way of ever confirming it. I mean, he might have—he might have a problem in one form and can translate it—but in general, there is a big issue about where the problems come from in the first place. And fundamentally the problem space is one way of trying to answer that: it says that the organism really does make a commitment that it has no way of validating; if it comes up with a solution to its problem then it will accept it. And that commitment is in some respects the central thing in problem spaces.

Let me go along—oh I can't remember what follows what in time. There's this issue in 1980—actually little bit before that—in which one moves from "problem spaces are good for problem solving", to "problem spaces are a way of organizing things for all action". Then that's this 1980 paper on problem spaces as a fundamental category (Newell 1980). In one sense there's nothing new about that idea, except now it got taken very seriously; it got laid out in a strong enough way, and a few of its properties got sketched out, particularly with respect to the possibility of moving continuously from problem solving behavior to skilled behavior without having to decide to shift representations. That is certainly not around in '65, I can tell you that. And it's not around in '72, either. In '72, it's all problem solving—of course the book was on problem solving. The areas of investigation were all problem solving. At that point some things like operators are still done in Lisp, but that's at least how you organize this problem solving.

None of that gets us to multiple problem spaces. Multiple problem spaces come with Soar so maybe we put that to one side.

Phil: Does your conception of problem spaces change in the context of there being multiple problem spaces, with new problem spaces created on impasses and so forth?

Allen: We have to say this a different way historically. With Soar come many things, one of which is multiple problem spaces—also finally getting rid of having the operators done as black boxes in Lisp. Now, the relationship between problem spaces doesn't arise as "I've got multiple problem spaces— I wonder what the relationship between the spaces is". It arises through the whole business of impasses and the creation of subproblem spaces to resolve them. You see, most of my view of problem spaces is that the new development is mostly just the gradual discovery of what was already there—I mean, already there in Soar. If one had set out to design a multiple problem space system—which nobody did, at least that I know of, and that's incredible when you think about it—the relationship between spaces would have been the relationship of implementation. You would have set it up so that the subproblem spaces implemented the stuff above them.

Phil: Like the classical notion of abstraction, or planning as it was called.

Allen: Or procedure realization: I have an operator and I have to realize it. It turns out that the relationship in Soar is a lot richer than that: it's any lack of knowledge at all. But that increased richness was not an object of scientific discovery. It simply flowed from impasses and we didn't think about it until we turned around later and thought about multiple problem space systems as opposed to thinking about Soar. Well, that's not quite true. We talked about the fact that this was a way of formulating any goal. We had a principle at one point called the "any-goal principle", which is that the system can formulate any goal that you need. Though it's gone from the theory now, that principle was actually a driving factor of one generation of Soar. In other words, if you can't decide what to do then you must be able to formulate that goal. If we are going to have a general intelligence, whatever comes up it has to be able to formulate goals of dealing with that. But looking at current systems at that time, most of them simply had K goal types *[that is, some fixed number of pre-programmed goal types]* that you could instantiate. And this certainly does not allow you to set up the goal of "finding the criteria for how I'm going to decide which type to use". And so we explicitly set out to solve this "any-goal problem". It turns out, along the way, that it just gets overcome by the dynamics of Soar and the insight into universal subgoaling and so forth. A very early stage in Soar actually had both deliberate goals and what we called then reactive goals. Reactive goals later turned into universal subgoaling. And so, you could have deliberate goals which you knew how to set up, and you would have the reactive goals. And then, looking at the programs we were running, we observed that you never used deliberate goals. And so we made this simultaneously bold and unbold decision, "to hell with it, we'll just get rid of the deliberate goals because all the goals can come out of reactive subgoaling", which then turns into universal subgoaling. Then the "any-goal principle", which was actually driving this arrangement, just sort of disappears. You know, principles are not the interesting things. They're just a way to get you from here to there.

Now, there is another insight as well; I don't recall offhand whether it occurs before or after what's called now the problem space hypotheses, the idea of using problem spaces for all cognitive activity. This is the distinction between the predicates that define goals and the invariants that are maintained, as really a representational matter, by the operators of a given problem space. These invariants do at least half the work, and the problem poser's task is to decide which properties of the final solution are simply invariants and then formulate the problem accordingly. This notion goes back to the generate versus test distinction, or at least back to the '72 book, and it has been a productive view for us.

Now that isn't the end of it actually. There is a notion of a problem space computational model (Newell et al. 1991).

Phil: Which was new to me just this afternoon.

Allen: I see, all right. Well, it is the notion, growing out of our work with Soar, of a separate and distinct computational model between a symbol level computational model and the knowledge level. One of the things that strongly informs our research—and I don't know how many other research groups hold so strongly to this—is a notion that the right way to characterize an intelligent system is in terms of approximation to the knowledge level, wherein the system brings all of its knowledge to bear on its decisions (Newell 1981). And there clearly is a symbol level system which is going to realize this. But in between there is this problem space computational model which is a way of autonomously talking about the problem space operation that does not have to refer to any of the lower level implementation. *[For later development of the problem space computational model, see (Newell 1991).]*

Phil: Is it a complete characterization?

Allen: Yeah, well that's what it means to be a computational model.

Phil: That's a strong claim.

Allen: Right, real strong. That's what was happening: when you look at all the people working with Soar, they're working entirely in terms of problem spaces. Of course, they actually do drop down—if you look at the Soar 5 manual, you have to go down and write these productions and so forth—but fundamentally it was all happening at the problem space level and it didn't seem to make much difference what the details were, except that you clearly had to program the thing. And so the notion gradually arose of a separate level. It's still a symbol level; it's not that there's a different kind of thing. It's talking about these spaces and these operators and those are all internal processing notions. So in fact we have gradually been recasting Soar in terms of this problem space computational model. Now of course we don't yet know what the computational model is. All we know is that such a thing seems clearly to be destined in Soar because that's what's happening empirically.

Phil: An interesting sort of empirically, right? You've got all of these programmers ...

Allen: Yes!

Phil: ... out there and this is what they seem to need. And they feel compelled by the practicalities of their work and being programmers into doing things a certain way and you can observe that. That's marvelous.

Allen: It's clear that Soar is a symbol level architecture that is saturated with problem space notions. It has the problem space and the state and the operator and all, but with no division. Okay? So we're talking about separating out a level that only deals with the problem space. We'll know it when we have it, because then we'll be able to treat all the productions and recognition memory and decision procedures as simply an implementation system for it. Okay? And since it's still Soar, that gives us the total set of phenomena, a huge list of them. To pick the most obvious one, Soar does this chunking. If you talk about problem spaces today, there's nothing that corresponds to chunking in them at all. I mean, we speak of problem spaces as this partial construct and we speak of chunking in terms of the underlying processes, the impasses and so forth. So Soar has chunking in it, but if I'm now going to divide Soar into two levels, either something has to correspond to chunking or you simply decide that a lot of the real action occurs at the lower level.

To take an analogy, Geoff Hinton and I once tried to enumerate all the possible ways that connectionist systems could relate to the symbol systems. And one of them is that all the learning really happens at the connectionist level. In between learnings, so to speak, you can find a symbol level description of what's going on, even though no learning occurs up on that symbolic level. In other words, the lower learning does all of its stuff and thereby produces another, new symbol level system whose relation to the previous one is kind of obscure.

Anyway, the idea here is to somehow play this same game. You can say that the problem space computational model doesn't include the learning. And that's clearly not the tack we're taking. The tack we're taking is everything that is reflected in Soar 5.2 (Laird et al. 1989). The point is that we have a really strong driver for this discovery process. There is no general notion of a multiple problem space model; all we have are problem spaces. All the glue that holds it together is down at the other level. And so another step has occurred—there's a paper on it called "Formulating the problem space computational model" (Newell et al. 1991)—in which we discovered how to describe a multiple problem system autonomously in its own terms. And so we solved half the problem.

But the essential idea is that you have a problem space. A problem space is a nondeterministic system because most of the action, like how the operators actually produce their results and so forth, is not specified. So we'll posit a set of components that are processes that do this: processes of "select an operator", "apply an operator", and "terminate the task". And then we have to specify those processes. But how do you specify a process when you don't want to commit yourself to the nature of it? You specify it with a knowledge level system. So we'll describe the knowledge level system to apply an operator. Now we need to implement that knowledge level system. But that's what problem spaces are for: they're devices to implement knowledge with. So then we'll have one big problem space to implement that. And so the gimmick is that the problem space computational model, which turns out to be a multiple problem space system, gets created by a recursive definition between the problem spaces and the knowledge level without ever going below that. Of course that recursion has to be grounded out, so there is a primitive process called "immediately available knowledge", where the thing just knows how to behave. And so we get a formulation of problem space computational model which is one step closer to what's required.

And that's where we stand as of May of this year *[1991]*. And all summer I've been pushing the next step on that. I think I understand it. I won't tell you about it only because I haven't told anybody else about it. There's a lot of pressure in the Soar group for a solution to this problem. It's not just an intellectual problem. Let me give you an example. We are reimplementing Soar, which one has to do every so often, but we are reimplementing it by building a formal specification.

Phil: That will make a lot of people very happy.

Allen: In Z, you know Z?

Phil: No.

Allen: There are a couple of public formal specification languages from the programming world. One is called Larch (Guttag 1990); you may have heard of Larch. Another one is called Z (Spivey 1989, Hayes 1985). It was developed around Tony Hoare and the Oxford group. It seems to have slightly better publicly available programs and a slightly larger user community. And there are more important differences too. Anyway, we first did it in home brew, mainly in mathematical notation, but we shifted over to a publicly available specification language. We actually have a formal specification of Soar which is 75 percent complete *[see Milnes et al. 1992]*. In other words, the Soar we'll produce is an implementation of that, so that whenever anything changes you'll change the specification first and then the implementation. That's going to be a pretty exciting adventure actually. Not many systems try to live that way—I mean not just for the first implementation but all the way through. There's a long story, which we shouldn't get into, about why we came to do this. The important thing is, everything in that specification ought to be justifiable against the problem space computational model. It's an implementation system, in short, for the problem space computational model. But of course we don't quite have a problem space computational model yet, so we end up having endless silly design arguments about why it's rational for it to be this way or that—the game we all play when we build systems. But ultimately our design decisions on the symbol level system will be justified first against the problem space computational model. And maybe, like all other implementation systems, it will have a bunch of extra properties, but once we're sure that it implements this model everything else will be matters of efficiency or simplicity.

Now this is all false in the following important way. We're making a huge assumption about human behavior, which is that humans are organized so that they have these extra levels too.

Phil: That wasn't an assumption all along?

Allen: No, what's driving this is just Soar, not evidence about human behavior.

Phil: I get it.

Allen: What's driving this is our understanding about the structure of this architecture. This understanding of the real nature of Soar comes by getting experience and thinking hard about it, so that gradually the view comes to prevail that it really has two-level organization. And only after that do you say to yourself, "God, I don't think humans are organized this way".

Phil: It's a big genuine empirical question you're saying.

Allen: Absolutely!

Phil: And somebody better go out and start testing it.

Allen: Well I'd just as soon have the problem space computational model in hand before you start testing it.

Phil: I understand.

Allen: Now, many of the descriptions, for example in *Human Problem Solving*, are all problem space level. So in some sense we can already describe human behavior this way, except you simply jump to the productions to give the rules. Take the crypto-arithmetic work: how do you know when you to go to the next level of modeling? In terms of the problem space computational model, you'll jump down to the symbol level and give the productions that will realize it. That's what Soar does too. But nevertheless, if you look hard at the regularities, they describe people as doing various kinds of operations and living within limited worlds. The big empirical result in cryptarithmetic is that people do in fact seem to solve that problem by only working with these four operators and not doing all the other things you might have thought they could do. So this is a slowly emerging big issue.

Phil: Maybe it just doesn't pan out. Maybe you can't quite get it together.

Allen: Yes, maybe we can't get the problem space computational model to pan out. Or, much worse, maybe we can get the problem space computational model to work fine for Soar, so that it's really the right way to organize the system, and yet it doesn't correspond to human behavior. In that case we're in deep, deep trouble, a real parting of ways.

Phil: Do you think of that as being a really big test of the Soar philosophy?

Allen: No. There's a possibility of a neat sharp result, especially in the negative direction, though we'd have to understand how to describe that empirically. But I just actually believe it's all going to work out, so I just don't think about it. Because I live in the world in which Soar is sort of the way the human mind is and so the issues for me are only how it's going to work out, not whether it's going to work out. Of course, lots of things could be wrong with this, but that's fine; I'll just change my mind later. But, I do think of it as a fairly interesting prediction. Now, maybe these levels end up being a useful descriptive abstraction but in fact in people there's a lot of leakage and the properties of the underlying systems show through in a lot of places. And that's why the properties of the underlying symbol level system are very important. Of course I started out here with a typical computer science statement, "it doesn't make any difference what the lower levels are like", but that was assuming the absolute implementation relationship. But if there's actually leakage then the actual properties of that system make a lot of difference.

Let's see; is there any more to say about problem spaces? A lot of commitments there. Although most of them are not additional commitments. They really flow out of it.

4. Search and planning

Phil: Now that we've established this trajectory from search spaces to problem spaces, let me ask about a particular widespread interpretation of search. It goes like this: You start off from the initial situation which corresponds to reality as it is right now and you try out by mental simulation a variety of possible actions; operators in this account are possible actions. And then when the search arrives at a goal, you traverse the winning path through the search space and you gather up the operator symbols into a plan that can now be executed. This story posits a certain relation between the internal world and the external world, that operators have two faces: internally they can simulate actions and externally they can actually perform these actions in the world. STRIPS is like this, and much else in the planning literature. And theorem proving is like this in the sense that executing the plan means actually carrying out the proof out in the world. This is a particular tidy story about the internal world and the external world. Now, did you ever believe such a thing?

Allen: No. Absolutely not.

Phil: Tell me more.

Allen: It never occurred to me. It came as a shock to me at one point in time, to hear people talking about the generation of behavior in the world as always an issue of planning.

Phil: Okay ...

Allen: I always thought that what GPS was doing was problem solving and not planning. Now, GPS did planning as one activity, which to say it did generate an internal string of operators which it then used as a guide for action, still internally. So planning for GPS had two faces: the internal generation of a data structure that was then used as a guide to implementation. And so in *Human Problem Solving*, do the people doing logic problems plan? Well you can look at the protocols and you see them working now at one level of productions and now down at another, and maybe finding that the plan doesn't work, or doesn't quite work and requires doing a little subproblem. And so I have always had a view that problem solving was not planning, and that in fact, people (and machines) did problem solving and that planning was just one method for doing that. It came as a shock to me one day to realize that once I had defined it that way, formally GPS did planning because it created a little data structure in its stack. Okay, so you could look at GPS at doing planning. On the other hand, there really is a difference if I do a bunch of search and look ahead and whatever I do, and I use that to decide upon the next move and I throw all that stuff away and I start to ...

Phil: By "the next move", do you mean the next physical action?

Allen: Right, the next physical action. So in fact there really is a distinction: you don't have to keep this as a plan around. You can, in fact, keep it as a plan around and use it if you want. You can, in fact, simply think about the world and consider and then decide to make a move and then consider again and then it seems to me you're not doing planning, however much reasoning or thinking ahead or imagining you might be doing before you decide on something.

Phil: Yeah.

Allen: One of the things that I found objectionable early on in the planning point of view was that I could never see how their programs, like STRIPS, were doing anything more than problem solving. And that's because it was only a plan in the eye of the observer who said, "now this plan is going to be executed", but the system itself never did that. Until it was hooked up to Shakey it was not executing a plan. It was problem solving in its head. And it was only because you wrapped it up in this larger view and said I'm now going to remember that ... And in fact it wasn't even clear to me that it actually remembered the plan as opposed to printing it out as it went so the experimenter could look at it and say, "oh, yes, it did this, it did this, it did this ...".

Phil: Well now there could be backtracking in the search.

Allen: That's right. Many of these systems did backtracking to remember something. But actually to begin with, at the end they didn't actually have that plan. They actually generated it by backtracking, and even then they were in fact doing it backwards—printing it out as they went along—so it's not clear they had the plan in this tidy picture. So I always said, I believe something was planning when it generated an actual data structure, where I could then see the implementation. But I've given up fighting that battle. In this view that you laid out planning and problem solving are the same thing. Although it's not clear that they haven't lost a great distinction.

Phil: I'm glad to have that all on tape.

Allen *[laughing]*: You did touch a button.

Phil: It strikes me about the planning literature that until recently there are few episodes in the planning literature where execution of plans is taken even seriously enough that there is a thing that executes the plans.

Allen: Right.

Phil: And that is both striking and fateful for the reason you said and I think for many other reasons as well.

Allen: The issue of planning, of course, is not really internal or external. It really is just two spaces. So if you look at GPS planning, the plan is generated internally and then applied to the internal problem space. So there are two problem spaces, one of which is an abstraction of the other. You solve the problem in this problem space and you keep the record of the operators that solved it. And then you use that in this problem space and you never go external. So it's not an issue of the real world, it's really just an issue of the multiple spaces.

5. Chunking and learning

[It will help to understand that this section proceeds through successive debunking and revisions of PA's first question. These successive revisions correspond roughly to the historical development of the ideas in Soar, and AN's formulation at the very end of the section corresponds roughly to the Soar group's current understanding of the issues.]

Phil: Let me put a devil's advocate position about chunking and learning to you and just ask you to debunk it. It goes like this. According to the devil, there's only a very limited sense, and an entirely inadequate sense, in which Soar can ever learn anything new. Chunking is the summarization of a search process that takes place in a problem space generated by an impasse, and so chunking is only summarizing something that's been discovered to be a generative possibility of things Soar could already do, applying operators it already had to states it already knew about. That's only discovering something new in the explanation-based learning sense, where you discovered an outpost in a search space, and explanation-based learning is clearly a search process. It's like discovering that Fermat's Last Theorem is true from Peano's axioms; you didn't learn anything new in one sense but in another sense you did. And so the devil would conclude that Soar can't be learning anything new about the outside world. Now plainly you don't believe this, because data chunking for example is ...

Allen: Plainly it's not true empirically.

Phil: ... and data chunking is intended as counterexample.

Allen: Right.

Phil: Now what's wrong with the devil's argument?

Allen: So the devil is actually Tom Dietterich.

Phil: Okay.

Allen: He wrote a neat paper called "Learning at the knowledge level" (1986) that lays out this point of view with crystal clarity. I think it was not abroad strongly before that. This article observes that there are two kinds of learning, symbol level learning, which can make you more efficient but adds no new knowledge, and knowledge level learning, which does, and that chunking was a symbol level learning device and therefore you could learn nothing new from it. QED. It is such a clean paper it's terrible to say that it has a flaw. (By the way, what's really funny about this is that Tom's was also one of the few papers which took the knowledge level seriously. In the "knowledge level" paper I 'say, "look, this is all chat until people begin to do technical things with it", which is one of my excuses for giving it as a presidential address rather than as a technical paper.) So our papers talk about how to refute that argument by showing that Soar can learn from the outside world. The flaw is that it is simply not the case that the knowledge to be attributed to a generative system is a transitive closure of the operators over the system. That is, the flaw is to believe that if I give you a set of axioms then the theory of the knowledge level says that you must attribute as knowledge the transitive closure of this thing. The right statement is that something can be described at the knowledge level if you can somehow state the knowledge of the system such that you can predict the behavior of the system from the goal and the knowledge. And if you try and use the transitive closure as the predictor, you will do terribly in predicting it because the system itself never gets close to its transitive closure. And all you've learned from that is, that you've made a lousy choice of how to attribute knowledge. And it is not part of the theory that you must attribute knowledge that way. But the whole argument about this separation between knowledge level and symbol level is based on saying that the knowledge associated with the problem space must be the transitive closure of its operations—or in a logical system that the knowledge associated with the set of axioms and so forth—must be the transitive closure. Now, maybe a given system *has* no knowledge level description, so that the only way to describe its behavior is in terms of its internal operations. Nothing says that every system can be described at the knowledge level.

Phil: Yes, that's right.

Allen: And that's the flaw in the argument. We thought it was useful to show that Soar could learn stuff from the outside world. There is this great compulsion to believe that you must assign the knowledge to be the transitive closure. It comes about as well because of the logical interpretation of knowledge. And of course it's more than the logical expression. That is, it doesn't do much good to describe the knowledge by saying it's what you've got here and here and here, plus this plus a match routine. And so, the only other option is to describe it as a transitive closure. That just turned out not to be true of these systems—I mean, us systems, any of us.

Phil: That is an adequate response to Dietterich's argument, because the latter turns on a mistaken interpretation of the knowledge level ...

Allen: But all I heard you give was a man-in-the-street version of that theory.

Phil: Well let me try stating the difference I see. I think it's just right to refuse to call knowledge the transitive closure of all the operations on representations. So fine let's call it ...

Allen: How about calling it "observer-inferred belief".

Phil: Good. It is the case that Soar acquires new knowledge—now taking knowledge in the narrow sense—and the question I thought I was asking is, does Soar acquire new observer-inferred belief? Does Soar acquire any new knowledge which is outside the transitive closure of its operators applied to its existing representations?

Allen: Clearly Soar has to learn from the outside world. And it does. And so the issue is only what's going on. And let me describe that in two ways, one of which also illuminates problem spaces. The first one starts with the observation that if Soar guesses the outside world by going to a space which will generate all possibilities, and can verify that, then in fact it has new knowledge. The search in the problem space is a way of doing that guessing and wide open guessing is in general intractable. However we can actually use the outside world to guide that search so that the guessing works faster. But in any event it acquires new knowledge. In terms of problem spaces, we observe that chunking only expresses what is achieved in terms of the operators, but not in terms of the selective rules that chose the operators. So if I use the external environment to select how to go through the space, the problem that it's solving is independent of that.

Let me back up and explain this in terms of a dilemma. The dilemma says that if I endeavor to create a memory that I can retrieve at a later time, so I have retrievable knowledge of the outside world, and I do that in the obvious way, then both the conditions that I want to use for retrieval and the thing that I want to retrieve show up in the condition side of the production. And consequently I can't—in logical terms—ever detach the knowledge that that stimulus was really associated with. The way of solving that problem in data chunking is to set up to recognize what's in the world. You can do that. So I actually acquired knowledge from the world fairly directly because I can set up to recognize it even if I can't generate it.

Phil: But to expect it?

Allen: Not to expect it, simply if it occurs a second time to recognize that that is in fact what was in the world before. That problem is straightforwardly solvable.

Phil: Yeah. So let me try a trivial case of that that might make that clear. Suppose you had a simple world in which events happened on a nice regular clock, and only four things could ever happen. The problem space then tries all four operators; it then looks to see which one just happened in the world and it prefers that one. Then it focuses on the newly created state and proceeds along to the next event. When you chunk that you have something that can recognize that same sequence happening again.

Allen: Right, though that's just recognition, which doesn't solve the problem of how I would be able to recall that information.

Phil: Oh, okay.

Allen: And the way you solve that recall problem is to say, if I could just guess by random generation that that's what was in the world, then I will build the right production. And that's not an intractable procedure but a highly efficient one because in a problem space the search control is not part of the chunking. And it's not part of the chunking because chunking only looks at the solution to this problem, which is just the operator sequence. And therefore I will use the external world to guide this search toward the thing I want to recognize. But then I recognize it, thus solving that problem, and then I actually put that knowledge away.

Now, the other way of describing it is to observe that the real problem was that EBL—that is the chunking—was doing just what it was supposed to do: the occurrence of this new information was contingent upon the original information that came in from the environment. So only if that environment information shows up again can you get this knowledge. And you really want to detach that information. That is, you want to make an induction. And so what's really going on in data chunking is simply untying the information you've just gotten from the time and place it came in. That's an induction; in other words, you have to throw away some conditions. When we discovered that the data chunking problem existed for Theo (Mitchell 1990) for instance, we asked Tom Mitchell how Theo would solve it and he said, "no problem, I'm just going to put in a Lisp program that'll throw that thing away", because it knows it wants to make that induction. And in some respects the procedure of data chunking is a way of justifying that induction, because the environment lets you do it, so to speak. So the real problem is how to get Soar to make that induction when the basic chunking does not have a process that says "I wish now to make an induction by throwing away these conditions".

Phil: Is it true then that Soar's ability to learn something new now in the full sense that we've established is dependent on chunking being inductive?

Allen: Let me just say, "yes", but that's just tautological if by "new" you mean something that the system did not already know was justified. In that sense, of course, anyone who is to learn anything new must make an induction.

Phil: And you're right that basically the answer to my question was, "yes, tautologically". The reason I asked it, though, is also the reason why I said that your formal specification of Soar will make a lot of people happy, namely that the obvious interpretation of chunking to many people is that it's some kind of lemma summarization: given these premises I've concluded that this follows from them monotonically. But no, chunking is not like that. Chunking is nonmonotonic, because there's all manner of nonmonotonic steps in the midst. And so chunking is inductive in that way. And the riposte then of people who are eager for that formal definition is: Okay, if that is not the formal, independently defined problem that chunking solves, then what is your definition of the problem that chunking solves, so that you can now verify that a particular proposal about chunking actually solves it?

Allen: The problem that chunking solves is to provide the knowledge—the symbolic representation of that knowledge—so that when you reach the same situation again you don't get the impasse. Now that's the problem that chunking solved, but it's not the total function that chunking plays. Those are not the same thing. For one thing, according to that definition, there would never be any transfer of chunking to other situations. And so the fact is, when chunking is applied in a different situation, the system makes an implicit inductive leap that it's relevant to that situation. And it can be wrong. In Soar that's called over-generalization. And we get lots of it. And so therefore, every act of applying a chunk which is not, in God's eye, the same situation is an act of induction. However, that's not what's going on in the data chunking. I mean some of that's going on in the data chunking, but ...

Phil: You could do data chunking without that, or what? There's a fine distinction in here somewhere.

Allen: I'd have to think about that, but I don't believe that data chunking depends upon the transfer of chunking. The act of abstraction occurs because Soar can believe anything. Okay? The way you believe anything is you simply set up a problem space which will generate everything. Now according to the devil's view Soar knows everything. The real problem is, Soar just doesn't know which of its beliefs are right. And so in one view Soar cannot have any more knowledge. It's got it all. It just doesn't know if it's right or not.

Phil: A hole in the devil's argument I hadn't understood until just then is, just because Soar generates something doesn't mean it believes it.

Allen: Yes! There's a paper on that by Paul Rosenbloom and Jens Aasman (1990). It talks about Soar in terms of moving things from low belief level to high belief level. The fact that something's in there in this problem space says that Soar believes this thing to some value, like zero maybe. And the act of chunking actually is a way of moving things from one space to the other. And the act of data chunking actually then increases the value of what's true in the outside world. You start out with all of these things being possible in the outside world, but you don't know which one is true. But now having seen the outside world, I can say that this one is, and therefore I move it to this other problem space. And I believe the things that are in this other problem space whereas this lower problem space is just a free generator of every damn thing in the world.

6. The Soar community

Phil: Tell me something about how the Soar community works.

Allen: The community has some pretty interesting social properties. Its main feature is that it's completely free-standing. For instance it has no membership list. The only criterion is whether you're serious about Soar. There are gatekeepers, so if you're not serious about Soar I guess you can be excluded. But fundamentally it is a community of people who are totally free standing in their interest and do their own research. In that respect there's no formal coordination of any kind.

Phil: Well one kind of formal coordination is when a new edition of Soar comes out, tapes are mailed out. *[The code and related materials are now available by anonymous FTP. Further information is available from The Soar Group at soar-requests@cs.cmu.edu or School of Computer Science, Carnegie Mellon University, 5000 Forbes Ave, Pittsburgh, PA 15213-3891, USA.]*

Allen: Yes that's right. And at another level it lives and exists because it's a network community. It's almost inconceivable to think of running this way in 1930. But there is indeed a commitment to use a single version of Soar, so that is a strong cohesive point of view. It raises the rate of intercommunication very quickly. It also raises the rate at which people contribute to other people's research very quickly because problems can show up in anybody's work anywhere, including problems at the lowest possible level. But, interestingly, there never was actually a decision to build such a thing. That happened pretty much because since Paul and John and I dispersed, we were already distributed in terms of these mechanics. And then the issue was simply whether someone wanted to come on and we just let that happen. It started out being just the three places and then since we had a little contract from Digital then clearly the guy from Digital would come and so it has grown that way. For instance there is absolutely no pooling of funds, even to make the workshop happen. Whoever gets to give the workshop has to stand in for all the expenses. So there are essentially no issues of funding reliance in this community. And I had no idea that we were going to do this. We've been around for several years; we have about ninety people. It clearly has taken on a kind of institutional shape. And so I actually do find it rather remarkable. I just sort of watch it happen, although it depends upon the effect of the leadership of the three people, Paul and John and myself. I actually spend over half of every day on it. So there are big managerial costs, aside from the intellectual ones. That has certainly gone on and I think it just gets worse. I have no idea what will happen if it ever grows to two hundred people.

Phil: I imagine, though, that there being ninety people out there doing serious Soar work changes your experience of making progress in Soar. What's that like?

Allen: Well, the funniest part of it, and I see this when I talk to potential funders, is that no one controls what problems are worked on in Soar. It operates like a science in a sense that individual investigators work on what they please and for their own purposes. So, when you try and draw a coherent picture, it is, in that respect, a patchwork, and is not about to be shaped. For instance it's got a strong HCI area. And that comes about in part because computationally oriented psychologists around the world have gravitated to HCI for lots of reasons. Therefore, they come in with HCI-like problems. So there are lots of things that focus it. But these are things that focus any science. And I just accept that.

Phil: There's vast amounts of accumulated experience now. And you're all in the network sharing it and you can now, in a way that couldn't be possible otherwise, discern a trend, or notice a regularity, such as the way problems spaces came out, as we were talking about before. Is that a basic way of working for you?

Allen: Sure. In fact this community is a lot more focused than others I've worked in. So, how does information get captured in this community? It fundamentally gets captured in papers. I mean, people write all these papers, so on a given day five new papers may come out. And that kind of dictates your reading for a while. So, a lot of time is spent on that assimilation. The only way that differs, I think, from the 1970's AI world is this strong focusing in this relationship to Soar and so forth. In these other communities, there's plenty of interaction in meetings and so forth, but it's all much more abstracted because you and Doug Lenat are not working on the same system. So you're interested in talking about Cyc, but you don't understand Cyc very well. You're only willing to make a certain investment, and so you exchange things at a certain level. And in this community the exchange runs a lot deeper. Still you don't understand everything that everyone is doing. I try pretty hard.

Another influence is the lack of a single leader. John and Paul and I share the leadership and have from day one, and certainly have by the time it became a larger community. There's just more manpower to read papers, so that this leadership can be expected to understand everything that's going on everywhere in the project. And if, as in most situations, there's a single person at the top to carry the intellectual load, you just get a different dynamics. I think that's a pretty interesting feature, and it may also have made the thing appear less arbitrary. We've never had fights about the architecture. We have had this guy from Holland, Ep Piersma, come to one of the Soar workshops and give a paper entitled, "Soar 6, what Soar 5 should be" (1990), which made a critique of the complexity of Soar 5 and so forth, and that was just great. But it didn't generate any sort of tussle. There have been many contributions of that type. The architecture evolves, and the concern with the architecture tends to be localized in about six or seven people. But it adds new people from time to time and people drop out. So despite the rule that there shall be one architecture, it is not given who makes the essential input. Right now it's driven by a process that includes not only John and Paul and myself, but Gary Pelton and Brian Milnes and a couple of other characters, but mostly Gary and Brian, who are the main guys doing this new formalization. So there's a group of about seven or eight people now for whom the institutional focus is really this issue of how to specify Soar and produce a new implementation. And two or three other people are involved in that because they're concerned about efficiency in production systems, all these lower level issues fundamentally.

So it's working moderately well. We raised an issue at one of the workshops: Were we organized right? Should the Soar community exist? Should we pool some funds? Is it maybe bad for the same three guys to be the leadership all the time? And there was a zero response to that. It just died. I was surprised. I raised it to get that issue out in the open sometime, since often when you take the lid off you discover a bunch of issues underneath. Now part of it is that money has never been involved. We all sort of struggle by in our own ways. And we've always be able to find enough internal funds to handle things like the Soar maintenance and development. And if anyone wants to get involved with Soar, we will put them on our machines. Some character showed up here from Amsterdam the other day, using one of the machines to run some Soar on. It sort of surprised me, since they were using a lot of cycles. So we're not indifferent. We believe that Soar is an interesting candidate to look at. But I have no idea how long such a loose voluntary organization can continue. And people do drop out. We have a group in Montreal, with the developmental psychologist Tom Shultz. And as time has gone on he's gotten more interested in connectionism. So he's still a member of the community, but fundamentally his own theoretical efforts have left Soar. That happens.

7. Chunking and interaction

[AN's comments in this section should be understood as a rough first pass on some radical new ideas about the eventual evolution of Soar. In recent

but still preliminary work the Soar group has found more limited solutions to the specific issues—the Soar term is "non-contemporaneous chunks"—that I raise here (John Laird and Paul Rosenbloom, personal communication.)]

Phil: Back on chunking and what it means. My concern is that the world is going on in real time the whole time you're thinking. You don't go into Soar I/O very much in the book.

Allen: It was not very well developed in the book.

Phil: But it has been developed, and certainly the book had a slot for a theory of real-time perception and motor control. What I wanted to know is how that interacts with chunking. You have some problem space and you've applied some sequence of operators and now it's time to chunk that. But the world's been changing the whole time, right? And in particular working memory's been changing the whole time. And the world may be a different place than it was when you started in on that subgoal. And I don't understand what chunking means when working memory can be changing out from under it as it goes along.

Allen: Well, let's see. Don't talk about working memory. You're at the wrong level. You ought to be at the problem space level. Anyway, I'm not sure I'm going to give you an answer, but I can poke away at it a little bit. The way to phrase your question is what happens if the state keeps changing? If the rest of the working memory keeps changing, that isn't going to bother the problem space. So you say, well suppose the state keeps changing, all right? So let's track that down a little bit. One view is, problem spaces can't be that static. The standard definition of problem spaces is, you've got this set of states and these operators, and these operators satisfy a certain set of conditions, which if I can remember them are DDSRV. Okay? *[AN is about to define most of the terms in this mnemonic: Discrete operators, Discrete representations, Serial operators, Reliable application of operators, and Voluntary application of operators.]* Operators are discrete, meaning that when I apply an operator nothing happens till we get the output. The representation is discrete, meaning I can represent it by a discrete symbolic structure. Only one operator gets applied at a time, so it's serial. They're all under the control of the agent, so the only operators you get applied are the ones the agent applies. And they're reliable: you apply the same operator you always get the same result. And this is just the way everybody formulates it.

So, first answer is, well, that's no way to run a problem space. Problem spaces have all these other properties: maybe the states can go flopping around and so forth. And so that's the problem. And within Soar it turns out to be a really big problem which shows up in a lot of the accumulating activity. Let me try and describe that. We have a language called TAQL (Yost and Altmann 1991). TAQL started out to be a task acquisition language. But it has turned out to be the problem space computational model. Because the hypothesis was—very early on—that the level at which you are to specify things to Soar was at the problem space level. But the expert system person just wants to think in terms of problem spaces of different kinds. We have two versions of the problem space computational model. One is that we simply describe Soar 5.2 this way in the manual. But we also have TAQL. Now it turns out that the problem space computational model assumed by TAQL and the one assumed by Soar 5 are not the same. For all the obvious reasons they're not the same. But in particular it turns out that TAQL tends to honor this DDSRV.

Phil: Yes.

Allen: Now the reason it does so is historical. Soar 4 honored DDSRV very strongly and the original version of TAQL worked for Soar 4. The essential simplification in Soar 4 was that nothing ever was changed in working memory and productions could only add information. So in a structural sense—not a logical sense—the system was totally monotonic. I went from an old state to a new state, I must build a brand new state from scratch. So I put the new stuff in then I copy over all the old stuff. That works well and I actually believe that if we hadn't done it that way the first time we could never have seen through all the issues. It's an extremely simple thing. Its most important property, conceptually speaking, is that on the right-hand side of a production are simply working memory elements to be instantiated. All you can do, after all, is to put those elements in memory, as opposed to a general production system with a whole command language. And so when you go to build chunks it's a simple matter to compose the right-hand side: you just put all those elements together. On the other hand, some things are really wrong with it. First of all is all that copying. But the other thing, which is even worse, is that you're saving all these states. Now that seems like a great idea for purposes of search. But in practice Soar never went back to old states. As you'll recall, this was one of the clues that problem spaces were not search spaces. So the working memory for this big production system suddenly contains all these dozens of highly similar states, and they make the production match lots more expensive. This wouldn't be so bad if you were actually using them, but as it is they're just a drag. The solution to this is what we call destructive state modification. You make an assumption that within a problem space there can only be a single state. And you take the state that you're now in and use it as material to construct the new state. With that, of course, comes an infinite set of complexities. But we don't really have time to talk about them right now. The point is, Soar 5 does destructive state modification. The move to destructive state modification is also driven by the connection to the external world, because if you say that I copy over a whole state every time something comes in from the external world, then you're in deep trouble if you're going to have any sort of asynchronous activity. So the motive for destructive state modification comes from efficiency issues and from the connection to the external world. So we have made that transition. TAQL, which was developed initially for Soar 4, had to move to Soar 5, but it kept that same sort of computational model. So it differs from what's natural for Soar 5 and for interaction. And so there has been a running discussion over a year and a half about what's the right semantics for operators. That's the way it's expressed itself. TAQL, in order to impose its model, actually has to do some buffering. And that's a little technical issue about the difference between insert–delete semantics and insert–replace–delete semantics. And in Soar 5 you don't really control the synchronization of the operators, so you can't make insert–delete semantics work quite like you want for insert–replace–delete semantics, which TAQL really presented to the user, without having some buffering and so forth. One of the interesting issues about Soar is you can't hide anything. I mean, you can hide the buffer but you can't hide it from chunking.

Phil: Yes, well that's why I asked, right? Chunking has that kind of omniscience, which is both its big advantage and its Achilles' heel if it's done wrong.

Allen: Oh, absolutely right. Now, that was all preparatory sloshing around the issue that this whole problem has raised. And so in some respects we are still seeking the solution to that. Namely, what do I do if the state keeps changing? And here's an answer, though this is all part of what I'm currently thinking about; I don't know whether this is the right answer and I haven't discussed it with anybody else. The answer is that you have to generalize the notion of problem spaces. You have to admit a much broader set of operators. You have to abandon the simplified DDSRV operators. And you have to allow many different kinds of operators, voluntary multiple operators applying and all these other kinds of things. And what you have to hang onto is this commitment: when the agent decides to use this problem space, it may have all this stuff flopping around in it but if I can get a path of operators from here to there then I can still build a chunk from that. The issue, in other words, is the commitment of the problem solver that this is a problem space, though maybe not this simplified form of problem space. If the agent says, "I don't know whether this problem space is going to solve my problem because everything is changing and it's all Alice in Wonderland", then that's the agent's problem and it had better not use that problem space.

Now the fly in this ointment is that the top problem space in Soar is fundamentally not a problem space. It was not one that the organism selected in order to solve the problem. It just exists. And so maybe the organism is just constrained by that, and it has to learn to work with the operators in that space. In other words, it has a constrained choice of the space but its problem is still how to conceive of that as a space that will solve its problems. And that's what it has to do. And I don't understand much about how that happens. So the fundamental solution is: your confusion should not be your confusion; it's the organism's confusion about whether it can still treat the thing as a problem space.

And there are two possibilities. One is that this whole framework isn't going to work. I mean, maybe this finally finds the Achilles' heel to this whole thing and we're going to have to think about this differently. My belief at the moment—I'm a bit conservative—is that it's all going to work out. And the organism is going to live with problem spaces that way. It's going to use other kinds of problems spaces. And it's going to be able to commit to those. And the issue of the justification for chunking goes along with that commitment. And therefore, things can flop around and you still take the stuff that it depended upon. And if you didn't depend on this stuff flopping around then it doesn't show up in the chunk. Isn't that something? I think that's the fundamental direction to look for an answer to the problem.

Phil: And the lesson to learn is that faced with a tension in the design in the system, there is some give. The give is in the fact that it is an architecture and that there's a whole variety of different ways to use it. And that is part of theory as much as the architecture itself is.

Allen: That's right, though I thought you were going to draw a different lesson. Which is: if you look at the architecture hard enough it will tell you how to solve that problem. Of course this isn't a true characterization, since you're changing the architecture. Actually it's more like, we're changing the way we describe it.

Phil: Yeah, that's right.

Allen: This is like my feeling about problem spaces all along, that mostly they are a discovery of what's there, although here a real generalization is going on. So I have a concept, problem spaces, and it won't work. And so I've generalized it and then the game is, what's the invariant to be maintained? I've told you what I think the invariant is. You can let go of the nature of the operators ... actually this is not entirely true; even if simultaneous operators are applying they need to result in a single path, so they have to build up a joint state. They can be additive or whatever. So the total set of invariants is not quite clear. I will keep this commitment that the agent says, "if I use this space and I hit the desired state and I recognize it, I'll say my problem is solved", so that anything else is not important. I think that's the right thing. That's one of the reasons I said the key issue in the problem space is this creative active decision on the part of the agent. It's a real existential act. That's how it's going to represent its world and its problems.

References

[1] K. Craik, *The Nature of Explanation* (Cambridge University Press, Cambridge, England, 1945).

[2] A.D. de Groot, *Thought and Choice in Chess* (Mouton, The Hague, Netherlands, 1965).

[3] T.G. Dieterich, Learning at the knowledge level, *Mach. Learn.* **1** (3) (1986) 287–316.

[4] E.A. Feigenbaum and J.A. Feldman, eds., *Computers and Thought* (McGraw-Hill, New York, 1963).

[5] R.E. Fikes and N.J. Nilsson, STRIPS: a new approach to the application of theorem proving to problem solving, *Artif. Intell.* **2** (3) (1971) 189–208.

[6] J.V. Guttag, Report on the Larch Shared Language, Tech. Rept. 58, Systems Research Center, Digital Equipment Corporation (1990).

[7] I. Hayes, *Specification Case Studies* (Prentice Hall, Hemel Hampstead, England, 1985).

[8] P.N. Johnson-Laird, *Mental Models: Towards a Cognitive Science of Language, Inference, and Consciousness* (Harvard University Press, Cambridge, MA, 1983).

[9] J.E. Laird, K. R. Swedlow, E. Altmann, and C.B. Congdon, Soar 5 user's manual, Tech. Rept., School of Computer Science, Carnegie Mellon University, Pittsburgh, PA (1989).

[10] R.L. Lewis, Situated data chunking: (very) preliminary explorations, Soar Workshop 9, Columbus, OH (1991).

[11] G.A. Miller, E. Galanter and K.H. Pribram, *Plans and the Structure of Behavior* (Henry Holt and Company, New York, 1960).

[12] B.G. Milnes, G. Pelton, R. Doorenbos, M. Hucka, J. Laird, P. Rosenbloom and A. Newell, A specification of the Soar cognitive architecture in Z, Rept. CMU-CS-92-169, School of Computer Science, Carnegie Mellon University, Pittsburgh, PA (1992).

[13] T.M. Mitchell, Becoming increasingly reactive, in: *Proceedings AAAI-90*, Boston, MA (1990).

[14] A. Newell, Studies in problem solving: subject 3 on the cryptarithmetic task: DONALD+GERALD=ROBERT, Computer Science Department, Carnegie Institute of Technology (1967).

[15] A. Newell, Reasoning, problem solving and decision processes: the problem space as a fundamental category, in: R. Nickerson, ed., *Attention and Performance* VIII (Erlbaum, Hillsdale, NJ, 1980) 693–718.

[16] A. Newell, The knowledge level, *AI Mag.* **2** (2) (1981) 1–20; also: *Artif. Intell.* **18** (1) (1982) 87–127.

[17] A. Newell, PSL: towards a complete PSCM (first try) (1991).

[18] A. Newell and G. Ernst, The search for generality, in: *Proceedings IFIP Congress 65*, Washington, DC (1965) 17–24.

[19] A. Newell, J.C. Shaw and H.A. Simon, Empirical explorations with the Logic Theory machine: a case study in heuristics, in: E.A. Feigenbaum and J.A. Feldman, eds., *Computers and Thought* (McGraw-Hill, New York, 1963).

[20] A. Newell and H.A. Simon, GPS: a program that simulates human thought, in: E.A. Feigenbaum and J.A. Feldman, eds, *Computers and Thought* (McGraw-Hill, New York, 1963).

[21] A. Newell and H.A. Simon, *Human Problem Solving* (Prentice-Hall, Englewood Cliffs, NJ, 1972).

[22] A. Newell, G.R. Yost, J.E. Laird, P.S. Rosenbloom and E. Altmann, Formulating the problem space computational model, in: R.F. Rashid, ed., *Carnegie Mellon Computer Science: A 25-Year Commemorative* (Addison-Wesley/ACM Press, Reading, MA, 1991).

[23] E.H. Piersma, Constructive criticisms on theory and implementation: The Soar 6 computational model, Tech. Rept. WR 90-1, Traffic Research Center, University of Groningen, Netherlands (1990).

[24] T. Polk and A. Newell, Modeling human syllogistic reasoning in Soar, in: *Proceedings Tenth Annual Conference of the Cognitive Science Society*, Montreal, Que. (1988) 181–187.

[25] Z.W. Pylyshyn, ed., *The Robot's Dilemma: The Frame Problem in Artificial Intelligence* (Ablex, Norwood, NJ, 1987).

[26] P.S. Rosenbloom and J. Aasman, Knowledge level and inductive uses of chunking (EBL), in: *Proceedings AAAI-90*, Boston, MA (1990) 821–827.

[27] J.R. Slagle, A heuristic program that solves symbolic integration problems in freshman calculus, in: E.A. Feigenbaum and J.A. Feldman, eds., *Computers and Thought* (McGraw-Hill, New York, 1963).

[28] J.M. Spivey, *The Z Notation* (Prentice Hall, Hemel Hampstead, England, 1989).

[29] D.M. Steier, Automating algorithm design within an architecture for general intelligence, CS-CMU-89-128, School of Computer Science, Carnegie Mellon University, Pittsburgh, PA (1989).

[30] K. VanLehn, *Mind Bugs: The Origins of Procedural Misconceptions* (MIT Press, Cambridge, MA, 1990).

[31] G.R. Yost and E. Altmann, TAQL 3.1.3: Soar task acquisition language user's manual, School of Computer Science, Carnegie Mellon University, Pittsburgh, PA (1991).

Index

Note: Page numbers in italics indicate illustrations.